SOCIAL WORK EDUCATION:

A Bibliography

by

HONG-CHAN LI

The Scarecrow Press, Inc.
Metuchen, N.J. & London
1978

Library of Congress Cataloging in Publication Data

Li, Hong-Chan, 1934-
  Social work education.

  Includes index.
  1. Social word education--Bibliography. I. Title.
Z7164.C4L49 [HV11]   016.361'007'1   77-19339
ISBN 0-8108-1108-1

For my father

and

to the memory of my mother

TABLE OF CONTENTS

vii

ix

FOREWORD

The social work profession, in the last two decades, has gone through a searching reexamination of functions, levels of education, and conceptual frames of reference. In the process, the literature has proliferated and it has been extremely difficult to find a systematic way of reviewing and analyzing this diverse material, as well as categorizing and compiling this literature in an ordered way.

Mr. Hong-Chan Li's Social Work Education: A Bibliography has filled this void brilliantly. He has developed a thorough, thoughtful, and extremely useful comprehensive and systematic guide to the literature in social work education. The bibliography is a necessary reference to everyone interested in this subject area. Mr. Li has provided those of us in social work education an ordered compilation of the literature that also clearly establishes areas where insufficient material exists.

The bibliography is a result of Mr. Li's creativeness, thoroughness, intelligence and most painstaking labor. The social work profession is deeply in his debt.

Morton Coleman, Dean
University of Connecticut
School of Social Work

PREFACE

Social work education has a relatively short history and is unique in many aspects in comparison with education in other disciplines and professions. In the past fifteen years, it has experienced tremendous growth and change as a result of the demands within the field of social work as well as societal changes. Consequently, a substantial body of literature has emerged as social work educators, practitioners and researchers have increasingly been sharing their views, experiences, and findings.

The rapid increase in the literature, coupled with the lack of adequate bibliographic control in this field, has created difficulties for its users. For example, readers often have to spend enormous time and effort by going through voluminous reference tools in searching for needed bibliographical material; yet, some significant and useful works are still likely to elude them.

A far more critical problem is that many valuable writings probably never come to their attention at all, since a considerable amount of older as well as newer professional literature in social work education has not been indexed or abstracted anywhere.

Purpose

This bibliography represents an attempt to alleviate the problem by bringing together in one volume extensive sources of references in various forms on a wide range of issues in social work education and by classifying them as precisely as possible according to the subject matter. It is hoped that this volume will not only provide social work educators, students, researchers, librarians, and concerned practitioners a ready access to the vast amount of literature, but also serve as a stimulus for further inquiry and development in the field.

Scope

The term "social work education" may imply a wide variance in meaning and scope for different people in different times; it is likely that no single definition would satisfy all users. This bibliography, however, is concerned primarily with formal social work education in academic settings. Consequently, it covers a continuum of educational programs from community and junior colleges to doctoral level and includes continuing education. References on agency-sponsored in-service training or staff development as well as training of social service volunteers are excluded.

Historically, social work education in the United States began with the training schools, flourished at the Master's level, then developed upward and downward. For half a century, the Master's degree program has constituted the backbone of social work education. This phenomenon accounts for the preponderance of references on graduate social work education in the present work.

Coverage

The bibliography includes books, periodical articles, proceedings, reports, pamphlets, documents, microfiches, and doctoral dissertations, all of which are specifically related to social work education. A special attempt has been made to include pertinent papers and chapters from books or collections on different subjects, so that fugitive, but valuable, literature is directly brought to the user's attention under its own author and title in its own subject category. The volume contains approximately 3,000 references drawn from a wide range of sources, in addition to about 300 duplicate entries.

The bibliography provides comprehensive coverage of the literature in the area of social work education after 1960 and selective coverage before 1960. Decisions about inclusion of items from the pre-1960 literature were guided by the following criteria: 1) the works bear on the history of social work education; 2) the works are still viewed as the best available on particular aspects of the field; and 3) the works represent timeless or classical contributions.

In order to provide an international perspective, foreign publications are also included. However, since the bibliography was designed chiefly for use in the United States, all foreign works cited are confined to publications in the English language.

Arrangement and Classification

The bibliography is divided into 17 general subject sections, with references arranged alphabetically by author under the section heading or specific topical headings. The general arrangement follows the scheme of classification indicated in the Table of Contents. This scheme was devised partly on the basis of the structure and pattern of knowledge in social work education and partly in response to the number of works presently available in various subject areas. Also, to facilitate its use, it was organized with an attempt to conform closely with the views of social work educators and to possess the merits of simplicity. Rigid and in-depth hierarchical division or subdivision therefore was not applied in developing the classification scheme, although in some instances it may have been highly desirable from a logical viewpoint.

The compiler is aware that this classification scheme is far from being ideal for every study purpose. Therefore, as a complement to the subject classification, the following features are included to help the user to locate desired references:

1. Subject cross-references are provided at the beginning of many subject categories and subcategories.
2. Multiple entries are made when a reference is applicable to more than one category.
3. An Author Index is supplied in the back of the volume. Authors' names are listed alphabetically, giving the assigned consecutive entry number. The index includes all individuals and organizations cited as author or co-authors of works in the bibliography.

How to Use the Bibliography

For the purpose of this bibliography, the broader term "graduate education" is viewed as synonymous with "Master's degree education," since the two terms are generally used interchangeably in the literature. Therefore, individuals interested in questions on

Master level education should consult Sections III through VII.
Those interested in doctoral level education should consult Section
VIII, but may also examine the preceding five sections for refer-
ences of possible interest.

In using the bibliography, the reader should start with the
Table of Contents and locate the category or categories that are
most likely to provide the references needed and, if necessary, fol-
low the cross-reference for possible additional entries from other
categories. The form of entry used in this bibliography is in general self-explanatory. It should be noted, however, that journal
titles cited in this bibliography are the ones used at the time of
publication of the cited articles.

Doctoral dissertations selected for this bibliography represent those completed by doctoral students from the field of social
work and other disciplines as well. Unless later published in book
form, they are designated with "Doctoral dissertation" in the entry.
Many dissertations are available on microfilm or in xerographic
copy in academic libraries with special interest in social work.
Microfilm and xerographic copy of individual dissertation, except
those submitted to the University of Chicago, may be purchased
from Xerox University Microfilms, Ann Arbor, Michigan 48106.
Dissertations of the University of Chicago may be purchased directly from the Department of Photoduplication, Joseph Regenstein Library, University of Chicago, 1100 East 57th Street, Chicago, Illinois 60637.

ERIC documents are distinguished by an ED number at the
end of the entry. ERIC is the acronym for the Educational Resources Information Center, National Institute of Education, U.S.
Department of Education, Health, and Welfare, Washington, D.C.
A complete collection of ERIC documents on microfiche is available
in many academic libraries and regional education resource centers.
Microfiche and paper copy of individual documents may be ordered
from ERIC Document Reproduction Service, P.O. Box 190, Arlington, Virginia 22210.

For the convenience of the user, United Nations documents

cited in this bibliography are provided, when available, with their
U. N. document number at the end of the entry.

Limitations

In compiling this bibliography, various means were used to
track down the relevant bibliographic information and to locate the
original works.   Virtually all works cited in this bibliography were
seen and examined for their contents and bibliographic accuracy.
A few whose texts could not be obtained were classified on the basis
of a published abstract.   Very few were classified merely on the
basis of the title.

For the purpose of limiting the volume to a reasonable size,
the overall number of duplicated entries has been kept to a minimum.   For the same reason, in cases of cited works that have
later been reprinted in multiple sources, only the original or the
best available source is cited.

The cut-off date for inclusion of references in this volume
is December 1976.   It should be noted that certain relevant articles
appearing in foreign journals issued in late 1976 may have been
left out.

Although an attempt was made to reach the goal of comprehensive coverage for the post-1960 literature, some vital omissions
may have occurred.   Deciding which pre-1960 literature to include
in the bibliography was a very difficult and largely subjective task.
Inclusions of some titles and exclusions of others may not be re-
garded as appropriate.   I truly regret these limitations as well as
others.   All suggestions for improvement of future supplements are
most sincerely welcome.

Acknowledgments

I wish to acknowledge my debt to many individuals who gave
their cooperation and assistance to the work.   My deep appreciation
goes to Dean Morton Coleman of the School of Social Work, University of Connecticut, whose consistent interest and support made this
bibliography a reality.

Many thanks are due those faculty members at the School of Social Work, University of Connecticut, who gave helpful advice either through formal or informal consultation. I am particularly grateful to Professor Anthony N. Maluccio of the same school. Professor Maluccio not only provided expert counsel on various complex conceptual problems in social work education, but also patiently read each section of the earlier drafts and contributed many valuable suggestions.

Special appreciation is expressed to the present and former staff of the School of Social Work Library, University of Connecticut, who built such a valuable collection that it made this undertaking possible. I especially want to acknowledge my appreciation to Mr. Lee E. Sellers, Chief Librarian, for his encouragement and generous support, and to Miss Elizabeth Dzurnak and Miss Iris King for their cooperation in many ways.

I am thankful to all other libraries that I visited to locate references and to review material. Special recognitions are owed to the Library of Congress, the Yale Libraries, Dag Hammarskjold Library of the United Nations, and the Social Work Libraries at Columbia University, Hunter College, Simmons College, and the University of Pennsylvania. The cooperation of colleagues at these and all other libraries consulted is warmly appreciated.

I am indebted to Dr. Dojelo C. Russell, School of Social Work, Virginia Commonwealth University, for sending a mimeographed bibliography compiled by her.

Sincere appreciation is extended to the staff of the Council on Social Work Education for having taken the trouble to investigate a number of my inquiries.

Personal thanks are given to Miss Karen Shlevin who spent many long and tedious hours assisting me in preparation and editing of the drafts, and to Mrs. Marie Gionfriddo for typing the manuscript with accuracy.

I am also very grateful to the Research Foundation of the University of Connecticut, which provided a grant to make this undertaking and the completion of the bibliography possible.

Finally, I wish to express my deep gratitude to my wife, Yun-Chun, and children, George and Linda, for their patience and understanding during the many lost evenings and weekends when the work kept me away from home.

Although I appreciate the contributions of these individuals, institutions, and all others who provided the assistance to the work, I am solely responsible for its contents as well as any flaws and errors.

Hong-Chan Li
West Hartford, Conn.

WHY A BIBLIOGRAPHY ON SOCIAL WORK EDUCATION?

by
Anthony N. Maluccio*

The optimistic predictions of a decade ago concerning the rapidly multiplying need for social workers have given way in the 1970's to the harsh realities of inflation and retrenchment. The field of social work, however, continues to be inundated by an ever expanding body of literature.

In particular, in recent years there has been a rapid growth in the number of publications related to social work education. A professional journal concerned exclusively with education for the field of social welfare was launched in 1965.[1] New books, articles, reports and papers are increasingly being published, in response to such influences as innovation and experimentation, expansion of programs along the continuum from community colleges to doctoral education, and ongoing examination of recurring questions concerning structure as well as quality.

This abundance in the literature is in some ways a mixed blessing. As is true in the field in general, the literature on social work education is characterized by considerable repetition and overlapping, limited cumulative building of knowledge, and insufficient systematic analysis. In addition, many references are not easily available, because they have appeared in "fugitive" periodicals or in agency publications with narrow circulation. Other potentially important references are frequently buried in volumes whose titles suggest little relevance for social work education.

The expansion, the complexity, and the peculiarities of the literature make it difficult to carry out research on any aspect of

---

*Doctor of Social Welfare, Professor, University of Connecticut, School of Social Work.

1

social work education in an efficient, orderly, and productive man-
ner. The bibliography in this volume therefore makes an essential
and timely contribution to the field at an important point in its development. Within the framework of ego psychology, the bibliography may in fact be viewed as a significant adaptive response to a
growing environmental challenge--the task of making sense out of a
complex, confusing, and exploding body of literature.

As a result of the painstaking labor and professional skills
of its compiler, this bibliography offers for the first time a comprehensive and systematic guide to a vast amount of published and un-
published material.

It covers a broad range of topics and titles, from the early
history of social work education to contemporary issues in curriculum building and program development. A unique feature is the inclusion of references from or about countries other than the United
States, thus helping to place social work education in a cross-na-
tional context.

The references are organized on the basis of a coherent
classification scheme that reflects a logical approach as well as
current realities in social work. It is evident that every effort was
made to place each title in a carefully chosen section.

For all of these reasons, anyone interested in social work
education should find this volume extremely useful as a basic reference work. In addition to its explicit purpose as a bibliographical
guide, the text should prove valuable in highlighting issues and trends
and suggesting leads for further analysis, debate, and research.

A quick review, for example, helps to identify important characteristics of social work education. The long-standing emphasis on
the M. S. W. degree and on social work methods is evident in the
preponderance of titles in these areas. Social workers' propensity
for self-scrutiny is reflected in the articles on reassessment and
self-appraisal scattered throughout most topical categories. The on-
going search for criteria and guidelines in the process of student
selection and recruitment is seen in the large number of articles
and studies devoted to these topics.

The bibliography also reveals critical gaps in knowledge. Very little has been written about issues that have become urgent more recently, such as the continuum of social work education, preparation of different types and levels of social work manpower, and involvement of persons from minority groups as students and faculty members. Similarly, there has been little systematic research on the effectiveness of different patterns of social work education. It seems that educational problems and questions have not attracted as much interest as practice and service delivery problems.

In short, this volume documents the changing landscape of social work in general and social work education in particular. Many of the newer titles point to the ferment in the field and the critical issues confronting practitioners, students, educators, and researchers. One gets the sense that social work education is on the road to somewhere. But the question is: WHERE?

It may be that, just as the 1940's gave rise to the Hollis-Taylor study[2] and the 1950's to the Boehm study,[3] events in the 1970's are crying out for an even more intensive examination of social work education and a thorough debate on the crucial issues of the day. The widespread response to the recent report of the CSWE Task Force on Structure and Quality of Social Work Education[4] attests to the concerns and interests existing throughout the profession.

As social workers continue in their struggle to find ways of shaping a more effective profession, this bibliography should prove valuable in guiding anyone interested in exploring various facets of social work education.

NOTES

1. The Journal of Education for Social Work, published three times a year by the Council on Social Work Education.

2. Ernest V. Hollis and Alice L. Taylor. Social Work Education in the United States (New York: Columbia University Press, 1951).

3. Werner W. Boehm, et al. Social Work Curriculum Study--Vols. I-XIII (New York: Council on Social Work Education, 1959).

4. Ralph Dolgoff. An Analysis of the Responses to the Reports of the Task Force on Structure and Quality in Social Work Education and the Task Force on Practice and Education (New York: Council on Social Work Education, August 1975).

I. GENERAL ASPECTS, HISTORY, PHILOSOPHY AND TRENDS OF SOCIAL WORK EDUCATION

A. GENERAL ASPECTS

1 Abbott, Edith. Social welfare and professional education. Chicago: University of Chicago Press, 1942. 321p.

2 "Appraisals of the Curriculum Study of the Council on Social Work Education." Social Casework, v. 41, no. 1, Jan. 1960. Entire issue.

3 Barlow, Henry M., editor. Higher education and the social professions; papers presented at Symposium on Higher Education and the Social Professions, Lexington, Kentucky, 1972. Lexington: College of Social Professions, University of Kentucky, 1973. 216p.

4 Bisno, Herbert. Structure and quality in social work education; report of the Task Force on Structure and Quality in Social Work Education. New York: Council on Social Work Education, 1974. 23p.

5 Boehm, Werner W. "Education for social work." Encyclopedia of social work. 16th issue, v. 1. New York: National Association of Social Workers, 1971. 257-273.

6 _____. Objectives of the social work curriculum of the future. The social work curriculum study, v. 1. New York: Council on Social Work Education, 1959. 291p.

7 Chenault, Joann. Human services education and practice: an organic model. New York: Behavioral Publications, 1975. 69p.

8 Council on Social Work Education. Approaches to innovation in social work education. New York: The Council, 1974. 104p.

9 _____. Bibliography of major out-of-print publications and documents previously published by Council on Social Work Education and the American Association of Schools of Social Work. New York: The Council, 1966. 9p.

10 _____. Catalogue of publications. New York: The Council, annual.

5

11   . Contemporary education for social work in the
        United States. New York: The Council, 1966. 31p.

12   . Education for social work; proceedings of Annual
        Program Meeting, Council on Social Work Education, 1953-
        1964. New York: The Council, 1953-1964. 12v.

13   . Facing challenge; plenary session papers from the
        1973 Annual Program Meeting. New York: The Council,
        1973. 85p.

14   . Index to articles appearing in Social Work Education
        and the Proceedings of Annual Program Meetings. New
        York: The Council, 1965. 23p.

15   . Index to articles appearing in Social Work Education
        Reporter and Journal of Education for Social Work, 1965-
        1967. New York: The Council, 1968. 27p.

16   . Social work curriculum study. New York: The
        Council, 1959-62. 14v.

17   . Statistics on social work education. New York:
        The Council, annual.

18 David, Henry. "Education for the professions: common is-
        sues, problems, and prospects." Journal of Education
        for Social Work, v. 3, no. 1, spring 1967. 5-12.

19 Deasy, Leila Calhoun, editor. Doctoral students look at social
        work education. New York: Council on Social Work Edu-
        cation, 1971. 150p.

20 Dixon, William G., editor. Social welfare and the preserva-
        tion of human values; anniversary papers of the School of
        Social Work of the University of British Columbia. Van-
        couver: J. M. Dent, 1957. 231p.

21 Dolgoff, Ralph. An analysis of the responses to the Reports
        of the Task Force on Structure and Quality in Social Work
        Education and the Task Force on Practice and Education.
        New York: Council on Social Work Education, 1975. 49p.

22 Finestone, Samuel. "A memorandum on research into social
        work education." Journal of Education for Social Work,
        v. 1, no. 1, spring 1965. 18-25.

22a Gartner, Alan. The preparation of human service professionals.
        New York: Human Sciences Press, 1976. 272p.

23 "Goals of social work education: reviews of 'The Social Work
        Curriculum Study.'" Social Service Review, v. 33, no.
        4, Dec. 1959. 360-445.

24 Gurin, Arnold. "Education for changing practice." Shaping the
    new social work. Edited by Alfred J. Kahn. New York:
    Columbia University Press, 1973. 169-198.

25 _____ and David Williams. "Social work education." Edu-
    cation for the professions of medicine, law, theology and
    social welfare; a report prepared for the Carnegie Com-
    mission on Higher Education. New York: McGraw-Hill,
    1973. 201-247.

26 Hagerty, James Edward. The training of social workers. New
    York: McGraw-Hill, 1931. 205p.

27 Hamilton, Gordon. "Some implications of social work education
    in the United States." Social Casework, v. 33, no. 2,
    Feb. 1952. 55-60.

28 Hollis, Ernest V. and Alice L. Taylor. Social work education
    in the United States; the report of a study made for the
    National Council on Social Work Education. New York:
    Columbia University Press. 1951. 422p.

29 Kindelsperger, Walter L. "Responsible entry into the profes-
    sion--some current issues." Journal of Education for
    Social Work, v. 2, no. 1, spring 1966. 41-51.

30 Loeb, C. Peter and John A. Slosar, Jr. "Sociatrogenic dys-
    functions: a concern for social work education." Journal
    of Education for Social Work, v. 10, no. 2, spring 1974.
    51-58.

31 Lyndon, Benjamin H., editor. Social need and education for
    social welfare; proceedings of the First Conference on
    Social Welfare Education in the State University of New
    York, 1968. Syracuse, New York: State University of
    New York, 1968. 69p.

32 Lyndon B. Johnson School of Public Affairs. Higher education
    for public affairs, public administration, and related fields
    in Texas: a survey. Austin: The School, 1975. 104p.

33 McGlothlin, William J. Patterns of professional education.
    New York: Putnam's Sons, 1960. 288p.

34 Marks, Rachel Bryant. "Education for social work." Encyclo-
    pedia of social work. 15th issue. Edited by Harry L.
    Lurie. New York: National Association of Social Work-
    ers, 1965. 277-283.

35 Parad, Howard J. "Form and substance in social work educa-
    tion." Child Welfare, v. 39, no. 2, Feb. 1960. 1-5.

36 Pins, Arnulf M., et al. The current scene in social work edu-

cation. New York: Council on Social Work Education, 1971. 39p.

37 Regensburg, Jeanette. "Charting directions in social work education in the United States." Social Casework, v. 32, no. 2, Feb. 1952. 47-54.

38 Ripple, Lilian. Report of the Task Force on Structure and Quality in Social Work Education. New York: Council on Social Work Education, 1974. 68p.

39 Rothman, Beulah. "Social work education." Nonprofessionals in the human services. Edited by Charles Grosser, William E. Henry and James G. Kelly. San Francisco: Jossey-Bass, 1969. 149-173.

40 Shaffer, Gary, Estie Bomzer and Mark P. Hale. "Social work education." Contemporary social work: an introduction to social work and social welfare. By Donald Brieland, et al. New York: McGraw-Hill, 1975. 395-416.

41 Smalley, Ruth E. "Reaction to the Curriculum Study." Social Work, v. 4, no. 4, Oct. 1959. 105-107.

42 Spencer, Sue W., editor. Social work: promise and pressures. Nashville, Tennessee: School of Social Work, University of Tennessee, 1968. 65p.

43 Stein, Herman D. "Cross-currents in practice, undergraduate, and graduate education in social work." Journal of Education for Social Work, v. 1, no. 1, spring 1965. 56-67.

44 Swedish Association of Graduates from Schools of Social Work and Public Administration. Some aspects on social work training. Skärholmen: Sveriges Socionomförbund, 1969.

45 Timms, Noel. "Education for social work." Social work: an outline for the intending student. London: Routledge & Kegan Paul, 1970. 137-164.

46 Towle, Charlotte. "Distinctive attributes of education for social work." Social Work Journal, v. 33, no. 1, April 1952. 63-72, 94.

47 _____. The learner in education for the professions, as seen in education for social work. Chicago: University of Chicago Press, 1954. 432p.

48 _____. "Objectives for the social work curriculum of the future, by Werner W. Boehm: review." Social Service Review, v. 33, no. 4, Dec. 1959. 362-387.

49 _____. Some reflections on social work education. London: Family Welfare Association, 1956. 55p.

50 Tufts, James Hayden. Education and training for social work.
New York: Russell Sage Foundation, 1923. 240p.

51 Vigilante, Joseph L. "Social work, Education for." Encyclopedia of education, v. 8. New York: Macmillan & Free
Press, 1971. 286-295.

52 Walker, Sydnor H. Social work and the training of social
workers. Chapel Hill: University of North Carolina
Press, 1928. 241p.

53 Wessel, Rosa. "Meaning of professional education for social
work." Social Service Review, v. 35, no. 2, June 1961.
153-160.

54 Witte, Ernest F. "The Curriculum Study: some personal observations." Social Work, v. 4, no. 3, July 1959.
3-14.

55 Wu, Y. C. Analytical survey of research related to social
work education. Arlington, Virginia: ERIC Document
Reproduction Service, 1969. 179p. ED 042201.

56 Younghusband, Eileen L., editor. Education for social work.
London: Allen & Unwin, 1968. 180p.

B. HISTORY [See also Section I.C.]

57 Abbott, Edith. Twenty-one years of university education for
social service, 1920-1941; a report to the alumni with
register of alumni who received higher degrees, 1920-
1942, and their dissertation subjects. Chicago: University of Chicago, 1943. 108p.

58 _____ . "Twenty-one years of university education for the
social services, 1920-1941." Social Service Review,
v. 15, no. 4, Dec. 1941. 670-705.

59 Barlow, Henry M. "Graduate social work education at the University of Kentucky: the history of a decision." Welfare
in Review, v. 10, no. 3, May-June 1972. 34-43.

60 Bernstein, Saul, et al. The New York School of Social Work,
1898-1941. New York: Institute of Welfare Research,
Community Service Society of New York, 1942. 161p.

61 Brackett, Jeffrey Richardson. Supervision and education in
charity. New York: Macmillan, 1903. 222p.

62 Broadhurst, Betty Page. "Social thought, social practice, and
social work education: Sanborn, Ely, Warner, Richmond."
Doctoral dissertation, Columbia University, 1971. 952p.

63 Brown, Esther L. Social work as a profession. 4th ed.
    New York: Russell Sage Foundation, 1942. 232p.

64 Bruno, Frank J. "Twenty-five years of schools of social
    work." Social Service Review, v. 18, no. 2, June 1944.
    152-164.

65 _____. "The universities and the social services."
    Trends in social work, 1874-1956; a history based on the
    Proceedings of the National Conference of Social Work.
    New York: Columbia University Press, 1957. 133-144.

66 Campbell, Thomas F. SASS: fifty years of social work edu-
    cation; a history of the School of Applied Social Sciences,
    Case Western Reserve University. Cleveland: Case
    Western Reserve University, 1967. 131p.

67 Channing, Alice. "Early years of a pioneer school." Social
    Service Review, v. 28, no. 4, Dec. 1954. 430-440.

68 Chatterjee, Prabodh Kumar. "The growth and development of
    community organization education in schools of social
    work in India, 1936-1969: an historical analysis." Doc-
    toral dissertation, Bryn Mawr College, 1971. 456p.

69 Cutler, James Elbert. A school with a quarter of a century
    behind it. Cleveland: School of Applied Social Sciences,
    Case Western Reserve University, 1941. 15p.

70 _____ and Maurice Rea Davie. Study in professional ed-
    ucation at Western Reserve University: the School of Applied
    Social Sciences, 1916-1930. Cleveland: Western Reserve
    University Press, 1930. 208p.

71 Dawes, Anna L. "The need of training schools for a new pro-
    fession." Sociology in institutions of learning, being a
    report of the seventh section of the International Congress
    of Charities, Correction and Philanthropy, Chicago, 1893.
    Edited by Amos G. Warner. Baltimore: Johns Hopkins
    Press, 1894. 14-20.

72 "Education for social work." Social work year book. 1st-10th
    issues. New York: Russell Sage Foundation, 1929-1949;
    11th-14th issues. New York: National Association of
    Social Workers, 1951-1960.

73 Eubank, Earl E. "The schools of social work of the United
    States and Canada: some recent findings." Social Ser-
    vice Review, v. 2, no. 2, June 1928. 263-273.

74 Glenn, John M., Lilian Brandt and F. Emerson Andrews.
    Russell Sage Foundation: 1907-1946. New York: Rus-
    sell Sage Foundation, 1947. 2v.

75 Hagerty, James Edward. "History of training in social work."
    The training of social workers. New York: McGraw-
    Hill, 1931. 39-60.

76 Harris, Rufus Carrollton. Social work education and the Eli-
    zabethan era. New Orleans: School of Social Work, Tu-
    lane University, 1958. 18p.

77 Hathway, Marion. "Twenty-five years of professional educa-
    tion for social work and a look ahead." Compass,
    v. 27, no. 5, June 1946. 13-18.

78 Hellenbrand, Shirley C. "Main currents in social casework,
    1918-1936: the development of social casework in the
    United States as reflected in the literature and in class-
    room teaching material." Doctoral dissertation, Colum-
    bia University, 1965. 334p.

79 Hendry, Charles E. Fiftieth Anniversary, 1914-1964: School
    of Social Work, University of Toronto. Toronto: School
    of Social Work, University of Toronto, 1964. 63p.

80 Hollis, Ernest V. and Alice L. Taylor. "Evolution of social
    work education." Social work education in the United
    States. New York: Columbia University Press, 1951.
    3-52.

81 Hynes, Eleanor Marie. "Some issues in Catholic social work
    education, 1910-1955." Doctoral dissertation, Tulane
    University, 1971. 174p.

82 Kahn, Dorothy C. A study of professional education for social
    work in Cleveland. Cleveland: School of Applied Social
    Sciences, Western Reserve University, 1938. 105p.

83 Kaiser, Clara A. "Group work education in the last decade."
    Group, v. 15, no. 5, June 1953. 3-10, 27-29.

84 Karpf, Maurice J. "Progress and problems in social work
    education during the Depression." Jewish Social Service
    Quarterly, v. 10, no. 4, June 1934. 257-262.

85 Kerry, Esther W. "Early professional development in Montre-
    al." Social Worker-Travailleur Social, v. 29, no. 3,
    June 1961. 35-42.

86 Kidneigh, John C. "A brief history of the School of Social
    Work at the University of Minnesota, 1917-1968." After
    fifty years; papers from the 50th anniversary year--1967-
    68. Compiled by the School of Social Work, University
    of Minnesota. Minneapolis: The School, 1969. 1-10.

87 King, Dorothy. "Canadian schools of social work in wartime."
    Family, v. 23, no. 5, July 1942. 180-185.

88 Kingsbury, Susan Myra. Carola Woerishoffer Graduate Department of Social Economy and Social Research of Bryn Mawr College, 1915-1925. Bryn Mawr, Pennsylvania: Department of Social Economy, Bryn Mawr College, 1925. 63p.

89 Klein, Philip. "Training schools of social work." From philanthropy to social welfare: an American cultural perspective. San Francisco: Jossey-Bass, 1968. 220-242.

90 Lawler, Loretto R. Full circle: the story of the National Catholic School of Social Service, 1918-1947. Washington, D. C.: Catholic University of America Press, 1951. 243p.

91 Levy, Charles S. Social work education and practice, 1898-1955. New York: Wurzweiler School of Social Work, Yeshiva University, 1968. 106p.

92 Lindsay, Dorothy. "A quarter century." Social Worker (Boston), v. 7, no. 2, June 1930. 37-40.

93 Lindsay, Samuel McCune. "Schools of philanthropy." New encyclopedia of social reform. Edited by William D. P. Bliss and Rudolph M. Binder. New York: Funk & Wagnalls, 1910; New York: Arno Press & The New York Times, 1970. 1101-1102.

94 Lunt, Sally Herman. "The professionalization of social work: the history of education for social work, with special reference to the School for Social Workers (Boston, 1904)." Doctoral dissertation, Harvard University, 1974. 211p.

95 Macadam, Elizabeth. The equipment of the social worker. London: Allen & Unwin, 1925. 224p.

96 _____. The social servant in the making; a review of the provision of training for the social services. London: Allen & Unwin, 1945. 145p.

97 Maloney, Sara E. "The development of group work education in schools of social work in the United States from 1919 through 1948." Doctoral dissertation, Western Reserve University, 1963. 464p.

98 Mark, Kenneth L. "The School for Social Workers." Delayed by fire; being the early history of Simmons College. Concord, N. H.: Rumford Press, 1945. 121-125.

99 Meier, Elizabeth G. A history of the New York School of Social Work. New York: Columbia University Press, 1954. 154p.

100 Michigan. University. Institute of Social Work. The first ten years, 1935-1945. Detroit: The Institute, 1946. 30p.

101 National Association of Social Workers. San Diego Chapter.
A major achievement, a major opportunity; report on the
establishment of a graduate school of social work at San
Diego State College. San Diego, Calif: The Chapter,
1964. 49p.

102 National Institute for Social Work Training. An introductory
account, 1961-1974. London: The Institute, 1974. 32p.

103 New York. State University at Stony Brook. Social welfare
at Stony Brook. Stony Brook, N. Y. : The University,
1971. 101p.

104 Parad, Howard J. "The Smith College School for Social Work
in perspective." Smith College Studies in Social Work,
v. 30, no. 2, Feb. 1960. 175-186.

105 Pederson, Lora Lee. "A case history of the Nashville School
of Social Work." Compass, v. 27, no. 2, Jan. 1946.
15-17, 42.

106 Pins, Arnulf M. "Development of social work recruitment:
a historical review." Social Service Review, v. 39,
no. 1, March 1965. 53-62.

107 Pittsburgh. University. School of Social Work. 1938-1948:
ten years of education and practice in social work; proceedings of 1949 Alumni-Faculty Conference. Pittsburgh:
The School, 1949. 177p.

108 Pumphrey, Ralph E. and Muriel W. Pumphrey. "The begin-
nings of education"; "Education for the new profession."
The heritage of American social work. New York: Columbia University Press, 1961. 202-211; 284-298.

109 Richmond, Mary E. "The need of a training school in applied
philanthropy." Proceedings of the National Conference of
Charities and Correction, Toronto, 1897. Boston: Geo.
H. Ellis, 1898. 181-186.

110 Robinson, Virginia Pollard. "University of Pennsylvania
School of Social Work in perspective: 1909-1959." Journal of Social Work Process, v. 11, 1960. 10-29.

111 Roemele, Victoria. "1918-1968: Challenge, innovation, and
the Smith tradition." Smith College Studies in Social
Work, v. 39, no. 3, June 1969. 177-183.

112 Severinson, Hellen Eloise. "A study of students entering the
University of Pennsylvania School of Social Work as their
selection by the School relates to trends in social work."
Doctoral dissertation, University of Pennsylvania, 1964.
257p.

113   Siegel, Sheldon. "Social work education in perspective." in- "Organization growth: expansion and diversity in schools of social work." Doctoral dissertation, University of Michigan, 1974. 40-112.

114   Sikkema, Mildred. "The objectives of field work in social casework, 1898-1955." Doctoral dissertation, University of Chicago, 1965. 229p.

115   Smith, Marjorie J. Professional education for social work in Britain; an historical account. London: Allen & Unwin, 1965. 114p.

116   "South's foremost school of social work: Atlanta U School is Dixie's oldest and largest." Ebony, v. 14, no. 12, Oct. 1959. 84-88.

117   Spaulding, Edith R. "The training school of psychiatric social work at Smith College." Proceedings of the National Conference of Social Worker, 1919. Chicago: Rogers & Hall, 1919. 606-611.

118   Spencer, Sue W. "Perspectives on the University of Tennessee School of Social Work--past, present, and future." Social work: promise and pressures. Nashville, Tenn: School of Social Work, University of Tennessee, 1968. 51-63.

119   Steiner, Jesse Frederick. Education for social work. Chicago: University of Chicago Press, 1921. 99p.

120   Stinson, Malcolm B. "Social work education in the United States, 1898 through 1966." Indian Journal of Social Work, v. 28, no. 1, April 1967. 11-24.

121   Teicher, Morton I. "The Wurzweiler School of Social Work: an historical overview." Jewish Social Work Forum, v. 11, spring 1975. 1-6.

122   Texas. University. Graduate School of Social Work. The history of The School of Social Work and the professional experience of its graduates, 1950-1960. Austin, Tex.: The School, 1961. 123p.

123   Twente, Esther E. and Shirley L. Patterson. "One hundred years of social work in Kansas: beginning before 1866 and ending after 1966." Journal of Social Welfare, v. 1, no. 2, winter 1974. 3-15.

124   Varner, Barbara. "History of Atlanta University School of Social Work." Crossing over. Edited by Charles L. Sanders. Atlanta: School of Social Work, Atlanta University, 1970. 1-7.

125 Walton, Ronald G. "Women and social work education"; "Two decades of training 1951-71." Women in social work. London: Routledge & Kegan Paul, 1975. 57-65, 209-220.

126 Werner, Ruth. "Sixty years of field work, 1916-1976 (Case Western Reserve University School of Applied Social Sciences)." SASS Currents, special anniversary issue, 1976. Unpaged.

127 _____. "Sixty years of working together--agencies and school--in the interests of social work education (Case Western Reserve University School of Applied Social Sciences)." SASS Currents, special anniversary issue, 1976. Unpaged.

128 Yelaja, Shankar A. "Schools of social work in India: historical development, 1936-1966." Indian Journal of Social Work, v. 29, no. 4, Jan. 1969. 361-378.

C. BIOGRAPHY OF SOCIAL WORK EDUCATORS

129 Abbott, Edith. "Grace Abbott: a sister's memories." Social Service Review, v. 13, no. 3, Sept. 1939. 351-407.

130 _____. "Grace Abbott and Hull House, 1908-1921." Social Service Review, v. 24, nos. 3-4, Sept.-Dec. 1950. 374-394, 493-518.

131 Addams, Jane. My friend, Julia Lathrop. New York: Macmillan, 1935. 228p.

132 Baker, Helen C. "The Abbotts of Nebraska." Survey Graphic, v. 25, no. 5, June 1936. 370-372.

133 Baldwin, Elizabeth H. "In memoriam--Annette Garrett, 1898-1957." American Journal of Orthopsychiatry, v. 28, no. 1, Jan. 1958. 9-11.

134 Boynton, Percy H. "Graham Taylor--Religion in social action." Social Service Review, v. 4, no. 3, Sept. 1930. 423-426.

135 Bruno, Frank J. "Porter R. Lee, 1879-1939: the growth of training for social work." Family, v. 20, no. 9, Jan. 1940. 282-286.

136 "Charlotte Towle memorial issue." S.S.A. Newsletter, v. 13, no. 3, autumn-winter 1966-67. 25p.

137 Chenery, William L. "A great public servant (Julia C. Lathrop)." Survey, v. 46, no. 18, 1 Sept. 1921. 637-638.

138 Cornelius, Sandra. "Edward Thomas Devine, 1867-1948: a pivotal figure in the transition from practical philanthropy to social work." Doctoral dissertation, Bryn Mawr College, 1976. 229p.

139 De Schweinitz, Karl. "Porter R. Lee, 1879-1939: his contribution to case work teaching." Family, v. 20, no. 9, Jan. 1940. 277-281.

140 "Edith Abbott memorial issue." S.S.A. Newsletter, v. 5, no. 1, Dec. 1957. 20p.

141 Fishbein, Helene. "Philosophy and practice: an encounter with the ideas of William A. Rosenthal." Jewish Social Work Forum, v. 12, spring 1976. 1-2.

142 Gallagher, Raymond J. "Tribute to Monsignor John O'Grady." Proceedings of the 52nd Annual Meeting of the National Conference of Catholic Charities, New Orleans, 1966. Washington, D.C.: Graphic Arts Press, 1968. 16-19.

143 Gane, E. Marguerite. "Henrietta L. Gordon." Child Welfare, v. 41, no. 10, Dec. 1962. 437-443.

144 Goldmeier, John. "The legacy of Mary Richmond in education and practice." Social Casework, v. 54, no. 5, May 1973. 276-283.

145 Gottlieb, Mel. "The emergency of the professional self in the thought of Bill Rosenthal." Jewish Social Work Forum, v. 12, spring 1976. 7-15.

146 Hamilton, Gordon. "Philip Klein." New directions in social work. Edited by Cora Kasius. Freeport, N.Y.: Books for Libraries Press, 1968. 1-12.

147 Hardwick, Katherine D., Rose Weston Bull and Louisa Brackett. Jeffrey Richardson Brackett: "Everyday puritan." Boston: Privately printed, 1956. 53p.

148 Johnson, Alexander. "Adventures in social education." Adventures in social welfare. Fort Wayne, Ind.: Fort Wayne Printing Co., 1923. 371-387.

149 Johnson, Arlien. "Tribute to Marion Hathway." Human values and social responsibility: Marion Hathway memorial lecture. Compiled by the Council on Social Work Education. New York: The Council, 1961. ix-xv.

150 Katz, Sanford N. "Lydia Rapoport: a personal reminiscence." Creativity in social work; selected writings of Lydia Rapoport. Edited by Sanford N. Katz. Philadelphia: Temple University Press, 1975. xxi-xxvii.

151 Katz, Sidney. "Dr. Harry Cassidy: an appreciation." Social Workers, v. 20, no. 2, Dec. 1951. 24-28.

152 Kendall, Katherine A. "A tribute to the founders." International Social Work, v. 9, no. 4, Oct. 1966. 55-58.

153 Konopka, Gisela. Eduard C. Lindeman and social work philosophy. Minneapolis, Minn.: University of Minnesota Press, 1958. 220p.

154 Lenroot, Katherine F. "Sophonisba Preston Breckinridge, social pioneer." Social Service Review, v. 23, no. 1, March 1949. 88-96.

155 Lundberg, Emma Octavia. "Pathfinders of the middle years: V. Julia C. Lathrop, 1858-1932, a great public servant. VII. Monsignor William J. Kerby, 1870-1936, Priest and teacher. IX. Grace Abbott, 1878-1939, valiant defender of the rights of children." Social Service Review, v. 21, no. 1, March 1947. 11-14, 17-20, 22-25.

156 _____. Unto the least of these: social services for children. New York: Appleton-Century, 1947. 424p.

157 McCormick, Mary J. "Legacy of values (Mary E. Richmond)." Social Casework, v. 42, no. 8, Oct. 1961. 404-409.

158 McMillen, Wayne. "Arlien Johnson: pioneer in community organization." Social Work Papers, v. 6, Dec. 1958. 1-8.

159 Marks, Rachel Bryant. "Published writings of Edith Abbott." Social Service Review, v. 32, no. 1, March 1958. 51-56.

160 Marshall, T. H. "Richard Titmuss--an appreciation." British Journal of Sociology, v. 24, no. 2, June 1973. 137-139.

161 Martin, E. W. "Professor Richard Titmuss, 1907-1973." Social and Economic Administration, v. 8, no. 1, spring 1974. 3-5.

162 "Mary E. Richmond, 1861-1928." Family, v. 9, no. 10, Feb. 1929. 319-359.

163 Ogilvie, Katherine. "Norma Parker's record of service." Australian Journal of Social Work, v. 22, no. 2, June 1969. 5-12.

164 Parker, Norma and Alma E. Hartshorn. "Hazel Mildred Smith, 1916-1970." Australian Journal of Social Work, v. 23, no. 4, Dec. 1970. 2-6.

165 Peebles, Allon. "Harry Morris Cassidy, 1900-1951." Canadian Welfare, v. 27, no. 8, Dec. 15, 1951. 3-7.

166 Perlman, Helen Harris, editor. "Charlotte Towle: an appreciation." Helping: Charlotte Towle on social work and social casework. Chicago: University of Chicago Press, 1969. 1-24.

167 Pettit, Walter W. "Porter R. Lee, 1879-1939: his philosophy and personality." Family, v. 20, no. 9, Jan. 1940. 275-276.

168 Pumphrey, Muriel W. "First step--Mary Richmond's earliest professional reading, 1889-91." Social Service Review, v. 31, no. 2, June 1957. 144-163.

169 _____. "Mary E. Richmond--The practitioner." Social Casework, v. 42, no. 8, Oct. 1961. 375-385.

170 _____. "Mary Richmond and the rise of professional social work in Baltimore: the foundations of a creative career." Doctoral dissertation, Columbia University, 1956. 493p.

171 Rawitscher, Audrey. "Charlotte Towle and the development of social work practice." Applied Social Studies, v. 2, no. 1, Feb. 1970. 3-13.

172 Reynolds, Bertha Capen. An uncharted journey: fifty years of growth in social work. New York: The Citadel Press, 1963. 352p.

173 Rich, Margaret E. "Mary E. Richmond, social worker: 1861-1928." Social Casework, v. 33, no. 9, Nov. 1952. 363-370.

174 _____. "Zilpha Drew Smith: 1852-1926." Family, v. 11, no. 5, May 1930. 67-79.

175 Robinson, Virginia Pollard, editor. Jessie Taft: therapist and social work educator, a professional biography. Philadelphia: University of Pennsylvania Press, 1962. 384p.

176 Sacks, Joel G. "Some of the purposes and methods of Bill Rosenthal: a philosopher of practice." Jewish Social Work Forum, v. 12, spring 1976. 3-6.

177 Schwartz, Barbara. "Re-viewing the social group work group: a beginning (William A. Rosenthal)." Jewish Social Work Forum, v. 12, spring 1976. 16-21.

178   Smith, Jef.   "Profile: Dame Eileen Younghusband."   Social
      Work Today, v. 3, no. 5, 1 June 1972.   2-3.

179   "Sophonisba Preston Breckinridge (memorial issue)."   Social
      Service Review, v. 22, no. 4, Dec. 1948.   417-450.

180   Taylor, Lea D.   "The social settlement and civic responsi-
      bility - The life work of Mary McDowell and Graham
      Taylor."   Social Service Review, v. 28, no. 1, March
      1954.   31-40.

181   Towle, Charlotte.   "Marion E. Kenworthy: a social worker's
      reflections."   Social Service Review, v. 30, no. 4, Dec.
      1956.   446-452.

182   Tulchin, Simon H.   "In memoriam--Lawson G. Lowrey, 1890-
      1957."   American Journal of Orthopsychiatry, v. 28, no.
      1, Jan. 1958.   1-8.

183   Wade, Louise C.   Graham Taylor: pioneer for social justice,
      1851-1938.   Chicago: University of Chicago Press, 1964.
      268p.

184   Waldron, F. E.   "Marjorie Brown: 1909-1964."   British
      Journal of Psychiatric Social Work, v. 8, no. 1, spring
      1965.   3-5.

185   William J. Kerby: democracy through Christ.   n.p.:   William
      J. Kerby Foundation, 1943.   32p.

186   Wisner, Elizabeth.   "Edith Abbott's contributions to social
      work education."   Social Service Review, v. 32, no. 1,
      March 1958.   1-10.

187   Wright, Helen R.   "Three against time: Edith and Grace Ab-
      bott and Sophonisba P. Breckinridge."   Social Service Re-
      view, v. 28, no. 1, March 1954.   41-53.

188   Wright, Lucy.   "Zilpha Drew Smith, 1852-1926; retrospect,
      1945."   Social Worker (Boston), August 1945.   2-
      5.

189   Yabura, Lloyd.   "The legacy of Forrester B. Washington:
      Black social work educator and Nation builder."   Cross-
      ing over.   Edited by Charles L. Sanders.   Atlan-
      ta: School of Social Work, Atlanta University, 1970.
      28-40.

190   Young, Whitney M., Jr. and Frankie V. Adams.   Some pio-
      neers in social work.   Atlanta: School of Social Work,
      Atlanta University, 1957.   43p.

D. PHILOSOPHY AND TRENDS

191 Aptekar, Herbert H. "Education for social responsibility." Journal of Education for Social Work, v. 2, no. 2, fall 1966. 5-11.

192 Barker, Mary W. "Education for social work: a teacher's viewpoint." Social Work Today, v. 1, no. 9, Dec. 1970. 18-23.

193 Boehm, Werner W. "Social work education: issues and problems in light of recent developments." Journal of Education for Social Work, v. 12, no. 1, winter 1976. 20-27.

194 Briar, Scott. "Flexibility and specialization in social work education." Social Work Education Reporter, v. 16, no. 4, Dec. 1968. 45-46, 62-63.

195 _____. "New patterns of education for social work." Social Work, v. 19, no. 3, May 1974. 258.

196 Brieland, Donald. "Social work education: impressions of the art, 1976/77. Public Welfare, v. 34, no. 3, summer 1976. 6-12.

197 Butler, Barbara. "Generalism and specialism in social work training." International Social Work, v. 18, no. 1, 1975. 9-17.

198 Cannon, William B. "Innovations in education in a time of financial adversity." Facing the challenge; plenary session papers from the 1973 Annual Program Meeting, Council on Social Work Education. New York: The Council, 1973. 51-74. Discussion by Leon H. Ginsberg. 75-85.

199 Carlton, Thomas Owen and Marshall Jung. "Adjustment or change: attitudes among social workers." Social Work, v. 17, no. 6, Nov. 1972. 64-71.

200 Chambers, Clarke A. "The slippery side of the curve--Social work education and the acceleration of history." Education for social work; proceedings of the 1964 Annual Program Meeting, Council on Social Work Education. New York: The Council, 1964. 23-36.

201 Class, Norris E. "Crisis and social work education: some challenges." Social Work Papers, v. 10, 1963. 45-49.

202 Couillard, Carmen. "Perspectives on education for social work." Social Worker-Travailleur Social, v. 28, no. 1, Jan. 1960. 57-63.

203 Coyle, Grace L. "Some principles and methods of social work education." International Social Work, v. 1, no. 3, July 1958. 1-6.

204 Dana, Bess S. "Social work education at risk." Mother-at-risk. Edited by Florence Haselkorn. Garden City, N. Y.: School of Social Work, Adelphi University, 1966. 116-125.

205 Duce, Leonard A. "Changes in higher education: new ways of thinking about problems." Journal of Education for Social Work, v. 1, no. 2, fall 1965. 11-18.

206 Falck, Hans S. "Twentieth-century philosophy of science and social work education." Journal of Education for Social Work, v. 6, no. 1, spring 1970. 21-27.

207 Fauri, Fedele F. "Achieving the Great Society: the contribution of social work education." Social Work Education Reporter, v. 14, no. 2, June 1966. 21-24, 40.

208 Feldman, Ronald A. and Ronda S. Connaway. "Toward individualized professional education for social work." Iowa Journal of Social Work, v. 5, no. 4, fall 1972. 21-33.

209 Fisher, Philip S. "A layman looks at social work education." Education for social work; proceedings of the 1964 Annual Program Meeting, Council on Social Work Education. New York: The Council, 1964. 67-74.

210 Fowler, David. "Specialization in professional courses." Social Work Today, v. 3, no. 2, 20 April 1972. 9-10.

211 Frankfurter, Felix. "Social work and professional training." Proceedings of the National Conference of Charities and Correction, Baltimore, 1915. Chicago: Hildmann Printing Co., 1915. 591-596.

212 Gardner, John W. "Remarks; delivered at the 1966 Annual Program Meeting, Council on Social Work Education." Journal of Education for Social Work, v. 2, no. 1, spring 1966. 5-9.

213 Gilbert, Neil and Harry Specht. "The incomplete profession." Social Work, v. 19, no. 6, Nov. 1974. 665-674.

214 Guzzetta, Charles. "Concepts and precepts in social work education." Journal of Education for Social Work, v. 2, no. 2, fall 1966. 40-47.

215 Hale, Mark P. "Focus and scope of a school of social work." Journal of Education for Social Work, v. 3, no. 2, fall 1967. 35-48.

216 Irvine, Elizabeth E. "Education for social work: science or humanity?" Social Work (London), v. 21, no. 1, Jan. 1969. 3-6.

217 _____. "The organization of social work training." International Social Work, v. 13, no. 1, 1970. 18-20.

218 Johnson, Arlien. "Preparing professional leaders for America's welfare program." Social work as human relations; anniversary papers of the New York School of Social Work and the Community Service Society. New York: Columbia University Press, 1949. 101-115.

219 Kendall, Katherine A. "Basic content in professional education for social work." International Social Work, v. 1, no. 2, April 1958. 29-39.

220 _____. "Change, challenge and continuity." Social Work Education Reporter, v. 13, no. 1, March 1965. 13-14.

221 _____. "Choices to be made in social work education." Social work practice, 1966; selected papers of 1966 Annual Forum of the National Conference on Social Welfare. New York: Columbia University Press, 1966. 108-116.

222 _____. "Dream or nightmare? The future of social work education." Journal of Education for Social Work, v. 9, no. 2, spring 1973. 12-23.

223 _____. "To fathom the future." Journal of Education for Social Work, v. 3, no. 1, spring 1967. 21-28.

224 Kidneigh, John C. "Social work education 1993." Goals for social welfare 1973-1993; an overview of the next two decades. Edited by Harleigh B. Trecker. New York: Association Press, 1973. 224-236.

225 Kindelsperger, Kenneth W. "Guidelines for the future." Social Work Education Reporter, v. 10, no. 6, Dec. 1962. 1-4.

226 Lee, Porter R. Social work as cause and function and other papers. New York: Columbia University Press, 1937. 270p.

227 Leonard, Peter. "The place of scientific method in social work education." Case Conference, v. 13, no. 5, Sept. 1966. 163-168.

228 Maas, Henry S. "Purpose, participation and education." Innovations in teaching social work practice. Edited by Lil-

ian Ripple. New York: Council on Social Work Education, 1970. 9-21.

229 _____ . "Social work, knowledge and social responsibility." Journal of Education for Social Work, v. 4, no. 1, spring 1968. 37-48.

230 MacLauchin, Anna Margaret and Helen Pinkus. "The role of a clinical social worker in a changing society." Journal of Education for Social Work, v. 10, no. 2, spring 1974. 59-64.

231 Orten, James D. "Do treatment practitioners need graduate training?" Arete, v. 2, no. 3, spring 1973. 125-133.

232 Pettes, Dorothy E. "The dilemma of social work education in the United States." Social work education in the 1970's. Compiled by the Association of Social Work Teachers. Bradford, Eng.: The Association, 1971. 1-17.

233 Pruyser, Paul W. "Existentialist notes on professional education." Social Work, v. 8, no. 2, April 1963. 82-87.

234 Reichert, Kurt. "Current developments and trends in social work education in the United States." Journal of Education for Social Work, v. 6, no. 2, fall 1970. 39-50.

235 Richmond, Mary E. "The need of a training school in applied philanthropy." Proceedings of the National Conference of Charities and Correction, Toronto, 1897. Boston: Geo. H. Ellis, 1898. 181-186.

236 Robins, Arthur J. "Constraints on innovation in social work education." Applied Social Studies, v. 3, no. 3, Oct. 1971. 147-154.

237 Schorr, Alvin L. "Poverty, politics, and people: the education of social workers." Personnel in anti-poverty programs: implications for social work education. By Sherman Barr, et al. New York: Council on Social Work Education, 1967. 29-35.

238 Silverstein, Max. "The fusion of knowledge and skill." Social Work Education Reporter, v. 15, no. 4, Dec. 1967. 22, 59-60.

239 Slavin, Simon and Felice Davison Perlmutter. "Perspectives for education and training." A design for social work practice. Edited by Felice Davison Perlmutter. New York: Columbia University Press, 1974. 243-265.

240 Smalley, Ruth E. "Freedom and necessity in social work
     education." Education for social work; proceedings of the
     1963 Annual Program Meeting, Council on Social Work
     Education. New York: The Council, 1963. 54-65.

241 _____ . "Values and directions in social work educa-
     tion." Journal of Social Work Process, v. 17, 1969.
     11-36.

242 _____ . "Today's frontiers in social work education."
     Frontiers for social work; a colloquium on the fiftieth
     anniversary of the School of Social Work of the University
     of Pennsylvania. Edited by W. Wallace Weaver. Phila-
     delphia: University of Pennsylvania Press, 1960. 95-
     125.

243 Smith, Zilpha D. "The education of the friendly visitor."
     Proceedings of the National Conference of Charities and
     Correction, Toronto, 1892. Boston: Geo. H. Ellis,
     1892. 445-449.

244 Snelling, Jean M. "Social work education and the American
     scene." Medical Social Work, v. 20, no. 5, Sept. 1967.
     177-183.

245 Stein, Herman D. "Reflections on competence and ideology
     in social work education." Journal of Education for So-
     cial Work, v. 5, no. 1, spring 1969. 81-90.

246 Stinson, Malcolm B. "Crisis and social work education: dan-
     ger plus opportunity." Social Work Papers, v. 10, 1963.
     49-52.

247 _____ . "Social work and the socially disadvantaged: im-
     plications for social work education." Social Work Pap-
     ers, v. 11, 1964. 48-51.

248 Stuart, Richard B. "The role of social work education in in-
     novative human services." Implementing behavioral pro-
     grams for schools and clinics; proceedings of the Banff
     International Conference on Behavior Modification, 1971.
     Edited by F. W. Clark, D. R. Evans and L. A. Hamer-
     lynck. Champaign, Ill.: Research Press, 1972. 3-39.

249 Swain, Doris D. "Coming of age--Social work education."
     Child Welfare, v. 46, no. 4, April 1967. 184, 221.

250 Teicher, Morton I. "Culture of concepts." Social Casework,
     v. 42, no. 10, Dec. 1961. 491-493.

251 Thursz, Daniel. "Professional education for expected political
     action by social workers." Journal of Education for So-
     cial Work, v. 9, no. 3, fall 1973. 87-93.

252 Towle, Charlotte. "General objectives of professional educa-
          tion." Social Service Review, v. 25, no. 4, Dec. 1951.
          427-440.

253 Tyler, Ralph W. "Scholarship and education for the profes-
          sions." Journal of Social Work Process, v. 15, 1966.
          135-151.

254 Vance, Patricia V. "The changing scene in social work edu-
          cation." Child Welfare, v. 51, no. 7, July 1972. 413-
          422.

255 Walker, Walter L. "Changing thought and action styles of
          students and faculty: imperatives for social work educa-
          tion?" Journal of Education for Social Work, v. 8,
          no. 1, winter 1972. 56-63.

256 Weil, Henry. "A new degree challenges tradition." Change,
          v. 6, no. 10, Dec./Jan. 1975. 18-20.

257 Wittman, Milton. "Preventive social work: a goal for prac-
          tice and education." Social Work, v. 6, no. 1, Jan.
          1961. 19-28.

258 Wright, Helen R. "Social work education: problems for the
          future." New directions in social work. Edited by Cora
          Kasius. Freeport, N. Y.: Books for Libraries Press,
          1968. 176-193.

259 Yarbrough, Roy D. "Operationalism: a philosophy for social
          work education." Journal of Education for Social Work,
          v. 11, no. 2, spring 1975. 116-121.

260 Yelaja, Shankar A. "Freedom and authority in professional
          education." Indian Journal of Social Work, v. 32, no. 4,
          Oct. 1971. 305-313.

E.   ACCREDITATION AND ACCOUNTABILITY [See also Sections
     II. C; III. F; IX. F.]

261 American Association of Schools of Social Work. Manual of
          accrediting. Chicago: American Association of Schools
          of Social Work, 1943. 59p.

262 Arkava, Morton L. and E. Clifford Brennen, editors. Com-
          petency-based education for social work: evaluation and
          curriculum issues. New York: Council on Social Work
          Education, 1976. 204p.

263 Biestek, Felix P. "Accreditation--Implications for social
          work education." Education for social work; proceedings
          of the 1960 Annual Program Meeting, Council on Social
          Work Education. New York: The Council, 1960. 93-99.

264 Bloom, Martin. "Analysis of the research on educating social work students." Journal of Education for Social Work, v. 12, no. 3, fall 1976. 3-10.

265 Boehm, Werner W. "Evaluating the effectiveness of the educational program." Objectives of the social work curriculum of the future. New York: Council on Social Work Education, 1959. 245-254.

266 Canadian Association of Schools of Social Work. Manual of standards and procedures for the accreditation of programmes of social work education. Ottawa: The Association, 1975. 50p.

267 Council on Social Work Education. Colleges and universities with accredited undergraduate social work programs. New York: The Council, annual.

268 _____. Major issues in curriculum policy and current practices in accreditation; a series of papers delivered at the 1961 Annual Program Meeting, Council on Social Work Education. New York: The Council, 1961. 29p.

269 _____. Manual of accrediting standards for graduate professional schools of social work. New York: The Council, 1953.

270 _____. _____. New York: The Council, 1965. 79p.

271 _____. _____. Revised. New York: The Council, 1971. 79p.

272 _____. Schools of social work with accredited Master's degree program. New York: The Council, annual.

273 _____. "Standards for the accreditation of baccalaureate degree programs in social work." Social Work Education Reporter, v. 21, no. 3, Sept. 1973. 13-16.

274 Hollis, Ernest V. and Alice L. Taylor. "Accreditation of social work education." Social work education in the United States. New York: Columbia University Press, 1951. 361-388.

275 Kidneigh, John C. "Accrediting of professional schools of social work." Education for social work; proceedings of the 1954 Annual Program Meeting, Council on Social Work Education. New York: The Council, 1954. 42-49.

276 Levy, Charles S. "A framework for planning and evaluating social work education." Journal of Education for Social Work, v. 8, no. 2, spring 1972. 40-47.

277 Loewenberg, Frank M. and Alfred Stamm. "Standard setting in social work education." The current scene in social work education. By Arnulf M. Pins, et al. New York: Council on Social Work Education, 1971. 29-39.

278 Nowak, Mary Jane and William E. Stilwell. Developmental models for accountability in undergraduate social work education. Arlington, Va.: ERIC Document Reproduction Service, 1974. 22p. ED 115149.

279 Nyquist, Ewald B. "The meaning and control of professional accreditation analyzed." Social Work Education Reporter, v. 10, no. 3, June-July 1962. 4-5.

280 _____. "The wing wherewith we fly to heaven or the real function of accreditation." Education for social work; proceedings of the 1964 Annual Program Meeting, Council on Social Work Education. New York: The Council, 1964. 105-122.

281 Oviatt, Boyd E., editor. Evaluation and accountability in social work education. Salt Lake City: Graduate School of Social Work, University of Utah, 1973. 50p.

282 Regensburg, Jeanette. "Some implications for the practicing agency arising from discontinuing the accreditation of specialized sequences." Education for social work; proceedings of the 1959 Annual Program Meeting, Council on Social Work Education. New York: The Council, 1959. 41-45. Comments by Roger Cumming and William Wilsnack. 45-50.

283 Reichert, Kurt. "Commission on Accreditation survey of non-discriminatory practice in accredited graduate schools of social work in the United States." Social Work Education Reporter, v. 16, no. 4, Dec. 1968. 20-23, 70.

284 _____. "Some national trends in accrediting and their relationship to graduate social work education." Social Work Education Reporter, v. 16, no. 1, March 1968. 39, 52-53.

285 United States. Social and Rehabilitation Service. Social work education planning and assessment system: handbook of fundamental assessment concepts; manual for project managers; appendices. Washington, D. C.: Government Printing Office, 1976. 1 v. (various pagings)

F. COUNCIL ON SOCIAL WORK EDUCATION

286 Conrad, Irene Farnham. "The organization, objectives and program of the National Council on Social Work Education." Compass, v. 28, no. 3, March 1947. 3-6.

287 Council on Social Work Education. "Future program and structure of the Council on Social Work Education; final report of Special Board Committee and action by Board of
Directors, March 24, 1966." Social Work Education Reporter, v. 14, no. 2, June 1966. 18-20.

288 _____. Meeting human needs by ensuring the quality
and quantity of social workers: the role of the Council
on Social Work Education. New York: The Council,
n. d.

289 Coyle, Grace L. "Mutuality--The foundation principle of the
Council on Social Work Education." Education for social
work; proceedings of the 1960 Annual Program Meeting,
Council on Social Work Education. New York: The
Council, 1960. 81-89.

290 Cumming, Roger. "Quantity and quality in social work education: a commitment for the future." Social Work Education Reporter, v. 14, no. 1, March 1966. 16-17, 44-45.

291 Grangrade, K. D. "The India Project seen through the eyes
of a Delhi participant." Social Work Education Reporter,
v. 10, no. 2, April 1962. 7-10.

292 Hartman, Nelie M. "A team member reviews the CSWE India Project." Social Work Education Reporter, v. 10,
no. 2, April 1962. 1-5.

293 Kendall, Katherine A. "Education for social work." Social
Work Journal, v. 35, no. 1, Jan. 1954. 19-22, 32.

294 _____. "Highlights of the new CSWE program of international cooperation in social work education." Social
Work Education Reporter, v. 15, no. 2, June 1967. 20-
23, 37, 42.

295 _____. "Issues and problems in social work education."
Social Work Education Reporter, v. 14, no. 1, March
1966. 15, 34-38, 48.

296 King, Anna E. "The place of the professional educational association in the field of social work." Compass, v. 27,
no. 3, March 1946. 20-24.

297 Pins, Arnulf M. "Challenge and change in social work education." Social Work Education Reporter, v. 17, no. 1,
March 1969. 34A-34D.

298 _____. "Current program and future priorities of the
Council on Social Work Education." Social Work Education Reporter, v. 16, no. 1, March 1968. 27A-38A.

299 _____ . "Current realities and future opportunities for social work education." Journal of Education for Social Work, v. 3, no. 1, spring 1967. 51-59.

300 _____ . "Entering the Seventies: changing priorities for social work education." Social Work Education Reporter, v. 18, no. 1, March 1970. 31R-38R.

301 Witte, Ernest F. "Profession of social work: professional associations." Encyclopedia of social work. 16th issue, v. 2. New York: National Association of Social Workers, 1971. 972-982.

II. PROFESSIONAL ISSUES AND SOCIAL WORK EDUCATION

A. VALUES AND ETHICS [See also Section III. E. 12.]

302 Aptekar, Herbert H. "The concept of social responsibility in social work education." International Social Work, v. 9, no. 4, Oct. 1966. 50-54.

303 Bowers, Swithun. "Social work policies, services and supporting values." Child Welfare, v. 39, no. 3, March 1960. 1-4.

304 Brown, Malcolm J. "Social work values in a developing country." Social Work, v. 15, no. 1, Jan. 1970. 107-112.

305 Bye, Lilian. "Social values and social work education." International Social Work, v. 12, no. 1, 1969. 48-63.

306 Cannon, Mary Antoinette. "The philosophy of social work and its place in the professional curriculum." Proceedings of the National Conference of Social Work, 1930. Chicago: University of Chicago Press, 1931. 520-527.

307 Costin, Lela B. "Values in social work education: a study." Social Service Review, v. 38, no. 3, Sept. 1964. 271-280.

308 Council on Social Work Education. The school's responsibility for explicit and implicit communication of value and ethical content; workshop report of the 1960 Annual Program Meeting. New York: The Council, 1960. 23p.

309 Frankel, Charles. "Social values and professional values." Journal of Education for Social Work, v. 5, no. 1, spring 1969. 29-35.

310 Frings, Margaret. "Professional acculturation of the social worker." Catholic Charities Review, v. 49, no. 7, Sept. 1965. 11-17.

311 Gibbons, W. Eugene. "Undergraduate social work: the influence on values of undergraduate social work education." Doctoral dissertation, University of Utah, 1974. 183p.

312 Halmos, Paul, editor. Moral issues in the training of teach-
     ers and social workers. Keele, Eng.: University Col-
     lege of North Staffordshire, 1960. 153p.

313 Hasan, Saiyid Zafar. "Programme of action for the profes-
     sion of social work to attain goals of social reconstruc-
     tion." Social Work Forum, v. 5, no. 2, April 1967.
     5-9.

314 Johnson, Arlien. "Educating professional social workers for
     ethical practice." Social Service Review, v. 29, no. 2,
     June 1955. 125-136.

315 Kendall, Katherine A., editor. Social work values in an age
     of discontent. New York: Council on Social Work Educa-
     tion, 1970. 106p.

316 Kohs, Samuel Calmin. The roots of social work. New York:
     Association Press, 1966. 189p.

317 Levy, Charles S. "Education for social work ethics." So-
     cial work ethics. New York: Human Sciences Press,
     1976. 226-238.

318 Lifshitz, Michaela. "Quality professionals: Does training
     make a difference? A personal construct theory study of
     the issue." British Journal of Social and Clinical Psy-
     chology, v. 13, part 2, June 1974. 183-189.

319 Lundy, Lawrence Allen. "Learning the ethical norms of prac-
     titioner-client relationships at a school of social work."
     Doctoral dissertation, University of Toronto, 1969. 213p.

320 McCormick, Mary J. "Dimensions of social work values in
     the United States: implications for social work educa-
     tion." International Social Work, v. 12, no. 3, 1969.
     14-28.

321 _____. "Professional codes and the educational pro-
     cess." Journal of Education for Social Work, v. 2, no.
     2, fall 1966. 57-65.

322 MacDonald, Mary E. "The teaching of values and ethics in
     social work education, by Muriel W. Pumphrey: review."
     Social Service Review, v. 33, no. 4, Dec. 1959. 437-
     442.

323 McLeod, Donna L. and Henry J. Meyer. "A study of the
     values of social workers." Behavioral science for social
     workers. Edited by Edwin J. Thomas. New York:
     Free Press, 1967. 401-416.

324 Marriage, Adrian J. and Gerald W. Pepper. "Experiment in stimulating the student's professional imagination." Social Casework, v. 43, no. 2, Feb. 1962. 59-64.

325 Nanavatty, Meher C. "Obligation of the profession of social work towards social reconstruction: its implications for social work education and practice." Social Work Forum, v. 5, no. 1, Jan. 1967. 11-14.

326 National Association of Social Workers. Ad Hoc Committee on Advocacy. "The social worker as advocate: champion of social victims." Social Work, v. 14, no. 2, April 1969. 16-22.

327 Papanoutsos, Evanghelos. "Human values in social work education." Public Welfare, v. 23, no. 3, July 1965. 167-170.

327a Perlman, Helen Harris. "Believing and doing: values in social work education." Social Casework, v. 57, no. 6, June 1976. 381-390. Commentary by Merl C. Hokenstad, 391-392; by Anne C. Schwartz, 393-396.

328 Preas, Mary E. "Human values and the self-concept in social process: essential factors in educating for social responsibility." Creative curricula in undergraduate social welfare education. Edited by Robert M. Ryan and Amy Reynolds. Atlanta: Southern Regional Education Board, 1970. 9-38.

329 Pumphrey, Muriel W. The teaching of values and ethics in social work education. The social work curriculum study, v. 13. New York: Council on Social Work Education, 1959. 164p.

330 Samoff, Zelda and Margaret Mitter. "Stimulating social awareness." Social Work Education Reporter, v. 11, no. 6, Dec.-Jan. 1964. 6-7, 29.

331 Sharwell, George R. "Can values be taught? A study of two variables related to orientation of social work graduate students toward public dependency." Journal of Education for Social Work, v. 10, no. 2, spring 1974. 99-105.

332 Stein, Herman D., et al. "Teachability and application of social work values; a panel discussion." International Social Work, v. 12, no. 1, 1969. 23-34.

333 Tanenbaum, David E. "Bibliography on social values and social work education." International Social Work, v. 12, no. 1, 1969. 80-86.

334 Valk, Margaret A. "Reflections on the teaching of ethics and social work." Case Conference, v. 13, no. 6, Oct. 1966. 209-212.

335 Vigilante, Joseph L. "Between values and science: education for the profession during a moral crisis or Is proof truth?" Journal of Education for Social Work, v. 10, no. 3, fall 1974. 107-115.

336 Yasas, Frances Maria. "Gandhian values and professional social work values with special emphasis on the dignity of man." Doctoral dissertation, Catholic University of America, 1962. 295p.

B. SOCIAL WELFARE MANPOWER [See also Sections III. E. 2, E. 11, F.]

337 Ad Hoc Committee on Manpower Issues of the Council on Social Work Education and National Association of Social Workers. "A plan for resolving the manpower issue." NASW News, v. 14, no. 2, Feb. 1969. 34-46.

338 Adler, Jack and Jacob L. Trobe. "The obligations of social work education in relation to meeting manpower needs at differential levels in social work." Child Welfare, v. 47, no. 6, June 1968. 346-353, 363.

339 Alexander, Chauncey A. "Implications of the NASW Standards for Social Service Manpower." Journal of Education for Social Work, v. 11, no. 1, winter 1975. 3-8.

340 Arden House Workshop on Manpower. Manpower: a community responsibility; proceedings of the workshop, 1967. New York: National Commission for Social Work Careers, National Association of Social Workers, 1968. 60p.

341 Austin, Michael J., Edward Kelleher and Philip L. Smith, editors. The field consortium: manpower development and training in social welfare and corrections. Tallahassee, Fla.: State University System of Florida, 1972. 121p.

342 _____ and Philip L. Smith. "Manpower utilization and educational articulation: the Florida experiment in collaborative planning." Approaches to innovation in social work education. Compiled by the Council on Social Work Education. New York: The Council, 1974. 1-14.

243 _____ and _____, editors. Statewide career planning for health and welfare. Tallahassee, Fla.: State University System of Florida, 1972. 217p.

344 Baker, Mary R. "Personnel needs and accountability: pro-
     blems and projects." Social Work Education Reporter,
     v. 10, no. 1, Feb. 1962. 3-6.

345 Barker, Robert L. and Thomas L. Briggs. Differential use
     of social work manpower; an analysis and demonstration-
     study. New York: National Association of Social Work-
     ers, 1968. 270p.

346 _____ and _____, editors. Manpower research
     on the utilization of baccalaureate social workers: impli-
     cations for education. Washington, D. C.: Government
     Printing Office, 1971. 109p.

347 _____ and _____. Using teams to deliver so-
     cial services. Syracuse, N. Y.: Syracuse University
     Press, 1969. 40p.

348 Barr, Sherman, et al. Personnel in anti-poverty programs:
     implications for social work education. New York:
     Council on Social Work Education, 1967. 66p.

349 Blum, Arthur. "Differential use of manpower in public wel-
     fare." Social Work, v. 11, no. 1, Jan. 1966. 16-21.

350 Boehm, Werner W. "The differential use of personnel--the
     contribution of education." Child Welfare, v. 47, no. 8,
     Oct. 1968. 455-460, 491.

351 _____. "Manpower planning in social welfare." Jour-
     nal of Education for Social Work, v. 6, no. 1, spring
     1970. 11-20.

352 Briggs, Thomas L. "A critique of the NASW manpower
     statement." Journal of Education for Social Work, v. 11,
     no. 1, winter 1975. 9-15.

353 _____. "Current conceptualizations of the B.A. level
     practitioner in human services: implications for under-
     graduate education." Developing programs in the helping
     services; field experience, methods courses, employment
     implications. Edited by Dutton Teague and Dorothy P.
     Buck. Boulder, Colo.: Western Interstate Commission
     for Higher Education, 1968. 1-13.

354 _____. "Social work manpower: developments and
     dilemmas of the 1970's." Educating MSW students to
     work with other social welfare personnel. Edited by
     Margaret Purvine. New York: Council on Social Work
     Education, 1973. 4-31. Discussion by Elsbeth Kahn.
     32-37.

355 Burbank, Edmund G. "What the schools of social work can do to increase the pool of trained correctional personnel." Education for social work; proceedings of the 1961 Annual Program Meeting, Council on Social Work Education. New York: The Council, 1961. 163-177.

356 Carlsen, Thomas, editor. Social work manpower utilization in mental health programs; proceedings of a workshop. Syracuse, N. Y.: Syracuse University Press, 1969. 41p.

357 Conference on International Social Welfare Manpower. Proceedings of the conference, 1964, Washington, D. C. Washington, D. C.: Government Printing Office, 1965. 112p.

358 Council on Social Work Education. Social work education and social welfare manpower; present realities and future imperatives; papers by Ellen Winston and others. New York: The Council, 1965. 71p.

359 Daly, Dorothy Bird. "The future baccalaureate degree social worker: implications for social work education." Continuities in undergraduate social welfare education. Compiled by the Council on Social Work Education. New York: The Council, 1969. 41-50.

360 _____, Martin B. Loeb and Frederick A. Whitehouse. The social services and related manpower. Washington, D. C.: Government Printing Office, 1971. 29p.

361 _____. "Social work manpower." Encyclopedia of social work. 16th issue, v. 2. New York: National Association of Social Workers, 1971. 1481-1486.

362 Dinerman, Miriam. "Options in social work manpower and education." Social Work, v. 20, no. 5, Sept. 1975. 348-352.

363 Euster, Gerald L. "The job market for undergraduate social work majors: implications for social work education." Social Work Education Reporter, v. 21, no. 2, April-May 1973. 39-43.

364 Fradkin, Helen, editor. Use of personnel in child welfare agencies; proceedings of the Arden House Conference, 1966, Harriman, N. Y. New York: School of Social Work, Columbia University, 1966. 47p.

365 French, David G. Needed research on social work manpower: with particular reference to program areas for which the federal government has responsibility; report to the Task Force on Social Work Education and Manpower. Washing-

ton, D. C.: U. S. Department of Health, Education, and Welfare, 1964. Various pagings.

366 Glover, E. Elizabeth. "Education, training, and manpower." Child Welfare, v. 45, no. 3, March 1966. 124, 158.

367 Gockel, Galen L. "Social work and recent college graduates: a report on two national surveys." Social Work Education Reporter, v. 15, no. 2, June 1967. 24-25, 38-39.

368 Herberg, Dorothy Chave. "Career patterns and work participation of graduate female social workers." Doctoral dissertation, University of Michigan, 1970. 266p.

369 _____. "A study of work participation by graduate female social workers: some implications for professional social work training." Journal of Education for Social Work, v. 9, no. 3, fall 1973. 16-23.

370 Illinois State Board of Higher Education. Master Plan Committee. Social work education in Illinois; report. Arlington, Va.: ERIC Document Reproduction Service, 1969. 36p. ED 040649

371 Kermish, Irving, Barbara Kohlman and Frank Kushin. The professionally educated social worker in public assistance programs: a California perspective. Berkeley: School of Social Welfare, University of California, 1970. 106p.

372 Linford, Alton A. "The B.L.S. Study and its import for social work education." Education for social work; proceedings of the 1962 Annual Program Meeting, Council on Social Work Education. New York: The Council, 1962. 100-105.

373 Loewenberg, Frank M. "Social work education responds to the manpower shortage: a statistical review, 1957-67." Social Service Review, v. 43, no. 1, March 1969. 69-73.

374 National Association of Social Workers. Standards for social service manpower. Washington, D. C.: The Association, 1973. 19p.

374a Ogren, Evelyn H. Social work manpower needs in the State of Maryland, mid 70's-mid 80's: an analysis of program and professional social work staff. Baltimore: School of Social Work and Community Planning, University of Maryland at Baltimore, 1975. 117p.

375 Padberg, William Hugo. "The social welfare labor market attachment of the undergraduate social work major." Doctoral dissertation, Columbia University, 1974. 267p.

376 Pins, Arnulf M. "The public welfare worker 1965-1975: implications for social work education." Public Welfare, v. 25, no. 1, Jan. 1967. 21-27.

377 _____. "Social work education and social welfare manpower: The United States picture." International Social Work, v. 9, no. 1, Jan. 1966. 5-11.

378 _____. Who chooses social work, when and why? New York: Council on Social Work Education, 1963. 212p.

379 Richan, Willard C. "A theoretical scheme for determining roles of professional and nonprofessional personnel." Social Work, v. 6, no. 4, Oct. 1961. 22-28.

380 Rosen, Alex. "Changing patterns in service delivery and utilization of manpower: implications for the MSW program." Social Work Education Reporter, v. 17, no. 2, June 1969. 34-37, 57.

381 Schreiber, Paul. "Social work need--social welfare education." Social need and education for social welfare. Edited by Benjamin Lyndon. Syracuse, N. Y.: State University of New York, 1968. 14-23.

382 Schwartz, Edward E., editor. Manpower in social welfare: research perspectives. New York: National Association of Social Workers, 1966. 160p.

383 Siegel, Sheldon. Social service manpower needs: an overview to 1980. New York: Council on Social Work Education, 1975. 19p.

384 Sobey, Francine S. "New educational content for a changing social work practice: focus on manpower." Educating MSW students to work with other social welfare personnel. Edited by Margaret Purvine. New York: Council on Social Work Education, 1973. 49-62.

385 Southern Regional Education Board. Action for social welfare manpower in the South; the final report of the Undergraduate Social Welfare Manpower Project. Atlanta: The Board, 1970. 70p.

386 Stein, Herman D. "Social work manpower and training." Social Work Education Reporter, v. 20, no. 1, Dec.-Jan. 1972. 23-24.

387 Swain, Doris D. "Social work education and manpower for child welfare." Child Welfare, v. 45, no. 8, Oct. 1966. 468-470.

388   Teare, Robert J. and Harold L. McPheeters. Manpower utili-
      zation in social welfare: a report based on a symposium
      on manpower utilization in social welfare services. At-
      lanta: Southern Regional Education Board, 1970. 74p.

389   Teeple, John. Implications of career openings in social wel-
      fare occupations for priorities in vocational-technical edu-
      cation; working papers. Arlington, Va.: ERIC Document
      Reproduction Service, 1968. 34p. ED 036611

390   United States. Department of Health, Education, and Welfare.
      Departmental Task Force on Social Work Education and
      Manpower. Closing the gap in social work manpower;
      report. Washington, D. C.: Government Printing Office,
      1965. 90p.

391   Vidaver, Robert M. Developments in human services educa-
      tion and manpower. New York: Behavioral Publications,
      1973. 363-524.

392   Watson, Elizabeth V. "Training and utilization of social work
      manpower." International social welfare research and
      demonstration. Los Angeles: Regional Research Institute
      in Social Welfare, School of Social Work, University of
      Southern California, 1974. 121-137.

393   Wedemeyer, J. M. "The development of social work programs
      in the California State colleges." Social Work Education,
      v. 9, no. 1, Feb. 1961. 16-17.

393a Western Interstate Commission for Higher Education. Man-
      power: Western graduate programs in social work.
      Boulder, Colo.: The Commission, 1971. 10p.

394   Winston, Ellen. Social welfare education and careers in the
      South. Atlanta: Southern Regional Education Board,
      1975. 33p.

395   Wisconsin. Coordinating Council for Higher Education. So-
      cial welfare education in Wisconsin; a coordinated ap-
      proach. Madison: The Council, 1968. 28p.

396   Wittman, Milton. "Implications of social welfare manpower
      needs in 1975 for professional education and social plan-
      ning." Social Service Review, v. 39, no. 4, Dec. 1965.
      459-467.

397   _____. "Meeting the challenge of change: new develop-
      ments in social work practice and education." Journal
      of Education for Social Work, v. 3, no. 2, fall 1967.
      90-98.

398 _____ . "Social work manpower in the health services."
American Journal of Public Health, v. 55, no. 3, March
1965. 393-399.

C. SOCIAL WORK PRACTICE [See also Sections III.C.2; XIII.]

399 Abbott, Edith. Social welfare and professional education.
Chicago: University of Chicago Press, 1942. 321p.

400 Anderson, Delwin. "Practice and education: a commentary."
Social Work, v. 19, no. 16, Nov. 1974. 651-653.

401 Baker, Ron. "The multirole practitioner in the generic orientation to social work practice." British Journal of Social
Work, v. 6, no. 3, autumn 1976. 327-352.

402 Bartlett, Harriett M. "Implications of the Hollis-Taylor report for social work practitioners." Medical Social Work,
v. 2, no. 1, Jan. 1953. 1-23.

403 _____ . "Responsibilities of social work practitioners
and educators toward building a strong profession." Social Service Review, v. 34, no. 4, Dec. 1960. 379-391.
Discussion by Louise A. Frey. 391-393.

404 _____ . "The study of social work education: its significance for the whole field of social work." Social
Work Journal, v. 32, no. 4, Oct. 1951. 172-177.

405 Bass, Deborah. "Learn from the nurses." Social Work,
v. 21, no. 1, Jan. 1976. 74.

406 Bell, William A. "Practice critique of social work curriculum in view of current trends and new developments in
practice." Social Work Education Reporter, v. 20, no.
3, Sept./Oct. 1972. 32-34.

407 Bishop, Julia Ann. "A consideration of the gaps between education and practice." Education for social work; proceedings of the 1963 Annual Program Meeting, Council on Social Work Education. New York: The Council, 1963.
206-213.

408 Blackey, Eileen. "Issues in social work education--new and
changing demands made of the profession." Education
for social work; proceedings of the 1964 Annual Program
Meeting, Council on Social Work Education. New York:
The Council, 1964. 75-89.

409 Brennan, Tom. "On becoming and being professional."
Australian Social Work, v. 25, no. 1, March 1972. 3-6.

410 Briar, Scott. "Changes in education will change practice."
      Social Work, v. 20, no. 5, Sept. 1975. 342, 424.

411 _____. "Practice and academia." Social Work, v. 18,
      no. 6, Nov. 1973. 2.

412 Chien, James M. N. "Does training meet the needs of the
      profession?" International Social Work, v. 19, no. 2,
      1976. 6-11.

413 Council on Social Work Education. Policy statements on so-
      cial work practice and education and structure and quality
      in social work education adopted by the House of Dele-
      gates, March 1976. New York: The Council, 1976.
      1 v. (various pagings)

414 Dawes, Anna L. "The need of training schools for a new
      profession." Sociology in institutions of learning, being
      a report of the seventh section of the International Con-
      gress of Charities, Correction and Philanthropy, Chicago,
      1893. Edited by Amos G. Warner. Baltimore: John
      Hopkins Press, 1894. 14-20.

415 Dolgoff, Ralph. An analysis of the responses to the Reports
      of the Task Force on Structure and Quality in Social Work
      Education and the Task Force on Practice and Education.
      New York: Council on Social Work Education, 1975.
      49p.

416 _____. Report to the Task Force on Social Work
      Practice and Education. New York: Council on Social
      Work Education, 1974. 33p.

417 Erlich, John L. and Jesse F. McClure. "The grassroots
      ivory tower." Social Work, v. 19, no. 6, Nov. 1974.
      653-655.

418 Family Service Association of America. "Position statement
      of family service agencies regarding graduate schools of
      social work." Smith College Studies in Social Work,
      v. 43, no. 2, Feb. 1973. 108-110.

419 Flexner, Abraham. "Is social work a profession?" Proceed-
      ings of the National Conference of Charities and Correc-
      tion, Baltimore, 1915. Chicago: Hildmann Printing Co.,
      1915. 576-590.

420 Gartner, Alan. "Four professions: how different, how alike."
      Social Work, v. 20, no. 5, Sept. 1975. 353-358.

421 Gingerich, Wallace J., Ronald A. Feldman and John S. Wo-
      darski. "Accuracy in assessment: Does training help?"
      Social Work, v. 21, no. 1, Jan. 1976. 40-48.

422 Goltermann, Glen E. Attitudes of social workers in a welfare department toward the usefulness of their education. Arlington, Va.: ERIC Document Reproduction Service, 1974. 11p. ED 123138.

423 Greenwood, Ernest. "Attributes of a profession." Social Work, v. 2, no. 3, July 1957. 45-55.

424 Hepworth, Dean H., editor. Assuring practitioner competence: whose responsibility? Salt Lake City: Graduate School of Social Work, University of Utah, 1974. 90p.

425 Kahn, Alfred J. "Current conceptualizations of social work practice: their significance for social work education." Education for social work; proceedings of the 1962 Annual Program Meeting, Council on Social Work Education. New York: The Council, 1962. 28-44.

426 Kendall, Katherine A. "Social work education: a responsibility of the total profession." Social Casework, v. 34, no. 1, Jan. 1953. 17-23.

427 Kidneigh, John C. "Significance of program developments in the National Association of Social Workers for social work education." Education for social work: proceedings of the 1960 Annual Program Meeting, Council on Social Work Education. New York: The Council, 1960. 175-186.

428 Kruse, Arthur. "An appraisal of the kind of talent that is apt to be attracted by the present status of social work practice." Education for social work; proceedings of the 1960 Annual Program Meeting, Council on Social Work Education. New York: The Council, 1960. 72-80.

429 Lechnyr, Ronald J. "Learn from the teachers." Social Work, v. 21, no. 1, Jan. 1976. 75.

430 Levy, Charles S. "A backdrop of values." Social Work, v. 21, no. 1, Jan. 1976. 71-72.

431 Lewis, Harold. "Standards in social work: implications for practice and education." Clinical Social Work Journal, v. 3, no. 3, fall 1975. 211-224.

432 Lovata, William M. "The appropriate performance activities of the beginning practitioner in social work based upon the opinions expressed by students, educators, and practitioners." Doctoral dissertation, St. Louis University, 1975. 146p.

433 Lubove, Roy. The professional altruist: the emergence of

social work as a career, 1880-1930. Cambridge, Mass.: Harvard University Press, 1965. 291p.

434 Lucas, Leon. "Can we reconcile generic education and specialized practice: Part II." Journal of Psychiatric Social Work, v. 23, no. 4, June 1954. 215-222.

435 Lurie, Abraham. The relationship between social work practice and education; report of the Task Force on Practice and Education. New York: Council on Social Work Education, 1974. 8p.

436 Mayadas, Nazneen S. and Wayne D. Duehn. "Toward an empirically based practice stance: another look at the relationship between social work education and professional practice." Iowa Journal of Social Work, v. 6, nos. 2 and 3, Dec. 1975. 81-99.

437 Melichercik, John. "Social work education and social work practice." Social Worker-Travailleur Social, v. 41, no. 3, spring 1973. 22-27.

438 Meyer, Henry J. "Profession of social work: contemporary characteristics." Encyclopedia of social work. 16th issue, v. 2. New York: National Association of Social Workers, 1971. 959-972.

439 Miller, Stephen J. "Professions, Human service." Encyclopedia of social work. 16th issue, v. 2. New York: National Association of Social Workers, 1971. 982-999.

440 Minahan, Anne. "Generalists and specialists in social work-- Implications for education and practice." Arete, v. 4, no. 2, fall 1976. 55-67.

441 National Association of Social Workers. "1975 NASW Delegate Assembly issues paper: social work practice-education relationships." NASW News, v. 20, no. 3, March 1975. 5-7.

442 _____. National Board of Directors. "Board takes practice/education stance." NASW News, v. 20, no. 10, Nov. 1975. 14-15, 23.

443 Palmera, Paul J. "One foot in academia, one in practice." Social Work, v. 20, no. 4, July 1975. 320-321.

444 Pins, Arnulf M. "Changes in social work education and their implications for practice." Social Work, v. 16, no. 2, April 1971. 5-15.

445 Piven, Herman. "The fragmentation of social work." Social Casework, v. 50, no. 2, Feb. 1969. 88-94.

446 "Practice/education relationship enriched." NASW News, v. 21, no. 5, May 1976. 6-7.

447 Ramachandran, P. "Students' changing views on social work." Indian Journal of Social Work, v. 33, no. 3, Oct. 1972. 191-198.

448 Rapoport, Lydia. "In defense of social work: an examination of stress in the profession." Social Service Review, v. 34, no. 1, March 1960. 62-74.

449 Reinitz, Freda E. "An assessment of essentiality and adequacy of social work education in relation to the demands of practice." Doctoral dissertation, University of Pennsylvania, 1971. 181p.

450 Richan, Willard C. "The social work profession and organized social welfare." Shaping the new social work. Edited by Alfred J. Kahn. New York: Columbia University Press, 1973. 147-168.

451 _____ and Allan R. Mendelsohn. Social work: the unloved profession. New York: New Viewpoints, 1973. 226p.

452 Shapiro, Solomon. "A study of the needs and satisfactions of social workers as perceived by college students and social workers." Doctoral dissertation, University of Minnesota, 1964. 165p.

453 Shey, Thomas H. "How American social work students view their profession: highlights of a recent survey." Applied Social Studies, v. 2, no. 3, Oct. 1970. 137-143.

454 Smalley, Ruth E. "Can we reconcile generic education and specialized practice? Part I." Journal of Psychiatric Social Work, v. 23, no. 4, June 1954. 207-214.

455 Smith, Elliott D. "Education and the task of making social work professional." Social Service Review, v. 31, no. 1, March 1957. 1-10.

456 _____. "Keeping social work and social work education truly professional." Social Service Review, v. 34, no. 4, Dec. 1960. 394-401.

457 Specht, Harry. "The deprofessionalization of social work." Social Work, v. 17, no. 2, March 1972. 3-15.

458 Stevenson, Olive. "Relationships between educators and practitioners in social work." Social work education in the 1970's. Compiled by the Association of Social Work Teachers. Bradford, Eng.: The Association, 1971. 103-112.

459 Stubbins, Henry. "The profession's expectations of undergraduate education." Social Worker-Travailleur Social, v. 35, no. 2, May 1967. 64-70.

460 Taylor, Alice L. "The responsibility of professional membership associations for social work education." Social Worker, v. 20, no. 2, Dec. 1951. 1-8.

461 Tragler, A., et al. "Students' perception of social work." Indian Journal of Social Work, v. 32, no. 4, Oct. 1971. 321-331.

462 Tropp, Emanuel. "Expectation, performance, and accountability." Social Work, v. 19, no. 3, March 1974. 139-148.

463 Tyler, Ralph W. "Distinctive attributes of education for the professions." Social Work Journal, v. 33, no. 2, April 1952. 55-62, 94.

464 Wasserman, Harry. "Early careers of professional social workers in a public child welfare agency." Social Work, v. 15, no. 3, July 1970. 93-101.

465 Weissman, Myrna M. "Some problems of the recent social work graduate in the integration of learning." Medical Social Work, v. 21, no. 5, Sept. 1968. 137-143.

466 White, Grace. "Generic education for social work: implications for fields of practice." Child Welfare, v. 39, no. 9, Nov. 1960. 10-16.

D. SOCIAL WORK KNOWLEDGE DEVELOPMENT [See also Sections VI. G; VIII; XVI.]

467 Arkava, Morton L. "Social work practice and knowledge: an examination of their relationship." Journal of Education for Social Work, v. 3, no. 2, fall 1967. 5-13.

468 Ballard, Rod. "Knowledge for use in social work practice: some problems of application." Social and Economic Administration, v. 9, no. 3, autumn 1975. 147-152.

469 Bloom, Martin. "The selection of knowledge from the behavioral sciences and its integration into social work curricula." Journal of Education for Social Work, v. 5, no. 1, spring 1969. 15-27.

470 Brieland, Donald. "Broadening the knowledge base through a social services center." Modes of professional education; functions of field instruction in the curriculum; report of a symposium, 1969, New Orleans. Edited by Helen Cassidy. New Orleans: School of Social Work, Tulane University, 1969. 106-121.

471 Burns, Mary E. "Paths to knowledge: some prospects and problems." Journal of Education for Social Work, v. 1, no. 1, spring 1965. 13-17.

472 Chilman, Catherine S. "Production of new knowledge of relevance to social work and social welfare: an examination of knowledge which underlies social work practice and permeates the curriculum." Social Work Education Reporter, v. 17, no. 3, Sept. 1969. 49-53, 57.

473 Finestone, Samuel. "Field teaching and knowledge development." Modes of professional education: functions of field instruction in the curriculum; report of a symposium, 1969, New Orleans. Edited by Helen Cassidy. New Orleans: School of Social Work, Tulane University, 1969. 122-130.

474 Hearn, Gordon, "Phases in the theory-building cycle." Education for social work; proceedings of the 1960 Annual Program Meeting, Council on Social Work Education. New York: The Council, 1960. 38-49.

475 _____. Theory building in social work. Toronto: University of Toronto Press, 1958. 83p.

476 Inlow, Ruby Strand. "Some implications of research in contemporary cultures for the education of social workers." Regional planning for social work education. Edited by Lora Lee Pederson. Nashville, Tenn.: School of Social Work, University of Tennessee, 1949. 71-81.

477 Jack, Barbara T. "Building social work knowledge: an approach to the problem." Social Work Education Reporter, v. 18, no. 1, March 1970. 51-54, 63.

478 Kadushin, Alfred. "The knowledge base of social work." Issues in American social work. Edited by Alfred J. Kahn. New York: Columbia University Press, 1959. 39-79.

479 Kahn, Alfred J. "The nature of social work knowledge." New directions in social work. Edited by Cora Kasius. Freeport, N. Y.: Books for Libraries Press, 1968. 194-214.

480 Kidneigh, John C. "A note on organizing knowledge." Modes of professional education: functions of field instruction in the curriculum; report of a symposium, 1969, New Orleans. Edited by Helen Cassidy. New Orleans: School of Social Work, Tulane University, 1969. 153-160.

481 Kindelsperger, Walter L. "An inquiry into the anatomy of social work knowledge." Modes of professional education:

functions of field instruction in the curriculum; report of a symposium, 1969, New Orleans. Edited by Helen Cassidy. New Orleans: School of Social Work, Tulane University, 1969. 161-198.

482 National Association of Social Workers. Building social work knowledge; report of a conference. New York: The Association, 1964. 115p.

483 Rosen, Aaron. "Doctoral education, professional culture and development of social work knowledge." Applied Social Studies, v. 1, no. 3, Oct. 1969. 151-159.

484 Studt, Elliot. "The contribution of practice and education to social work theory building." Education for social work; proceedings of the 1960 Annual Program Meeting, Council on Social Work Education. New York: The Council, 1960. 50-59.

485 Taber, Merlin. "A knowledge base for social work: three positions." Modes of professional education: functions of field instruction in the curriculum; report of a symposium, 1969, New Orleans. Edited by Helen Cassidy. New Orleans: School of Social Work, Tulane University, 1969. 143-152.

E. SOCIAL CHANGE

486 Blackey, Eileen. "Patterns of social work education in meeting the needs of societies." International Social Work, v. 13, no. 3, 1970. 13-23.

487 Burns, Eveline M. "Reconversion and its implications for the schools of social work." Social Service Review, v. 19, no. 2, June 1945. 194-200.

488 _____. "Tomorrow's social needs and social work education." Journal of Education for Social Work, v. 2, no. 1, spring 1966. 10-20.

489 Council on Social Work Education. Current issues in social work seen in historical perspective; compilation of six papers presented at a workshop held during Annual Program Meeting, St. Louis, Missouri, Jan. 1962. New York: The Council, 1962. 80p.

490 Guzzetta, Charles. "Social change and education for the social professions." Higher education and the social professions. Edited by Henry M. Barlow. Lexington, Ky.: College of Social Professions, University of Kentucky, 1973. 93-112.

491 International Association of Schools of Social Work. Educa-
     tion for social change; human development and national
     progress; proceedings of the 17th International Congress
     of Schools of Social Work, Nairobi, 1974. New York:
     The Association, 1975. 167p.

492 Lebeaux, Charles N. "Learning to live on the curve." Edu-
     cation for social work; proceedings of the 1964 Annual
     Program Meeting, Council on Social Work Education.
     New York: The Council, 1964. 37-46.

493 Lewis, Harold. "Societal crises--strategies for social work
     education." Journal of Education for Social Work, v. 5,
     no. 1, spring 1969. 57-67.

494 Lowy, Louis. "Whither social work education amid social
     change?" Journal of Education for Social Work, v. 4,
     no. 1, spring 1968. 31-36.

495 Pearman, Jean R. and Robert A. Lombardo. "The impact of
     social change on social work education." Arete, v. 3,
     no. 2, fall 1974. 81-92.

496 Smith, Russell E. and John N. Hester. "Social services in
     a technological society." Journal of Education for Social
     Work, v. 10, no. 1, winter 1974. 81-89.

497 Witte, Ernest F. "Some major social problems which chal-
     lenge social work education." Social Work Education Re-
     porter, v. 10, no. 6, Dec. 1962. 1-5, 10.

498 Younghusband, Eileen L. "The challenge of social change to
     education for social work." International Social Work,
     v. 6, no. 2, April 1963. 1-4.

III. GRADUATE SOCIAL WORK EDUCATION
AND SCHOOLS OF SOCIAL WORK

A. GENERAL ASPECTS OF GRADUATE PROGRAMS [See also
Sections I. E; VIII; XI; XII.]

499 Ammons, Paul. "Advanced placement in MSW programs."
Journal of Education for Social Work, v. 11, no. 3, fall
1975. 12-15.

500 Bateman, Richard. "Should our schools of social work do
more than educate?" Proceedings of the 51st Annual
Meeting of the National Conference of Catholic Charities,
Philadelphia, 1965. Washington, D. C.: Graphic Arts
Press, 1968. 44-52.

501 Breckinridge, Sophonisba P. "The new horizons of professional education for social work." Social Service Review, v.
10, no. 3, Sept. 1936. 437-449.

502 Brink, Charles B. "Expansion of education and training facili-
ties." Education for social work; proceedings of the 1964
Annual Program Meeting, Council on Social Work Education. New York: The Council, 1964. 131-138.

503 Carroll, Nancy K. and Ronda S. Connaway. "Ideology and ra-
tionality in social work education." Journal of Education
for Social Work, v. 11, no. 3, fall 1975. 30-37.

504 Cooper and Company. The cost and output of graduate social
work education: an exploratory study. Washington, D. C.:
Government Printing Office, 170. 188p.

505 Council on Social Work Education. Concentrations and special
learning opportunities in the Master of Social Work curricula of graduate schools of social work. New York: The
Council, annual.

506 _____. Schools of social work with accredited Master's
degree program. New York: The Council, annual.

507 _____. Summary information on Master of Social Work
programs. New York: The Council, annual.

48

508 Eades, Joe C. "Starting where the student is: an experiment in accelerated graduate social work education." Journal of Education for Social Work, v. 12, no. 3, fall 1976. 22-28.

509 Family Service Association of America. "Position statement of family service agencies regarding graduate schools of social work." Smith College Studies in Social Work, v. 43, no. 2, Feb. 1973. 108-109.

510 Fellin, Phillip A. "Long-range planning: implications for social work education." Journal of Education for Social Work, v. 10, no. 2, spring 1974. 27-33.

511 Hollis, Ernest V. and Alice L. Taylor. "The graduate professional education for social work." Social work education in the United States. New York: Columbia University Press, 1951. 210-279.

512 Hyde (Laurin) Associates. Planning professional social work education in New York State. Albany: University of the State of New York, 1969. 81p.

513 Jones, Robert Paul, Theodore Ernst, and Constance Osgood. Evaluation of the University of Missouri School of Social Work Experimental Program. Kansas City, Mo.: Institute for Community Studies, 1969. 100p.

514 Kadushin, Alfred. A proposal for an accelerated program in social work education and design for evaluation. Madison: School of Social Work, University of Wisconsin, 1967. 119p.

515 Kelling, George Lee. "The accelerated program of professional social work education at the University of Wisconsin, Madison, compared with the traditional program." Doctoral dissertation, University of Wisconsin, 1973. 439p.

516 Kendall, Katherine A. "Orthodoxy and paradoxes: dilemmas of social work education." Social Work, v. 1, no. 3, July 1956. 43-49.

517 Loewenberg, Frank M. Time and quality in graduate social work education; report of the Special Committee to Study the Length of Graduate Social Work Education. New York: Council on Social Work Education, 1972. 58p.

518 Lyndon, Benjamin H. "The future of master's and doctoral programs in social work education." Undergraduate social work education for practice: a report on curriculum content and issues. Edited by Lester J. Glick. Washington, D. C.: Government Printing Office, 1972. 117-123.

519 McCann, Charles W., editor. Exploring the interfaces of social work education; report of a program in continuing
education for deans and faculties of graduate schools of
social work. Boulder, Colo.: Western Interstate Commission for Higher Education, 1970. 117p.

520 McGlothlin, William J. The professional schools. New York:
Center for Applied Research in Education, 1964. 118p.

521 Meyer, Gregory C. "Systems models and the graduate school
of social work." Doctoral students look at social work
education. Edited by Leila Calhoun Deasy. New York:
Council on Social Work Education, 1971. 53-67.

522 Pins, Arnulf M. "The number, size, output, and programs
of schools of social work and the need for professional
manpower: implications for expansion of graduate social
work education." Social work education and social welfare manpower: present realities and future imperatives.
By Ellen Winston, et al. New York: Council on Social
Work Education, 1965. 27-54.

523 Rosenblatt, Aaron, Marianne Welter and Sophie Wojciechowski.
The Adelphi experiment: accelerating social work education. New York: Council on Social Work Education,
1976. 189p.

524 Schlesinger, Elfriede G. and Isabel Wolock. "An accelerated
and traditional MSW program compared." Journal of Education for Social Work, v. 10, no. 1, winter 1974.
68-76.

525 Siegel, Sheldon. "Organization growth: expansion and diversity in schools of social work." Doctoral dissertation,
University of Michigan, 1974. 364p.

526 Silberman, Samuel J., et al. Support for social work education. New York: Council on Social Work Education,
1972. 24p.

527 South Dakota. State Legislative Research Council. Feasibility
of establishing a graduate program of social work in
South Dakota. Pierre: The Council, 1969. 36p.

B. SCHOOL ADMINISTRATION, GOVERNANCE AND ORGANIZA-
TION [See also Sections III.C.1, D, E.9.]

528 Bell, Winifred. "Educational bases for student involvement in
the administration of social work schools." Social Work
Education Reporter, v. 17, no. 4, Dec. 1969. 56-61.

529 Blackey, Eileen. "The challenges of the post of dean in so-
     cial work education." Journal of Education for Social
     Work, v. 7, no. 1, winter 1971. 23-31.

530 Boylan, Richard. "Issues in governance in schools of social
     work: a student's perspective." Exploring the interfaces
     of social work education. Edited by Charles W. McCann.
     Boulder, Colo.: Western Interstate Commission for High-
     er Education, 1970. 91-97.

531 Brink, Charles B. "A structure for student representation in
     the governance of a school of social work: the University
     of Washington model." Exploring the interfaces of social
     work education. Edited by Charles W. McCann. Boul-
     der, Colo.: Western Interstate Commission for Higher
     Education, 1970. 75-79.

532 Clark, Frank W. and Eugene I. Bender. "Does faculty congru-
     ence work? The case of social work education." Cana-
     dian Journal of Social Work Education, v. 1, no. 1, fall
     1974. 4-13.

533 Hage, Jerald. "Organizational perspectives about education in
     social rehabilitation schools." Higher education and the
     social professions. Edited by Henry M. Barlow. Lex-
     ington: College of Social Professions, University of Ken-
     tucky, 1973. 115-137.

534 Hollis, Ernest V. and Alice L. Taylor. "Organization and
     administration of schools of social work." Social work
     education in the United States. New York: Columbia
     University Press, 1951. 280-322.

535 Jennings, Daniel E., et al. An exploratory study of commun-
     ity participation in the governance of schools of social
     work in the United States. Portland, Ore.: Portland
     State University, 1970. 31p.

536 Kraft, Ivor. "Governance and the professional school." Jour-
     nal of Education for Social Work, v. 11, no. 2, spring
     1975. 68-75.

537 Pifer, Alan. "Some reflections on lay advisory councils for
     schools of social work." Social Work Education Report-
     er, v. 14, no. 2, June 1966. 25-27, 45.

538 Rosen, Alex. "Can schools of social work survive the current
     crisis?" Social Work Education Reporter, v. 18, no. 2,
     June 1970. 8-9, 51.

539 Schreiber, Paul. "Student involvement in administration and
     policy formation and in educational programs and curricu-

lum development." Social Work Education Reporter,
v. 16, no. 4, Dec. 1968. 55-58, 67-68.

540 Stickney, Patricia J., editor. Student participation in decision making in graduate schools of social work and in
higher education. New York: Council on Social Work
Education, 1972. 181p.

541 Vigilante, Joseph L. "Student participation in decision-making
in schools of social work." Journal of Education for Social Work, v. 6, no. 2, fall 1970. 51-60.

542 Youngdahl, Benjamin E. "Leadership in a graduate school of
social work." Social action and social work. New York:
Association Press, 1966. 145-155.

543 _____. "Who's what in Who's Who and why." Social
Work Education Reporter, v. 11, no. 6, Dec.-Jan.
1964. 5, 23.

C. SCHOOL RELATIONSHIPS

1. School-University Relationship

544 Anderson, G. Lester. "The professional school in the university." Education for social work; proceedings of the
1956 Annual Program Meeting, Council on Social Work
Education. New York: The Council, 1956. 79-88.

545 Cohen, Nathan Edward. "The school of social work within
the university system." Exploring the interface of social
work education. Edited by Charles W. McCann. Boulder, Colo.: Western Interstate Commission for Higher
Education, 1970. 19-36. Discussion. 37-42.

546 Dumpson, James R. "Social welfare education in a university:
its objectives and implementation." Social need and education for social welfare. Edited by Benjamin Lyndon.
Syracuse, N. Y.: State University of New York, 1968.
24-36.

547 Frankel, Charles. "Professional education as university education." Social Service Review, v. 32, no. 3, Sept.
1958. 234-246.

548 Hamovitch, Maurice B. "Social work education; its place in
the modern university." The Dorothy King Memorial lec-
tures. Montreal: McGill University, 1971. 56-74.

549 Katz, Israel and Harold Silver, editors. The university and
social welfare; papers delivered at the colloquium held in

Jerusalem, April 1967. Jerusalem: Magnes Press, Hebrew University, 1969. 251p.

550 Kristenson, Avis. "Autonomy in the administrative relationships of professional schools of social work in the United States to their universities and colleges." Doctoral dissertation, Columbia University, 1967. 565p.

551 _____. "Autonomy in the administrative relationships of schools of social work in the United States to their parent institutions." Journal of Education for Social Work, v. 4, no. 1, spring 1968. 21-30.

552 McConnell, T. R. "The professional school and the university." Social Work Education Reporter, v. 16, no. 1, March 1968. 24-26, 51-52.

553 Schenk, Quentin F. and George L. Kelling. "Schools of social professions in contemporary urban universities." Journal of Home Economics, v. 60, no. 6, June 1968. 441-443.

554 Stein, Herman D. and Avis Kristenson. The professional school and the university: the case of social work. New York: Council on Social Work Education, 1970. 93p.

2. School-Agency Relationship
[See also Sections II. C; VII. M.]

555 Arnold, Mildred, chairman. "The relationship of schools of social work to child welfare agencies: a panel discussion." Organization of services that will best meet needs of children; proceedings of Arden House Conference, 1965, Harriman, N. Y. Edited by Helen Fradkin. New York: School of Social Work, Columbia University, 1966. 136-150.

556 Berkowitz, Sidney J. "Agency-school communications and relationships: redefinition of agency-school partnerships." Social Work Education Reporter, v. 16, no. 4, Dec. 1968. 59-60, 69.

557 Council on Social Work Education. Joint responsibilities of school and agency in education for social work; workshop report of the 1955 Annual Program Meeting, Council on Social Work Education. New York: The Council, 1955. 41p.

558 _____. Potentials and problems in the changing school-agency relationships in social work education; background materials and papers prepared for discussion at CSWE House of Delegates Meeting, 1967, Salt Lake City, Utah. New York: The Council, 1967. 37p.

559 Daniel, Margaret. "Agency as a teaching center: responsibility of the agency." Education for social work; proceedings of the 1961 Annual Program Meeting, Council on Social Work Education. New York: The Council, 1961. 130-136.

560 Downes, Laura B. "Collaboration between the school and the agency in professional education for social work." Journal of Social Work Process, v. 10, 1959. 21-26.

561 Downing, Ruppert A. "Bridging the gap between education and practice." Social Casework, v. 55, no. 6, June 1974. 352-359.

562 Glover, E. Elizabeth. "Agency-school partnership." Child Welfare, v. 43, no. 3, March 1964. 108, 132.

563 Hale, Mark P. "The parameters of agency-school social work educational planning." Journal of Education for Social Work, v. 2, no. 1, spring 1966. 32-40.

564 Hamilton, Gordon. "Education for social work: the interaction of school and agency." Social Work Journal, v. 30, no. 2, April 1949. 76-87.

565 Itzin, Frank H. "Social work education and the social work enterprise." Child Welfare, v. 52, no. 5, May 1973. 277-286.

566 Kendall, Katherine A. "Commitment, communication, and co-operation: the essence of school-agency relations." Social Casework, v. 48, no. 1, Jan. 1967. 33-37.

567 _____. "The crucial role of the agency in social work education." Social Work Education, v. 12, no. 4, Aug.-Sept. 1964. 1, 10-11.

568 Kumar, Krishna. "The place of social service agencies in social work education." Indian Journal of Social Work, v. 23, no. 3, Oct. 1962. 243-252.

569 Leader, Arthur L. "An agency's view toward education for practice." Journal of Education for Social Work, v. 7, no. 3, fall 1971. 27-34.

570 _____. "The clinical professorship in social work education." Social Casework, v. 46, no. 6, June 1965. 339-344.

571 Middleman, Ruth R. "Social work education: the myth of the agency as partner." Social welfare forum, 1973; proceedings of the National Conference on Social Welfare. New York: Columbia University Press, 1974. 196-212.

572 Tennant, Violet E. "The agency as a teaching center: responsibility of the school of social work." Education for social work; proceedings of the 1961 Annual Program Meeting, Council on Social Work Education. New York: The Council, 1961. 123-129.

573 Werner, Ruth. "Sixty years of working together - agencies and school - in the interests of social work education (Case Western Reserve University School of Applied Social Sciences)." SASS Currents, special anniversary issue, 1976. Unpaged.

3. School-Community Relationship
[See also Section VII. R.]

574 Baum, Martha and Barbara B. Jameson. "Trends in higher education and community placements." Journal of Education for Social Work, v. 12, no. 1, winter 1976. 11-19.

575 Brieland, Donald. "A social services center for a multi-problem community." Social Work Education Reporter, v. 15, no. 3, Sept. 1967. 30-32, 41.

576 Collacott, Robert H. "The community team in social work education: the community." Education for social work; proceedings of the 1956 Annual Program Meeting, Council on Social Work Education. New York: The Council, 1956. 17-26.

577 Hamovitch, Maurice B. "New directions for social work education's relationship with government." Journal of Education for Social Work, v. 10, no. 3, fall 1974. 36-41.

578 Heitman, Beverly Tom. "Community service philosophy and activity: a case study of four schools of social work." Doctoral dissertation, University of Pennsylvania, 1970. 293p.

579 Hoffer, Joe R. "A school of social work alumni association--an asset in university and community relationships." Social Work Education Reporter, v. 19, no. 2, April-May 1971. 38-39.

580 Levy, Charles S. "(The graduate) school (of social work) and society." Journal of Education for Social Work, v. 7, no. 2, spring 1971. 25-30.

581 Lide, Pauline D. and Gayle Alexander. "An educational partnership: preparing social workers for a changing society." Journal of Education for Social Work, v. 11, no. 1, winter 1975. 94-98.

582 Lloyd, Gary A. "Tulane and 'Betsy': community service of a school of social work after a natural disaster." Social Work Education Reporter, v. 14, no. 1, March 1966. 26-27, 39-41, 45.

583 Rashid, Rifat, "Schools of social work and social policy: the experience of a new school." International Social Work, v. 8, no. 1, Jan. 1965. 17-21.

584 Reichert, Kurt. "Schools of social work and inner-city concerns, racial problems and anti-poverty activities." Social Work Education Reporter, v. 16, no. 1, March 1968. 2, 49-51.

585 Siporin, Max. "The experience of aiding the victims of hurricane 'Betsy'." Social Service Review, v. 40, no. 4, Dec. 1966. 378-389.

586 Titmuss, Richard M. "The relationship between schools of social work, social research, and social policy." Journal of Education for Social Work, v. 1, no. 1, spring 1965. 68-75.

587 _____. "Social administration: teaching and research." Commitment to welfare. New York: Pantheon Books, 1968. 13-55.

588 Vasey, Wayne. "The community team in social work education: the schools." Education for social work; proceedings of the 1956 Annual Program Meeting, Council on Social Work Education. New York: The Council, 1956. 27-35.

D. FACULTY [See also Section IV. B.]

589 American Association of Schools of Social Work. Committee on Faculty Work Loads and Salaries. Work loads and salaries in 49 schools of social work; report. New York: The Association, 1952. 32p.

590 Balian, Pereta, et al. "Induction of Puerto Rican faculty in New York City schools of social work." Social Work Education Reporter, v. 19, no. 1, Dec.-Jan. 1971. 41-42.

591 Blackey, Eileen. "Selection and preparation of faculty for schools of social work." Journal of Education for Social Work, v. 1, no. 1, spring 1965. 5-12.

592 Boehm, Werner W. "Academic freedom and professional education in social work." Journal of Education for Social Work, v. 7, no. 1, winter 1971. 33-42.

593 Brown, Allan G. and Christine Webb. "Social work teachers and social work practice." British Journal of Social Work, v. 3, no. 1, spring 1973. 101-111.

594 Cheetham, Juliet. "From social work to teaching--the first year." Case Conference, v. 14, no. 8, Dec. 1967. 285-289.

595 Council on Social Work Education. "Systemic barriers to recruitment, retention, and promotion of ethnic minority faculty in schools of social work." Social Work Education Reporter, v. 20, no. 3, Sept.-Oct. 1972. 25-27.

596 Curren, D. J., editor. The Chicano Faculty Development Program: a report. New York: Council on Social Work Education, 1973. 134p.

597 De Colstoun, M. Brown. "Teachers in schools of social work: functions and qualifications." Report of the European Seminar on Training for Senior Social Welfare Personnel, Paris, 1962. Geneva: United Nations, 1963. 58-74. SOA/ESWP/1962/2.

598 Feldman, Ronald A. "The evaluation of social work teaching competence: issues, pseudo-issues, and future directions." Iowa Journal of Social Work, v. 3, no. 3, summer 1970. 63-77.

599 _____. "Towards the evaluation of teaching competence in social work." Journal of Education for Social Work, v. 8, no. 2, spring 1972. 5-15.

600 Frey, Louise A. "The evaluation of teacher competence in continuing education." Social Work Education Reporter, v. 20, no. 3, Sept.-Oct. 1972. 43-47.

601 Gould, Ketayun H. and Bok-Lim C. Kim. "Salary inequities between men and women in schools of social work: myth or reality?" Journal of Education for Social Work, v. 12, no. 1, winter 1976. 50-55.

602 Grinnell, Richard M., Jr. and Nancy S. Kyte. "Measuring faculty competence: a model." Journal of Education for Social Work, v. 12, no. 3, fall 1976. 44-50.

603 Hartford, Margaret E. "Faculty development: the continuing preparation of the social work education teacher." Journal of Education for Social Work, v. 11, no. 2, spring 1975. 44-51.

604 Jennings, Daniel E. "Characteristics of social work faculty members." Social Work Education Reporter, v. 14, no. 3, Sept. 1966. 23-26, 49.

605 _____. "An exploratory study of characteristics of
    faculty members of graduate professional schools of so-
    cial work in the United States and Canada." Doctoral
    dissertation, Catholic University of America, 1965. 176p.

606 Jorgensen, James D. "Communication and social work facul-
    ties." Journal of Education for Social Work, v. 8,
    no. 2, spring 1972. 25-31.

607 Kennedy, Charles Joseph. "Comparative ideologies: law and
    social work educators." Doctoral dissertation, Tulane
    University, 1975. 126p.

608 Kidneigh, John C. "A study of factors associated with size
    of faculty in schools of social work." Social Work Edu-
    cation, v. 5, no. 3, June 1957. 1-4.

609 _____, chairman. "Training of social work educators:
    panel discussion." International Social Work, v. 4,
    no. 4, Oct. 1961. 20-25.

610 Kolevzon, Michael S. and Kermit T. Wiltse. "Student ratings
    and teacher effectiveness: a reappraisal." Journal of
    Education for Social Work, v. 9, no. 2, spring 1973.
    24-30.

611 Krill, Don. "Faculty development: antidote for crisis." Ex-
    ploring the interfaces of social work education. Edited
    by Charles W. McCann. Boulder, Colo.: Western Inter-
    state Commission for Higher Education, 1970. 67-72.

612 Longres, John. "Schools of social work and minority group
    faculty." Perspectives from the Puerto Rican Faculty
    Training Project. New York: Council on Social Work
    Education, 1973. 19-29.

613 Lower, Katherine D. "Faculty work loads in schools of so-
    cial work." Social Work Education, v. 12, no. 2, April-
    May 1964. 1-5, 18-21.

614 Macarov, David. "Faculty identifications and graduate-im-
    ages." International Social Work, v. 12, no. 4, 1969.
    30-34.

615 McDaniel, Clyde O., Jr. "Some procedures for appointment
    and promotion in professional schools." Social Work
    Education Reporter, v. 19, no. 2, April-May 1971.
    40-44.

616 _____. "Some suggestions for weighing the categories
    and items of faculty workload." Indian Journal of Social
    Work, v. 35, no. 3, Oct. 1974. 221-225.

617 Meier, Elizabeth G. "Preparation for teaching social work."
Social Work Education Reporter, v. 13, no. 3, Sept.
1965. 14-15, 34-35.

618 Onken, Richard. A survey of faculty in graduate schools of
social work. New York: Council on Social Work Education, 1968. 81p.

619 Robins, Arthur J. "Evaluation of Social work teaching." Indian Journal of Social Work, v. 31, no. 1, April 1970.
1-10.

620 Shachter, Burt. "Relevance of direct practice for today's social work educator." Journal of Education for Social
Work, v. 5, no. 2, fall 1969. 39-46.

621 Skidmore, Rex A. "Evaluation and accountability in schools
of social work." Evaluation and accountability in social
work education. Edited by Boyd E. Oviatt. Salt Lake
City: Graduate School of Social Work, University of
Utah, 1973. 27-38.

622 Smalley, Ruth E. "The attributes of a social work educator."
Social Work Education Reporter, v. 13, no. 2, June
1965. 10-11, 27, 30.

623 Smith, George and David Bradbury. "Staff tensions in social
work education." Social Work Today, v. 3, no. 6, 15
June 1972. 8-9.

624 Soffen, Joseph. Faculty development in professional education;
problems of, and proposals for recruitment, pre-service,
induction, and continuing development in social work education. New York: Council on Social Work Education,
1967. 187p.

625 _____. "The Faculty Development Project: objectives
and plans." Social Work Education Reporter, v. 13,
no. 4, Dec. 1965. 20-22, 45.

626 _____, editor. The social work educator; readings on
the preparation and induction of social work faculty. New
York: Council on Social Work Education, 1969. 129p.

627 Towle, Charlotte. "Classroom teacher as practitioner." Social Service Review, v. 22, no. 3, Sept. 1948. 312-323.

628 _____. "Helping the casework practitioner become a
classroom teacher." Education for social work; proceedings of the 1959 Annual Program Meeting, Council on Social Work Education. New York: The Council, 1959.
84-95.

629 Werley, Harriet H., et al. "Medicine, nursing, social work: professionals and birth control: student and faculty attitudes." Family Planning Perspectives, v. 5, no. 1, winter 1973. 42-49.

630 Younghusband, Eileen L. "Developing the faculty: the opportunities and demands of teaching." International Social Work, v. 10, no. 1, Jan. 1967. 29-35.

E. STUDENTS

1. Advising

631 Beck, Deborah Lisansky. "A counseling program for social work students." Social Casework, v. 57, no. 10, Dec. 1976. 651-655.

632 Finestone, Samuel. "Some issues in faculty advising." Education for social work; proceedings of the 1963 Annual Program Meeting, Council on Social Work Education. New York: The Council, 1963. 214-219.

633 Lantz, Marian Gertrude. "The significance of the school adviser in social work education." Doctoral dissertation, University of Pennsylvania, 1956. 254p.

634 Merle, Sherman. "Student advising." Social Work Education Reporter, v. 17, no. 2, June 1969. 51-53, 61.

635 Nolan, Lydia Glover. "Faculty consultant in relation to the social work student." Social Casework, v. 34, no. 4, April 1953. 156-161.

636 Rapoport, Lydia and Jona M. Rosenfeld. "The nature of student advising in social work education." Applied Social Studies, v. 1, no. 2, June 1969. 113-124.

637 Rosenbloom, Maria, Greta W. Stanton and Phyllis Caroff. "Faculty advisement--A proposal for the 1970's." Social Work Education Reporter, v. 21, no. 1, Dec.-Jan. 1973. 64-67.

638 Russell, Dojelo Crabaugh. "The faculty advisor in graduate education for social work: an exploratory-descriptive study of experiences and perceptions of advisors and advisees." Doctoral dissertation, Catholic University of America, 1971. 377p.

639 _____. "The faculty advisor in social work education." Doctoral students look at social work education. Edited by Leila Calhoun Deasy. New York: Council on Social Work Education, 1971. 69-86.

640 Yelaja, Shankar A. "Student advising in social work educa-
     tion." Journal of Education for Social Work, v. 8,
     no. 1, winter 1972. 64-70.

2. Career Choice
[See also Section III. E. 11.]

641 Canada. Women's Bureau. A new career after 30; report of
     an enquiry into the experience of women who had taken
     professional social work training at thirty years of age
     or over. Ottawa: Department of Labour of Canada,
     1960. 34p.

642 Diangson, Pat and Diane F. Kravetz and Judy Lipton. "Sex-
     role stereotyping and social work education." Journal of
     Education for Social Work, v. 11, no. 3, fall 1975. 44-
     49.

643 Fuller, Albert D. "Career choice and values." in "The values
     of social workers." Doctoral dissertation, University of
     Southern California, 1962. 181-236.

644 Gockel, Galen L. Silk stockings and blue collars: social
     work as a career choice of America's 1961 college gradu-
     ates. Chicago: National Opinion Research Center, 1966.
     171p.

645 _____. "Social work as a career choice." Manpower
     in social welfare: research perspectives. Edited by Ed-
     ward E. Schwartz. New York: National Association of
     Social Workers, 1966. 89-98.

646 Golden, Deborah, Arnulf M. Pins and Wyatt Jones. Students
     in schools of social work; a study of characteristics and
     factors affecting career choice and practice concentration.
     New York: Council on Social Work Education, 1972. 88p.

647 Goodwin, Marjorie. Correlates of career choice; a compara-
     tive study of recruits to the health professions and other
     professional fields. Vancouver: School of Social Work,
     University of British Columbia, 1972. 191p.

648 Kadushin, Alfred. "Determinants of career choice and their
     implications for social work." Social Work Education,
     v. 6, no. 2, April 1958. 17-22.

649 Katz, Israel. "Some background correlates of occupational
     choice." Doctoral dissertation, Case Western Reserve
     University, 1962. 173p.

650 Lahav, Elkhanan. "Social incongruency and occupational
     choice." Doctoral dissertation, University of Connecticut,
     1968. 190p.

651 Lauffer, Armand A. "The future of social work in the Jewish community center; the case of the disinclined student." Journal of Jewish Communal Service, v. 46, no. 1, fall 1969. 45-58.

652 _____. "Old and new routes: an exploration into the factors that led students to schools of social work." in "Social actionists come to social work: comparison of community organization students with their peers in casework and group work." Doctoral dissertation, Brandeis University, 1969. 103-153.

653 Miller, Joseph Pearce, Jr. "A study of career choice among undergraduate social science majors: social work, psychology and sociology, with emphasis upon social work." Doctoral dissertation, University of Pittsburgh, 1974. 132p.

654 Mutschler, Phyllis. "Factors affecting choice of and perseveration in social work with the aged." Gerontologist, v. 11, no. 3, autumn 1971. Part I, 231-241.

655 Pins, Arnulf M. Who chooses social work, when and why? New York: Council on Social Work Education, 1963. 212p.

656 Ramachandran, P. and B. C. Barah. "Motivation for social work." Indian Journal of Social Work, v. 33, no. 2, July 1972. 117-123.

657 Steinman, Richard. Values in occupational choice and occupational selection: a comparative study of admissions in social work education. Doctoral dissertation, Brandeis University, 1968. 526p.

658 Taietz, Philip, Bert Ellenbogen and Charles E. Ramsey. "Occupational choice--some implications for recruitment of social workers." Social Work, v. 3, no. 2, April 1958. 44-48.

659 Walther, Regis H. Personality variables and career decisions; a pilot study of law and social work students. Arlington, Va.: ERIC Document Reproduction Service, 1966. 52p. ED 012937.

660 Young, Whitney M., Jr. "Minorities and social work career." Careers in social work; 1967 annual review, National Commission for Social Work Careers. New York: The Commission, 1967. 9-10, 19.

3. Characteristics and Background

661 Brager, George and John A. Michael. "The sex distribution

in social work: causes and consequences." Social Casework, v. 50, no. 10, Dec. 1969. 595-601.

662 Demarest, Lorraine E. Student body characteristics useful in admissions and teaching. New Orleans: School of Social Work, Tulane University, 1963. 16p.

663 Edwards, Raymond Lewis, Jr. "Familial characteristics and personality profiles of graduate social work students." Doctoral dissertation, Florida State University, 1966. 237p.

664 Gilbert, Dorothea. "Social work students and their educational outcome: an examination of characteristics of students who dropped out and who graduated from the Master's curriculum of the University of Pennsylvania School of Social Work, September 1954 to June 1960." Doctoral dissertation, University of Pennsylvania, 1963. 346p.

665 Goldmeier, John. "Association of personality characteristics of the caseworker and selected aspects of the treatment process." Doctoral dissertation, University of Chicago, 1966. 170p.

666 _____. "Study of selected personality attributes and treatment preferences of caseworkers and casework students." Social Service Review, v. 42, no. 2, June 1968. 232-240.

667 Goldstein, Harris K. and Rachel Dedmon. "A computer-assisted analysis of input, process, and output of a social work educational program." Journal of Education for Social Work, v. 12, no. 2, spring 1976. 17-20.

668 Hess, Dolph and Martha Williams. "Personality characteristics and value stances of students in two areas of graduate study." Journal of Education for Social Work, v. 10, no. 3, fall 1974. 42-49.

669 Kidneigh, John C. and Horace W. Lundberg. "Are social work students different?" Social Work, v. 3, no. 3, July 1958. 57-61.

670 Lauffer, Armand A. "A new breed of social actionist comes to social work: the community organization student." Journal of Education for Social Work, v. 7, no. 1, winter 1971. 43-55.

671 _____. "Social actionists come to social work: comparison of community organization students with their peers in casework and group work." Doctoral dissertation, Brandeis University, 1969. 260p.

672   Loewenberg, Frank M. and Thomas H. Shey. "Ethnic charac-
       teristics of full-time Master's degree students in U. S.
       schools of social work, 1969." Social Work Education
       Reporter, v. 18, no. 2, June 1970. 14-17, 48.

673   McCune, Shirley Dickinson. "An exploratory study of the
       measured behavioral styles of students in five schools of
       social work." Doctoral dissertation, Catholic University
       of America, 1966. 210p.

674   Pins, Arnulf M. "A bird's eye view of the students in schools
       of social work." Education for social work; proceedings
       of the 1964 Annual Program Meeting, Council on Social
       Work Education. New York: The Council, 1964. 47-52.

675   _____ . "The Jewish social work student: some re-
       search data about him and their implications for the
       shortage of Jewish community center workers." Journal
       of Jewish Communal Service, v. 41, no. 1, fall 1964.
       88-100.

676   Plotnick, Harold L. "The relation between selected personal-
       ity characteristics of social work students and accuracy
       in predicting the behavior of clients." Doctoral disserta-
       tion, Columbia University, 1961. 178p.

677   Warkov, Seymour. "Social work students and other graduate
       students: a comparison." Manpower in social welfare:
       research perspectives. Edited by Edward E. Schwartz.
       New York: National Association of Social Workers, 1966.
       99-107.

4. Dropout and Transfer Students

678   Beckerman, Aaron Harry. "Ethnicity, retention, and pre-grad-
       uate variables;" "Ethnicity, retention, and graduate per-
       formance." in "Ethnicity and graduate social work educa-
       tion; an exploratory study of first year full-time students
       enrolled in six Greater New York City schools of social
       work, 1965-1966." Doctoral dissertation, Columbia Uni-
       versity, 1971. 165-231.

679   Gilbert, Dorothea. "Social work students and their educational
       outcome; an examination of characteristics of students who
       dropped out and who graduated from the Master's curricu-
       lum of the University of Pennsylvania School of Social
       Work, September 1954 to June 1960." Doctoral disserta-
       tion, University of Pennsylvania, 1963. 346p.

680   Loewenberg, Frank M. "Drop-outs and transfer students."
       Social Work Education Reporter, v. 16, no. 2, June 1968.
       19, 21.

681 Quaranta, Mary Ann. "Discontinuance in social work education: a study of pre-admissions and post-admissions variables." Doctoral dissertation, Columbia University, 1973. 216p.

5. Educationally Disadvantaged Students
[See also Section XIV.]

682 Council on Social Work Education. Educationally disadvantaged students in social work education; opening and expanding opportunities in graduate schools of social work. New York: The Council, 1968. 168p.

683 Greenberg, Harold I. and Carl A. Scott. "Ethnic minority-group recruitment and programs for the educationally disadvantaged in schools of social work." Social Work Education Reporter, v. 17, no. 3, Sept. 1969. 32A-32D.

684 Griffiths, Kenneth A. "Support systems for educationally disadvantaged students." Assuring practitioner competence: whose responsibility? Edited by Dean H. Hepworth. Salt Lake City: Graduate School of Social Work, University of Utah, 1974. 66-72. Group discussion. 72-74.

685 Holland, Nora. Students at a disadvantage in higher education with special reference to social work programs. New York: Council on Social Work Education, 1972. 72p.

686 Thursz, Daniel and Elaine Rothenberg. "The educationally disadvantaged student: the challenge to social work education." Social Work Education Reporter, v. 16, no. 3, Sept. 1968. 26-29.

6. Financial Aids

687 Arnhoff, Franklin N., Beatrice M. Shriver and Milton Wittman. Student research stipend program in social work: a followup survey. Bethesda, Md.: National Institute of Mental Health, 1966. 10p.

688 Council on Social Work Education. Establishing and administering student financial aid programs in social work education; a guide to standards and practices. New York: The Council, 1966. 12p.

689 _____. In pursuit of excellence; a guide to local communities in organizing scholarship programs for social work education. New York: The Council, 1959. 26p.

690 Graves, Conrad. "Financing social work education." Social Work Education Reporter, v. 14, no. 4, Dec. 1966. 20-21, 59-60.

691 Mumm, Louise N., editor. Student financial aid for master's program in graduate schools of social work in the U. S. A. and Canada. New York: Council on Social Work Education, 1968. 184p.

692 National Commission for Social Work Careers. Social work fellowships and scholarships in Canada and the United States for the academic years 1965-66 and 1966-67. New York: The Commission, 1964. 91p.

693 Pins, Arnulf M. Financial aid to social work students. New York: Council on Social Work Education, 1965. 130p.

694 Wittman, Milton and F. Marie McNabola. "Major trends of support for social work education under the National Institute of Mental Health Training Program." Social Work Education, v. 11, no. 6, Dec.-Jan. 1964. 1-4.

7. Foreign Students

695 Arndt, Hilda C. M., et al. A study of field instruction for international students in schools of social work in the United States and Canada. New York: Council on Social Work Education, 1957. 105p.

696 Clarke, Helen I. and Martha Ozawa. The foreign student in the United States, with special reference to Martha (Naoko Ozawa). Madison: School of Social Work, University of Wisconsin, 1970. 189p.

697 Desai, Armaity Sapur. "Attitudes and learning experiences of foreign students in American schools of social work." Doctoral dissertation, University of Chicago, 1970. 271p.

698 _____ and Donald Brieland. "An empirical study of first-year foreign students--Implications for social work education." Social Work Education Reporter, v. 18, no. 3, Sept.-Oct. 1970. 36-40.

699 Gangrade, K. D. "Study abroad, as seen through the eyes of a participant." International Social Work, v. 5, no. 4, Oct. 1962. 7-10.

700 Hochwald, Hilde Landenberger. "Teaching the principle of self-determination to foreign students." Social Casework, v. 38, no. 7, July 1957. 362-365.

701 Leslie, Alison M. "Two years of social work training at Boston University, U. S. A." Case Conference, v. 7, no. 10, April 1960. 254-258.

702 Livingstone, Arthur S. "International students: Part I--The

student group, their selection and placement." International Social Work, v. 5, no. 4, Oct. 1962. 1-6.

703 _____. "International students: Part II--Entrance requirements and placement procedures." International Social Work, v. 6, no. 1, Jan. 1963. 4-12.

704 _____. "International students: Part III--Academic provisions and the study experience." International Social Work, v. 6, no. 4, Oct. 1963. 18-29.

705 _____. "International students: Part IV--Personal and social experience--the return home." International Social Work, v. 7, no. 1, Jan. 1964. 29-35.

706 Murase, Kenneth. "Cross-cultural education: some implications for social work." Social Service Review, v. 33, no. 1, March 1959. 43-54.

707 _____. "International students in education for social work: an assessment by international graduates of schools of social work in North America, 1948-57." Social Service Review, v. 35, no. 2, June 1961. 171-183.

708 _____. "International students in education for social work: an assessment of the educational experience by international graduates of schools of social work in North America, 1948-57." Doctoral dissertation, Columbia University, 1961. 358p.

709 Palmer, Barbara B. "Foreign student: a challenge to the social work educator." Social Service Review, v. 31, no. 3, Sept. 1957. 277-289.

710 Sanders, Irwin T., editor. The professional education of students from other lands; based on conference materials and discussion of the Inter-professional Conference on Professional Training in North America for Students from Other Countries, held at Boston University, 1961. New York: Council on Social Work Education, 1963. 264p.

711 Santiago, Cayetano. The effect of cultural differences on the value of American social work education to foreign students. New York: Council on Social Work Education, 1965. 22p.

712 Stinson, Malcolm B. "The foreign student in the school of social work." Social Work Papers, v. 9, 1962. 49-54.

713 United States. Social Security Administration. International students in schools of social work in the United States. Washington, D. C.: Government Printing Office, 1953. 57p.

714 _____. _____. Social workers abroad assess their
    training in the United States. Washington, D. C. Govern-
    ment Printing Office, 1955. 27p.

715 Vakharia, Parin. "Studies abroad: principles of teaching and
    learning in the preparation of international students. "
    International Social Work, v. 1, no. 1, Jan. 1958. 21-24.

716 Wojciechowski, Sophie, editor. A second vocation: educating
    emigre professionals for social work. New York: Coun-
    cil on Social Work Education, 1974. 70p.

8. Handicapped Students

717 Barnett, Eleanor M. "A plan of social work education for a
    deaf person. " Orientation of social workers to the prob-
    lems of deaf persons. Edited by Beryl Godfrey. Wash-
    ington, D. C.: U. S. Department of Health, Education,
    and Welfare, Vocational Rehabilitation Administration,
    1964. 96-98.

718 Blank, Marion Sidman. "Field work for blind students in a
    school of social work. " Social Service Review, v. 26,
    no. 3, Sept. 1952. 310-318.

719 Burnett, Mary C. Studies of blind students in schools of
    social work. Chicago: American Association of Schools
    of Social Work, 1943. 6p.

720 Grossberg, Sidney M. and Barbara L. Beyer. "Field in-
    struction with blind students. " Social Work Education
    Reporter, v. 20, no. 1, Dec.-Jan. 1972. 60-63.

721 New York State Federation of Workers for the Blind. Com-
    mittee on the Employment of Blind Individuals in the Pro-
    fessions. Blind persons as social workers and rehabili-
    tation counselors. Arlington, Va.: ERIC Document Repro-
    duction Service, 1967. 9p. ED 027561.

722 Poor, Joanna Lucille. "Field work training of a visually
    handicapped student. " Social Casework, v. 26, no. 10,
    Feb. 1946. 368-371.

723 Roberts, Gary. "Field work in community organizations for
    the deaf. " Journal of Rehabilitation of the Deaf, v. 6,
    no. 2, Oct. 1972. 73-75.

9. Organization, Participation and Role

724 Bell, Winifred. "Educational bases for student involvement in
    the administration of social work schools. " Social Work
    Education Reporter, v. 17, no. 4. Dec. 1969. 56-61.

725 Boylan, Richard. "Issues in governance in schools of social
     work: a student's perspective." Exploring the inter-
     faces of social work education. Edited by Charles W.
     McCann. Boulder, Colo.: Western Interstate Commis-
     sion for Higher Education, 1970. 91-97.

726 Brink, Charles B. "A structure for student representation in
     the governance of a school of social work: the University
     of Washington model." Exploring the interfaces of social
     work education. Edited by Charles W. McCann. Boulder,
     Colo.: Western Interstate Commission for Higher Educa-
     tion, 1970. 75-79.

727 Carlton, Thomas Owen. "Student participation and political
     efficacy: perception of decision making at three graduate
     schools of social work." Doctoral dissertation, University
     of Pennsylvania, 1975. 354p.

728 Erlich, John L. and John M. Riley. "A new breed of social
     workers?" Renewal, v. 8, no. 1, Jan.-Feb. 1968. 23-24.

729 _____ and John E. Tropman. "The politics of participation:
     student power." Social Work, v. 14, no 4, Oct. 1969.
     64-72.

730 _____. "The 'turned-on' generation: new antiestablishment
     action roles." Social Work, v. 16, no. 4. Oct. 1971.
     22-27.

731 Erony, Michael. "A philosophical and practice perspective on
     the goals, function, and contribution of NFSSW in today's
     world." Social Work Education Reporter, v. 17, no. 2.
     June 1969. 54-57.

732 Haddad, Joseph. "A student organization of a school of social
     work and its relationship to social and legal change."
     Social Work Education Reporter, v. 14, no. 2, June 1966.
     37, 50-51.

733 Jennings, Daniel E., et al. An exploratory study of community
     participation in the governance of schools of social work
     in the United States. Portland, Ore.: Portland State
     University, 1970. 31p.

734 McCuan, Patrick. "The student movement in social work."
     Social Work Education Reporter, v. 17, no. 2, June 1969.
     29-30, 58.

735 Main, Marjorie White. "Orientation to the student role: the
     role of student in a professional school." Social Work
     Education Reporter, v. 16, no. 4, Dec. 1968. 51-52,
     66-67.

736 Pavlin, Frank. "Generation gap: student social worker and
      the A. A. S. W. " Australian Journal of Social Work, v. 22,
      no. 4, Dec. 1969. 35-36.

737 Peirce, Frank J. "Student involvement: participatory democ-
      racy or adult socialization?" Journal of Education for
      Social Work, v. 6, no. 2, fall 1970. 21-26.

738 Poulard, Othello W. "Orientation to the student role: today's
      student in the school of social work. " Social Work Educa-
      tion Reporter, v. 16, no. 4, Dec. 1968. 53-54, 62.

739 Reid, Kenneth L. "The activities of a student organization as
      a means of community problem-solving. " Social Work
      Education, v. 12, no. 4, Aug.-Sept. 1964. 3, 11-13.

740 Ripple, Lilian. "Students' rights and responsibilities in
      graduate schools of social work: survey of current prac-
      tice. " Social Work Education Reporter, v. 17, no. 2,
      June 1969. 48-50.

741 Robertson, Mary Ella. "The role of students. " Journal of
      Education for Social Work, v. 4, no. 1, spring 1968.
      55-64.

742 Sawdy, Mavis. "A social work students' association? Moves
      to form national body to exchange views and to comment
      on training. " Social Work Today, v. 4, no. 23, 21 Feb.
      1974. 731-732.

743 Schreiber, Paul, et al. "Responses to student participation
      and student involvement. " Journal of Education for Social
      Work, v. 7, no. 1, winter 1971. 5-10.

744 _____. "Student involvement in administration and policy
      formation and in educational programs and curriculum
      development. " Social Work Education Reporter, v. 16,
      no. 4, Dec. 1968. 55-58, 67-68.

745 Stickney, Patricia J. "Some issues identified by the graduate
      schools of social work regarding student rights and re-
      sponsibilities. " Social Work Education Reporter, v. 18,
      no. 1, March 1970. 25-27, 64.

746 _____, editor. Student participation in decision making in
      graduate schools of social work and in higher education.
      New York: Council on Social Work Education, 1972. 181p.

747 Vigilante, Joseph L. "Student participation in decision-making
      in schools of social work. " Journal of Education for
      Social Work, v. 6, no. 2, fall 1970. 51-60.

10. Performance and Evaluation
[See also Sections III. E. 11; VII. I.]

748 Beckerman, Aaron Harry. "Ethnicity and graduate social work education: an exploratory study of first year full-time students enrolled in six Greater New York City schools of social work, 1965-1966." Doctoral dissertation, Columbia University, 1971. 448p.

749 Berengarten, Sidney. Admissions prediction and student performance in social work education; an unduplicated count study of applicants for admission and enrolled students entering schools of social work, fall term 1961/62. New York: Council on Social Work Education, 1964. 64p.

750 _____. "The unduplicated count study of 2,741 enrolled students entering schools of social work in the United States and Canada in 1961-62." Education for social work; proceedings of the 1964 Annual Program Meeting, Council on Social Work Education. New York: The Council, 1964. 53-60.

751 Bloom, Martin and Marcella Farra. "Becoming a professional social worker: two conceptual models." Social Work Education Reporter, v. 20, no. 2, April-May 1972. 23-26.

752 Bloom, Tybel. "Learning to use the self for professional service: a study of teachers' and supervisors' judgments on social work students' performance in class and field work." Doctoral dissertation, University of Pennsylvania, 1960. 316p.

753 Briar, Scott. "The effects of client social class, social class distance, and social work experience on the judgments of social work students." Doctoral dissertation, Columbia University, 1961. 178p.

754 _____. "Use of theory in studying effects of client social class on students' judgments." Social Work, v. 6, no. 3, July 1961. 91-97.

755 Buran, Gretchen and Thomas H. Walz. A study of the differences in background and performance of pre-social work and non-pre-social work undergraduate majors in a graduate school of social work. Minneapolis: University of Minnesota, 1969. 41p.

756 Clark, Raymond H. "Preinstructional testing of students entering graduate schools of social work, fall term 1971." Doctoral dissertation, University of Utah, 1972. 139p.

757 Clemenger, Florence. "Assessment of students' performance in the classroom." Teaching and learning in social work education. Edited by Marguerite Pohek. New York: Council on Social Work Education, 1970. 27-33.

758 Cox, Cordelia. "Performance of undergraduate social welfare majors in graduate schools of social work." Social Work Education Reporter, v. 13, no. 2, June 1965. 20-21.

759 Francel, Edward W. "Factors associated with the successful outcome of professional training for social work." Doctoral dissertation, University of Minnesota, 1960. 223p.

760 Fredericks, Marcel, William J. Mackey and Paul Mundy. "An analysis of academic achievement and personality characteristics of students in a school of social work." Iowa Journal of Social Work, v. 5, no. 4, fall 1972. 14-20.

761 _____, Paul Mundy and William J. Mackey. "The relationship between social class, stress-anxiety responses, academic achievement and professional attitudes of students in a school of social work." Arete, v. 3, no. 2, fall 1974. 61-70.

762 Garzino, Salvatore J. "Objective tests in training." Social Work, v. 20, no. 6, Nov. 1975. 468-473.

763 Goldmeier, John. "Association of personality characteristics of the caseworker and selected aspects of the treatment process." Doctoral dissertation, University of Chicago, 1966. 170p.

764 _____. "Study of selected personality attributes and treatment preferences of caseworkers and casework students." Social Service Review, v. 42, no. 2, June 1968. 232-240.

765 Hess, Dolph. "Prediction of success in casework practice from performance in the graduate program." Doctoral dissertation, University of Minnesota, 1966. 151p.

766 Kadushin, Alfred. A proposal for an accelerated program in social work education and design for evaluation. Madison: School of Social Work, University of Wisconsin, 1967. 119p.

767 _____. Testing the discriminatory capabilities of a series of evaluation measures as applied to a program of social work education. Madison: University of Wisconsin, 1968. 96p.

768 Kirlin, Betty A. In search of a consistency model for evaluation of student performance in graduate education for the social professions. Lexington, Ky.: College of Social Professions, University of Kentucky, 1974. 53p.

769   Lane, Terry and Philip Lichtenberg. "Toward negating authoritarianism in appraisals of performance in social work education." Journal of Education for Social Work, v. 7, no. 3, fall 1971. 19-26.

770   Leon, Herman. "Factors predictive of successful educational performance in social work school." Doctoral dissertation, Columbia University, 1970. 247p.

771   Marin, Rosa C. "The relationship of three psychological tests to grades earned in classroom courses in the School of Social Work of the University of Puerto Rico." Doctoral dissertation, University of Pittsburgh, 1963. 88p.

772   Merriam, Thornton Ward. The relations between scholastic achievement in a school of social work and six factors in students' background. New York: Teachers' College, Columbia University, 1934; New York: AMS Press, 1972. 136p.

773   Metz, Marian Westwick. "The relationship between intelligence rankings of social work students and the quality of perceptiveness which they demonstrate in an experimental situation." Doctoral dissertation, University of Chicago, 1969. 150p.

774   Otto, Herbert A. and Kenneth A. Griffiths. "New approach to developing the student's strengths." Social Casework, v. 44, no. 3, March 1963. 119-124.

775   Plotnick, Harold L. "The relation between selected personality characteristics of social work students and accuracy in predicting the behavior of clients." Doctoral dissertation, Columbia University, 1961. 178p.

776   Quaranta, Mary Ann. "Discontinuance in social work education: a study of pre-admissions and post-admissions variables." Doctoral dissertation, Columbia University, 1973. 216p.

777   Stein, Shayna R., Margaret W. Linn and James Furdon. "Predicting social work student performance." Journal of Education for Social Work, v. 10, no. 3, fall 1974. 85-92.

778   Sterne, Richard and Peter W. Chommie. "Pass/Fail, a comparative analysis of grading systems." Social Work Education Reporter, v. 21, no. 2, April-May 1973. 69-75.

779   Sturges, Jack and Roy D. Yarbrough. Ability of social work students to determine the appropriateness of solutions to problems encountered in social work practice. Arlington, Va.: ERIC Document Reproduction Service, 1975. 25p. ED 104273.

780 _____ and _____. "Ability of social work students to
identify and formulate helpful response statements."
Journal of Social Welfare, v. 2, no. 3, winter 1975. 27-39.

781 Torre, Elizabeth Lassiter. "Student performance in solving
social work problems and work experience prior to entering the MSW program." Journal of Education for
Social Work, v. 10, no. 2, spring 1974. 114-117.

782 Vail, Susan. "The effects of socio-economic class, race, and
level of experience on social workers' judgments of clients."
Smith College Studies in Social Work, v. 40, no. 3, June
1970. 236-246.

783 Walz, Thomas H. and Gretchen Buran. "Graduate school performance of the undergraduate social work major." Social
Work Education Reporter, v. 16, no. 3, Sept. 1968. 32-
33, 44-45.

11. Recruitment, Selection, and
Prediction of Success
[See also Sections III. E. 2; III. E. 10.]

784 Auerbach, Arnold J. "Quotas in schools of social work."
Social Work, v. 17, no. 2, March 1972. 102-105.

785 Berengarten, Sidney. Admissions prediction and student performance in social work education; an unduplicated count
study of applicants for admission and enrolled students
entering schools of social work, fall term 1961/62. New
York: Council on Social Work Education, 1964. 64p.

786 _____ and Irene H. Kerrigan. Interviewing and personality
assessment; selection of social work students. New York:
Council on Social Work Education, 1968. 91p.

787 _____. "Pilot study: criteria in selection for social work."
Social work as human relations; anniversary papers of the
New York School of Social Work and the Community Service
Society. New York: Columbia University Press, 1949.
170-194.

788 _____. "A pioneer workshop in student selection." Bulletin
of the New York School of Social Work, v. 44, no. 4,
July 1951. 3-12.

789 _____. "The unduplicated count study of 2,741 enrolled
students entering schools of social work in the United
States and Canada in 1961-62." Education for social work;
proceedings of the 1964 Annual Program Meeting, Council
on Social Work Education. New York: The Council, 1964.
53-60.

790 Bishop, Margaret E. The selection and admission of students in a school of social work. Philadelphia: University of Pennsylvania Press, 1948. 58p.

791 Brigham, Thomas M. "Philosophical issues and trends in student selection today." Journal of Education for Social Work, v. 4, no. 2, fall 1968. 27-34.

792 Burns, Mary E. "Criteria for selection of students for advanced study." Social Work Education Reporter, v. 13, no. 2, June 1965. 12-13, 25-26.

793 Burt, Winston Donald. "Admission criteria for Black students in graduate social work education: traditional and non-traditional approaches." Doctoral dissertation, University of Michigan, 1973. 254p.

794 Caroff, Phyllis. "A comparative study of applicants to schools of social work, 1961-1962: a secondary analysis." Doctoral dissertation, Columbia University, 1969. 276p.

795 _____. "A comparative study of applicants to schools of social work, 1961-62, a secondary analysis." Social Work Education Reporter, v. 18, no. 3, Sept.-Oct. 1970. 32-35.

796 _____ and Florence Vigilante. "Selection at admissions: a perspective for the 1970s." Social Work Education Reporter, v. 21, no. 1, Dec.-Jan. 1973. 21-23.

797 Chatterjee, Pranab. "Recruitment in law, medicine, and social work: some comparative trends." Social Work Education Reporter, v. 21, no. 1, Dec.-Jan. 1973. 24-27.

798 Council on Social Work Education. The admissions process in schools of social work; 2nd National Workshop on Admissions, 1962, St. Louis, Missouri. New York: The Council, 1964. 84p.

799 _____. The assessment process in selection for professional education; workshop report of the 1957 Annual Program Meeting. New York: The Council, 1957. 19p.

800 _____. The role of the undergraduate college, the agency and the professional school in selection for graduate education in social work; workshop report of the 1960 Annual Program Meeting. New York: The Council, 1960. 29p.

801 _____. Committee on Admissions. Selection of students for schools of social work: the National Workshop on Admissions, 1953, and progress in implementation of recommendations, 1954 and 1955. New York: The Council, 1955. 84p.

802 Dailey, Dennis M. "The validation of admissions predictions: implications for social work education." Doctoral dissertation, Washington University, 1972. 144p.

803 _____. "The validity of admissions predictions: implications for social work education." Journal of Education for Social Work, v. 10, no. 2, spring 1974. 12-19.

804 Educational Testing Service. Admission to graduate schools of social work: Practices, problems, and prospects; a report submitted to the Council on Social Work Education. Princeton, N. J.: The Service, 1965. 174p.

805 Edwards, M. Elizabeth. "The interview as an instrument of selection for professional education: a study of its use by schools of social work." Doctoral dissertation, University of Pennsylvania, 1969. 293p.

806 _____. "Selection interviews and admissions decisions in professional education for social work." Social Work Education Reporter, v. 18, no. 3, Sept.-Oct. 1970. 41-46.

807 _____. "Selection interviews in relation to the process of reaching admissions decisions in schools of social work; report of a survey." Applied Social Studies, v. 3, no. 1, Feb. 1971. 39-50.

808 Ellis, June. "Selecting students for social work training." British Journal of Social Work, v. 5, no. 2, summer 1975. 137-147.

809 Esser, Barbara F. and Clarice Freud. Testing as a tool in the admissions process: an overview of research. New York: Council on Social Work Education, 1966. 58p.

810 Golden, Janet M. "Scores on admissions tools used by the National Catholic School of Social Service for the academic years 1969, 1970, and 1971 in relation to first year students' differential performance in the Master's degree program." Doctoral dissertation, Catholic University of America, 1973. 214p.

811 Greenberg, Harold I. and Carl A. Scott. "Ethnic minority-group recruitment and programs for the educationally disadvantaged in school of social work." Social Work Education Reporter, v. 17, no. 3, Sept. 1969. 32A-32D.

812 Guilford, Richard G. "What is the best undergraduate preparation for entrance into graduate schools? The viewpoint of the graduate school of social work." Social Work Education Reporter, v. 14, no. 2, June 1966. 33, 46-48.

813 Hanks, John W. "Graduate school admission requirements."

Social Work Education Reporter, v. 21, no. 1, Dec.-Jan. 1973. 51-53.

814 Harward, Naomi. "Two Arizona studies related to undergraduate background for social workers." _Social Work Education Reporter_, v. 15, no. 4, Dec. 1967. 48-50, 55-56.

815 Hepworth, Dean H. "The predictive validity of admissions criteria used by the Graduate School of Social Work, University of Utah, to select students for the fall-term, 1966." Doctoral dissertation, University of Utah, 1968. 170p.

816 _____. "The use of reference letters and certain other criteria in student selection." _Social Work Education Reporter_, v. 20, no. 2, April-May 1972. 47-51.

817 Hess, Dolph and Martha Williams. "Personality characteristics and value stances of students in two areas of graduate study." _Journal of Education for Social Work_, v. 10, no. 3, fall 1974. 42-49.

818 Jacobs, Elizabeth R. _Recruiting for social work._ New York: National Association of Social Workers, 1961. 72p.

819 Jones, Dorothy. "Recommendations for undergraduate preparation for graduate school--from the viewpoint of the undergraduate college." _Social Work Education Reporter_, v. 14, no. 2, June 1966. 32, 49, 51.

820 Lentschner, Esther Meltzer. "Perception of the candidate: the double image in admissions." Doctoral dissertation, Columbia University, 1974. 338p.

821 Leon, Herman. "Factors predictive of successful educational performance in the social work school." Doctoral dissertation, Columbia University, 1970. 247p.

822 Levitt, Louis. "Recruiting minority group students to social work." _Manpower: a community responsibility; proceedings of the Arden House Workshop, 1967._ New York: National Commission for Social Work Careers, National Association of Social Workers, 1968. 39-40.

823 _____. "Social Work Recruiting Center of Greater New York." _Educationally disadvantaged students in social work education._ Compiled by the Council on Social Work Education. New York: The Council, 1968. 96-98.

824 Lower, Katherine D. "Undergraduate preparation prerequisite to admission to graduate schools of social work--from the graduate point of view." _Undergraduate education; a series of papers delivered at the 1958 Annual Program Meeting, Council on Social Work Education._ New York: The Council, 1958. 6-10.

825 Marin, Rosa C. "Puerto Ricans are not being attracted to United States schools of social work." Social Work Education Reporter, v. 19, no. 1, Dec.-Jan. 1971. 45.

826 Marks, Rachel Bryant. "An examination of applications for admissions to programs of advanced education: analysis and interpretation." Social Work Education Reporter, v. 13, no. 1, March 1965. 6-7, 15.

827 Matson, Margaret B. "Undergraduate preparation prerequisite to admission to graduate schools of social work--from the undergraduate point of view." Undergraduate education; a series of papers delivered at the 1958 Annual Program Meeting, Council on Social Work Education. New York: The Council, 1958. 1-5.

828 Merle, Sherman. "The selection of students at a graduate school of social work: a study of the incremental value of a pre-admission interview and the use of the undergraduate grade point average and Miller Analogy Test in identifying the successful and unsuccessful student." Doctoral dissertation, Brandeis University, 1968. 151p.

829 Muzumdar, Ammu M. "Selection of students to the schools of social work--A challenge to social work educators." Social Work Forum. v. 1, no. 1, Jan. 1963. 27-28.

830 National Workshop on Admissions. The admissions process in schools of social work; papers presented at the workshop, St. Louis, 1962. New York: Council on Social Work Education, 1964. 84p.

831 Olander, Helen L. "Selection of students for social work education: factors predictive of successful achievement." Doctoral dissertation, University of Southern California, 1964. 265p.

832 Ontell, Robert. "Criteria employed and the reliability of judgments in making decisions about the acceptance of applicants into the Columbia University School of Social Work." Doctoral dissertation, Columbia University, 1965. 170p.

833 O'Reilly, Charles T. "Issues in student recruitment and selection." Educationally disadvantaged students in social work education. Compiled by the Council on Social Work Education. New York: The Council, 1968. 85-95.

834 _____. "S-U grades and admission to graduate schools of social work." Journal of Education for Social Work, v. 10, no. 2, spring 1974. 65-67.

835 Pins, Arnulf M. "Development of social work recruitment: a historical review." Social Service Review, v. 39, no. 1, March 1965. 53-62.

836 Quaranta, Mary Ann. "Discontinuance in social work educa-
     tion: a study of preadmissions and post-admissions vari-
     ables. " Doctoral dissertation, Columbia University, 1973.
     216p.

837 Ranade, S. N. "Recruitment to social work. " Social Work
     Forum, v. 1, no. 1, Jan. 1963. 13-18.

838 Riskin, Leona L. "Sampling social work: how summer social
     work programs for selected undergraduates can serve as an
     effective aid to recruitment. " Child Welfare, v. 39, no. 2,
     Feb. 1960. 11-14.

839 Rivera, Julian. "Recruitment of Puerto Rican students into
     schools of social work. " Social Work Education Reporter,
     v. 19, no. 1, Dec. -Jan. 1971. 43-44.

840 Robertson, Mary Ella. "Attracting minority group members to
     social work--professional education's responsibility. "
     Manpower: a community responsibility; proceedings of the
     Arden House Workshop, 1967. New York: National Com-
     mission for Social Work, National Association of Social
     Workers, 1968. 36-38.

841 _____, et al. Observations on admission to graduate social
     work education. New York: Council on Social Work Ed-
     ucation, 1967. 34p.

842 Ross, Bernard and Philip Lichtenberg. Enrollment in schools
     of social work, 1950-1960. New York: Council on Social
     Work Education, 1963. 36p.

843 Sarnat, Rhoda Gerard. "Prediction versus performance in
     student selection. " Social Work Education Reporter, v. 16,
     no. 1, March 1968. 45-46, 59-61.

844 Schubert, Margaret. "Admissions decisions. " Social Service
     Review, v. 37, no. 2, June 1963. 154-165.

845 _____. "Admissions decisions: repetition of a study. "
     Social Service Review, v. 38, no. 2, June 1964. 147-152.

846 Seidl, Frederick W. "Rejection by a school of social work:
     some consequences for the applicant. " Social Work-
     er--Travailleur Social, v. 42, no. 2, summer 1974.
     117-124.

847 Severinson, Hellen Eloise. "A study of students entering the
     University of Pennsylvania School of Social Work as their
     selection by the School relates to trends in social work. "
     Doctoral dissertation, University of Pennsylvania, 1964.
     257p.

848 Spence, John M. and Robert W. Weinbach. "The preadmissions interview as an element in the admissions process of schools of social work." Arete, v. 3, no. 2, fall 1974. 71-79.

849 Stein, Shayna R., Margaret W. Linn and James Furdon. "Predicting social work student performance." Journal of Education for Social Work, v. 10, no. 3, fall 1974. 85-92.

850 Steinman, Richard. "Values in occupational choice and occupational selection: a comparative study of admissions in social work education." Doctoral dissertation, Brandeis University, 1968. 526p.

851 Teicher, Morton I. "Reverse discrimination." Social Work, v. 17, no. 6, Nov. 1972. 3-4.

852 Thursz, Daniel. "Recruiting community planners." Social Work Education Reporter, v. 15, no. 2, June 1967. 28-31, 41-42.

853 Towle, Charlotte. "Implications of contemporary human values for selection of social work students." Social Service Review, v. 33, no. 3, Sept. 1959. 260-273.

854 Wells, Mabel G. "Report on a successful social work recruitment program." Journal of Education for Social Work, v. 10, no. 1, winter 1974. 109-117.

855 Wickham, E. R. "The use of students in admissions interviewing." Journal of Education for Social Work, v. 10, no. 2, spring 1974. 118-120.

856 Williams, Mark J. K. "The validity of demographic, and evaluation admissions criteria and status of rater variables, to predict educational performance in a graduate school of social work." Doctoral dissertation, Rutgers University, 1976. 208p.

12. Values and Attitudes
[See also Sections II. A; III. E. 3.]

857 Beckman, C. Wesley. "Aging: attitudes of social work students as predicted by selected socio-demographic variables, life, and educational experiences." Doctoral dissertation, University of Utah, 1974. 170p.

858 Behroozi, Cyrus S. "Relationships among value definitions and practice competence in social work: a study of a group of first-year graduate students." Doctoral dissertation, University of Pennsylvania, 1974. 198p.

859 Bernard, L. Diane. "The impact of the first year of professional education in social work on student value positions."

Doctoral dissertation, Bryn Mawr College, 1967. 170p.

860 Crowns, Arthur John, Jr. "Attitude differential and professional socialization of successful and unsuccessful graduate social work students attending Florida State University." Doctoral dissertation, Florida State University, 1965. 158p.

861 Desai, A. N. "Attitudinal study of students on social work education." Social Action (Indian), v. 17, no. 1, Jan. - Feb. 1967. 20-33.

862 Durfee, Richard. "Personality characteristics and attitudes toward the disabled of students in the health professions." Rehabilitation Counseling Bulletin, v. 15, no. 1, Sept. 1971. 35-44.

863 Eckardt, Ralph W., Jr. "Evangelical Christianity and social work: a study of the beliefs and practice of graduates of the social work majors at Philadelphia College of Bible and Temple University." Doctoral dissertation, University of Pennsylvania, 1974. 322p.

864 Edwards, Raymond Lewis, Jr. "Familial characteristics and personality profiles of graduate social work students." Doctoral dissertation, Florida State University, 1966. 237p.

865 Erard, Glen. "Student skepticism as a variable in professional education: implications for clinical and didactic learning." Doctoral dissertation, Smith College, 1972. 159p.

866 Erlich, John L. and John E. Tropman. "Social work students, other graduate students, and issues of student protest." Journal of Education for Social Work, v. 10, no. 1, winter 1974. 22-26.

867 Feinstein, Ronald Myron. "Social work value orientation and satisfaction with education program." Doctoral dissertation, University of Pittsburgh, 1972. 353p.

868 Fredericks, Marcel, William J. Mackey and Paul Mundy. "An analysis of academic achievement and personality characteristics of students in a school of social work." Iowa Journal of Social Work, v. 5, no. 4, fall 1972. 14-20.

869 _____, Paul Mundy and William J. Mackey. "The relationship between social class, stress-anxiety responses, academic achievement and professional attitudes of students in a school of social work." Arete, v. 3, no. 2, fall 1974. 61-70.

870 _____, et al. "Social backgrounds, attitudes, and aspira-
tions of students in a school of social work." Iowa
Journal of Social Work, v. 6, nos. 2 and 3, Dec. 1975.
100-117.

871 Fuller, Albert D. "The values of social workers." Doctoral dissertation, University of Southern California,
1962. 269p.

872 Goode, Norma Lee Montague. "Attitudes of professional
and social work value orientations in undergraduate
social welfare majors: a comparative study of professionalism attitudes and social work value orientations
at two levels of professional social work education."
Doctoral dissertation, University of Minnesota, 1974.
208p.

873 Grimm, James W. and James D. Orten. "Student attitudes
toward the poor." Social Work, v. 18, no. 1, Jan. 1973.
94-100.

874 Gruener, Jennette R. "Values of social work students in
two cultures." Social Work Education Reporter, v. 16,
no. 1, March 1968. 44, 57-59.

875 Hanna, Herbert Wayne. "The associations between social
work value orientations, social work education, professional attitudes and organizational structure with the job
satisfaction of social workers." Doctoral dissertation,
Ohio State University, 1975. 182p.

876 Harris, Linda Hall and Margaret Exner Lucas. "Sex-role
stereotyping." Social Work, v. 21, no. 5, Sept. 1976.
390-394.

877 Hayes, Dorothy D. and Barbara K. Varley. "Impact of
social work education on students' values." Social Work,
v. 10, no. 3, July 1965. 40-46.

878 Hepworth, Dean H. and E. Gene Shumway. "Changes in
open-mindedness as a result of social work education."
Journal of Education for Social Work, v. 12, no. 1, winter
1976. 56-62.

879 Keefe, Thomas W. "Empathy and social work education: a
study." Journal of Education for Social Work, v. 11, no.
3, fall 1975. 69-75.

879a _____. "Empathy: impact of social work education and
enhancement techniques." Doctoral dissertation,
University of Utah, 1973. 176p.

880 _____. "Empathy: the critical skill." Social Work,

v. 21, no. 1, Jan. 1976. 10-14.

881 Knott, Ben H. "Symbolic interaction and social work education." Journal of Education for Social Work, v. 9, no.
3, fall 1973. 24-30.

882 Kohn, Ezra Asher. "Selected characteristics of social work
students and education for social work at the University
of Nebraska." Doctoral dissertation, University of
Nebraska, 1972. 121p.

883 Kurtz, Nancy, Richard A. Kurtz and Robert Hoffnung.
"Attitudes toward the lower- and middle-class psychiatric
patient as a function of authoritarianism among mental
health students." Journal of Consulting and Clinical
Psychology, v. 35, no. 3, Dec. 1970. 338-341.

884 Kurtz, Richard A. and David J. Giacopassi. "Medical and
social work students' perceptions of deviant conditions
and sick role incumbency." Social Science and Medicine,
v. 9, no. 4-5, April-May 1975. 249-256.

885 Laycock, A. L. "Attitude changes in adult students during
social work training." Social Work (London), v. 25, no. 3,
July 1968. 17-23.

886 Lincoln, Lois, Margaret Berryman and Margaret W. Linn.
"Drug abuse: a comparison of attitudes." Comprehensive Psychiatry, v. 14, no. 5, Sept./Oct. 1973. 465-471.

887 Lowy, Louis. "Clarification of self and role perceptions in
social work students during training: a study of incor-
poration of a professional role." Doctoral dissertation,
Harvard University, 1966. 403p.

888 Lundberg, Horace W. "Some distinctive characteristics of
students entering graduate social work education." Doctoral dissertation, University of Minnesota, 1957. 168p.

889 Mangum, Paul D. and Kevin M. Mitchell. "Attitudes toward
the mentally ill and community care among professionals
and their students." Community Mental Health Journal,
v. 9, no. 4, winter 1973. 350-353.

890 Munday, Brian. "What is happening to social work students?"
Social Work Today, v. 3, no. 6, 15 June 1972. 3-6.

891 Myers, Clara Louise Hanser. "An experiment in the development and measurement of empathy in social work
students." Brown Studies, 1966. 84-86.

892 _____. "An experiment in the development and measurement of empathy in social work students." Doctoral

dissertation, Washington University, 1966. 119p.

893 Oren, Anne Winslow. "The construction of an instrument for the measurement of social worker attitudes associated with aptitude for interpersonal relationships." Doctoral dissertation, University of Minnesota, 1958. 117p.

894 Parlow, J. and A. Rothman. "Attitudes towards social issues in medicine of five health science faculties (Dentistry, medicine, nursing, pharmacy, and social work)." Social Science and Medicine, v. 8, no. 6, June 1974. 351-358.

895 Pavlin, Frank F. "Professional socialization: a study of attitudes and personality traits change during a course of professional education for social work." Australian Social Work, v. 26, no. 4, Dec. 1973. 7-27.

896 Plotnick, Harold L. "The attitudinal orientation of the worker and accuracy in predicting client behavior." Social Service Review, v. 39, no. 1, March 1965. 23-30.

897 Ramachandran, P. "Students' changing views on social work." Indian Journal of Social Work, v. 33, no. 3, Oct. 1972. 191-198.

898 Rothman, Beulah. "Processes of socialization to the profession of social work." Doctoral dissertation, Columbia University, 1963. 295p.

899 Rubenstein, Hiasaura. "Student orientations and faculty definitions of the professional role." Doctoral dissertation, University of Chicago, 1971. 205p.

900 Ryle, Anthony and Dana Breen. "Change in the course of social work training: a repertory grid study." British Journal of Medical Psychology, v. 47, part 2, June 1974. 139-147.

901 _____ and _____. "Social-work tutors' judgment of their students." British Journal of Medical Psychology, v. 47, part 2, June 1974. 149-152.

902 Schlesinger, Elfriede G. "Graduate social work education: impact on social change and behavioral science orientation." Journal of Education for Social Work, v. 12, no. 1, winter 1976. 113-120.

903 Shey, Thomas H. "How American social work students view their profession: highlights of a recent survey." Applied Social Studies, v. 2, no. 3, Oct. 1970. 137-143.

904 _____. "The professional socialization of social work students: how length of schooling, prior work exper-

ience, and other variables, affect some aspects of the professional socialization of graduate social work students. " Doctoral dissertation, New School for Social Research, 1969. 271p.

905 Shulder, Lois B. "A comparison of attitudes of law students, social work students, and gerontology students toward the aged and toward income-security programs and social welfare services for the aged. " Doctoral dissertation, University of Southern California, 1973. 226p.

906 Stein, Shayna R. and Margaret W. Linn. The effect of drug use on social work students' treatment attitudes. " Journal of Education for Social Work, v. 11, no. 2, spring 1975. 109-115.

907 Stempler, Benj L. "Effects of aversive racism on white social work students. " Social Casework, v. 56, no. 8, Oct. 1975. 460-467.

908 Todres, Rubin. "The professional socialization of attitudes toward social action tactics among social work students. " Doctoral dissertation, University of Pittsburgh, 1974. 266p.

909 Tragler, A. , et al. "Students' perception of social work." Indian Journal of Social Work, v. 32, no. 4, Oct. 1971. 321-331.

910 Varley, Barbara Knowles. "Social work values: changes in value commitments of students from admission to MSW graduation. " Journal of Education for Social Work, v. 4, no. 2, fall 1968. 67-76.

911 _____. "Socialization in social work education. " Social Work, v. 8, no. 3, July 1963. 102-109.

912 _____. "Socialization in social work education: a study of the value areas of change and non-change during social work training. " Doctoral dissertation, Case Western Reserve University, 1963. 125p.

913 Weagant, Robert. "Attitude change of professional social work students. " Doctoral dissertation, University of Chicago, 1976. 184p.

914 Werley, Harriet H. , et al. "Medicine, nursing, social work: professionals and birth control: student and faculty attitudes. " Family Planning Perspectives, v. 5, no. 1, winter 1973. 42-49.

915 Western, John S. "Social work and professional socialization. " Australian Journal of Social Issues, v. 1, no. 4, spring 1963. 53-65.

916 Whiteman, Martin and Irving F. Lukoff. "Attitudes toward blindness and other physical handicaps." Journal of Social Psychology, v. 66, no. 1, June 1965. 135-145.

917 _____ and _____. "Attitudes toward blindness in two college groups." Journal of Social Psychology, v. 63, no. 1, June 1963. 179-191.

918 Willis, Jerry, Warner Wilson and Joan Willis. "Religious orientations of three samples of graduate students in clinical psychology, social work, and counseling and guidance." Psychological Reports, v. 26, no. 2, April 1970. 623-630.

919 Wilson, Elizabeth. "A reply to Brian Munday: another view of What is happening to social work students." Social Work Today, v. 3, no. 9, 27 July 1972. 15-16.

920 Witte, Ernest F. "Student wisdom and values: the positive force of disaffection." Social work values in an age of discontent. Edited by Katherine A. Kendall. New York: Council on Social Work Education, 1970. 87-104.

921 Zober, Edith and Bill C. F. Snider. "A comparison of Iowa social work students with the general public in their perceptions of Black people and their struggle for equality." Iowa Journal of Social Work, v. 4, no. 1, winter 1971. 26-33.

F. SURVEYS OF GRADUATES AND THEIR EMPLOYMENT PATTERNS

922 Adams, David M. "Expectations of young social work graduates." Australian Social Work, v. 25, no. 1, March 1972. 29-33.

923 Bishop, Margaret E. "The mobility of professional social workers: a study of mobility of the graduates of the University of Pennsylvania School of Social Work, 1936-1954." Doctoral dissertation, University of Pennsylvania, 1958. 172p.

924 _____. "A report to the alumni on the mobility of the graduates of the University of Pennsylvania School of Social Work, 1936 to 1954." Journal of Social Work Process, v. 11, 1960. 140-144.

925 Golden, Deborah. "Social work graduates: the third study." NASW Personnel Information, v. 9, no. 2, March 1966. 1, 46-47.

926 Graham-Smith, Heather and John W. D. Davies. "Professional training and afterwards-- two former students reflect." Case Conference, v. 11, no. 1, May 1964. 3-8.

927 Herberg, Dorothy Chave. "Career patterns and work participation of graduate female social workers." Doctoral dissertation, University of Michigan, 1970. 266p.

928 _____. "A study of work participation by graduate female social workers: some implications for professional social work training." Journal of Education for Social Work, v. 9, no. 3, fall 1973. 16-23.

929 Hess, Dolph. "Prediction of success in casework practice from performance in the graduate program." Doctoral dissertation, University of Minnesota, 1966. 151p.

930 "Highlights of Howard University's study of MSW recipients 1946-1962." Social Work Education Reporter, v. 11, no. 4, Aug. 1963. 1, 12-13.

931 Kingsbury, Susan Myra. Carola Woerishoffer Graduate Department of Social Economy and Social Research of Bryn Mawr College, 1915-1925. Bryn Mawr, Pa.: Department of Social Economy, Bryn Mawr College, 1925. 63p.

932 Lewin, Thomas Fred. "The employment experience of married women social caseworkers: a study of one hundred graduates of the New York School of Social Work, Columbia University." Doctoral dissertation, University of Chicago, 1962. 124p.

933 McGee, Ruth. "A postgraduate lament." Perceptions, v. 1, no. 1, spring 1967. 5-8.

933a Meld, Murray B. "The employment experience of community organization graduates: a pilot study." Journal of Education for Social Work, v. 10, no. 1, winter 1974. 60-67.

934 Mitchell, Florence. "The first two years: review article." Medical Social Work (London), v. 18, no. 7, Nov. 1965. 209-212.

935 New York School of Social Work. "A brief study of the work histories of 368 two-year graduates as of January, 1931." Bulletin of New York School of Social Work, alumni number, July 1931. 3-14.

936 Pascoe, A. W. "Married women graduates in part-time practice." Social Worker-Travailleur Social, v. 38, no. 3, July 1970. 8-10.

937 Radin, Norma. "A follow-up study of social work graduates."
       Journal of Education for Social Work, v. 12, no. 3, fall
       1976. 103-107.

938 _____. A profile of social work graduates: the Univer-
       sity of Michigan School of Social Work. Ann Arbor:
       School of Social Work, University of Michigan, 1974. 24p.

939 Regensburg, Jeanette. "Testing the product of schools of
       social work." Social Work Journal, v. 32, no. 4, Oct.
       1950. 164-170.

940 Ryland, Gladys. Employment responsibilities of social group
       work graduates; a study of employment characteristics of
       social group workers in their first year of employment;
       prepared for the Committee on Group Work. New York:
       Council on Social Work Education, 1958. 70p.

941 Sarri, Rosemary C. and John M. Riley. "Graduates of the
       social welfare administration curriculum: where they
       are and how they view the curriculum." Social Work
       Education Reporter, v. 19, no. 2, April-May 1971. 53-56.

942 Sauber, Mignon. "Social work graduates: salaries and char-
       acteristics." NASW Personnel Information, v. 8, no. 1,
       Jan. 1965. 1, 33-36.

943 Schultz, Virginia M. "Employment trends of recent gradu-
       ates." NASW News, v. 16, no. 1, Nov. 1970. 15, 26.

944 Stamm, Alfred M. "1967 social work graduates: salaries
       and characteristics." NASW Personnel Information, v. 11,
       no. 2, March 1968. 1, 50-54.

945 Texas. University. Graduate School of Social Work. The
       history of The School of Social Work and the professional
       experience of its graduates, 1950-1960. Austin, Tex.:
       The School, 1961. 123p.

946 Thompson, Joseph Victor. "The social work generalist: a
       study of recent graduates of the University of Southern
       California School of Social Work." Doctoral dissertation,
       University of Southern California, 1969. 267p.

947 Turner, Frank J. A study of the alumni of the University of
       Ottawa School of Social Welfare, 1950-1963. Ottawa:
       School of Social Welfare, University of Ottawa, 1964.
       62p.

948 Turner, Robert O. and Alexis H. Skelding. "Results of a
       survey of March 1970 MSW graduates of Florida State
       University." Curriculum building for the continuum in
       social welfare education. Edited by Michael J. Austin,

et al. Tallahassee, Fla.: State University System of
Florida, 1972. 127-130.

949 Yeakel, Margaret. "The 1968 graduate survey: a profile of
Smith alumni." Smith College Studies in Social Work,
v. 39, no. 3, June 1969. 184-188.

950 _____. "The Smith alumni survey." Smith College
Studies in Social Work, v. 41, no. 2, Feb. 1971. 147-171.

IV.   GENERAL ASPECTS OF GRADUATE SOCIAL WORK
       CURRICULUM, TEACHING AND LEARNING

A.   SOCIAL WORK CURRICULUM AND CURRICULUM DESIGN

951   Amacher, Kloh-Ann. "Relevance and revolution: issue in
      curricular change." Social Work Education Reporter,
      v. 18, no. 2, June 1970. 39-46.

952   Andrew, Gwen. "Forecasting social work practice as a
      base for curriculum development." Journal of Education
      for Social Work, v. 10, no. 3, fall 1974. 3-8.

953   Aptekar, Herbert H. "The curriculum-building process."
      Journal of Education for Social Work, v. 4, no. 2, fall
      1968. 5-13.

954   Armitage, Andrew and Frank W. Clark. "Design issues in
      the performance-based curriculum." Journal of Educa-
      tion for Social Work, v. 11, no. 1, winter 1975. 22-29.

955   Bartlett, Harriett M. "The generic-specific concept in
      social work education and practice." Issues in American
      social work. Edited by Alfred J. Kahn. New York:
      Columbia University Press, 1959. 159-190.

956   Bernard, L. Diane. "Graduate curriculum for the future--
      Master's level." Curriculum building for the continuum
      in social welfare education. Edited by Michael J. Austin,
      et al. Tallahassee, Fla.: State University System of
      Florida, 1972. 66-70.

957   Blackey, Eileen. "Building the curriculum: the foundation
      for professional competence." International Social Work,
      v. 10, no. 1, Jan. 1967. 8-17.

958   Block, Alvan M. "The dilemma of social work education:
      restructuring the curriculum." Journal of Education for
      Social Work, v. 8, no. 1, winter 1972. 19-23.

959   Boehm, Werner W. "Common and specific learning for a
      graduate of a school of social work." Journal of
      Education for Social Work, v. 4, no. 2, fall 1968.
      15-26.

960 Bowers, Swithun. "Main problems of curriculum planning."
International Social Work, v. 4, no. 2, April 1961. 33-40.

961 Brown, Eddie F. "The inclusion of ethnic minority content
in the curricula of graduate schools of social work."
Doctoral dissertation, University of Utah, 1975. 148p.

962 Buell, Bradley. "Implications for social work education of
a conception of prevention." Education for social work;
proceedings of the 1960 Annual Program Meeting,
Council on Social Work Education. New York: The
Council, 1960. 139-150. Discussion by Mary R. Baker.
150-156.

963 Burian, William A. "The laboratory as an element in
social work curriculum design." Journal of Education
for Social Work, v. 12, no. 1, winter 1976. 36-43.

964 Carroll, Nancy K. "Areas of concentration in the graduate
curriculum: a three-dimensional model." Journal of
Education for Social Work, v. 11, no. 2, spring 1975.
3-10.

965 Council on Social Work Education. Building the social work
curriculum; report of the National Curriculum Workshop,
Allerton, Ill., 1960. New York: The Council, 1961.
85p.

966 _____. Concepts of prevention and control: their use in
the social work curriculum; report of the Workshop on
Use in Curriculum of the Concepts of Prevention and
Control, New York, 1961. New York: The Council,
1961. 32p.

967 _____. "Curriculum policy for the Master's degree program in graduate school of social work." Social Work
Education Reporter, v. 17, no. 4, Dec. 1969. 25R-27R.

968 _____. Curriculum policy statement, adopted by the
American Association of Schools of Social Work, 1952.
New York: The Council, 1952. 3p.

969 _____. Major issues in curriculum policy and current
practices in accreditation; a series of papers delivered
at the 1961 Annual Program Meeting. New York: The
Council, 1961. 29p.

970 _____. Official statement of curriculum policy for the
Master's degree program in graduate professional
schools of social work. New York: The Council, 1962
8p.

971 _____. Policy on curriculum experimentation and
innovation. New York: The Council, 1962. 2p.

972 _____. Problems and methods of curriculum evaluation;
workshop report of the 1957 Annual Program Meeting.
New York: The Council, 1957. 29p.

973 Desai, Armaity Sapur and Angelina C. Almanzor, editors.
Curriculum development and teaching; proceedings of the
South East Asian Seminar for Social Work Educators.
Bombay: Athenaeum Press, 1972. 240p.

974 Dieppa, Ismael. "Ethnic minority content in the social work
curriculum: a position statement!" Perspectives on
ethnic minority content in social work education.
Edited by Charles W. McCann. Boulder, Colo.:
Western Interstate Commission for Higher Education,
1972. 5-15.

975 Fellin, Phillip A. and Robert D. Vinter. "Curriculum development for contemporary social work education:
University of Michigan." Modes of professional education: functions of field instruction in the curriculum;
report of a symposium, 1969, New Orleans. Edited by
Helen Cassidy. New Orleans: School of Social Work,
Tulane University, 1969. 52-68.

976 Foster, Marion G. "The process of planning for curriculum
change." Doctoral students look at social work education. Edited by Leila Calhoun Deasy. New York:
Council on Social Work Education, 1971. 29-51.

977 _____. "The process of planning for curriculum change:
a case study in a school of social work." Doctoral
dissertation, Catholic University of America. 1970.
217p.

978 Geismar, Ludwig L. "The options of a school of social work
for curriculum-building in a period of urban crisis."
Social Service Review, v.43, no.2, June 1969. 184-193.

979 Glenn, Mary Willcox. "The history of social work and its
place in the professional curriculum." Proceedings of
the National Conference of Social Work, 1930. Chicago:
University of Chicago Press, 1931. 511-519.

980 Goldstein, Howard. "Students' perceptions of curriculum:
a resource for curriculum construction." Perceptions,
v.1, no.1, spring 1967. 18-23.

981 Guzzetta, Charles. "Curriculum alternatives." Journal of
Education for Social Work, v.8, no.1, winter 1972.
24-30.

982 _____. "The curriculum continuum." Curriculum building
for the continuum in social welfare education. Edited by

Michael J. Austin, et al. Tallahassee, Fla.: State University System of Florida, 1972. 15-26.

983 Hale, Mark P. "Curriculum models for social work education." Modes of professional education: functions of field instruction in the curriculum; report of a symposium, 1969, New Orleans. Edited by Helen Cassidy. New Orleans: School of Social Work, Tulane University, 1969. 211-228.

984 Hamilton, Gordon. "Some problems of the second-year curriculum of the professional schools." Social Service Review, v. 16, no. 2, June 1942, 212-223.

985 Haselkorn, Florence. "An ounce of prevention...." Journal of Education for Social Work, v. 3, no. 2, fall 1967. 61-70.

986 Kadushin, Alfred. "Two problems of the graduate program: level and content." Journal of Education for Social Work, v. 1, no. 1, spring 1965. 33-46.

987 Kendall, Katherine A. "A conceptual framework for the social work curriculum of tomorrow." Social Service Review, v. 27, no. 1, March 1953. 15-26.

988 Lewis, Harold. "Agology, animation, conscientization: implications for social work education in the USA." Journal of Education for Social Work, v. 9, no. 3, fall 1973. 31-38.

989 _____. "Developing a program responsive to new knowledge and values." Evaluation of social intervention. Edited by Edward F. Mullen and James R. Dumpson. San Francisco, Jossey-Bass, 1972. 71-89.

990 McDaniel, Clyde O., Jr. and Deryl G. Hunt. "Toward a revision of the curriculum for masters-level education in urban schools of social work." Indian Journal of Social Work, v. 34, no. 3, Oct. 1973. 259-274.

991 McGrath, Frances C. and Roger Owen. A survey of genetics and genetic counselling in social work education. Miami, Fla.: Mailman Center for Child Development, University of Miami, 1975. Various pagings.

992 Main, Marjorie White. "Restructuring social work education: knowledge, curriculum, instruction." Journal of Education for Social Work, v. 7, no. 2, spring 1971. 31-38.

993 Merle, Sherman. "The social work teacher and the social work curriculum." Exploring the interfaces of social work education. Edited by Charles W. McCann. Boulder, Colo.:

Western Interstate Commission for Higher Education, 1970. 43-54.

994 Nann, Richard C. and Henry S. Maas. "Purpose and framework for curriculum development in social work." International Social Work, v. 17, no. 1, 1974. 54-61.

995 "New Curriculum Policy Statement: three views." "Freedom and/or regulation-1," by Gideon Horowitz; "Freedom and/or regulation-2," by Arthur J. Katz; "Professional cohesion-3," by Willard C. Richan. Journal of Education for Social Work, v. 7, no. 2, spring 1971. 39-60.

996 Piven, Frances Fox. "Political science content and the social work curriculum." Social Work Education Reporter, v. 15, no. 2, June 1967. 26-27, 40.

997 Rockmore, Myron J. and John J. Conklin. "Contemporary social work education and psychoanalysis." Journal of Education for Social Work, v. 10, no. 2, spring 1974. 68-75.

998 Rothman, Beulah and Joseph L. Vigilante. "Curriculum planning in social work education." Journal of Education for Social Work, v. 10, no. 2, spring 1974. 76-85.

999 Sanders, Daniel S. "Educating social workers for the role of effective change agents in a multicultural, pluralistic society." Journal of Education for Social Work, v. 10, no. 2, spring 1974. 86-91.

1000 Segal, Brian. "A commentary on curriculum components." Canadian Journal of Social Work Education, v. 2, no. 1, spring 1976. 44-48.

1001 Sikkema, Mildred. "Some aspects of curriculum-building." Social Service Review, v. 32, no. 1, March 1958. 11-23.

1002 Slavin, Simon. "Concepts of social conflict: use in social work curriculum." Journal of Education for Social Work, v. 5, no. 2, fall 1969. 47-60.

1003 Smalley, Ruth E. "Place of specialized courses in a generic curriculum." Child Welfare, v. 34, no. 4, April 1955. 10-16.

1004 _____. Specialization in social work education. New York: Council on Social Work Education, 1956. 13p.

1005 Stein, Herman D. Curriculum study: New York School of Social Work, Columbia University. New York: New York School of Social Work of Columbia University, 1960. 105p.

1006 _____. "Implications of social change theory for social work practice and education." Education for social work; proceedings of the 1960 Annual Program Meeting, Council on Social Work Education. New York: The Council, 1960. 24-37.

1007 _____. "Observations on the 1962 Curriculum Policy Statement." Education for social work; proceedings of the 1963 Annual Program Meeting, Council on Social Work Education. New York: The Council, 1963. 47-53.

1008 Stevenson, Olive. "Knowledge for social work." British Journal of Social Work, v. 1, no. 2, summer 1971. 225-237.

1009 Stinson, Malcolm B. "Authority in the social work curriculum." Social Work Papers, v. 8, 1961. 31-34.

1010 Taber, Merlin. "Curriculum development on the Urbana Campus, University of Illinois." Modes of professional education: functions of field instruction in the curriculum; report of a symposium, 1969, New Orleans. Edited by Helen Cassidy. New Orleans: School of Social Work, Tulane University, 1969. 5-21.

1011 Thomlison, Raymond J. and Frederick W. Seidl. "An experiment in curriculum innovation in graduate social work education." Journal of Education for Social Work, v. 10, no. 3, fall 1974. 93-98.

1012 Towle, Charlotte. "Education for social work: issues and problems in curriculum development." Social Work Journal, v. 30, no. 2, April 1949. 67-75, 102.

1013 _____. Generic trends in education for social work. London: Association of Social Workers, 1956. 13p.

1014 Tyler, Ralph W. The basic principles of curriculum and instruction. Chicago: University of Chicago Press, 1950. 83p.

1015 Vasey, Wayne. "The Curriculum Study: implications for graduate and undergraduate curricula." Social Casework, v. 41, no. 1, Jan. 1960. 7-13.

1016 Wasserman, Harry and Rosalyn Benitez. "Dissonances in social work education." Social Work Education Reporter, v. 17, no. 1, March 1969. 47-50, 58-60.

1017 Wisner, Elizabeth. "Uses of historical material in the social work curriculum." Social Service Review, v. 34, no. 3, Sept. 1960. 265-272.

1018 Youngdahl, Benjamin E. "Criteria for an integrated curriculum." Social work as human relations; anniversary papers of the New York School of Social Work and the Community Service Society. New York: Columbia University Press, 1949. 116-126.

B. TEACHING AND LEARNING [See also Sections III. D; IV. C. D. E. F; VII. E.]

1019 Anderson, G. Lester. "Learning theory and teaching method." Education for social work; proceedings of the 1961 Annual Program Meeting, Council on Social Work Education. New York: The Council, 1961. 102-108.

1020 Andrew, Gwen. "A structural model for MSW education." Social Work Education Reporter, v. 20, no. 1, Dec. / Jan. 1972. 25-28.

1021 Barrett, Elwin M. "Contract learning: negotiation and agreement in the teaching-learning process." Doctoral dissertation, University of Southern California, 1974. 141p.

1022 Berengarten, Sidney. "Identifying learning patterns of individual students: an exploratory study." Social Service Review, v. 31, no. 4, Dec. 1957. 407-417.

1023 Bloom, Tybel. "Achieving professional identity: a conception of social work education." Journal of Social Work Process, v. 17, 1969. 37-54.

1024 Blum, Arthur. "Faculty involvement in utilization of community conflict situations in teaching." Social Work Education Reporter, v. 18, no. 2, June 1970. 24-26, 46-47.

1025 Brown, Leonard N. , Daniel Katz and Theodore Walden. "Student-centered teaching: the analog to client-centered practice." Journal of Education for Social Work, v. 12, no. 3, fall 1976. 11-17.

1026 Canfield, Stephen F. , et al. "A laboratory training model for the development of effective interpersonal communications in social work." Journal of Education for Social Work, v. 11, no. 1, winter 1975. 45-50.

1027 Carlson, Raymond W. "Expanding educational assumptions for social work education." Journal of Education for Social Work, v. 10, no. 3, fall 1974. 17-24.

1028 Cassidy, Helen E. "Meeting the needs of work-experienced students." Public Welfare, v. 25, no. 1, Jan. 1967. 29-37.

1029 Clark, Frank W. and Albert Comanor. "Implications of the
      socio-behavioral framework for social work education."
      Social Worker-Travailleur Social, v. 41, no. 4, winter
      1973. 291-303.

1030 Council on Social Work Education. Methods of formulating
      and teaching the common elements of social work prac-
      tice; workshop report no. 6 of the 1953 Annual Program
      Meeting. New York: The Council, 1953. 24p.

1031 _____. A source book of readings on teaching in social
      work. New York: The Council, 1965. Various pagings.

1032 _____. The use of record material in teaching; workshop
      report of the 1956 Annual Program Meeting, Council on
      Social Work Education. New York: The Council, 1956.
      26p.

1033 Coyle, Grace L. "The role of the teacher in the creation of
      an integrated curriculum." Social Work Journal, v. 33,
      no. 2, April 1952. 73-82.

1034 _____. "Securing student participation in practice courses."
      Family, v. 26, no. 2, April 1945. 50-54.

1035 Crichton, Anne. "Developing understanding of group behaviour
      in social studies students." Social Work (London), v. 23,
      no. 3, July 1966. 19-24.

1036 Crompton, Don W. "Transition from a closed teaching sys-
      tem to an open learning system: a demonstration project."
      International Social Work, v. 19, no. 3, 1976. 38-50.

1037 Cullen, Yvonne M. "Some reflections of an existential ap-
      proach to education in social work." Australian Social
      Work, v. 24, nos. 3 & 4, Sept. -Dec. 1971. 20-25.

1038 Cummings, Joan Elizabeth. "Integration of learning in gra-
      duate social work education." Doctoral dissertation, Uni-
      versity of Toronto, 1973. 302p.

1039 Desai, Armaity Sapur and Angelina C. Almanzor, editors.
      Curriculum development and teaching; proceedings of the
      South East Asian Seminar for Social Work Educators.
      Bombay: Athenaeum Press, 1972. 240p.

1040 Duehn, Wayne D. and Enola K. Proctor. "A study of cog-
      nitive complexity in the education for social work prac-
      tice." Journal of Education for Social Work, v. 10, no.
      2, spring 1974. 20-26.

1041 Ericksen, Stanford C. "Transfer of learning and the matura-
      tion of private knowledge." Journal of Education for Social

Work, v. 3, no. 1, spring 1967. 13-20.

1041a Fischer, Joel. "Training for effective therapeutic practice."
Psychotherapy, v. 12, no. 1, spring 1975. 118-123.

1042 Flanigan, Beverly. "Planned change and contract negotiation
as an instructional model." Journal of Education for Social Work, v. 10, no. 2, spring 1974. 34-39.

1043 Foeckler, Merle M. and Gerald Boynton. "Creative adult
learning-teaching: who's the engineer of this train?"
Journal of Education for Social Work, v. 12, no. 3, fall
1976. 37-43.

1044 Guzzetta, Charles. "The student as learner." Journal of
Education for Social Work, v. 3, no. 2, fall 1967. 27-34.

1045 Hamilton, Gordon. "Self-awareness in professional education."
Social Casework, v. 35, no. 9, Nov. 1954. 371-379.

1046 Ho, Man Keung. "Fishbowl experience in social work learning, teaching, and practice." Iowa Journal of Social Work,
v. 6, nos. 2 and 3, Dec. 1975. 122-136.

1047 _____. "Implications of teacher-student relationships in
social work education." Journal of Education for Social
Work, v. 11, no. 1, winter 1975. 74-82.

1048 _____. "Team teaching--for better or for worse." Social
Work Education Reporter, v. 21, no. 2, April-May 1973.
49-52.

1049 Hollis, Florence. "'...and what shall we teach?' The social work educator and knowledge." Social Service Review,
v. 42, no. 2, June 1968. 184-196.

1050 Hunt, Linda, Kenneth Harrison and Michael Armstrong. "Integrating group dynamics training and the education and
development of social work students." British Journal of
Social Work, v. 4, no. 4, winter 1974. 405-423.

1051 Kapoor, J. M. "Resistance in social work education and practice." Indian Journal of Social Work, v. 27, no. 1, April
1966. 31-37.

1052 Kay, Kazuko. "Need for development of self-awareness in
social work education." Social Work (Manila), v. 15, no.
3, July-Oct. 1970. 9-12.

1053 Knott, Ben H. "Conceptual learning: implications for social
work education." Indian Journal of Social Work, v. 32,
no. 4, Jan. 1972. 353-368.

1054 Knowles, Malcolm S. "Innovations in teaching styles and approaches based upon adult learning." Journal of Education for Social Work, v. 8, no. 2, spring 1972. 32-39.

1055 Larsen, Jo Ann. "A comparative study of traditional and competency-based methods of teaching interpersonal skills in social work education." Doctoral dissertation, University of Utah, 1975. 145p.

1056 Lawrence, Richard G. The use of research results in teaching social work practice. Arlington, Va.: ERIC Document Reproduction Service, 1967. 23p. ED 014112.

1057 Leonard, Peter. "Explanation and education in social work." British Journal of Social Work, v. 5, no. 3, autumn 1975. 325-333.

1058 Lowy, Louis, Leonard M. Bloksberg and Herbert J. Walberg. Integrative learning and teaching in schools of social work; a study of organizational development in professional education. New York: Association Press, 1971. 285p.

1059 _____, _____, and _____. Teaching records: integrative learning and teaching project. New York: Council on Social Work Education, 1973. 107p.

1060 Macarov, David. "The concept of empathy and the educational process." Applied Social Studies, v. 2, no. 2, May 1970. 107-113.

1061 _____. "Some aspects of teaching from foreign records." Indian Journal of Social Work, v. 24, no. 4, Jan. 1964. 315-320.

1062 _____. "Sustaining discussion in the small class." Social Service Review, v. 37, no. 2, June 1963. 177-183.

1063 MacIntyre, J. McEwan. "The development of cohesion in student learning groups." Social Worker-Travailleur Social, v. 41, no. 4, winter 1973. 304-309.

1064 Mehta, Vera D. "Innovative teaching methods and materials in social work education." Social Work Education and Development Newsletter, no. 15, March 1976. 4-9.

1065 Middleman, Ruth R. and Gale Goldberg. "The interactional way of presenting generic social work concepts." Journal of Education for Social Work, v. 8, no. 2, spring 1972. 48-57.

1066 Miller, Steven L. and Patricia Miller. "Social work concepts and language analysis." Social Casework, v. 52, no. 3, March 1971. 142-147.

1067   Moore, Stewart. "Classroom: heart of student involvement."
        Social Work Education Reporter, v. 19, no. 2, April-May
        1971. 45-48.

1068   Morgan, Robert. "Telegraphic personalized instructional
        packages for students." Journal of Education for Social
        Work, v. 11, no. 2, spring 1975. 91-101.

1069   Morris, Clare. "Individual tutorials: a teacher's view of
        their educative and therapeutic values." Social Work To-
        day, v. 3, no. 6, 15 June 1972. 9-11.

1070   Neely, Ann Elizabeth. "The development of teaching mater-
        ials in North America." International Social Work, v. 3,
        no. 3, July 1960. 22-25.

1071   Olds, Victoria. "Activities to improve the quality of instruc-
        tion at a school of social work." Social Work Education
        Reporter, v. 14, no. 3, Sept. 1966. 37, 48-49.

1072   Ottaway, Andrew Kenneth Cosway. Learning through group
        experience. London: Routledge & K. Paul, 1966. 168p.

1073   Paterson, Jacqueline. "The role of tutor on a social work
        practice." International Social Work, v. 15, no. 3, 1972.
        42-47.

1074   Perlman, Helen Harris. "... and gladly teach." Journal
        of Education for Social Work, v. 3, no. 1, spring 1967.
        41-50.

1075   Pohek, Marguerite V. "Report on developments in teaching
        and teaching methodology." Social Work Education Re-
        porter, v. 16, no. 2, June 1968. 20-21.

1076   _____, editor. The teacher's compendium. New York:
        Council on Social Work Education, 1963. 72p.

1077   _____, editor. Teaching and learning in social work ed-
        ucation. New York: Council on Social Work Education,
        1970. 87p.

1078   _____. "Toward a methodology of teaching." Education
        for social work; proceedings of the 1964 Annual Program
        Meeting, Council on Social Work Education. New York:
        The Council, 1964. 149-161.

1079   Price, Hazel G. "Achieving a balance between self-directed
        and required learning." Journal of Education for Social
        Work, v. 12, no. 1, winter 1976. 105-112.

1080   Pritchard, David C. "The student as learner." Social Work
        Education Reporter, v. 15, no. 2, June 1967. 18, 36-37.

1081 Reynolds, Bertha Capen. Learning and teaching in the practice of social work. New York: Russell & Russell, 1965. 390p.

1082 Rose, Sheldon D. "Incident method as a technique in social work training." Social Work Forum, v. 4, no. 1, Jan. 1966. 16-19.

1083 Rubin, Gerald K. "General systems theory: an organismic conception for teaching modalities of social work intervention." Smith College Studies in Social Work, v. 43, no. 3, June 1973. 206-219.

1084 Schaub, Elisabeth. "Learning principles applicable to classroom teaching in social work." Doctoral students look at social work education. Edited by Leila Calhoun Deasy. New York: Council on Social Work Education, 1971. 3-25.

1085 Schmidt, Teresa M. "The development of self-awareness in first-year social work students." Smith College Studies in Social Work, v. 46, no. 3, June 1976. 218-235.

1086 Seidl, Frederick W. "When students make the decisions: group decision and learning in a course in social work." Applied Social Studies, v. 3, no. 2, May 1971. 91-105.

1087 Shapiro, Charles R. "The development of a model for the integration of classroom and practicum learning experiences in social work education." Doctoral dissertation, University of Denver, 1976. 134p.

1088 Sharlin, Shlomo and Richard Goldman. "A laboratory for the development of specific skills by social workers." Educational Technology, v. 15, no. 1, Jan. 1975. 39-42.

1089 Somers, Mary Louise. "Contributions of learning and teaching theories to the explication of the role of the teacher in social work education." Journal of Education for Social Work, v. 5, no. 2, fall 1969. 61-73.

1090 _____. "Dimensions and dynamics of engaging the learner." Journal of Education for Social Work, v. 7, no. 3, fall 1971. 49-57.

1091 _____. "The small group in learning and teaching." Learning and teaching in public welfare; v. 1 of Report of the Cooperative Project on Public Welfare Staff Training. Washington, D. C.: U. S. Children's Bureau, 1963. 158-173.

1092 _____. "Toward the improvement of social work teaching

methods and materials." Social Work Education Reporter, v. 14, no. 4, Dec. 1966. 28-32, 54.

1093 Stevenson, Olive. "Integration of theory and practice in professional training." Case Conference, v. 8, no. 2, June 1961. 45-49.

1094 _____. "Problems in the use of theory in social work education." British Journal of Psychiatric Social Work, v. 9, no. 1, spring 1967. 27-29.

1095 Tarail, Theodore T. "The student as consumer in social work education." Australian Social Work, v. 25, no. 1, March 1972. 35-39.

1096 Thomas, M. Duane and Thomas L. Morrison. "New perspectives in social work education." International Social Work, v. 17, no. 2, 1974. 21-27.

1097 Towle, Charlotte. "The emotional element in learning in professional education for social work." Professional education; five papers delivered at the 1948 Annual Meeting, American Association of Schools of Social Work. New York: The Association, 1948. 19-30.

1098 _____. "Learning process and educational process." The learner in education for the professions, as seen in education for social work. Chicago: University of Chicago Press, 1954. 3-230.

1099 _____. "Professional education--A humanizing process." Some reflections on social work education. London: Family Welfare Association, 1956. 3-14.

1100 Walberg, Herbert J. "Can educational research contribute to the practice of teaching?" Journal of Education for Social Work, v. 4, no. 2, fall 1968. 77-85.

1101 Walden, Theodore, Greta Singer and Winifred Thomet. "Students as clients: the other side of the desk." Clinical Social Work Journal, v. 2, no. 4, winter 1974. 279-290.

1102 Williams, Mark J. K. "The practice seminar in social work education." The dynamics of field instruction: learning through doing. Compiled by the Council on Social Work Education. New York: The Council, 1975. 94-101.

1103 Wolins, Martin. "Toward the freedom of individualized education." Social Work Education Reporter, v. 17, no. 4, Dec. 1969. 44-45, 61.

1104 Younghusband, Eileen L. "The teacher in education for social work." Social Service Review, v. 41, no. 4, Dec. 1967. 359-370.

C. PROGRAMMED INSTRUCTION, COMPUTER ASSISTED INSTRUCTION, AND SIMULATION GAMES

1105 Boags, William. "A comparison of affective reaction and cognitive learning of participants in a simulation-game experience." Doctoral dissertation, Syracuse University, 1970. 94p.

1106 Ehlers, Walter H. "Computer-assisted instruction in social work." Social Work Education Reporter, v. 17, no. 4, Dec. 1969. 20-23, 61.

1107 _____ and John C. Prothero. "Performances and attitudes of social work students using programmed instruction texts." Programmed Learning and Educational Technology, v. 8, no. 4, Oct. 1971. 225-234.

1108 Gentry, Martha. "Social simulation games in social work education and practice." Social Work Education Reporter, v. 20, no. 2, April-May 1972. 29-30, 39-42.

1109 Meinert, Ronald G. "Simulation technology: a potential tool for social work education." Journal of Education for Social Work, v. 8, no. 3, fall 1972. 50-59.

1110 Rosen, Aaron. "Programmed instruction in social work education: an evaluative study." Brown Studies, 1967. 17-32.

1111 Thomas, Edwin J. and Roger M. Lind. "Programmed instruction as potentially useful in social work education: an annotated bibliography." Social Work Education Reporter, v. 15, no. 1, March 1967. 22-27, 33.

1112 Wallace, Henry M. "Programmed instruction and social work: an analysis of problems and possibilities." Social Work Education Reporter, v. 17, no. 3, Sept. 1969. 41-44, 59-60.

D. SENSITIVITY TRAINING AND T GROUPS

1113 Balgopal, Pallassana R. "Sensitivity training: a conceptual model for social work education." Journal of Education for Social Work, v. 10, no. 2, spring 1974. 5-11.

1114 _____. "Sensitivity training: a study in theory and its applicability to social work education." Doctoral dissertation, Tulane University, 1971. 154p.

1115   Brook, Bryan Dunn. "Sensitivity training in social work ed-
       ucation." Doctoral dissertation, University of Denver,
       1974. 167p.

1116   Davies, Evan. "The use of T groups in training social wor-
       kers." British Journal of Social Work, v. 3, no. 1, spring
       1973. 65-77.

1117   Gifford, C. G. "Sensitivity training and social work." So-
       cial Work, v. 13, no. 2, April 1968. 78-86.

1118   O'Connor, Gerald and John Alderson. "Human relations
       groups for human services practitioners." Small Group
       Behavior, v. 5, no. 4, Nov. 1974. 495-505.

1119   Papell, Catherine P. "Sensitivity training: relevance for
       social work education." Journal of Education for Social
       Work, v. 8, no. 1, winter 1972. 42-55.

E.   USE OF AUDIO-VISUAL AIDS

1120   Atkins, Jacqueline Marx, compiler. Audio-visual resources
       for population education and family planning: an interna-
       tional guide for social work educators. New York: Inter-
       national Association of Schools of Social Work, 1975.
       148p.

1121   Benschoter, Reba Ann, Charles Garetz and Pringle Smith.
       "The use of closed circuit TV and videotape in the train-
       ing of social group workers." Social Work Education Re-
       porter, v. 15, no. 1, March 1967. 18-19, 30.

1122   Bohm, Peter E. "Focussed videotape feedback in supervised
       interpersonal skills training for social work practice."
       Canadian Journal of Social Work Education, v. 2, no. 2,
       1976. 22-30.

1123   Burian, William A. "The laboratory as an element in social
       work curriculum design." Journal of Education for Social
       Work, v. 12, no. 1, winter 1976. 36-43.

1124   Elwell, Mary Ellen, compiler. Films for use in teaching
       social welfare and where to find them. Atlanta: Southern
       Regional Education Board, 1971. 49p.

1125   Howard, John and Pat Gooderham. "Closed circuit TV in
       social work training." Social Work Today, v. 6, no. 7,
       26 June 1975. 194-197.

1126   Itzin, Frank H. "Use of tape recording in field work." So-
       cial Casework, v. 41, no. 4, June 1960. 314-315.

1127 Katz, David, Nazneen S. Mayadas and Donald E. O'Brien. "Starting out in television: a student-centered approach to media development in social work." Journal of Education for Social Work, v. 11, no. 1, winter 1975. 83-88.

1128 Kelley, Minnie E. "Additional uses of tape recordings in social work education." Social Casework, v. 43, no. 1, Jan. 1962. 26-29.

1129 Litrio, John. "Closed circuit television: implications for social work education." Social work continuing education yearbook, 1973. Edited by Selima Faruqee and Armand Lauffer. Ann Arbor: Michigan, School of Social Work, University of Michigan, 1973. 64-79.

1130 National Center for School and College Television. Television in higher education: social work education. Bloomington, Ind.: The Center, 1969. 17p.

1131 Norwood, Frank. "Instructional television survey: 1966." Social Work Education Reporter, v. 14, no. 4, Dec. 1966. 22, 62.

1132 O'Brien, Donald E. and Nazneen S. Mayadas. "Technology and social casework: a review of the literature." Teaching for competence in the delivery of direct services. Compiled by the Council on Social Work Education. New York: The Council, 1976. 83-94.

1133 Oswald, Ida M., compiler. An annotated bibliography on audiovisual instruction in professional education. New York: Council on Social Work Education, 1966. 61p.

1134 _____ and Suzanne Wilson. This bag is not a toy; a handbook for the use of videorecording in education for the professions. New York: Council on Social Work Education, 1971. 133p.

1135 _____. "Through the looking glass: adventure in television." Journal of Education for Social Work, v. 1, no. 1, spring 1965. 47-55.

1136 _____. "Use of media in training." Social workers as trainers in health programs. Edited by Laura Bertino and Robert C. Jackson. Berkeley: Program in Public Health Social Work, University of California, 1972. 42-52.

1137 Perlmutter, Morton S. and Gary Gumpert. "An analysis of an instructional television approach to the teaching of social work methods." Social Work Education Reporter, v. 14, no. 1, March 1966. 19-21, 43, 47.

1138 _____ and _____ . "Field instruction and group process: an experiment in the use of television." Social Work Education Reporter, v. 15, no. 3, Sept. 1967. 26-29.

1139 _____ . "Theory and educational objectives in the use of new teaching media." Teaching and learning in social work education. Compiled by Marguerite Pohek. New York: Council on Social Work Education, 1970. 35-42.

1140 Ruhl, Erving C. "The use of video tape systems in teaching social work practice." Doctoral dissertation, University of Southern California, 1975. 236p.

1141 Shotland, Leonard. "A social work film festival: a teaching technique." Social Work Education Reporter, v. 20, no. 3, Sept.-Oct. 1972. 83-84.

1142 Silverman, Eva Olive, compiler. Films for teaching in social work and social studies. Birmingham, Eng.: Department of Social Studies, Selly Oak Colleges, 1971. 72p.

1143 Stockbridge, M. E. and B. E. Wooller. "Skill teaching in community work: a videocorder technique." Australian Social Work, v. 27, no. 3, Sept. 1974. 31-35.

1144 Vigilante, Joseph L., Paul Pitcoff and Beulah Rothman. "The making of a training film, 'The Way It Is.'" Social Work Education Reporter, v. 19, no. 1, Dec.-Jan. 1971. 50-53.

1145 Vinson, A. "Television and group-centered learning." Social Work Education Reporter, v. 16, no. 2, June 1968. 32-33.

1146 Youth Service Information Center. Audio visual resources in social education. Leicester, Eng.: The Center, 1972. 151p.

F. LIBRARY SERVICE AND INFORMATION SCIENCE

1147 Beattie, Walter M., Jr. "The changing role of social work library services." Social Work Education Reporter, v. 18, no. 2, June 1970. 27-29.

1148 Bloom, Martin. "Information science in the education of social work students." Journal of Education for Social Work, v. 11, no. 1, winter 1975. 30-35.

1149 _____ . "Training the helping professional to use computer-delivered information: a preliminary report." The information conscious society; proceedings of the American Society for Information Science, v. 7. Edited by Jeanne B. North. Washington, D. C.: American Society for Information Science, 1970. 185-187.

1150 Brittain, Michael. "Information services for social welfare." Social Service Quarterly, v. 49, no. 1, summer 1975. 5-7.

1151 Butler, Evelyn. "Institute for Professional Social Welfare Librarians, Nov. 20-22, 1968, University of Pennsylvania." Special Libraries, v. 60, no. 1, Jan. 1969. 54-55.

1152 Council on Social Work Education. Building a social work library; a guide to the selection of books, periodicals, and reference tools. New York: The Council, 1962. 105p.

1153 _____. Role of the library in professional education; report of workshop discussion and recommendations and papers presented at the 1954 Annual Program Meeting. New York: The Council, 1954. Various pagings.

1154 _____. The role of the library in social work education; proceedings of the 1956 Annual Program Meeting, Concurrent Session. New York: The Council, 1956. 14p.

1155 Crossley, Charles A. "Sources of information in applied social studies." Applied Social Studies, v. 1, no. 3, Oct. 1969. 137-149.

1156 _____. "Sources of information in applied social studies." Social work research and the analysis of social data. By Alistair E. Philip, J. Wallace McCulloch and Norman J. Smith. New York: Pergamon Press, 1975. 47-73.

1157 Elder, Charles and Terence Walton. "The function of the library in a school of social work." Journal of Education for Social Work, v. 10, no. 1, winter 1974. 19-21.

1158 Hoffer, Joe R. A document retrieval system for social welfare. Columbus, Ohio: National Conference on Social Welfare, 1963. 24p.

1159 _____. "Information and document retrieval in social welfare." Social welfare forum, 1964; proceedings of the National Conference on Social Welfare. New York: Columbia University Press, 1964. 217-226.

1160 _____. "Information exchange in social welfare: a myth or a reality?" Special Libraries, v. 60, no. 4, April 1969. 193-202.

1161 _____. "Information retrieval in social welfare: experiences with an edge-notched information retrieval system." American Documentation, v. 13, no. 2, April 1962. 169-175.

1162 _____. "Information science in social work education: the

NCSW approach." Journal of Education for Social Work, v. 11, no. 2, spring 1975. 52-59.

1163 _____. Manual for a handsort punch-card system for indexing social welfare publications. Columbus, Ohio: National Conference on Social Welfare, 1966. 81p.

1164 _____. "Precise terminology means better communication." Community organization, 1960; papers presented at the Annual Forum of the National Conference on Social Welfare. New York: Columbia University Press, 1960. 22-41.

1165 _____ and Eugene Price, editors. Readings on social welfare documentation; selected papers from the National Conference on Social Welfare. Columbus, Ohio: National Conference on Social Welfare, 1967. 13p.

1166 _____. Toward an international social welfare information and document retrieval system. Columbus, Ohio: National Conference on Social Welfare, 1966. 22p.

1167 Jones, Kathleen. "Teaching of social administration in universities: how libraries could help." Library Association Record, v. 73, no. 11, Nov. 1971. 205-206.

1168 Lopez, Manuel D., compiler. Guide to the literature of social welfare. Buffalo, N. Y.: Reference Department, Lockwood Memorial Library, State University of New York at Buffalo, 1969. 24p.

1169 Lovejoy, Eunice. "Social work students and libraries." Social Work Education, v. 11, no. 2, April 1963. 1, 16-18.

1170 Mann, M. G. and T. D. Wilson, editors. Forum on social welfare/information research; report of proceedings together with background papers prepared for the Forum, Sheffield, 1974. Sheffield, Eng.: Postgraduate School of Librarianship and Information Science, Sheffield, University, 1974. 94p.

1171 Otto, Margaret M. "Mary E. Richmond archive." Social Casework, v. 42, no. 8, Oct. 1961. 410-412.

1172 _____. "Role of the library in professional education." Social Work Journal, v. 35, no. 4, Oct. 1954. 157-160, 175.

1173 Shepperd, Judy. Social work reference aids in the University of Toronto Library. Toronto: Reference Department, University of Toronto Library, 1973. 100p.

1174 Stewart, Martha L. "Black-white curriculum content: School of Applied Social Sciences Library (Case Western Reserve University)." Special Libraries, v. 65, no. 4, April 1974. 194-195.

1175 _____. "Social work education: the librarian's role." Special Libraries, v. 60, no. 6, July-Aug. 1969. 347-348.

1176 Webley, Maureen. "The Aslib Social Sciences Working Group on Social Welfare Information: a review of its development and current activities." Aslib Proceedings, v. 28, nos. 6-7, June-July 1976. 243-247.

V. FOUNDATION KNOWLEDGE IN GRADUATE EDUCATION

A. HUMAN BEHAVIOR AND THE SOCIAL ENVIRONMENT [See also Section XVI. C. 1.]

1177 Abramowitz, Naomi R. "Human sexuality in the social work curriculum." Family Coordinator, v. 20, no. 4, Oct. 1971. 349-354.

1178 Archinard, Enolia B. "An approach to coordinated teaching of Growth and Behavior in class and field." Journal of Education for Social Work, v. 2, no. 2, fall 1966. 12-21.

1179 Bennett, Ivy B. "A plea for personality theory." Social Work, v. 20, no. 1, Jan. 1975. 58-59.

1180 Butler, Ruth M. An orientation to knowledge of human growth and behavior in social work education. The social work curriculum study, v. 6. New York: Council on Social Work Education, 1959. 80p.

1181 _____. Social functioning framework; an approach to the Human Behavior and Social Environment sequence. New York: Council on Social Work Education, 1970. 52p.

1182 Chilman, Catherine S. "Some knowledge bases about human sexuality for social work education." Journal of Education for Social Work, v. 11, no. 2, spring 1975. 11-17.

1183 Council for Training in Social Work. Human growth and behavior as a subject for study by social workers; report of the Working Party on Human Growth and Behavior. London: The Council, 1967.

1184 Faith, Goldie Basch. "Knowledge and methods in social work education: Human Growth and Behavior in social work education." Child Welfare, v. 39, no. 7, Sept. 1960. 14-17.

1185 Fraiberg, Selma. "Teaching psychoanalytic theory to social work students." Social Casework, v. 36, no. 6, June 1955. 243-252.

1186 Gochros, Harvey L. "A concentration in social work practice with sex-related problems." Journal of Education for

Social Work, v. 10, no. 2, spring 1974. 40-46.

1187 _____. "Educating graduate social work students to deal
with sexual problems." Human sexuality and social work.
Edited by Harvey L. Gochros and LeRoy R. Young. New
York: Association Press, 1972. 244-251.

1188 _____. "Introducing human sexuality into the graduate
social work curriculum." Social Work Education Reporter, v. 18, no. 3, Sept. -Oct. 1970. 47-50.

1189 _____. "Teaching more or less straight social work students to be helpful to more or less gay people." Homo-
sexual Counseling Journal, v. 2, no. 2, April 1975. 58-67.

1190 Haworth, Glenn Oscar. "Social work students' theoretical
orientations toward human behavior." Doctoral dissertation, University of California, 1967. 177p.

1191 Heyman, Margaret M. "An examination of the Human Be-
havior and Social Environment sequence at the Hunter
College School of Social Work." Social Work Education
Reporter, v. 17, no. 4, Dec. 1969. 48-51, 59-60.

1192 _____. "A new design for an old sequence: the revised
Human Growth and Behavior sequence at the Hunter College School of Social Work, 1966-67." Social Work Education Reporter, v. 15, no. 4, Dec. 1967. 47, 54, 56-
58.

1193 Hyde, Alice and Jean Murphy. "Experiment in integrative
learning." Social Service Review, v. 29, no. 4, Dec. 1955.
358-371.

1194 Jehu, Derek. "A scientific psychological approach in the
teaching of Human Growth and Behaviour." Case Conference, v. 14, no. 2, June 1967. 48-52.

1195 Johnson, Joy and Ord Matek. "Critical issues in teaching
human sexuality to graduate social work students." Journal of Education for Social Work, v. 10, no. 3, fall 1974.
50-55.

1196 Kadushin, Alfred. "Content on aging in the Growth and Behavior sequence." Social work education for better services to the aging; proceedings of the Seminar on the
Aging, Aspen, Colorado, 1958. New York: Council on
Social Work Education, 1959. 67-72.

1197 Kamerman, Sheila B. , et al. "Knowledge for practice: social science in social work." Shaping the new social work.
Edited by Alfred J. Kahn. New York: Columbia University Press, 1973. 97-146.

1198 Leonard, Peter. "Some questions on the teaching of Human
       Growth and Behaviour to social work students." Social
       Work (London), v. 24, no. 4, Oct. 1967. 26-28.

1199 Lichtenberg, Philip. "Introduction of radical theory and prac-
       tice in social work education: personality theory." Jour-
       nal of Education for Social Work, v. 12, no. 2, spring 1976.
       10-16.

1200 Lister, Larry and Harvey L. Gochros. "Preparing students
       for effective social work practice related to death." Jour-
       nal of Education for Social Work, v. 12, no. 1, winter
       1976. 85-90.

1201 Littner, Ner. "Is social work education keeping pace with
       our deepening knowledge of children?". Education for
       social work; proceedings of the 1962 Annual Program
       Meeting, Council on Social Work Education. New York:
       The Council, 1962. 135-151. Discussion by Charlotte
       Towle. 152-161.

1202 Loewenstein, Sophie F. "Integrating content on feminism and
       racism into the social work curriculum." Journal of Ed-
       ucation for Social Work, v. 12, no. 1, winter 1976. 91-96.

1203 Maas, Henry S. "Human Behaviour/Social Environment cour-
       ses: penumbra from the past, projections into the future."
       Canadian Journal of Social Work Education, v. 1, no. 3,
       summer 1975. 24-27.

1204 McBroom, Elizabeth. "Individual, group, and community in
       the Behavior sequence." Journal of Education for Social
       Work, v. 1, no. 2, fall 1965. 27-34.

1205 Meisel, Susan Schilling and Alice Perkins Friedman. "The
       need for women's studies in social work education."
       Journal of Education for Social Work, v. 10, no. 3, fall
       1974. 67-74.

1206 Minnesota. University. School of Social Work. Health and
       disability concepts in social work education; proceedings
       of a workshop conference. Minneapolis: The School,
       1964. 46p.

1207 Neser, William B. and Grace B. Sudderth. "Genetics and
       casework." Social Casework, v. 46, no. 1, Jan. 1965.
       22-25.

1208 Page, Mary and Mildred Pratt. "Community laboratory: an
       innovation in higher education." Journal of Education for
       Social Work, v. 9, no. 3, fall 1973. 45-50.

1209 Perlman, Helen Harris. "An orientation to knowledge of hu-

man growth and behavior in social work education, by
Ruth M. Butler: review." Social Service Review, v. 33,
no. 4, Dec. 1959. 409-411.

1210 Prince, G. Stewart. "The teaching of mental health in schools
of social work." International Social Service Review, no.
8, March 1961. 31-35.

1211 Rayner, Eric H. "Elementary education in human develop-
ment--some considerations in social work training." Case
Conference, v. 14, no. 1, May 1967. 3-10.

1212 Rockmore, Myron J. and John J. Conklin. "Contemporary
social work education and psychoanalysis." Journal of
Education for Social Work, v. 10, no. 2, spring 1974. 68-
75.

1213 Ruiz, Juliette S. "A structure for organizing ethnic minority
content in the Human Behavior sequence." The Chicano
Faculty Development Program: a report. Edited by D.
J. Curren. New York: Council on Social Work Education, 1973. 91-98.

1214 Schlesinger, Benjamin. "Human Behavior and Social Environment in the two-year graduate social work curriculum--
An overview." Social Work Education Reporter, v. 16, no.
3, Sept. 1968. 38-41, 49.

1215 _____. "Sexuality and social work: a course in Human
Behaviour and Social Environment: a note and bibliography."
Social Work Education Reporter, v. 20, no. 3, Sept. -Oct.
1972. 80-82.

1216 Schwartz, Mary C. "Sexism in the social work curriculum."
Journal of Education for Social Work, v. 9, no. 3, fall
1973. 65-70.

1217 Stein, Herman D. "Comments on social science in the social
work curriculum." International Social Work, v. 6, no. 2,
April 1963. 24-25.

1218 Tanner, Libby A. "Teaching a course in human sexuality in
a graduate school of social work: strategy and content."
Family Coordinator, v. 23, no. 3, July 1974. 283-289.

1219 Towle, Charlotte. "Social work approach to courses in growth
and behavior." Social Service Review, v. 34, no. 4, Dec.
1960. 402-414.

1220 Tropp, Emanuel. "Approaching the concept of change in education for social work." Journal of Education for Social
Work, v. 9, no. 3, fall 1973. 99-106.

1221   Upham, Frances. "Use of analysis of content in curriculum
       development." Journal of Education for Social Work, v. 3,
       no. 2, fall 1967. 80-89.

1222   Valentich, Mary and James Gripton. "Teaching human sex-
       uality to social work students." Family Coordinator, v.
       24, no. 3, July 1975. 273-280.

B.   SOCIAL WELFARE POLICY AND SERVICES

1223   Bell, Winifred. "Obstacles to shifting from the descriptive
       to the analytic approach in teaching social services."
       Journal of Education for Social Work, v. 5, no. 1, spring
       1969. 5-13.

1224   Bowers, Swithun. "Social work policies, services and sup-
       porting values." Child Welfare, v. 39, no. 3, March 1960.
       1-4.

1225   Breul, Frank R. "Social welfare policy and services in so-
       cial work education, by Irving Weissman: review." So-
       cial Service Review, v. 33, no. 4, Dec. 1959. 433-437.

1226   Conference on Social Policy and Social Work Education. Pa-
       pers and proceedings of the conference, Arden House,
       1957. New York: School of Social Work, Columbia
       University, 1957. 208p.

1227   Council on Social Work Education. Social policy content in
       graduate education for social work; workshop report of
       the 1961 Annual Program Meeting. New York: The Coun-
       cil, 1961. 16p.

1228   _____. Testing an approach to curriculum development
       in the Social Welfare Policy and Social Services sequence;
       a report of two workshops on the Social Services sequence
       held in Oklahoma City, 1960 and Montreal, 1961. New
       York: The Council, 1962. 42p.

1229   Galper, Jeffry. "Introduction of radical theory and practice
       in social work education: social policy." Journal of Ed-
       ucation for Social Work, v. 12, no. 2, spring 1976. 3-9.

1230   Gil, David G. "Research, a basic ingredient in the study of
       social policy and social services." Journal of Education
       for Social Work, v. 4, no. 1, spring 1968. 14-20.

1231   Hannon, Eleanor Mary. "The Social Welfare Policy and Ser-
       vices curriculum in the Master's degree program in so-
       cial work, 1968-1969: a descriptive analysis focusing on
       content and its organization as developed in the courses

in this sequence offered in fifteen schools of social work."
Doctoral dissertation, Catholic University of America,
1970. 199p.

1232 Jaffe, Benson and Rino J. Patti. "An experiment in the
teaching of social welfare policy." Journal of Education
for Social Work, v. 9, no. 1, winter 1973. 23-33.

1233 Klingler, Dorothy. "Social Welfare Policy and Services:
Social policy the curriculum's stepchild no longer?" Social Work Education, v. 12, no. 3, June-July 1964. 1-3,
18.

1234 Levin, Herman. "Social welfare policy: base for the curriculum." Social Work Education Reporter, v. 17, no. 3,
Sept. 1969. 38-40, 58-59.

1235 McVeigh, Frank J. "An experimental class in 'Social Problems and Social Welfare.'" Social Work Education Reporter, v. 20, no. 3, Sept. -Oct. 1972. 65-69.

1236 Murase, Kenji. "Ethnic minority content in the social work
curriculum: social welfare policy and social research."
Perspectives on ethnic minority content in social work
education. Edited by Charles W. McCann. Boulder, Colo.:
Western Interstate Commission for Higher Education,
1972. 17-38.

1237 Parsons, Jack R. "The Social Welfare Policy and Services
sequence: teaching the concepts for use." Social Work
Education, v. 12, no. 3, June-July 1964. 4-6, 16-18.

1238 Richman, Harold A. "Social welfare policy as a specialization in the graduate social work curriculum." Journal of
Education for Social Work, v. 6, no. 1, spring 1970. 53-
60.

1239 Rose, Albert. "Teaching Social Welfare Policy and Services
in the social work curriculum of Canadian schools." Canadian Journal of Social Work Education, v. 1, no. 3, summer 1975. 4-12.

1240 Weissman, Irving. Social welfare policy and services in social work education. The social work curriculum study,
v. 12. New York: Council on Social Work Education,
1959. 94p.

1241 Winston, Ellen. "Preparation of social workers for a role
in the formulation of public social policy: whose responsibility?" Education for social work; proceedings of the
1960 Annual Program Meeting, Council on Social Work
Education. New York: The Council, 1960. 166-174.

1242 Yelaja, Shankar A. "Social welfare policy and services curriculum in Indian schools of social work." Doctoral dissertation, University of Pennsylvania, 1967. 329p.

VI. GRADUATE EDUCATION FOR SOCIAL WORK METHODS

A. GENERAL

1243 Briar, Scott. "Effective social work intervention in direct practice: implications for education." Facing the challenge; plenary session papers from the 1973 Annual Program Meeting, Council on Social Work Education. New York: The Council, 1973. 17-30.

1244 Council on Social Work Education. Teaching for competence in the delivery of direct services. New York: The Council, 1976. 117p.

1245 Crane, John A. "Utilizing the fundamentals of science in educating for social work practice." Journal of Education for Social Work, v. 2, no. 2, fall 1966. 22-29.

1246 Ginet, Marie L. "Comments on specialization in social work education." International Social Work, v. 6, no. 2, April 1963. 26-27.

1247 Hamilton-Smith, Elery. "A paradigm for consideration of the nature of social work processes." Australian Journal of Social Work, v. 22, no. 1, March 1969. 12-20.

1248 Mullen, Edward J. and James R. Dumpson, editors. Evaluation of social intervention; proceedings of a symposium held January 1971 at the Lincoln Center Campus of Fordham University. San Francisco: Jossey-Bass, 1972. 267p.

1249 Ripple, Lilian, editor. Innovations in teaching social work practice; papers presented at the Workshop on Current Directions in the Teaching of Methods of Social Work Practice, Cleveland, March 1969. New York: Council on Social Work Education, 1970. 89p.

B. SOCIAL CASEWORK [See also Section VII. N.]

1250 Ackerman, Nathan W. "The training of case workers in psychotherapy." American Journal of Orthopsychiatry, v. 19, no. 1, Jan. 1949. 14-24.

1251 Allan, Eunice and Esther Clemence. "Toward a philosophy of teaching casework." Smith College Studies in Social Work, v. 30, no. 2, Feb. 1960. 137-143.

1252 Alpine, George C., et al. "Interviewing techniques for social work student training." Mental Hygiene, v. 49, no. 1, Jan. 1965. 126-131.

1253 Appelberg, Esther. "Teaching casework from students' own material." Child Welfare, v. 50, no. 10, Dec. 1971. 593-598.

1254 Bandler, Bernard. "Ego-centered teaching." Smith College Studies in Social Work, v. 30, no. 2, Feb. 1960. 125-136.

1255 Bardill, Donald R. "The ego ideal and clinical activity." Social Work, v. 16, no. 2, April 1971. 75-80.

1256 _____. "The ego-ideal and clinical activity: an investigation of the effect of a formal explication of a client's ego-ideal elements on student workers' orientation to the client." Doctoral dissertation, Smith College, 1968. 147p.

1257 Bellsmith, Virginia S. "New Frontiers in the teaching of social casework." Ego-oriented casework: problems and perspectives. Edited by Howard J. Parad and Roger R. Miller. New York: Family Service Association of America, 1963. 259-272.

1258 Berkowitz, Sidney J. "Comment on the implications of the Curriculum Study for social casework." Journal of Jewish Communal Service, v. 37, no. 2, winter 1960. 143-147.

1259 Boehm, Werner W. The social casework method in social work education. The social work curriculum study, v. 10. New York: Council on Social Work Education, 1959. 164p.

1260 Briar, Scott. "The casework predicament." Social Work, v. 13, no. 1, Jan. 1968. 5-11.

1261 Cannon, Mary Antoinette and Philip Klein, editors. Social casework; an outline for teaching, with annotated case records and sample course syllabi. New York: Columbia University Press, 1933. 627p.

1262 Clemence, Esther H. "The dynamic use of ego psychology in casework education." Smith College Studies in Social Work, v. 35, no. 3, June 1965. 157-172.

1263 De Romero, Luz Tocornal. "Curriculum planning in relation to social service to individuals." International Social Work, v. 4, no. 4, Oct. 1961. 12-16.

1264 Donadello, Gloria. "An exploration of progress toward professional autonomy during the first year of social casework
education." Doctoral dissertation, Smith College, 1973.
153p.

1265 Erard, Glen. "Student skepticism as a variable in professional
education: implications for clinical and didactic learning."
Doctoral dissertation, Smith College, 1972. 159p.

1266 Fraiberg, Selma. "Psychoanalysis and the education of caseworkers." Smith College Studies in Social Work, v. 31,
no. 3, June 1961. 196-221.

1267 Garrett, Annette. "Casework teaching by the case method."
Family, v. 20, no. 7, Nov. 1939. 211-216.

1268 _____. "Historical survey of the evolution of casework."
Journal of Social Casework, v. 30, no. 6, June 1949. 225-
228.

1269 Goldmeier, John. "Association of personality characteristics
of the caseworker and selected aspects of the treatment
process." Doctoral dissertation, University of Chicago,
1966. 170p.

1270 _____. "Study of selected personality attributes and treatment preferences of caseworkers and casework students."
Social Service Review, v. 42, no. 2, June 1968. 232-240.

1271 Halmos, Paul. The faith of the counsellors: a study in the
theory and practice of social case work and psychotherapy.
New York: Schocken Books, 1966. 220p.

1272 Hellenbrand, Shirley C. "Main currents in social casework,
1918-1936: the development of social casework in the
United States as reflected in the literature and in classroom teaching material." Doctoral dissertation, Columbia
University, 1965. 334p.

1273 Heywood, Jean S. An introduction to teaching casework skill.
New York: Humanities Press, 1964. 180p.

1274 Hofstein, Saul. "Preparation of workers for casework practice in the Jewish agency." Journal of Jewish Communal
Service, v. 45, no. 2, winter 1968. 156-164.

1275 Hollis, Florence. "Contemporary issues for caseworkers."
Smith College Studies in Social Work, v. 30, no. 2, Feb.
1960. 157-174.

1276 _____. "Generic and specific in social casework reexam-
ined." Social Casework, v. 37, no. 5, May 1956. 211-219.

1277 _____. "The implications of the Curriculum Study for social casework." Journal of Jewish Communal Service, v. 37, no. 2, winter 1960. 135-142. Comments by Sidney J. Berkowitz and Bess Dana. 143-150.

1278 Institute on Education for Social Work with "Unmotivated" Clients. Education for social work with "unmotivated" clients; proceedings of an institute, Brandeis University, January 1965. Waltham, Mass.: Florence Heller Graduate School for Advanced Studies in Social Welfare, Brandeis University, 1965. 250p.

1279 James, Maria. "Basic concepts common to casework and groupwork." International Social Work, v. 1, no. 3, July 1958. 7-13.

1280 Kamphuis, Marie. "Report of discussion groups on curriculum planning in relation to social services for individuals." International Social Work, v. 4, no. 4, Oct. 1961. 17-19.

1281 Karpf, Maurice J. The scientific basis of social work: a study in family case work. New York: Columbia University Press, 1931. 424p.

1282 Lee, Porter R. "Providing teaching material." Proceedings of the National Conference of Social Work, 1920. Chicago: University of Chicago Press, 1920. 465-473.

1283 Lide, Pauline D. "An experiment in teaching social casework." Social Service Review, v. 33, no. 3, Sept. 1959. 253-259.

1284 Marzialli, Elsa and Heather Munroe Blum. "Clinical research: a model for teaching and learning." Canadian Journal of Social Work Education, v. 2, no. 2, 1976. 45-52.

1285 Mayadas, Nazneen S. and Donald E. O'Brien. "Teaching casework skills in the laboratory: methods and techniques." Teaching for competence in the delivery of direct services. Compiled by the Council on Social Work Education. New York: The Council, 1976. 72-82.

1286 Milford Conference. Social casework, generic and specific; an outline: a report of the Milford Conference. New York: American Association of Social Workers, 1929. 92p.

1287 Mitchell, Gust William. "The application of a behavioral objectives model in social work education." Doctoral dissertation, Catholic University of America, 1975. 149p.

1288 Nelsen, Judith C. "Uses of systems theory in Casework I and II: a proposal." Journal of Education for Social

Work, v. 8, no. 3, fall 1972. 60-64.

1289 Neser, William B. and Grace B. Sudderth. "Genetics and
      casework." Social Casework, v. 46, no. 1, Jan. 1965.
      22-25.

1290 O'Brien, Donald E. and Nazneen S. Mayadas. "Technology
      and social casework: a review of the literature." Teach-
      ing for competence in the delivery of direct services.
      Compiled by the Council on Social Work Education. New
      York: The Council, 1976. 83-94.

1291 Orcutt, Ben Avis Adams. "Anchoring effects in the clinical
      judgments of social work students and experienced case-
      workers." Doctoral dissertation, Columbia University,
      1962. 124p.

1292 Oxley, Genevieve B. "The methods lab--An experiment in
      experiential classroom teaching." Social Work Education
      Reporter, v. 21, no. 1, Dec. -Jan. 1973. 60-63.

1293 Pascoe, Wray. "Education for clinical practice." Clinical
      Social Work Journal, v. 3, no. 1, spring 1975. 46-54.

1294 Perlman, Helen Harris. "The charge to the Casework se-
      quence." Social Work, v. 9, no. 3, July 1964. 47-55.

1295 _____ . "Lecture as a method in teaching case work."
      Social Service Review, v. 25, no. 1, March 1951. 19-32.

1296 _____ . "The social casework method in social work edu-
      cation, by Werner W. Boehm: review." Social Service
      Review, v. 33, no. 4, Dec. 1959. 423-428.

1297 _____ . "Teaching casework by the discussion method."
      Social Service Review, v. 24, no. 3, Sept. 1950. 334-346.

1298 Phillips, David G. "Swing toward clinical practice." Social
      Work, v. 20, no. 1, Jan. 1975. 61-63.

1299 Plotnick, Harold L. "The relation between selected person-
      ality characteristics of social work students and accuracy
      in predicting the behavior of clients." Doctoral disserta-
      tion, Columbia University, 1961. 178p.

1300 Regensburg, Jeanette. "The Curriculum Study: implications
      for the practice of social casework." Social Casework,
      v. 41, no. 1, Jan. 1960. 13-18.

1301 Reid, William J. "The center for social casework research:
      its potential for social work education." Social Work Edu-
      cation Reporter, v. 15, no. 4, Dec. 1967. 20-21, 60-62.

1302 _____ . "An experimental study of methods used in casework treatment." Doctoral dissertation, Columbia University, 1963. 163p.

1303 Reynolds, Bertha Capen. "Preparation of social workers for
meeting the emotional needs of people." Regional planning for social work education. Edited by Lora Lee Pederson. Nashville, Tenn.: School of Social Work, University
of Tennessee, 1949. 64-70.

1304 Santilli, Muriel P. "Treatment intervention is for better or
for worse." Canadian Journal of Social Work Education,
v. 2, no. 2, 1976. 15-21.

1305 Schwartz, Arthur. "The place of operant procedures in the
social work curriculum." Teaching for competence in
the delivery of direct services. Compiled by the Council
of Social Work Education. New York: The Council, 1976.
95-106.

1306 Setleis, Lloyd. "Teaching social casework practice: a social
process." Doctoral dissertation, University of Pennsylvania, 1959. 151p.

1307 Shachter, Burt. "The client as a collaborator in social work
teaching." Teaching for competence in the delivery of
direct services. Compiled by the Council on Social Work
Education. New York: The Council, 1976. 107-117.

1308 Sherman, Sanford N. "Teaching casework through participant
observation." Social Casework, v. 49, no. 10, Dec. 1968.
595-601.

1309 Smalley, Ruth E. "The teaching of social casework--A basic
process in social work education." Doctoral dissertation,
University of Pittsburgh, 1949. 312p.

1310 Sullivan, Ina G. "System oriented social work administration:
some effects of casework versus administration training on
social work administrators." Doctoral dissertation, Rutgers University, 1976. 201p.

1311 Swell, Lila. "Role-playing in the context of learning theory
in casework teaching." Journal of Education for Social
Work, v. 4, no. 1, spring 1968. 70-76.

1312 Towle, Charlotte. "Applications in teaching social casework."
The learner in education for the professions, as seen in
education for social work. Chicago: University of Chicago Press, 1954. 233-411.

1313 _____ . "Contribution of education for social casework to practice." Social Casework, v. 31, no. 8, Oct. 1950. 318-326.

1314 _____. "Selection and arrangement of case material for orderly progression in learning." Social Service Review, v. 27, no. 1, March 1953. 27-54.

1315 _____. "Social case record from a psychiatric clinic: with teaching notes." Social Service Review, v. 14, no. 1, March 1940. 83-118.

1316 _____. "Teaching psychiatry in social casework." Family, v. 20, no. 10, Feb. 1940. 324-331.

1317 Turner, Frank J. "Interlocking theoretical approaches to clinical practice: some pedagogical perspectives." Canadian Journal of Social Work Education, v. 2, no. 2, 1976. 6-14.

1318 Vasey, Wayne. "Implication for social work education." Multi-problem dilemma: a social research demonstration with multi-problem families. Edited by Gordon E. Brown. Metuchen, N. J.: Scarecrow Press, 1968. 32-46.

1319 Walsh, Ethel. "Research and teaching of casework." Journal of Education for Social Work, v. 1, no. 2, fall 1965. 47-52.

1320 Wasserman, Harry. "Some thoughts about teaching social casework today." Smith College Studies in Social Work, v. 43, no. 2, Feb. 1973. 111-143.

1321 Wells, Richard A. and Don Miller. "Developing relationship skills in social work students." Social Work Education Reporter, v. 21, no. 1, Dec. -Jan. 1973. 68-73.

1322 Wessel, Rosa. "Knowledge and methods in social work education: the social casework method in social work education." Child Welfare, v. 39, no. 7, Sept. 1960. 17-23.

C. SOCIAL GROUP WORK [See also Section VII. O.]

1323 American Association of Group Workers. "Professional education for group work practice." Group, v. 9, no. 2, June 1947. 6-9.

1324 Clarke, Helen I. "Evaluation processes in social work teaching." Group, v. 14, no. 2, Jan. 1952. 9-12, 20-21.

1325 Council on Social Work Education. A conceptual framework for the teaching of the social group work method in the classroom. New York: The Council, 1964. 43p.

1326 _____ . Educational developments in social group work; an examination of learning objectives, teaching methods, field instruction and student performance. New York: The Council, 1962. 81p.

1327 _____ . Methods of teaching social group work; workshop report of the 1959 Annual Program Meeting. New York: The Council, 1959. 34p.

1328 _____ . Theory building in social group work; workshop report of the 1960 Annual Program Meeting. New York: The Council, 1960. 22p.

1329 Glass, Robert. "The current dilemma in social group work methodology." Journal of Jewish Communal Service, v. 44, no. 4, summer 1968. 310-315.

1330 Gold, Bertram H. and Arnulf M. Pins. "Effective preparation for Jewish community center work." Journal of Jewish Communal Service, v. 39, no. 2, winter 1962. 121-141.

1331 Greene, Allan, Barry Kasdan and Brian Segal. "Jewish social group work students view the Jewish community center field as a placement and career." Journal of Jewish Communal Service, v. 44, no. 2, winter 1972. 168-176.

1332 Hartford, Margaret E. "The preparation of social workers to practice with people in groups." Journal of Education for Social Work, v. 3, no. 2, fall 1967. 49-60.

1333 Heap, Kenneth. "The teaching of intervention in social group work--some problems and a point of view." Case Conference, v. 13, no. 10, Feb. 1967. 349-356.

1334 James, Maria. "Basic concepts common to casework and groupwork." International Social Work, v. 1, no. 3, July 1958. 7-13.

1335 Kaiser, Clara A. "Group work education in the last decade." Group, v. 15, no. 5, June 1953. 3-10, 27-29.

1336 Lawrence, Harry and Martin Sundel. "Self-modification in groups: a student training method for social groupwork." Journal of Education for Social Work, v. 11, no. 2, spring 1975. 76-83.

1337 Levy, Charles S. Education for social group work practice. New York: School of Social Work, Yeshiva University, 1959. 124p.

1338 _____. "From education to practice in social group work." Doctoral dissertation, Columbia University, 1958. 411p.

1339 _____. From education to practice in social group work. New York: School of Social Work, Yeshiva University, 1960. 147p.

1340 Maier, Henry W. "Application of psychological and sociological theory to teaching social work with the group." Journal of Education for Social Work, v.3, no.1, spring 1967. 29-40.

1341 Maloney, Sara E. "The development of group work education in schools of social work in the United States from 1919 through 1948." Doctoral dissertation, Western Reserve University, 1963. 464p.

1342 Murphy, Marjorie. The social group work method in social work education. The social work curriculum study, v.11. New York: Council on Social Work Education, 1959. 176p.

1343 Paterson, Jacqueline and Margaret Burnett. Group work theory and the social work student; an analysis of its subsequent application. Birmingham: Faculty of Commerce and Social Science, University of Birmingham, 1973. 25p.

1344 Phillips, Helen U. "Knowledge and methods in social work education: education for social group work." Child Welfare, v.39, no.7, Sept. 1960. 23-25.

1345 _____. "The teaching of group work theory in the field and practice in the class." Journal of Social Work Process, v.17, 1969. 69-80.

1346 Ryland, Gladys. Employment responsibilities of social group work graduates; a study of employment characteristics of social group workers in their first year of employment; prepared for the Committee on Group Work. New York: Council on Social Work Education, 1958. 70p.

1347 Somers, Mary Louise. "Four small-group theories: an analysis and frame of reference for use as teaching content in social group work." Doctoral dissertation, Case Western Reserve University, 1957. 266p.

1348 _____. "The social group work method in social work education, by Marjorie Murphy: review." Social Service Review, v.33, no.4, Dec. 1959. 428-433.

1349 Vinik, Abe. "Role of the group service agency." Social

Work, v. 9, no. 3, July 1964. 98-105.

D. COMMUNITY ORGANIZATION AND SOCIAL PLANNING [See also Section VII. D.]

1350 Ahearn, Frederick L. , Jr. , Richard S. Bolan and Edmund M. Burke. "A social action approach for planning education in social work." Journal of Education for Social Work, v. 11, no. 3, fall 1975. 5-11.

1351 Bevis, Leona. "The Curriculum Studies of administration and community organization." Child Welfare, v. 39, no. 4, April 1960. 1-4.

1352 Brooks, Michael P. and Michael A. Stegman. "Urban social policy, race, and the education of planners." Journal of the American Institute of Planners, v. 34, no. 5, Sept. 1968. 275-286.

1353 Burns, Eveline M. "Social policy and the social work curriculum." Objectives of the social work curriculum of the future. By Werner W. Boehm. New York: Council on Social Work Education, 1959. 255-274.

1354 _____. "Social policy: the stepchild of the curriculum." Education for social work; proceedings of the 1961 Annual Program Meeting, Council on Social Work Education. New York: The Council, 1961. 23-34.

1355 Central Council for Education and Training in Social Work. The teaching of community work; a study group discussion paper. London: The Council, 1975. 84p.

1356 Chatterjee, Prabodh Kumar. "The growth and development of community organization education in schools of social work in India, 1936-1969: an historical analysis." Doctoral dissertation, Bryn Mawr College, 1972. 456p.

1357 Conference on Social Policy and Social Work Education. Papers and proceedings of the Conference, held in Harriman, New York, 1957. New York: New York School of Social Work, Columbia University, 1957. 208p.

1358 Council on Social Work Education. Community organization, community planning and community development; some common and distinctive elements. New York: The Council, 1961. 55p.

1359 _____. Curriculum content in community organization; workshop report of the 1959 Annual Program Meeting.

New York: The Council, 1959. 38p.

1360 _____. New developments in community organization practice and their significance for this sequence in the curriculum area; workshop report of the 1961 Annual Program Meeting. New York: The Council, 1961. 37p.

1361 De Jongh, J. F. "Schools of social work and social policy: old and new experience." International Social Work, v. 8, no. 1, Jan. 1965. 10-16.

1362 Downing, Willard E. "Social work creativity within the system." Journal of Education for Social Work, v. 12, no. 3, fall 1976. 18-21.

1363 Dunham, Arthur. "Training for community organization and social welfare administration." Compass, v. 27, no. 2, Jan. 1946. 9-11.

1364 Education for social welfare planning; proceedings of a Conference held under the joint auspices of the Florence Heller School for Advanced Studies in Social Welfare, Brandeis University and the Graduate School of Social Work, Rutgers University, 1970. New Brunswick, N. J.: Graduate School of Social Work, Rutgers University, 1971. 50p.

1365 Falck, Hans. "Social policy as an integral part of social work education and practice." Social Work Education Reporter, v. 14, no. 4, Dec. 1966. 33, 60-61.

1366 Goetschius, George. "Some difficulties in introducing a community work option into social work training." Community work; two. Edited by David Jones and Marjorie Mayo. London: Routledge & Kegan Paul, 1975. 90-103.

1367 Grosser, Charles F. and Gertrude S. Goldberg, editors. Dilemmas of social work leadership: issues in social policy, planning, and organizing. New York: Council on Social Work Education, 1974. 73p.

1368 _____. "The legacy of the federal comprehensive projects for community organization." Social Work Education Reporter, v. 15, no. 4, Dec. 1967. 46, 63-65.

1369 Gruber, Murray. "Policy planning models: heuristics for education." Journal of Education for Social Work, v. 8, no. 3, fall 1972. 30-39.

1370 Gummer, Burton. "Social planning and social administration: implications for curriculum development." Journal of Education for Social Work, v. 11, no. 1, winter 1975. 66-73.

1371　Gurin, Arnold.　"The Community Organization Curriculum Development Project: a preliminary report." Social Service Review, v. 42, no. 4, Dec. 1968.　421-434.

1372　＿＿＿＿＿. Community organization curriculum in graduate social work education: report and recommendations; report of the Community Organization Curriculum Development Project. New York: Council on Social Work Education, 1970.　200p.

1373　＿＿＿＿＿.　"Current issues in community organization practice and education." Social work practice, 1966; selected papers of 1966 Annual Forum of the National Conference on Social Welfare. New York: Columbia University Press, 1966.　20-31.

1374　＿＿＿＿＿.　"The new Community Organization Curriculum Development Project: its aims and methods." Social Work Education Reporter, v. 13, no. 2, June 1965.　14-15.

1375　＿＿＿＿＿ and Robert Perlman.　"An overview of the Community Organization Curriculum Development Project and its recommendations." Journal of Education for Social Work, v. 5, no. 1, spring 1969.　37-48.

1376　Hamovitch, Maurice B.　"Social policy and social work education." Social Work Papers, v. 13, 1975.　39-46.

1377　Hendry, Charles E.　"Implications for social work education in community planning, community development and community organization." Education for social work; proceedings of the 1961 Annual Program Meeting, Council on Social Work Education. New York: The Council, 1961.　49-64.

1378　Hokenstad, Merl C., Jr.　"Preparation for social development: issues in training for policy and planning positions." International Social Work, v. 18, no. 1, 1975.　3-8.

1379　Howard, Donald S., chairman.　"Social progress through social planning: the role of social work education; report of Study Group 8." Social progress through social planning--The role of social work; proceedings of the 12th International Conference of Social Work, Athens, Greece, 1964. New York: International Conference of Social Work, 1965.　313-318.

1380　Interregional Meeting of Experts on the Training of Social Welfare Personnel for Participation in Development Planning. Report of the Meeting, Geneva, 1969. New York: United Nations, 1970.　27p.　ST/SOA/97.

1381 Jones, John F. and Mary Bradley Witkins. "Skills for social development." Social Work Education and Development Newsletter, no. 9, March 1974. 15-17.

1382 Jones, Wyatt C. and Armand A. Lauffer. Implications of the Community Organization Curriculum Project for practice and education. New York: National Association of Social Workers, 1968. 15p.

1383 Kelley, Joseph B. "Educating effective social workers for a changing society: social policy." Journal of Education for Social Work, v. 11, no. 1, winter 1975. 89-93.

1384 Kindelsperger, Kenneth W. "Schools of social work throughout the world and social policy." International Social Work, v. 8, no. 3, July 1965. 14-18.

1385 Lappin, Ben W. "Social work education and community practice." Community workers and the social work tradition. Toronto: University of Toronto Press, 1971. 153-177.

1386 Lauffer, Armand A. "A new breed of social actionist comes to social work: the community organization student." Journal of Education for Social Work, v. 7, no. 1, winter 1971. 43-55.

1387 _____. "Social actionists come to social work: comparison of community organization students with their peers in casework and group work." Doctoral dissertation, Brandeis University, 1969. 260p.

1388 Levy, Charles S. Education and training for the fundraising function. New York: The Lois and Samuel Silberman Fund, 1974. 104p.

1389 _____, Marjorie Buckholz and Albert Comanor. Experiences in offering community organization courses for all students; reports from three schools. New York: Council on Social Work Education, 1964. 59p.

1390 _____. "Student observation visits as education for social responsibility." Social Casework, v. 46, no. 10, Jan. 1965. 626-628.

1391 Lockhart, George and Joseph L. Vigilante. "Community organization, planning and the social work curriculum." Community Development Journal, v. 9, no. 1, Jan. 1974. 64-70.

1392 Lurie, Harry L. The community organization method in social work education. The social work curriculum study, v. 4. New York: Council on Social Work Education, 1959. 270p.

1393   Magill, Robert S.   "An introductory policy planning course
        for graduate students."   Journal of Education for Social
        Work, v. 11, no. 1, winter 1975.   99-104.

1394   Meld, Murray B.   "The employment experience of community
        organization graduates: a pilot study."   Journal of Edu-
        cation for Social Work, v. 10, no. 1, winter 1974.   60-67.

1395   Melzer, Arden E. , Willard C. Richan and John B. Turner.
        "Analysis of social planning problems: a new design for
        a component of the community organization curriculum."
        Journal of Education for Social Work, v. 3, no. 2, fall
        1967.   71-79.

1396   Misrahi, Cecil, rapporteur.   "Social progress through social
        planning: the role of social work education; report of
        English-speaking group."   International Social Work, v. 8,
        no. 2, April 1965.   5-8.

1397   Mohsini, S. R.   "New orientation to social work education
        in preparation for social development."   Social Work For-
        um, v. 12, no. 4, Jan. 1975.   5-12.

1398   Morris, Robert.   "Social work preparation for effectiveness
        in planned change."   Education for social work; proceedings
        of the 1963 Annual Program Meeting, Council on Social
        Work Education.   New York: The Council, 1963.   166-180.

1399   Neill, Desmond G.   "On the teaching of social policy."   Inter-
        national Social Work, v. 8, no. 1, Jan. 1965.   26-28.

1400   Perlman, Helen Harris.   "On the teaching of social policy."
        International Social Work, v. 8, no. 1, Jan. 1965.   22-25.

1401   Ross, Murray.   "Conceptual problems in community organi-
        zation."   Community organization; workshop report of the
        1956 Annual Program Meeting, Council on Social Work
        Education.   New York: The Council, 1956.   5-18.

1402   Sanders, Daniel S.   "Trends in education for community de-
        velopment and community work: basic issues."   Interna-
        tional Social Work, v. 19, no. 1, 1976.   38-41.

1403   Segal, Brian.   "Policy science and social policy: implications
        for the social work curriculum."   Journal of Education for
        Social Work, v. 12, no. 2, spring 1976.   36-42.

1404   Shaffer, Anatole.   "Community organization and the oppressed."
        Journal of Education for Social Work, v. 8, no. 3, fall
        1972.   65-75.

1405   Sherrard, Thomas D.   "The community organization method

in social work education, by Harry L. Lurie: review."
Social Service Review, v. 33, no. 4, Dec. 1959. 397-404.

1406 Slavin, Simon. "Concepts of social conflict: use in social
work curriculum." Journal of Education for Social Work,
v. 5, no. 2, fall 1969. 47-60.

1407 Wilson, Thelma and Eileen L. Younghusband, editors. Teaching community work: a European exploration. New York:
International Association of Schools of Social Work, 1976.
62p.

1407a Winthrop, Henry. "Policy and planning programs as goals
of scientific work: interdisciplinary training for social
planning as a case study in applied social science."
American Journal of Economics and Sociology, v. 34, no. 3,
July 1975. 225-245.

1408 Yelaja, Shankar A. "Social policy practice." Journal of
Education for Social Work, v. 11, no. 3, fall 1975. 101-
106.

1409 Zweig, Franklin M. "The new thrust of the community social work curriculum: what implications for Jewish communal services?" Journal of Jewish Communal Service,
v. 43, no. 1, fall 1966. 93-99.

E.   ADMINISTRATION [See also Section VII. B.]

1410 Austin, David M. and Michael L. Lauderdale. "Social work
education: preparing public welfare administrators." Public Welfare, v. 34, no. 3, summer 1976. 13-18.

1411 Baron, D. W. B. "Report of the English-Speaking Section
of the Study Group on the Curriculum Planning for Social
Welfare Administration." International Social Work, v. 4,
no. 3, July 1961. 17-18.

1412 Bevis, Leona. "The Curriculum Studies of administration
and community organization." Child Welfare, v. 39, no. 4,
April 1960. 1-4.

1413 Council on Social Work Education. New approaches to administration and research in social work education. New
York: The Council, 1957. 41p.

1414 Dunham, Arthur. "Training for community organization and
social welfare administration." Compass, v. 27, no. 2,
Jan. 1946. 9-11.

1415 Fauri, David P. "Social work education for leadership roles in state government." Journal of Education for Social Work, v. 12, no. 1, winter 1976. 44-49.

1416 Fitzgerald, Harold Kenneth. "Education for public welfare administration." Doctoral dissertation, Catholic University of America, 1953. 190p.

1417 Giambruno, Anna. "Curriculum planning for social welfare administration." International Social Work, v. 4, no. 3, July 1961. 8-12.

1418 Godwin, Frances P. "Analysis of knowledge and skills needed by administrators of social service systems." Doctoral dissertation, Catholic University of America, 1975. 199p.

1419 Howard, Donald S. "Administration as a component of professional social work education." Social work in the current scene, 1950; selected papers, National Conference of Social Work, Atlantic City, 1950. New York: Columbia University Press, 1950. 240-252.

1420 Kazmerski, Kenneth J. and David Macarov. Administration in the social work curriculum: report of a survey. New York: Council on Social Work Education, 1976. 84p.

1421 Lewin, Thomas Fred. "A format for an educational sequence in administration." Social work practice, 1964; selected papers of the 1964 Annual Forum, National Conference on Social Welfare. New York: Columbia University Press, 1964. 178-182.

1422 Madou, Andree. "Summary report of group discussions on curriculum planning for social welfare administration." International Social Work, v. 4, no. 3, July 1961. 13-16.

1423 Marquiss, A. R. C. "Teaching the social services." Social Service Quarterly, v. 47, no. 3, Jan. -March 1974. 91-92.

1424 Michigan. University. School of Social Work. Social welfare administration: curriculum documents. Ann Arbor, Mich. : The School, 1969. Various pagings.

1425 Patti, Rino J. and Herman Resnick. "Educating for organizational change." Social Work Education Reporter, v. 20, no. 2, April-May 1972. 62-66.

1426 Pennsylvania. University. School of Social Work. National project on education for management, v. 1. Philadelphia: The School, 1975. 1v. (various pagings)

1427 Pennsylvania. University. School of Social Work and the

Wharton Entrepreneurial Center, Wharton School. Management in social welfare: casebook studies. Philadelphia: The School and The Center, 1976. 234p.

1428 Pennsylvania. University. Wharton School. Wharton Entrepreneurial Center. National project on education for management, v. 2. Philadelphia: The Center, 1975. 183p.

1429 Ranade, S. N. "Teaching of social administration in schools of social work." Social Work Forum, v. 3, no. 3, July 1965. 36-39.

1430 Sarri, Rosemary C. "Effective social work intervention in administrative and planning roles: implications for education." Facing the challenge; plenary session papers from the 1973 Annual Program Meeting, Council on Social Work Education. New York: The Council, 1973. 31-48.

1431 _____ and John M. Riley. "Graduates of the social welfare administration curriculum; where they are and how they view the curriculum." Social Work Education Reporter, v. 19, no. 2, April-May 1971. 53-56.

1432 Schwartz, Edward E. "The administration method in social work education, by Sue Spencer: review." Social Service Review, v. 33, no. 4, Dec. 1959. 393-397.

1433 _____. "Some views of the study of social welfare administration." Research in social welfare administration: its contributions and problems; report of the Institute on Research in Social Work Administration and Community Welfare Organization, Chicago, 1960. Edited by David Fanshell. New York: National Association of Social Workers, 1962. 33-43.

1434 Shapira, Monica. "Reflections on the preparation of social workers for executive positions." Journal of Education for Social Work, v. 7, no. 1, winter 1971. 55-68.

1435 Shastree, Tara. "Teaching of administration of social work." Indian Journal of Social Work, v. 25, no. 3, Oct. 1964. 273-276.

1436 Shiffman, Bernard M. and Martin Abramowitz. "Preparation of the MSW graduate for early assumption of administrative roles: the agency perspective." Social Work Education Reporter, v. 16, no. 3, Sept. 1968. 30-31, 42-43.

1437 Spencer, Sue W. The administration method in social work education. The social work curriculum study, v. 3. New York: Council on Social Work Education, 1959. 75p.

1438 Sprague, Linda G. , Alan Sheldon and Curtis P. McLaughlin.
      Teaching health and human services administration by the
      case method. New York: Behavioral Publications, 1973.
      33-138p.

1439 Stein, Herman D. "The teaching of administration in the
      master's curriculum. " Smith College Studies in Social
      Work, v. 35, no. 1, Oct. 1964. 1-10.

1440 Sullivan, Ina G. "System oriented social work administration:
      some effects of casework versus administration training
      on social work administrators. " Doctoral dissertation,
      Rutgers University, 1976. 201p.

1441 Trecker, Harleigh B. , Frank Z. Glick and John C. Kidneigh.
      Education for social work administration. New York:
      American Association of Social Workers, 1953. 25p.

1442 United Nations. European Social Welfare Programme. Re-
      port of the European Seminar on Training of Senior Per-
      sonnel for the Social Services, Amersfoort, Netherlands,
      1963. Geneva: United Nations, 1964. 158p. SOA/ESWP/
      1963/2.

1443 _____ . Office of Social Affairs, Geneva. Report of the
      European Seminar on Training for Senior Social Welfare
      Personnel, Paris, 1962. Geneva: United Nations, 1963.
      162p. SOA/ESWP/1962/2.

1444 Watson, Angelica. "Making administration live in class and
      field. " Case Conference, v. 13, no. 7, Nov. 1966. 249-
      253.

F. CONSULTATION, TEACHING, AND SUPERVISION

1445 Bontje, Adrian and John Longres. "Preparing MSW students
      to supervise paraprofessionals: the social service edu-
      cator training component. " Social Work Education Re-
      porter, v. 20, no. 3, Sept. -Oct. 1972. 35-38.

1446 Green, Rose and Maurice B. Hamovitch. "Education of so-
      cial workers for mental health consultation. " American
      Journal of Orthopsychiatry, v. 32, no. 2, March 1962.
      225-226.

1447 Jones, Shirley J. and Margaret Purvine. Report of the
      Workshop on Preparing Graduate Social Work Students
      to Work with Paraprofessionals. New York: Council on
      Social Work Education, 1971. 34p.

1448   Mullaney, John W. "Introducing teaching as an alternative career line in social work at the Master's level." Social Work Education Reporter, v. 19, no. 3, Sept. -Oct. 1971. 47-50.

1449   Purvine, Margaret, editor. Educating MSW students to work with other social welfare personnel. New York: Council on Social Work Education, 1973. 98p.

1450   Rapoport, Lydia. "Consultation: an overview--Education and training for consultation." Consultation in social work practice. Edited by Lydia Rapoport. New York: National Association of Social Workers, 1963. 15-18.

1451   Smith, Joanne M. B. "Social work consultation: implications for social work education." Doctoral dissertation, University of Utah, 1975. 171p.

G.   RESEARCH [See also Section VII. L.]

1452   Anderson, Claire M. "Information systems for social welfare: educational imperatives." Journal of Education for Social Work, v. 11, no. 3, fall 1975. 16-21.

1453   Avison, Margaret. The research compendium; review and abstracts of graduate research, 1942-1962. Toronto: University of Toronto Press, 1964. 276p.

1454   Cambria, Sophie T. "The responsibility of school and agency in student research." Smith College Studies in Social Work, v. 21, no. 2, Feb. 1951. 95-102.

1455   Chambers, Donald E. "The trouble with secrets: a radical revision of the teaching of research in the social work curriculum." Arete, v. 4, no. 1, spring 1976. 1-13.

1456   Council on Social Work Education. Aids for research teachers. New York: The Council, 1970. 5 units.

1457   _____. New approaches to administration and research in social work education. New York: The Council, 1957. 41p.

1458   _____. Selected papers in methods of teaching research in the social work curriculum. New York: The Council, 1959. 46p.

1459   Dadlani, G. G. "Learning values of group research project." Social Work Review, v. 8, July 1961. 47-51.

1460 Dailey, Dennis M. "A learning paradigm for the teaching of social work research." Journal of Education for Social Work, v. 11, no. 2, spring 1975. 25-31.

1461 Danzig, Martin E. "Team approach in conducting student research projects." Social Casework, v. 43, no. 7, July 1962. 372-375.

1462 Eaton, Joseph W. "Training social work researchers: a curriculum innovation." Social Work Education Reporter, v. 15, no. 1, March 1967. 16-17, 32.

1463 Fellin, Phillip A. "The standardized interview in social work research." Social Casework, v. 44, no. 2, Feb. 1963. 81-85.

1464 Finestone, Samuel. "The school center for research and demonstration: its potential for social work education." Social Work Education Reporter, v. 15, no. 4, Dec. 1967. 23-24, 45, 62-63.

1465 Francel, Edward W., chairman. "Task force report on research in MSW curriculum." Social Work Education Reporter, v. 16, no. 1, March 1968. 13, 20-21.

1466 Ganister, Marie. "An agency view of student research." Journal of Social Work Process, v. 10, 1959. 43-50.

1467 Goldstein, Harris K. Identifying and maximizing research learning potential for social work students. New Orleans: School of Social Work, Tulane University, 1967. 91p.

1468 Goldstein, Harris K. and Linda Horder. "Suggested teaching plans for maximizing research learning of three types of social work students." Journal of Education for Social Work, v. 10, no. 3, fall 1974. 30-35.

1469 Gordon, William E. "A conceptual framework for research in social work education: questions of boundaries and priorities." Education for social work; proceedings of the 1964 Annual Program Meeting, Council on Social Work Education. New York: The Council, 1964. 123-130.

1470 _____. The focus and nature of research completed by graduate students in approved schools of social work, 1940-1949, as indicated by theses and project titles. New York: American Association of Schools of Social Work, 1951. 10p.

1471 _____. "Research project: its educational value and its contribution to social work knowledge." Social Work Journal, v. 31, no. 3, July 1950. 110-116.

1472 Greenwood, Ernest. "Social work research: the role of the schools." Social Service Review, v. 32, no. 2, June 1958. 152-166.

1473 Kantrow, Ruth. "Innovations in the research sequence." Social Work Education Reporter, v. 17, no. 1, March 1969. 43-46, 60-61.

1474 Kelly, M. V. "Educating social workers for research." Social Worker-Travailleur Social, v. 41, no. 3, autumn 1973. 252-258.

1475 Kirk, Stuart A. and Joel Fischer. "Do social workers understand research?" Journal of Education for Social Work, v. 12, no. 1, winter 1976. 63-70.

1476 _____, Michael J. Osmalov and Joel Fischer. "Social workers' involvement in research." Social Work, v. 21, no. 2, March 1976. 121-124.

1477 Kolevzon, Michael S. "Integrational teaching modalities in social work education: promise or pretence?" Journal of Education for Social Work, v. 11, no. 2, spring 1975. 50-67.

1478 Lewis, Harold. "Perspectives on social work research in a school's curriculum." Journal of Social Work Process, v. 17, 1969. 81-96.

1479 _____. "The place of the research project in the Master's curriculum." Journal of Social Work Process, v. 10, 1959. 35-42.

1480 _____. "The significance for social work education of the student's approach to the formulation of a research question." Social Work Education Reporter, v. 9, no. 2, April 1961. Supplement. 7p.

1481 Linn, Margaret W. and Shayna R. Greenwald. "Student attitudes, knowledge, and skill related to research training." Journal of Education for Social Work, v. 10, no. 1, winter 1974. 48-54.

1482 Lower, Katherine D. "Responsibilities for research in the profession of social work." Education for social work; proceedings of the 1955 Annual Program Meeting, Council on Social Work Education. New York: The Council, 1955. 49-56.

1483 McDaniel, Clyde O., Jr. "Imperatives for a second-year research experience in graduate schools of social work." Social Work Education Reporter, v. 21, no. 1, Dec.-Jan. 1973. 54-59.

1484 MacDonald, Mary E. "Use of the group study in teaching
research." Social Service Review, v. 24, no. 4, Dec.
1950. 427-441.

1485 Mahadeva, Bani. "Training in research methods." Social
Work Forum, v. 4, no. 3, July 1966. 17-19.

1486 Marks, Rachel Bryant. "The research method in social work
education, by Samuel Mencher: review." Social Service
Review, v. 33, no. 4, Dec. 1959. 420-422.

1487 Marzialli, Elsa and Heather Munroe Blum. "Clinical research: a model for teaching and learning." Canadian
Journal of Social Work Education, v. 2, no. 2, 1976. 45-
52.

1488 Mencher, Samuel. The research method in social work education. The social work curriculum study, v. 9. New
York: Council on Social Work Education, 1959. 61p.

1489 Mullen, Edward J. "Evaluative research in social work."
Evaluation of social work services in community health
and medical care programs; based on the proceedings of
the 1973 Annual Institute for Public Health Social Workers.
Edited by Robert C. Jackson and Jean Morton. Berkeley:
Program in Public Health Social Work, University of California, 1973. 37-51. Summary of discussion. 52-54.

1490 Northwood, Lawrence K. "Enriched training for research in
the Master's degree program." Social Work Education
Reporter, v. 4, no. 2, June 1966. 34-35, 44-45.

1491 Polansky, Norman A. "Why research in the social work curriculum?" Smith College Studies in Social Work, v. 22,
no. 3, June 1952. 147-154.

1492 Rose, Charles L. "Group research by student social workers
in a Veterans Hospital." Journal of Psychiatric Social
Work, v. 23, no. 2, Jan. 1954. 93-98.

1493 Roth, Norman R. Ethnic content in the research component
of the social work curriculum: a report of a survey of
graduate schools of social work. Boulder, Colo.: Western Interstate Commission for Higher Education, 1973.
34p.

1494 Sacks, Joel G. "A study of the imformation and attitude
changes brought about by one social work research curriculum." Doctoral dissertation, Columbia University, 1970.
200p.

1495 Seaman, Richard. "Case method in the teaching and learning of social work research." Social Work Journal, v. 35, no. 3, July 1954. 119-120, 130.

1496 Seidl, Frederick W. "Teaching social work research: a study in teaching method." Journal of Education for Social Work, v. 9, no. 3, fall 1973. 71-77.

1497 Thomas, P. T. "Training in research methodology." Social Work Forum, v. 4, no. 1, Jan. 1966. 9-15.

1498 Walker, Helen Mabel. Manual: the use of the group research project in social work education. Cleveland: Press of Western Reserve University, 1959. 16p.

1499 Walsh, Ethel. "Research and teaching of casework." Journal of Education for Social Work, v. 1, no. 2, fall 1965. 47-52.

1500 Wodarski, John S. and Ronald A. Feldman. "The research practicum: a beginning, formulation of process and educational objectives." International Social Work, v. 16, no. 4, 1973. 42-48.

1501 Zimbalist, Sidney E. "The research component of the Master's degree curriculum in social work: a survey summary." Journal of Education for Social Work, v. 10, no. 1, winter 1974. 118-123.

H. INTEGRATED AND COMBINED METHODS [See also Section VII. H.]

1502 Ainsworth, Frank and Joan Hunter, editors. A unitary approach to social work practice--implications for education and organization. Dundee, Scotland: School of Social Administration, University of Dundee, 1975. 58p.

1503 Bertrand, Patricia T. Teaching multi-methods as an integral part of problem-centered social work practice. Madison: School of Social Work, University of Wisconsin, 1968. 17p.

1504 Blackey, Eileen. "The teaching of social work with individuals, groups, and communities; report of a European Regional Seminar, Edinburgh, Scotland, September 10-20, 1962: introduction and conclusion." International Social Work, v. 6, no. 3, July 1963. 1-7.

1505 Churchill, Sallie R. "The demand for competency in two social work methods: questions and challenges for education and practice." Social Work Education Reporter,

v. 14, no. 1, March 1966. 22-23, 31.

1506 Clearfield, Sidney M. "Merged method in social work educa-
      tion: a group worker's somewhat jaundiced view." Doc-
      toral students look at social work education. Edited by
      Leila Calhoun Deasy. New York: Council on Social Work
      Education, 1971. 87-105.

1507 Dea, Kay L. , editor. New ways of teaching social work
      practice. New York: Council on Social Work Education,
      1972. 50p.

1508 De Martinez, Leonor Mardones. "Some opinions on the teach-
      ing of social work with individuals, groups and communi-
      ties." International Social Work, v. 6, no. 2, April 1963.
      22-23.

1509 Doolan, Margaret B. and Winnifred A. Herington. "An edu-
      cational model for teaching practice with individuals, fam-
      ilies, and small groups." Social Worker-Travailleur So-
      cial, v. 40, no. 4, Dec. 1972. 245-255.

1510 Garvin, Charles. "Education for generalist practice: a com-
      parative analysis of current modalities." Teaching for
      competence in the delivery of direct services. Compiled
      by the Council on Social Work Education. New York:
      The Council, 1976. 18-30.

1511 Greenblatt, Bernard and Daniel Katkin. "Prolegomena to a
      curriculum for some occasions." Social Work Education
      Reporter, v. 20, no. 3, Sept. -Oct. 1972. 55-61.

1512 Johnson, Louise C. "Social work practice models: Teaching
      the differential aspects of practice." Teaching for com-
      petence in the delivery of direct services. Compiled by
      the Council on Social Work Education. New York: The
      Council, 1976. 40-50.

1513 Kadushin, Alfred and Quentin F. Schenk. "An experiment in
      teaching an integrated method course." Social Casework,
      v. 38, no. 8, Oct. 1957. 417-422.

1514 Kendall, Katherine A. "New Dimensions in casework and
      group work practice: implication for professional educa-
      tion." Social Work, v. 4, no. 4, Oct. 1959. 49-56.

1515 Kolevzon, Michael S. "Integrational teaching modalities in
      social work education: promise or pretence?" Journal
      of Education for Social Work, v. 11, no. 2, spring 1975.
      50-67.

1516 Kramer, Ralph M. "Community organization and administration: integration or separate but equal?" Journal of Education for Social Work, v. 2, no. 2, fall 1966. 48-56.

1517 Lloyd, Gary A. "Integrated methods and the field practice course." Social Work Education Reporter, v. 16, no. 2, June 1968. 28, 39-42.

1518 Northen, Helen. "An integrated practice sequence in social work education." Social Work Education Reporter, v. 16, no. 2, June 1968. 29-31, 37-39.

1519 Overton, Alice. "The issue of integration of casework and group work." Social Work Education Reporter, v. 16, no. 2, June 1968. 25-27, 47.

1520 Paraiso, Virginia A. "Common elements in education for social work practice with individuals, groups and communities." International Social Work, v. 6, no. 2, April 1963. 12-18.

1521 Sainsbury, Eric. "The teaching of social work with individuals, groups and communities; report of a European Regional Seminar, Edinburgh, Scotland, September 10-20, 1962: general report and critique." International Social Work, v. 6, no. 3, July 1963. 8-14.

1522 Shafer, Carl M. "Teaching social work practice in an integrated course: a general systems approach." The general systems approach. Edited by Gordon Hearn. New York: Council on Social Work Education, 1969. 22-36.

1523 Spencer, Sue W. "The first-year sequence in social casework/social group work at the University of Tennessee." Education for social work; proceedings of the 1963 Annual Program Meeting, Council on Social Work Education. New York: The Council, 1963. 220-230.

1524 Stumpf, Jack. "Teaching an integrated approach to social work practice." Innovations in teaching social work practice. Edited by Lilian Ripple. New York: Council on Social Work Education, 1970. 22-33.

1525 Thompson, Joseph Victor. "The social work generalist: a study of recent graduates of the University of Southern California School of Social Work." Doctoral dissertation, University of Southern California, 1969. 267p.

1526 Westbury, Ian and John Korbelik. Evaluation of a goal-focused educational program in social work. Arlington, Va.: ERIC Document Reproduction Service, 1973. 50p. ED 074136.

1527   _____, Bernece K. Simon and John Korbelik, editors. The generalist program: description and evaluation. Chicago: School of Social Service Administration, University of Chicago, 1973. 373p.

VII. FIELD INSTRUCTION AT THE GRADUATE LEVEL

A. GENERAL

1528 Abbott, Edith. "Field work and the training of the social worker." Proceedings of the National Conference of Charities and Correction, 1915, Baltimore. Chicago: Hildmann Printing Co., 1915. 615-621.

1529 Austin, Michael J., Edward Kelleher and Philip L. Smith, editors. The field consortium: manpower development and training in social welfare and corrections. Tallahassee, Fla.: State University System of Florida, 1972. 121p.

1530 Berengarten, Sidney. "Educational issues in field instruction in social work." Social Service Review, v. 35, no. 3, Sept. 1961. 246-257.

1531 Berg, Renee. "Developing a broadened view of the educational contribution of field practice." Journal of Social Work Process, v. 17, 1969. 55-68.

1532 Cassidy, Helen E., editor. Modes of professional education: functions of field instruction in the curriculum; report of a symposium, New Orleans, 1969. New Orleans: School of Social Work, Tulane University, 1969. 253p.

1533 Chitnis, Nancy and Gae Tigelaar. "Impact of a strike on graduate students." Social Work, v. 16, no. 2, April 1971. 65-68.

1534 Clark, Carol Miriam. The role of the field work consultant in social work education; a selective bibliography. Johannesburg: University of the Witwatersrand, Department of Bibliography, Librarianship and Typography, 1972. 48p.

1535 Collins, Mildred. "Some conflicts and issues in field teaching." Social Worker-Travailleur Social, v. 38, no. 2, May 1970. 15-18.

1536 Cook, Maxwell A. "The rationale of the field instruction program: the Carolina experience." Arete, v. 1, no. 1, spring 1970. 8-12.

1537   Council for Training in Social Work. The teaching of field-
        work; report of the Working Party on Fieldwork. London:
        The Council, 1971. 44p.

1538   Council on Social Work Education. The dynamics of field
        instruction: learning through doing. New York: The
        Council, 1975. 101p.

1539   _____. Field instruction in graduate social work educa-
        tion: old problems and new proposals. New York: The
        Council, 1966. 68p.

1540   Dana, Bess S. and Mildred Sikkema. "Field instruction--fact
        and fantasy." Education for social work; proceedings of
        the 1964 Annual Program Meeting, Council on Social Work
        Education. New York: The Council, 1964. 90-101.

1541   Davies, Hilary and Paul Taylor. "Two-agency placements in
        social work training." Social Work Today, v. 4, no. 8, 12
        July 1973. 245-250.

1542   Family Service Association of America. Trends in field work
        instruction; articles reprinted from Social Casework, 1955-
        65. New York: The Association, 1966. 71p.

1543   Finestone, Samuel. "Selected features of professional field
        instruction." Journal of Education for Social Work, v. 3,
        no. 2, fall 1967. 14-26.

1544   Foeckler, Merle M. "Orientation to field instruction in light
        of current needs of social work education." Social Work
        Education Reporter, v. 16, no. 3, Sept. 1968. 34-35, 45-
        46.

1545   Gadol, Morris. "Some observations on points of relevance
        between undergraduate field experience and field instruc-
        tion in the graduate school of social work." Social
        Work Education Reporter, v. 14, no. 2, June 1966.
        36, 51-52.

1546   Gilpin, Ruth S. Theory and practice as a single reality; an
        essay in social work education. Chapel Hill: University
        of North Carolina Press, 1963. 139p.

1547   Great Britain. Department of Health and Social Security.
        Advisory Council on Child Care. Fieldwork training for
        social work. London: HMSO, 1971. 215p.

1548   Henry, Cecil St. George. "An examination of fieldwork mo-
        dels at Adelphi University School of Social Work." Jour-
        nal of Education for Social Work, v. 11, no. 3, fall 1975.
        62-68.

1549 Hill, Mary A. "Introduction to field practice: the UBC practicum." Social Worker-Travailleur Social, v. 40, no. 3, Sept. 1972. 186-197.

1550 Jones, Betty Lacy, editor. Current patterns in field instruction in graduate social work education. New York: Council on Social Work Education, 1969. 175p.

1551 Kapoor, J. M. "The role of field work in modern social work education." Indian Journal of Social Work, v. 22, no. 2, Sept. 1961. 113-119.

1552 Kendall, Katherine A. "Selected issues in field instruction in education for social work." Social Service Review, v. 33, no. 1, March 1959. 1-9.

1553 Kindelsperger, Kenneth W. "Innovation in field instruction in social work education." Exploring the interfaces of social work education. Edited by Charles W. McCann. Boulder, Colo. : Western Interstate Commission for Higher Education, 1970. 55-66.

1554 Kohn, Regina. "Field instruction techniques." Social Work Education Reporter, v. 18, no. 1, March 1970. 39-41, 61.

1555 Kramer, Sidney. "Developing a field placement program." Social Casework, v. 42, no. 9, Nov. 1961. 456-460.

1556 Levy, Charles S. "A conceptual framework for field instruction in social work education." Child Welfare, v. 44, no. 8, Oct. 1965. 447-452.

1557 Llewellyn, Grace M. "Orientation: a conceptual approach to field work." Social Casework, v. 45, no. 7, July 1964. 404-406.

1558 Loeser, Drake. "A structural view of student involvement in field instruction." Social Work Education Reporter, v. 20, no. 3, Sept. -Oct. 1972. 62-64.

1559 Lurie, Abraham and Sidney Pinsky. "Queens Field Instruction Center: a field instruction center for multilevel education in social work." Journal of Education for Social Work, v. 9, no. 3, fall 1973. 39-44.

1560 Manis, Francis. "Education for social work: field work in developing nations." International Social Work, v. 14, no. 2, 1971. 17-20.

1561 _____ . Field practice in social work education; perspectives from an international base. Fullerton, Calif. : Sultana Press, 1972. 160p.

1562 Merrifield, Aleanor. "Changing patterns and programs in
field instruction." Social Service Review, v. 37, no. 3,
Sept. 1963. 274-282.

1563 National Conference on Social Welfare. Selected bibliography
on field work. Columbus, Ohio: The Conference, 1968.
Various pagings.

1564 Pinsky, Sidney. "The Queens Field Instruction Center: an
innovative model for field instruction in social work education." Doctoral dissertation, Columbia University, 1974.
174p.

1565 Quaranta, Mary Ann. "Curriculum Policy Statement of 1969:
implications for field instruction." Social Work Education
Reporter, v. 19, no. 3, Sept. -Oct. 1971. 58-60.

1566 Robertson, Jean M. "Problems related to practical training
in social work." International Social Service Review, no.
4, Sept. 1958. 15-18.

1567 Scott, Lyndell. "The function of field work in professional
education." Social Service Review, v. 25, no. 4, Dec. 1951.
441-454.

1568 Taber, Merlin. "A sampling of techniques for evaluative research in field instruction." Social Work Education Reporter, v. 15, no. 3, Sept. 1967. 22-25, 33.

1569 Werner, Ruth. "Sixty years of field work, 1916-1976 (Case
Western Reserve University School of Applied Social Sci-
ences)." SASS Currents, special anniversary issue, 1976.
Unpaged.

1570 Wessel, Rosa and Goldie Basch Faith. Professional education based in practice; two studies in education for social
work. Philadelphia: University of Pennsylvania School
of Social Work, 1953. 170p.

1571 Wilkens, Anne. Guides for field instruction for graduate
schools of social work, field experience of undergraduate
students, and summer employment of undergraduate students. Washington, D. C.: U. S. Bureau of Family
Services and U. S. Children's Bureau, 1963. 33p.

B. ADMINISTRATION AS A METHOD [See also Section VI. E.]

1572 Arndt, Hilda C. M. "The teaching of administration in first
year field instruction." Doctoral dissertation, University
of Chicago, 1966. 159p.

1573 Atwater, Pierce. "Outlines of field-work instruction in administration." Problems of administration in social work. Minneapolis: University of Minnesota Press, 1940. 296-312.

1574 Carroll, Donald and Patrick McCuan. "A specialized role function approach to field instruction in social administration." The dynamics of field instruction: learning through doing. Compiled by the Council on Social Work Education. New York: The Council, 1975. 1-9.

1575 Donovan, Frances. "Field work in social administration." Australian Journal of Social Work, v. 23, no. 2, June 1970. 30-36.

1576 Ford, Malcolm. "Administration and the fieldwork placement." Case Conference, v. 15, no. 10, Feb. 1969. 401-403.

1577 Glick, Frank Z. "Teaching administration in social work." Education for social work administration. By Harleigh B. Trecker, Frank Z. Glick and John C. Kidneigh. New York: American Association of Social Workers, 1953. 14-19.

1578 Henry, Sue, editor. The field experience in education for management in social welfare. Philadelphia: School of Social Work and Wharton Entrepreneurial Center, Wharton School, University of Pennsylvania, 1976. 78p.

1579 _____. "Guidelines for field experience in social work education for management in social welfare." National project on education for management, v. 1. Prepared by the School of Social Work, University of Pennsylvania. Philadelphia: The School, 1975. 16p. in blue covers.

1580 Neugeboren, Bernard. "Developing specialized programs in social work administration in the master's degree program: field practice component." Journal of Education for Social Work, v. 7, no. 3, fall 1971. 35-47.

C. BLOCK PLACEMENT AND CONCURRENT PLAN

1581 Council on Social Work Education. "Curriculum planning and field work administration on the block basis." Curriculum planning and reorganization; workshop report of the 1955 Annual Program Meeting. New York: The Council, 1955. 18-25.

1582 Gilpin, Ruth S. "Concurrence in the block plan of social work education." Doctoral dissertation, University of Pennsylvania, 1960. 255p.

1583 Schutz, Margaret L. "The potential of concurrent field instruction for learning." Current patterns in field instruction in graduate social work education. Edited by Betty Lacy Jones. New York: Council on Social Work Education, 1969. 99-107.

1584 Selyan, Alice A. "Learning theories and patterns in block and concurrent field instruction." Current patterns in field instruction in graduate social work education. Edited by Betty Lacy Jones. New York: Council on Social Work Education, 1969. 87-97.

1585 Timms, Noel. "The block placement in training for social work." Case Conference, v. 9, no. 8, Feb. 1963. 216-221.

D. COMMUNITY ORGANIZATION AND SOCIAL PLANNING [See also Section VI. D.]

1586 Barry, Mildred C. "Field work training in community organization." The community organization method in social work education. By Harry L. Lurie. New York: Council on Social Work Education, 1959. 67-84.

1587 Brager, George and John A. Michael. The student community organizer and his training in the field: a comparison of community organizers with other social work students, and their reactions to field training; the final report of the C. O. Curriculum Development Project of the Columbia University School of Social Work. New York: School of Social Work, Columbia University, 1969. Various pagings.

1588 Bryant, Richard. "Fieldwork training in community work." Community Development Journal, v. 9, no. 3, Oct. 1974. 212-216.

1589 _____. "Teaching practice skills in community work." Community Development Journal, v. 11, no. 1, Jan. 1976. 10-16.

1590 Dawley, David, Judson Stone and John L. Erlich. "Legislative action: new vistas for student placement." Social Work Education Reporter, v. 16, no. 1, March 1968. 40, 53-54.

1591 Ellis, Jack A. N. "The executive office of state government: a site for field instruction in community organization."

Social Work Education Reporter, v. 16, no. 1, March 1968. 41-42, 54-55.

1592 Holmes, Barbara, Richard Bryant and Donald Houston. "Student unit in community work: an experimental approach." Social Work Today, v. 4, no. 14, 18 Oct. 1973. 424-430.

1593 Jones, Shirley J. "New teaching settings and their relevance for social work education." Social Work Education Reporter, v. 20, no. 2, April-May 1972. 52-56.

1594 Kurren, Oscar and Paul Lister. "Social work internship in public housing: an interdisciplinary experience." Journal of Education for Social Work, v. 12, no. 3, fall 1976. 72-79.

1595 Lightman, J. B. "A unified field work theory of training for international social work." Social Worker-Travailleur Social, v. 26, no. 3, April 1958. 37-45.

1596 Lipscomb, Nell. "The teaching-learning setting in a first-year field instruction program." The dynamics of field instruction: learning through doing. Compiled by the Council on Social Work Education. New York: The Council, 1975. 68-75.

1597 McDonnell, David John. "An exploratory study of nontraditional community organization field practice placements." Doctoral dissertation, University of Pennsylvania, 1973. 131p.

1598 Masi, Fidelia A. Field instruction in community organization: a recent experiment. New York: National Urban League, 1967. 101p.

1599 Monk, Abraham and Fred Newdom. "The outposting method of community services: a multistaged field experience." Journal of Education for Social Work, v. 12, no. 3, fall 1976. 88-94.

1600 Rothman, Jack and Wyatt C. Jones. A new look at field instruction; education for application of practice skills in community organization and social planning; report of the Community Organization Curriculum Development Project. New York: Association Press, 1971. 224p.

1601 _____. "A pre-structured and faculty-directed approach to practice skill development." Current patterns in field instruction in graduate social work education. Edited by Betty Lacy Jones. New York: Council on Social Work Education, 1969. 109-122.

1602 Stephens, Bernice. "An experiment: a brief field experience
      in social welfare planning and social action for casework
      students." Social Work Education Reporter, v. 14, no. 1,
      March 1966. 24-25, 47.

1603 Travis, Georgia. "A research-centered project in social work
      with organizations and communities." Social Work Educa-
      tion Reporter, v. 16, no. 3, Sept. 1968. 36-37, 47-48.

1604 Waite, Eloise B. "Red Cross as a community organization
      field work agency." Social Work Education Reporter, v.
      18, no. 1, March 1970. 55-58, 62-63.

1605 Zweig, Franklin M. "The social worker as legislative om-
      budsman." Social Work, v. 14, no. 1, Jan. 1969. 25-33.

E. CURRICULUM, TEACHING AND LEARNING [See also Sections VII. F, G, P, Q.]

1606 Abrahamson, Arthur C. "Curriculum objectives in field teach-
      ing." Social Worker-Travailleur Social, v. 26, no. 3, April
      1958. 31-36.

1607 Allen, Jo Ann, et al. "A plan for orientation as the first
      phase in field experience." Social Work Education Re-
      porter, v. 17, no. 1, March 1969. 39-42, 66.

1608 Amacher, Kloh-Ann. "Explorations into the dynamics of learn-
      ing in field work." Doctoral dissertation, Smith College,
      1971. 283p.

1609 _____. "Explorations into the dynamics of learning in
      field work." Smith College Studies in Social Work, v.
      46, no. 3, June 1976. 163-217.

1610 Arndt, Hilda C. M. "The learner in field work." Educa-
      tion for social work; proceedings of the 1956 Annual Pro-
      gram Meeting, Council on Social Work Education. New
      York: The Council, 1956. 36-54.

1611 Atherton, Charles R. "The effect of work experience on the
      self concept and anxiety level of the social work graduate
      student." British Journal of Social Work, v. 4, no. 4,
      winter 1974. 435-444.

1612 _____ and Frank Itzin. "Learning value of the first-year
      field experience: student opinion." Social Work Educa-
      tion Reporter, v. 20, no. 1, Dec/Jan. 1972. 29-30, 47-50.

1613 Barker, Leslie. "Reassurance for the student." Case Conference, v. 9, no. 9, March 1963. 254-258.

1614   Cochrane, Hortense. "Some reality features of social work field work practice." Social Work Journal, v. 35, no. 2, April 1954. 73-75.

1615   Council on Social Work Education. Field learning and teaching; explorations in graduate social work education; proceedings of the symposium working party on field learning and teaching, New Orleans, 1967. New York: The Council, 1968. 138p.

1616   Davis, Dorothy. "Psychological maturation and student fieldwork learning." Australian Journal of Social Work, v. 17, no. 3, Nov. 1964. 42-46.

1617   Dekker, Andreas G. "Didactic principles and field work instruction." Social Casework, v. 38, no. 7, July 1957. 350-354.

1618   Gelfand, Bernard. "The work evaluation setting as a student learning laboratory." Rehabilitation Literature, v. 33, no. 3, Feb. 1972. 40-43.

1619   Gelman, Sheldon R. "Integrated learning through a post-placement seminar." Social Work Education Reporter, v. 19, no. 3, Sept.-Oct. 1971. 42-44.

1620   Goldberg, Ruth L. and Sidney M. Grossberg. "The role of the learning center on family functioning in social work education." Family Coordinator, v. 24, no. 3, July 1975. 273-280.

1621   Grover, Elizabeth L. "Field work teaching of new emphases in social work curriculum content in areas other than primary method: an exploratory study of field work teaching of sociocultural content." Doctoral dissertation, Columbia University, 1964. 282p.

1622   Hale, Mark P. "Innovations in field learning and teaching." Social Work Education Reporter, v. 15, no. 3, Sept. 1967. 20, 38-41.

1623   Hammond, Pauline H. "Patterns of learning in fieldwork." Case Conference, v. 13, no. 3, July 1966. 83-88.

1624   Herbert, George K. "A study of learning outcomes in a generic first-year program of graduate social work education." Doctoral dissertation, Tulane University, 1970. 219p.

1625   Hesselberg-Meyer, Grace. "Integration of theory and practice in social work training." Some aspects on social work training. Compiled by the Swedish Association of Graduates from Schools of Social Work and Public Administration. Kumla, Sweden: The Association, 1969. 20-35.

1626 Hollis, Florence. "Relationship of classroom teaching to field placement from the standpoint of the teacher." Social Casework, v. 33, no. 3, March 1952. 91-98.

1627 Husband, Diane and Henry R. Scheunemann. "The use of group process in teaching termination." Child Welfare, v. 51, no. 8, Oct. 1972. 505-513.

1628 James, Adrian. "The student in social work." Social Work Today, v. 2, no. 10, 12 Aug. 1971. 21-23.

1629 Kindelsperger, Kenneth W. "Innovations in field learning and teaching." Social Work Education Reporter, v. 15, no. 3, Sept. 1967. 21, 42-44.

1630 Krop, Lois P. Developing and evaluating a training manual for social work field instructors using elements of the behavioristic system of learning. Arlington, Va. : ERIC Document Reproduction Service, 1975. 67p. ED 116581.

1631 _____. Evaluating the effectiveness of a modern systems approach to field instruction in graduate social work education: curriculum development module. Arlington, Va. : ERIC Document Reproduction Service, 1973. 41p. ED 104305.

1632 _____. A strategy for obtaining a performance-oriented training program for social work field instructors. Arlington, Va. : ERIC Document Reproduction Service, 1975. 38p. ED 118032

1633 Lehrman, Louis J. "The integration of class and field in professional education." Social Casework, v. 33, no. 6, June 1952. 250-255.

1634 Leigh, James W. "Ethnic content in field instruction." Perspectives on ethnic minority content in social work education. Edited by Charles W. McCann. Boulder, Colo. : Western Interstate Commission for Higher Education, 1972. 49-63.

1635 Levin, Morris. "Learning and teaching in field work." Journal of Jewish Communal Service, v. 43, no. 3, spring 1967. 270-274.

1636 Lewis, Mary E. , Dorothy Howerton and Walter L. Kindelsperger. An experimental design for first year field in-

struction. New Orleans: School of Social Work, Tulane
University, 1962. 163p.

1637 _____, _____, and_____. "A research design and
findings in a research experiment in field instruction at
Tulane University." Education for social work; proceedings of the 1961 Annual Program Meeting, Council on
Social Work Education. New York: The Council, 1961.
149-162.

1638 Macarov, David. "Identification of factors reported by social
work students as hindering their learning in field work."
Indian Journal of Social Work, v. 26, no. 1, April 1965.
39-47.

1639 McGuire, Rita A. "Forecasting the future of field learning
and teaching." Current patterns in field instruction in
graduate social work education. Edited by Betty Lacy
Jones. New York: Council on Social Work Education,
1969. 13-20.

1640 Maurya, Moti Ram. "Field work training in social work."
Indian Journal of Social Work, v. 23, no. 1, April 1962.
2-14.

1641 Mayer, John E. and Aaron Rosenblatt. "Sources of stress
among student practitioners in social work: a sociological
view." Journal of Education for Social Work, v. 10, no. 3,
fall 1974. 56-66.

1642 Nathanson, Theresa. "Self-awareness in the educative process." Social Work, v. 7, no. 2, April 1962. 31-38.

1643 Quaranta, Mary Ann and Greta Stanton. "Planning curriculum
change in a large traditional field instruction program."
Journal of Education for Social Work, v. 9, no. 1, winter
1973. 55-67.

1644 Regensburg, Jeanette. "Report of exploratory project in
field instruction." Field instruction in graduate social work education. Compiled by the Council on
Social Work Education. New York: The Council,
1966. 23-56.

1645 Reynolds, Rosemary Ross. "Relationship of field placement
to classroom teaching from the standpoint of the supervisor." Social Casework, v. 33, no. 3, March 1952. 99-
105.

1646 Schubert, Margaret. "Curriculum policy dilemmas in field
instruction." Journal of Education for Social Work, v. 1,
no. 2, fall 1965. 35-46.

1647 _____. "The field work curriculum: a search for descriptive terms." Social Service Review, v. 42, no. 3, Sept. 1968. 297-313.

1648 _____. "A research design for research in field instruction at the University of Chicago." Education for social work; proceedings of the 1961 Annual Program Meeting, Council on Social Work Education. New York: The Council, 1961. 137-148.

1649 Selby, Lola G. "Helping students in field practice identify and modify blocks to learning." Social Service Review, v. 29, no. 1, March 1955. 53-63.

1650 Shapiro, Ben Zion. "Authenticity and control in professional education." Canadian Journal of Social Work Education, v. 2, no. 1, spring 1976. 36-43.

1651 Shulman, Lawrence. "Social systems theory in field instruction: a case example." The general systems approach. Edited by Gordon Hearn. New York: Council on Social Work Education, 1969. 37-44.

1652 Sikkema, Mildred. "A proposal for an innovation in field learning and teaching." Field instruction in graduate social work education. Compiled by the Council on Social Work Education. New York: The Council, 1966. 1-22.

1653 Simon, Bernece K. "Design of learning experiences in field instruction." Social Service Review, v. 40, no. 4, Dec. 1966. 397-409.

1654 Sterne, Richard. "The initial influence of structural variations in casework field instruction upon students' mastery of classroom knowledge." Doctoral dissertation, Washington University, 1967. 360p.

1655 Strubel, Peter and Mary Hutton. "Creative social work education: a student-designed practicum." The dynamics of field instruction: learning through doing. Compiled by the Council on Social Work Education. New York: The Council, 1975. 86-93.

1656 Torre, Elizabeth Lassiter. "An exploratory study of cognitive linkage to prior experience and the adult learner's problem-solving activities, as observed in the practicum component of graduate social work education." Doctoral dissertation, Tulane University, 1972. 251p.

1657 Vreugdenhil, Elizabeth. "Field education and the shy student." Australian Social Work, v. 29, no. 3, Sept. 1976. 5-14.

1658 Walsh, Margaret A. "Supervisory appraisal of the second-year student in field work." Social Casework, v. 41, no. 10, Dec. 1960. 530-533.

1659 Woodcock, G. D. C. "Tutor, supervisor and student: an evaluation of roles in social work training, with especial reference to new courses." British Journal of Psychiatric Social Work, v. 8, no. 3, spring 1966. 52-60.

F. FIELD INSTRUCTORS AND FIELD DIRECTOR [See also Sections III. D; VII. E, M, P, Q.]

1660 Boggs, Bessie. "Advance preparation of caseworkers for the supervision of graduate students." Journal of Social Work Process, v. 12, 1961. 57-71.

1661 Cassidy, Helen E. "Role and function of the coordinator or director of field instruction." Current patterns in field instruction in graduate social work education. Edited by Betty Lacy Jones. New York: Council on Social Work Education, 1969. 145-155.

1662 Cummerton, Joan Marie. "Expectations of social work field instructors." Doctoral dissertation, Washington University, 1970. 223p.

1663 DiPaola, Josephine. "Helping field instructors retool when a school changes its approach to the teaching of methods." Current patterns in field instruction in graduate social work education. Edited by Betty Lacy Jones. New York: Council on Social Work Education, 1969. 165-175.

1664 Fellin, Phillip A., Edwin J. Thomas and Clarice Freud. "Institutes on behavioral science knowledge for field instructors." Journal of Education for Social Work, v. 4, no. 1, spring 1968. 5-13.

1665 Garber, Ralph. "The field instructor's responsibility to his field of practice." Jewish Social Work Forum, v. 5, no. 2, fall 1968. 34-44.

1666 _____. "Role and task expectations for the part-time field instructor in social group work." Doctoral dissertation, University of Pennsylvania, 1963. 149p.

1667 Gitterman, Alex. "The faculty field instructor in social work education." The dynamics of field instruction: learning through doing. Compiled by the Council on Social Work Education. New York: The Council, 1975. 31-39.

1668 _____ . "The field instructor in social work education: a study of role strain." Doctoral dissertation, Columbia University, 1972. 211p.

1669 Irving, Howard H. "A social science approach to a problem in field instruction: the analysis of a three-part role-set." Journal of Education for Social Work, v. 5, no. 1, spring 1969. 49-56.

1670 Krop, Lois P. Developing and evaluating a performance-oriented training program for community-based faculty of a school of social work. Arlington, Va. : ERIC Document Reproduction Service, 1974. 45p. ED 100262.

1671 Landon, Lucy. A plan for orientation of incoming field instructors to an institution for the mentally retarded. New Brunswick, N. J. : School of Social Work, Rutgers University, 1965. 63p.

1672 McCall, Laura. "Manpower in field instruction: a 1970 exploration of the relationship between faculty position, faculty characteristics, and faculty movement in class and field instructors of casework who were respondents to the 1966 Council on Social Work Education survey of faculty in graduate schools of social work." Doctoral dissertation, Catholic University of America, 1972. 247p.

1673 Neustaedter, Eleanor. "Field supervisor as educator." Social work as human relations; anniversary papers of the New York School of Social Work and the Community Service Society. New York: Columbia University Press, 1949. 127-139.

1674 Selby, Lola G. "The field work supervisor as educator." Education for social work. Edited by Eileen L. Younghusband. London: Allen & Unwin, 1968. 152-166.

1675 Timberlake, Elizabeth March. "Career identity development of the agency-employed field instructor." Doctoral dissertation, Catholic University of America, 1974. 157p.

1676 Werner, Ruth. "The director of field work--Administrator and educator." Current patterns in field instruction in graduate social work education. Edited by Betty Lacy Jones. New York: Council on Social Work Education, 1969. 157-164.

1677 Zimmerman, Jerome. Experimentation with short term preparation for a teaching role: social work education. New Orleans: School of Social Work, Tulane University, 1971. 83p.

G.   GROUP SUPERVISION AND STUDENT UNIT [See also Section
VII. R.]

1678   Bernstein, Saul. Group supervision of social work students;
workshop report of the 1961 Annual Program Meeting,
Council on Social Work Education. New York: The Council, 1962. 40p.

1679   Cowan, Barbara, et al. "Group supervision as a teaching/
learning modality in social work." Social Worker-Travai-
lleur-Social, v. 40, no. 4, Dec. 1972. 256-261.

1680   Curnock, Kathleen. Student units in social work education.
London: Central Council for Education and Training in
Social Work, 1975. 116p.

1681   Ferns, Valda.   "The group method in supervising students. "   Australian Social Work, v. 29, no. 1, March
1976.   49-56.

1682   Harper, John. "Group supervision of students. " Social Work
(London), v. 26, no. 4, Oct. 1969. 18-22.

1683   Herington, Winnifred. "An experimental field practice unit:
a report of two years' experience. " Social Work Education Reporter, v. 20, no. 1, Dec. -Jan. 1972. 64-66.

1684   Holmes, Barbara, Richard Bryant and Donald Houston.   "Student unit in community work: an experimental approach. "
Social Work Today, v. 4, no. 14, 18 Oct. 1973. 424-430.

1685   Jambor, Helen M.   "An experiment in group interaction as a
method of student supervision. " Journal of Psychiatric
Social Work, v. 20, no. 3, March 1951. 117-122.

1686   Khinduka, Shanti K. "Group supervision of social work students. " Indian Journal of Social Work, v. 23, no. 1, April
1962. 105-114.

1687   Kirby, Betty A. "Group field work and tutorial experience. "
Social work practice, 1970; selected papers of the 1970
Annual Forum, National Conference on Social Welfare.
New York: Columbia University Press, 1970. 178-182.

1688   Lammert, Marilyn H. and Jan Hagen.   "A model for community-oriented field experience. " The dynamics of field instruction: learning through doing. Compiled by the Council on Social Work Education. New York: The Council,
1975. 60-67.

1689   McNew, Emily and Anne DeYoung. "Field instruction at Mary-
wood: it's micro, macro, and modular. " Journal of Ed-

ucation for Social Work, v. 6, no. 1, spring 1970. 29-40.

1690 Mayers, Friedericka. "Differential use of group teaching in first-year field work." Social Service Review, v. 44, no. 1, March 1970. 63-75.

1691 Pavlin, Frank. "Student unit: the advantages and disadvantages of group placement." Australian Journal of Social Work, v. 22, no. 4, Dec. 1969. 10-13.

1692 Rosolen, Nelida. "Group-teaching and group-work." International Social Work, v. 14, no. 3, 1971. 26-31.

1693 Sales, Esther. Individual and group supervision in field instruction; a research report. Ann Arbor: School of Social Work, University of Michigan, 1970. 83p.

1694 Solovey, Sylvia. "Seven years' experience of centralized training for students." Dynamic approaches to serving families. Compiled by Community Service Society of New York. New York: The Society, 1970. 91-100.

1695 Underwood, Barbara Ann. "A content analysis of small group seminar discussions in first-year field instruction." Doctoral dissertation, Tulane University, 1970. 124p.

1696 Waddington, Miriam. "The student unit: some problems and psychological implications." Journal of Social Casework, v. 30, no. 3, March 1949. 113-117.

1697 Wilson, Doreen. "The role of the student unit in social work education." Social Work Today, v. 2, no. 3, 6 May 1971. 3-6.

H. INTEGRATED AND COMBINED METHODS [See also Section VI. H.]

1698 Franks, Virginia. The autonomous social worker. Madison: University of Wisconsin, 1967. 12p.

1699 Henry, Cecil St. George. "The application of generic principles and theory to the practice of generic social work in the field." Journal of Education for Social Work, v. 10, no. 1, winter 1974. 27-33.

1700 Knouff, Scotia B. "Description of the joint multi-method project: implications for in-service training in probation and graduate social work education." Social Work Education Reporter, v. 14, no. 2, June 1966. 31, 42-44.

1701   McNew, Emily and Anne DeYoung.   "Field instruction at
       Marywood: it's micro, macro, and modular."   Jour-
       nal of Education for Social Work, v. 6, no. 1, spring
       1970.   29-40.

1702   Mehta, Vera D.   "Integrated methods approach--a challenge
       possibility in field work instruction."   Indian Journal of
       Social Work.   v. 35, no. 4, Jan. 1975.   335-344.

1703   Rothman, Beulah.   "Contributions of probation to social work
       education emerging from a joint project on multi-methods."
       Social Work Education Reporter, v. 14, no. 2, June 1966.
       30, 41-42.

1704   Sirotta, Dorothy.   "The use of the combined-methods place-
       ment in field instruction."   Social Worker-Travailleur
       Social, v. 35, no. 4, Nov. 1967.   273-275.

1705   Sumner, Dorothy.   "Experiment with field work in generic
       social work."   Social Casework, v. 37, no. 6, June 1956.
       288-294.

I.   PERFORMANCE AND EVALUATION [See also Section III. E. 10.]

1706   Baker, Eric.   "Supervision and assessment: impossible--and
       inescapable."   Social Work Today, v. 6, no. 7, 26 June
       1975.   207-208.

1707   Bruck, Max.   "Relationships between student anxiety, self-
       awareness, and self-concept and student competence in
       casework."   Social Casework, v. 44, no. 3, March 1963.
       125-131.

1708   Chamberlain, Edna.   "Testing with a treatment typology."
       Australian Journal of Social Work, v. 22, no. 4, Dec. 1969.
       3-8.   Commentary by Florence Hollis.   9.

1709   Council on Social Work Education.   Student evaluation; work-
       shop report of the 1956 Annual Program Meeting.   New
       York: The Council, 1956.   46p.

1710   Crane, John A.   Interpersonal competence and performance
       in social work.   Vancouver: School of Social Work, Uni-
       versity of British Columbia, 1974.   149p.

1711   Green, Solomon H.   "The bases for judgments: a use of the
       critical-incident technique to study field instructor judg-
       ments of the performance of first-year casework students
       in their field instruction placements."   Doctoral disserta-
       tion, University of Pennsylvania, 1965.   257p.

1712 _____ . "Educational assessments of student learning through practice in field instruction." Social Work Education Reporter, v. 20, no. 3, Sept. -Oct. 1972. 48-54.

1713 _____ . "Field instructor judgments: practice expectations for casework students." Social Work (London), v. 24, no. 4, Oct. 1967. 3-11.

1714 Hepworth, Dean H. and E. Gene Shumway. "Changes in open-mindedness as a result of social work education." Journal of Education for Social Work, v. 12, no. 1, winter 1976. 56-62.

1715 Johnson, Gladys. "Advanced standing in practicum I by examination: one school's experience." Journal of Education for Social Work, v. 12, no. 3, fall 1976. 59-64.

1716 Kagan, Morris. "The field instructor's evaluation of student performance: between fact and fiction." Social Worker-Travailleur Social, v. 31, no. 3, June-July 1963. 15-25.

1717 Kelley, Nancy, Morton S. Perlmutter and G. Visweswaran. "Assessment of student performance in the field course." Current patterns in field instruction in graduate social work education. Edited by Betty Lacy Jones. New York: Council on Social Work Education, 1969. 125-134.

1718 Korbelik, John and Laura Epstein. "Evaluating time and achievement in a social work practicum." Teaching for competence in the delivery of direct services. Compiled by the Council on Social Work Education. New York: The Council, 1976. 51-59.

1719 Lechnyr, Ronald J. "Evaluation of student effectiveness." Social Work, v. 20, no. 2, March 1975. 148-150.

1720 Logan, Frances Walker. "Development and testing of an improved method of measuring first-year field work performance of social group work students." Doctoral dissertation, University of Pennsylvania, 1965. 184p.

1721 Merrifield, Aleanor, Jan Linfield and Edythe Jastram. A standard for measuring the minimum acceptable level of performance in first-year field work in social work. Chicago: School of Social Service Administration, University of Chicago, 1964. 36p.

1722 Millard, D. W. "The examination of students' field-work." Social Work Today, v. 3, no. 14, 19 Oct. 1972. 13-16.

1723 Rankin, Geoffrey. "Supervision and assessments: science, art, therapy, or mumbo-jumbo." Social Work Today, v. 5, no. 8, 11 July 1974. 246.

1724 Reynolds, Rosemary Ross. Evaluating the field work of students. New York: Family Service Association of America, 1946. 58p.

1725 Schubert, Margaret. Assessment of social work student performance in field work. Minneapolis: School of Social
Work, University of Minnesota, 1966. 14p.

1726 _____. "Field work performance: achievement levels of
first-year students in selected aspects of casework service." Social Service Review, v. 32, no. 2, June 1968.
120-137.

1727 _____. "Field work performance: repetition of a study
of first-year casework performance." Social Service Review, v. 34, no. 3, Sept. 1960. 286-299.

1728 _____. "Field work performance: suggested criteria for
grading." Social Service Review, v. 32, no. 3, Sept. 1958.
247-257.

1729 _____. "Field work performance: the quality of the student's casework service at the end of the first year in a
public assistance setting." Doctoral dissertation, University of Chicago, 1958. 136p.

1730 Strean, Herbert Samuel. "Role expectations of first-semester
casework students and their field work instructors." Doctoral dissertation, Columbia University, 1968. 370p.

1731 _____. "Role expectations of students and teachers in a
graduate school of social work: their relationship to the
students' performance." Applied Social Studies, v. 3, no.
2, May 1971. 117-122.

1732 Wilson, Doreen. "Supervision and assessment: education or
injustice?" Social Work Today, v. 6, no. 7, 26 June 1975.
206-207.

J.   PLACEMENT SETTINGS [See also Section VII. R.]

1733 Brewer, Jack L. Working with older people--A field placement
program for second-year graduate social work students.
San Diego, Calif. : Graduate School of Social Work, San
Diego State College, 1970. 20p.

1734 Bristow, Thomas C. , Jr. "Field placement in Williamsburg
County." Arete, v. 2, no. 1, spring 1972. 31-41.

1735 Cowan, Barbara and Frank J. Turner. "Overseas field place-
      ment: an educational experiment." Journal of Education
      for Social Work, v. 11, no. 2, spring 1975. 18-24.

1736 "Field instruction placements in public welfare agencies."
      Social Work Education, v. 9, no. 3, June 1961. 4-5.

1737 Ginsberg, Leon H., et al. "An experiment in overseas field
      instruction." Journal of Education for Social Work, v. 8,
      no. 2, spring 1972. 16-24.

1738 Green, Solomon H. "Seeking Jewish dimensions in field in-
      struction." Jewish Social Work Forum, v. 5, no. 1, spring
      1968. 5-19.

1739 Hawkins, Mable T. "Interdisciplinary team training: social
      work students in public school field placement settings."
      The dynamics of field instruction: learning through doing.
      Compiled by the Council on Social Work Education. New
      York: The Council, 1975. 40-49.

1740 Hudson, Katherine. "Initiating a field work placement in a
      public health setting." Social Casework, v. 45, no. 2, Feb.
      1964. 91-95.

1741 Koegler, Ronald R., Enery Reyes Williamson and Corazon
      Grossman. "Individualized educational approach to field-
      work in a community mental health center." Journal of
      Education for Social Work, v. 12, no. 2, spring 1976. 28-
      35.

1742 Kurren, Oscar and Paul Lister. "Social work internship in
      public housing: an interdisciplinary experience." Journal
      of Education for Social Work, v. 12, no. 3, fall 1976. 72-
      79.

1743 Lee, Hei-Man. "Culture learning fieldwork: an educational
      experiment for the development of intercultural understand-
      ing." Social Work Education and Development Newsletter,
      no. 15, March 1976. 10-15.

1744 Lipscomb, Nell. "The teaching-learning setting in a first-
      year field instruction program." The dynamics of field
      instruction: learning through doing. Compiled by the
      Council on Social Work Education. New York: The Coun-
      cil, 1975. 68-75.

1745 McNary, Willette. The Jefferson County field course; report
      of a four-year project in mental retardation. Madison:
      School of Social Work, University of Wisconsin, 1967. 23p.

1746 Masi, Fidelia A. "International field placements." Journal

of Education for Social Work, v. 10, no. 1, winter 1974.
55-59.

1747 Maxwell, Jean M. "New settings for field instruction: the
response of schools of social work to changing patterns
of practice and agency clientele and new developments in
field placements designed to increase student learning potential." Social Work Education Reporter, v. 14, no. 3,
Sept. 1966. 30-31, 42-43.

1748 Meyer, Rose and Virginia L. Tannar. "The use of the public assistance setting for field practice." Social Work, v.
4, no. 3, July 1959. 35-40.

1749 Monk, Abraham and Fred Newdom. "The outposting method
of community services: a multistaged field experience."
Journal of Education for Social Work, v. 12, no. 3, fall
1976. 88-94.

1750 Roberts, Gary. "Field work in community organizations for
the deaf." Journal of Rehabilitation of the Deaf, v. 6, no.
2, Oct. 1972. 73-75.

1751 Rooney, Herbert L., et al. "The field work student as a
volunteer: an added dimension in social work education."
Social Work Education Reporter, v. 15, no. 4, Dec. 1967.
51, 55.

1752 Schubert, Margaret and Dorothy Pettes. "Selection of field
settings for casework students." Social Service Review,
v. 32, no. 4, Dec. 1958. 362-373.

1753 Sedio, Edward, Gordon Nelson and Beulah Compton. "Social
work student placement in a probation setting." NPPA
Journal, v. 2, no. 3, July 1956. 233-238.

1754 Shannon, Ruth. "Developing a framework for field work instruction in a public assistance agency." Social Casework,
v. 43, no. 7, July 1962. 355-360.

1755 Waite, Eloise B. "Red Cross as a community organization
field work agency." Social Work Education Reporter, v.
18, no. 1, March 1970. 55-58, 62-63.

1756 Wallace, Joan S. "Black studies and social work education:
new life styles for social workers." Journal of Black
Studies, v. 6, no. 2, Dec. 1975. 208-216.

1757 Watkins, Ted R. "The comprehensive community health center as a field placement for graduate social work students."
Community Mental Health Journal, v. 11, no. 1, spring
1975. 27-32.

1758 Wilbur, Mary. "Training of social work students in a narco-
tics treatment center: an impressionistic study." Drug
Forum, v. 1, no. 4, July 1972. 417-425.

K. RECORDING

1759 Desai, M. M. "Student recording in field work supervision."
Indian Journal of Social Work, v. 35, no. 4, Jan. 1975.
345-352.

1760 Dwyer, Margaret and Martha Urbanowski. "Student process
recording: a plea for structure." Social Casework, v.
46, no. 5, May 1965. 283-286.

1761 Feldman, Yonata. "Student training needs as reflected in
their recorded material." Smith College Studies in Social Work, v. 27, no. 2, Feb. 1957. 103-114.

1762 Holden, William. "Process recording." Social Work Education Reporter, v. 20, no. 1, Dec. -Jan. 1972. 67-69.

1763 Rose, Sheldon D. "Student perceptiveness--A content analysis
of process recording." Social Work Forum, v. 1, no. 1,
Jan. 1963. 6-10.

1764 Sytz, Florence. "Teaching recording." Social Casework, v.
30, no. 10, Dec. 1949. 399-405.

L. RESEARCH [See also Section VI. G.]

1765 Brenner, Melvin N. "The research field placement in social
work." Social Work Education Reporter, v. 21, no. 2,
April-May 1973. 31-34.

1766 Moore, Dorothy E. "Help Line: an integrated field-research
learning experience." The dynamics of field instruction:
learning through doing. Compiled by the Council on Social
Work Education. New York: The Council, 1975. 76-85.

1767 Schwartz, Saya S. "Field work for research students in public welfare agency." Compass, v. 21, no. 1, Oct. 1939.
7-9, 17-19.

M. SCHOOL-FIELD AGENCY RELATIONSHIP [See also Section III.
C. 2.]

1768 Borsuk, Howard W. "Agency-school communication: the influence of changing patterns of education." Current patterns in field instruction in graduate social work education. Edited by Betty Lacy Jones. New York: Council on Social Work Education, 1969. 51-59.

1769 Cassie, Louis and Elizabeth Ruiz. "'Them' and 'Us'--Mutuality as a theme in field settings." Social Work in Atlantic Canada, v. 1, 1975. 73-80.

1770 Council on Social Work Education. Agency board, executive and supervisory support conducive to productive field instruction; workshop report of the 1962 Annual Program Meeting. New York: The Council, 1962. 8p.

1771 _____. The future for field instruction: agency-school commitment and communication; three papers presented by Tybel Bloom, Robert M. Mulford, Sidney Berengarten and minutes of 11th Annual Meeting of the House of Delegates, Jan. 1963. New York: The Council, 1963. 24p.

1772 Dana, Bess S. "The role of national agencies in stimulating the improvement and expansion of field instruction resources; conference highlights." Field instruction in graduate social work education. Compiled by the Council on Social Work Education. New York: The Council, 1966. 57-68.

1773 Daniel, Patricia. "Fieldwork training--responsibilities of the agency." Case Conference, v. 14, no. 1, May 1967. 11-15.

1774 Gangrade, K. D. "School of social work--field work agency liaison." Indian Journal of Social Work, v. 35, no. 4, Jan. 1975. 353-357.

1775 Krop, Lois P. Developing and implementing effective modes of communication between the school of social work and agency-based faculty. Arlington, Va.: ERIC Document Reproduction Service, 1974. 52p. ED 100265.

1776 Nolan, Lydia Glover. "Faculty consultant in relation to supervisor and agency." Social Casework, v. 35, no. 2, Feb. 1954. 62-68.

1777 Olds, Victoria, editor. School-agency partnership in field instruction; proceedings of meetings with agency executives and field instructors, 1960-1961. Washington, D. C.: School of Social Work, Howard University, 1961. 86p.

1778 Sentman, Lois. "Some observations on role of the faculty representative in field work." Social Service Review, v. 23, no. 3, Sept. 1949. 337-346.

1779 Wineman, David and Adrienne James. "The advocacy challenge to schools of social work." Social Work, v. 14, no.
 2, April 1969. 23-32.

N. SOCIAL CASEWORK [See also Section VI. B.]

1780 Anderson, Mary E. , et al. "The content of first-year field
 work in a casework setting, part I: The orientation process." Social Casework, v. 34, no. 2, Feb. 1953. 61-
 67; "...part II: Basic knowledge and skills." Social
 Casework, v. 34, no. 3, March 1953. 112-119.

1781 Berkowitz, Sidney J. "Field training experiment with two
 first year students." Social Casework, v. 36, no. 1, Jan.
 1955. 33-35.

1782 Boyer, Ruth Gasink. "Identification of operative objectives
 of field instruction in casework for first semester, first
 year students at the National Catholic School of Social
 Service, 1962-1963." Doctoral dissertation, Catholic
 University of America, 1966. 141p.

1783 Caudell, Norman L. "Medical social work students and ma-
 trimonial casework." Medical Social Work, v. 21, no. 7,
 Nov. 1968. 205-210.

1784 Chicago. University. School of Social Service Administration. Guide to the content of second-year field teaching
 in casework. Chicago: The School, 1961. 42p.

1785 Dover, Frances T. Field instruction in casework, a report
 on a student training unit in casework. New York: Jewish
 Guild for the Blind, 1962. 104p.

1786 Duncan, Minna Green. "Experiment in applying new methods
 in field work." Social Casework, v. 44, no. 4, April 1963.
 179-184.

1787 Elmer, Elizabeth. "Mental health emphasis in casework field
 instruction." Social Work, v. 7, no. 3, July 1962. 77-83.

1788 Family Service Association of America. Techniques of student and staff supervision; reprinted from Social Casework.
 New York: The Association, 1962. 80p.

1789 Finestone, Samuel. "Scientific component in the casework
 field curriculum." Social Casework, v. 36, no. 5, May
 1955. 195-202.

1790 Golden, Kenneth M. "Client transfer and student social workers." Social Work, v. 21, no. 1, Jan. 1976. 65-66.

1791 Goldstein, Harris K. "A determination and description of some elemental task requirements of social casework as found in the field practice of third semester social casework students." Doctoral dissertation, Washington University, 1957. 149p.

1792 _____. "Some task-originated requirements found in student casework practice." Social Work, v. 3, no. 3, July 1958. 104-108.

1793 Green, Judy Kopp and William R. Morrow. "Precision social work: general model and illustrative student projects with clients." Journal of Education for Social Work, v. 8, no. 3, fall 1972. 19-29.

1794 Hannon, Eleanor Mary. "Shared experience: student and client learn about each other." Social Casework v. 49, no. 3, March 1968. 156-160.

1795 Holtzman, Reva Fine. "Major teaching methods in field instruction in casework." Doctoral dissertation, Columbia University, 1966. 278p.

1796 Howarth, Elizabeth. "An introduction to casework supervision." Case Conference, v. 8, no. 6, Nov. 1961. 159-163.

1797 Joelson, Jack Bernard. "The effects of optimism on the prognostic judgments of second-year casework students." Doctoral dissertation, University of Pittsburgh, 1968. 177p.

1798 Kadushin, Alfred. "Interview observation as a teaching device." Social Casework, v. 37, no. 7, July 1956. 334-341.

1799 Kohn, Regina. "Differential use of the observed interview in student training." Social Work Education Reporter, v. 19, no. 3, Sept. -Oct. 1971. 45-46.

1800 Large, Dorothy. "Four processes of field instruction in casework: the field instructor's contribution to instructor-student interaction in second-year field work." Social Service Review, v. 37, no. 3, Sept. 1963. 263-273.

1801 Leyendecker, Gertrude. "A family agency reviews its educational program." Social Casework, v. 44, no. 4, April 1963. 185-192.

1802 Marcus, Grace. "How case work training may be adapted to meet the worker's personal problems." Mental Hygiene, v. 11, no. 3, July 1927. 449-459.

1803 Pearlman, Lou W. , Jerome Hammerman and Sheldon S. To-
       bin. Social casework--Field work training in a geriatric
       institutional setting: review of a five-year experience.
       Chicago: American Public Welfare Association, 1968.
       16p.

1804 Robinson, Virginia Pollard. Dynamics of supervision under
       functional controls: a professional process in social case-
       work. Philadelphia: University of Pennsylvania Press,
       1949. 154p.

1805 _____. "Educational problems in preparation for social
       casework. " Mental Hygiene, v. 14, no. 4, Oct. 1930.
       828-836.

1806 _____. Supervision in social case work, a problem in
       professional education. Chapel Hill: University of North
       Carolina Press, 1936. 199p.

1807 _____, editor. Training for skill in social case work.
       Philadelphia: University of Pennsylvania Press, 1942.
       126p.

1808 Rubin, Gerald K. "Termination of casework: the student,
       client and field instructor. " Journal of Education for So-
       cial Work, v. 4, no. 1, spring 1968. 65-69.

1809 Ryan, Francis J. and Donald R. Bardill. "Joint interviewing
       by field instructor and student. " Social Casework, v. 45,
       no. 8, Oct. 1964. 471-474.

1810 Schlesinger, Rosa, et al. "Using policy in teaching casework
       principles to field work students. " Public Welfare, v. 15,
       no. 1, Jan. 1957. 21-24.

1811 Schubert, Margaret. Field instruction in social casework; a
       report of an experiment. Chicago: School of Social Ser-
       vice Administration, University of Chicago, 1963. 242p.

1812 _____ and Dorothy Pettes. "Selection of field settings for
       casework students. " Social Service Review, v. 32, no. 4,
       Dec. 1958. 362-373.

1813 Sikkema, Mildred. "The objectives of field work in social
       casework, 1898-1955. " Doctoral dissertation, University
       of Chicago, 1965. 229p.

1814 Urdang, Esther. "Educational project for first-year students
       in a field placement. " Social Casework, v. 45, no. 1, Jan.
       1964. 10-15.

1815 _____. "An experiment in teaching social work tasks. "

Social Casework, v. 47, no. 7, July 1966. 451-455.

1816 Wells, Richard A. "The use of joint field instructor-student participation in casework treatment as a teaching method." Social Work Education Reporter, v. 19, no. 1, Dec. -Jan. 1971. 58-62.

O. SOCIAL GROUP WORK [See also Section VI. C.]

1817 Abels, Paul. "New settings for group work: on a clear day." Current patterns in field instruction in graduate social work education. Edited by Betty Lacy Jones. New York: Council on Social Work Education, 1969. 45-50.

1818 Benschoter, Reba Ann, Charles Garetz and Pringle Smith. "The use of closed circuit TV and videotape in the training of social group workers." Social Work Education Reporter, v. 15, no. 1, March 1967. 18-19, 30.

1819 Garber, Ralph. "Role and task expectations for the part-time field instructor in social group work." Doctoral dissertation, University of Pennsylvania, 1963. 149p.

1820 Golden, Irwin. "Teaching a model of group work skill: a field instructor's report." Journal of Education for Social Work, v. 2, no. 2, fall 1966. 30-39.

1821 Kolodny, Ralph L. and John J. Tretton. "Students and new workers: an additional perspective on the use of groups in public welfare." Public Welfare, v. 29, no. 3, summer 1971. 320-327.

1822 McGuire, Rita A. "The group work field instructor-in-action: a study of field instruction using the critical incident technique." Doctoral dissertation, Columbia University, 1963. 188p.

1823 Somers, Mary Louise and Paul Gitlin. "Innovations in field instruction in social group work." Journal of Education for Social Work, v. 2, no. 1, spring 1966. 52-58.

P. STUDENT-INSTRUCTOR RELATIONSHIP [See also Sections VII. E, Q.]

1824 Connaway, Ronda S. "Some notes on field instruction as process." Brown Studies, 1965. 96-102.

1825 Kagan, Morris. "A study of selected dimensions of the field instructor-student relationship." Doctoral dissertation, University of Minnesota, 1968. 201p.

1826 MacGuffie, Robert A., Frederick V. Janzen and William M. McPhee. "The expression and perception of feelings between students and supervisors in a practicum setting." Counselor Education and Supervision, v. 9, no. 4, summer 1970. 263-271.

1827 Moffatt, R. A. "The student-supervisor relationship in social work education." Australian Journal of Social Work, v. 22, no. 3, Sept. 1969. 27-33.

1828 Murdaugh, Jessica. "Student supervision unbound." Social Work, v. 19, no. 2, March 1974. 131-132.

1829 Rose, Sheldon D., Jane Lowenstein and Phillip Fellin. "Measuring student perception of field instruction." Current patterns in field instruction in graduate social work education. Edited by Betty Lacy Jones. New York: Council on Social Work Education, 1969. 135-144.

1830 _____. "Students view their supervision: a scale analysis." Social Work, v. 10, no. 2, spring 1965. 90-96.

1831 Rosenblatt, Aaron and John E. Mayer. "Objectionable supervisory styles: students' views." Social Work, v. 20, no. 3, May 1975. 184-189.

1832 Starak, Igor. "Student dependence and independence in field instruction." Social Worker-Travailleur Social, v. 38, no. 1, Feb. 1970. 24, 29-31.

1833 Strean, Herbert Samuel. "Role expectations of first-semester casework students and their field work instructor." Doctoral dissertation, Columbia University, 1968. 370p.

1834 _____. "Role expectations of students and teachers in a graduate school of social work: their relationship to the students' performance." Applied Social Studies, v. 3, no. 2, May 1971. 117-122.

1835 Texas. University. Graduate School of Social Work. The field instructor-student relationship in social work. Austin, Tex.: The School, 1964. 93p.

Q. SUPERVISION [See also Sections VII. E, F, G, P.]

1836 Austin, Lucille N. "Basic principles of supervision." Social Casework, v. 33, no. 10, Dec. 1952. 411-419.

1837   Bishop, Julia Ann. "The agency's role in field supervision
        of social work students." Journal of Social Work Process,
        v. 10, 1959. 27-34.

1838   Crawford, Blaine. "Use of color charts in supervision." So-
        cial Casework, v. 52, no. 4, April 1971. 220-222.

1839   Foster, Marjorie W. "Agency supervision of students." Child
        Welfare, v. 36, no. 6, June 1957. 10-16.

1840   Garrett, Annette. "Learning through supervision." Smith
        College Studies in Social Work, v. 24, no. 2, Feb. 1954.
        109p.

1841   George, K. N. and N. Subramanian. "The concept of rela-
        tionship in field-work supervision." Social Work Forum,
        v. 1, no. 1, Jan. 1963. 31-33.

1842   Haan, Pieterdiena M. "A study of the activity of the
        supervisor of group work students in the first year of
        advanced social work education in the Netherlands."
        Doctoral dissertation, University of Pennsylvania, 1974.
        229p.

1843   Hammond, Pauline H. "Supervision in professional develop-
        ment." British Journal of Psychiatric Social Work, v. 8,
        no. 2, autumn 1965. 37-45.

1844   Howarth, Elizabeth. "An introduction to casework supervi-
        sion." Case Conference, v. 8, no. 6, Nov. 1961. 159-
        163.

1845   Hunt, Marguerite. "Field work supervision of graduate stu-
        dents." Child Welfare, v. 36, no. 6, June 1957. 6-9.

1846   Kadushin, Alfred. "Games people play in supervision." So-
        cial Work, v. 13, no. 3, July 1968. 23-32.

1847   Kennedy, Miriam and Lydia Keitner. "What is supervision--
        The need for a redefinition." Social Worker-Travailleur
        Social, v. 38, no. 1, Feb. 1970. 50-52.

1848   Kent, Bessie. Social work supervision in practice. New York:
        Pergamon Press, 1969. 159p.

1849   Khinduka, Shanti. "The role of supervision in social work ed-
        ucation." Indian Journal of Social Work, v. 24, no. 3, Oct.
        1963. 169-180.

1850   Mathew, Grace. "Educational and helping aspects of field
        work supervision." Indian Journal of Social Work, v. 35,
        no. 4, Jan. 1975. 325-333.

1851 Nelsen, Judith C. "Early communication between field instructors and casework students." Doctoral dissertation,
Columbia University, 1973. 427p.

1852 _____. "Teaching content of early fieldwork conferences."
Social Casework, v. 55, no. 3, March 1974. 147-153.

1853 Pathak, S. H. "Supervision in social work: historical development and current trends." Indian Journal of Social
Work, v. 35, no. 4, Jan. 1975. 317-323.

1854 Patterson, Charles M. and William H. Clayton. "One-to-one
method of field work training." Social Casework, v. 42,
no. 4, April 1961. 180-183.

1855 Pettes, Dorothy E. Supervision in social work; a method of
student training and staff development. London: Allen &
Unwin, 1967. 180p.

1856 Rapoport, Lydia. "The role of supervision in professional
education." Health Education Monographs, no. 15.
New York: Society of Public Health Educators, 1963.
3-15.

1857 Raymond, Frank B. "Consultation as a mode of field instruction." Journal of Sociology and Social Welfare, v. 3, no.
5, May 1976. 565-577.

1858 Reynolds, Bertha Capen. "The art of supervision." Family,
v. 17, no. 4, June 1936. 103-107.

1859 Robinson, Virginia Pollard. Dynamics of supervision under
functional controls: a professional process in social casework. Philadelphia: University of Pennsylvania, 1949.
154p.

1860 St. John, David. "Goal-directed supervision of social work
students in field placement." Journal of Education for
Social Work, v. 11, no. 3, fall 1975. 89-94.

1861 Sarnat, Rhoda Gerard. "Supervision of the experienced student." Social Casework, v. 33, no. 4, April 1952. 147-
152.

1862 Smalley, Ruth E. "Some elements of supervision in school
social work." Helping the troubled school child. Edited
by Grace Lee. New York: National Association of Social
Workers, 1959. 420-429.

1863 Thangavelu, R. "Field work supervision: its place in social
work education." Indian Journal of Social Work, v. 35,
no. 4, Jan. 1975. 359-366.

1864 Towle, Charlotte. "The place of help in supervision." Social Service Review, v. 37, no. 4, Dec. 1963. 403-415.

1865 _____. "Role of supervision in the union of cause and function in social work." Social Service Review, v. 36, no. 4, Dec. 1962. 396-407. Comments by Mazie F. Rappaport and C. Wilson Anderson. 407-411.

1866 Travis, Georgia. "Notes on supervision." Australian Journal of Social Work, v. 22, no. 2, June 1969. 19-42.

1867 Woodcock, G. D. C. "A study of beginning supervision." British Journal of Psychiatric Social Work, v. 9, no. 2, autumn 1967. 66-74.

1868 Young, Priscilla H. The student and supervision in social work education. New York: Humanities Press, 1967. 113p.

R. TEACHING AND SERVICE CENTERS

1869 Abels, Paul. "New settings for group work: on a clear day." Current patterns in field instruction in graduate social work education. Edited by Betty Lacy Jones. New York: Council on Social Work Education, 1969. 45-50.

1870 Aptekar, Herbert H. "Differentiating types of knowledge introduced in the classroom and teaching centers." Modes of professional education: functions of field instruction in the curriculum; report of a symposium, 1969, New Orleans. Edited by Helen Cassidy. New Orleans: School of Social Work, Tulane University, 1969. 79-94.

1871 Briar, Scott. "Teaching center design as a function of curriculum objectives." Modes of professional education: functions of field instruction in the curriculum; report of a symposium, 1969, New Orleans. Edited by Helen Cassidy. New Orleans: School of Social Work, Tulane University, 1969. 69-78.

1872 Brieland, Donald. "Broadening the knowledge base through a social services center." Modes of professional education: functions of field instruction in the curriculum; report of a symposium, 1969, New Orleans. Edited by Helen Cassidy. New Orleans: School of Social Work, Tulane University, 1969. 106-121.

1873 _____. "A social services center for a multi-problem community." Social Work Education Reporter, v. 15, no. 3, Sept. 1967. 30-32, 41.

1874   Finestone, Samuel.   "Field teaching and knowledge develop-
       ment."   Modes of professional education: functions of
       field instruction in the curriculum; report of a symposium,
       1969, New Orleans.   Edited by Helen Cassidy.   New Or-
       leans, School of Social Work, Tulane University, 1969.
       122-130.

1875   Johnston, Janet R.   "New methods of field instruction in the
       U. S. A.--An overview."   Australian Social Work, v. 26,
       no. 1, March 1973.   5-10.

1876   Kindelsperger, Kenneth W.   "Emerging structure and objec-
       tives of teaching centers: Kent School of Social Work."
       Modes of professional education: functions of field instruc-
       tion in the curriculum; report of a symposium, 1969, New
       Orleans.   Edited by Helen Cassidy.   New Orleans: School
       of Social Work, Tulane University, 1969.   22-35.

1877   Kindelsperger, Walter L. and Helen E. Cassidy.   Social work
       training centers: tentative analysis of the structure and
       learning environment.   New Orleans: School of Social
       Work, Tulane University, 1966.   27p.

1878   Knappe, Mildred E.   "The training center concept: educating
       social workers for a changing world."   The dynamics of
       field instruction: learning through doing.   Compiled by
       the Council on Social Work Education.   New York: The
       Council, 1975.   50-59.

1879   Lieberman, Lucile.   "The social services center: an exper-
       iment in education and community service."   Social Work
       Education Reporter, v. 17, no. 4, Dec. 1969.   46-47, 60.

1880   Meyer, Carol H.   "Integrating practice demands in social
       work education."   Social Casework, v. 49, no. 8, Oct. 1968.
       481-486.   Discussion by Mary B. Baker, 486-488.

VIII. DOCTORAL DEGREE AND
POST-MASTER'S EDUCATION

[See also Sections III. A; XII.]

1881   Aptekar, Herbert H.   Relevant knowledge in advance education
       for social work.   Waltham, Mass. :   Florence Heller
       School for Advanced Study in Social Welfare, Brandeis
       University, n. d.   21p.

1882   Baldi, John J.   "Doctorates in social work, 1920-1968. "   Jour-
       nal of Education for Social Work, v. 7, no. 1, winter 1971.
       11-22.

1883   Beckerman, Aaron Harry.   "Basic Literature in Social Re-
       search: an exploration of issues. "   Jewish Social Work
       Forum, v. 11, spring 1975.   73-84.

1884   Bolte, Gordon L.   "Current trends in doctoral programs in
       schools of social work in the United States and Canada. "
       Doctoral students look at social work education.   Edited
       by Leila Calhoun Deasy.   New York: Council on Social
       Work Education, 1971.   109-126.

1885   Burns, Eveline M.   "The doctoral program: progress and
       problems. "   Social Service Review, v. 26, no. 4, Dec.
       1952.   387-398.

1886   Burns, Mary E.   "Criteria for selection of students for ad-
       vanced study. "   Social Work Education Reporter, v. 13,
       no. 2, June 1965.   12-13, 25-26.

1887   _____.   "Paths to knowledge: some prospects and prob-
       lems. "   Journal of Education for Social Work, v. 1, no. 1,
       spring 1965.   13-17.

1888   _____.   "Social science content in doctoral programs. "
       Social Work Education Reporter, v. 13, no. 3, Sept. 1965.
       16-17, 34.

1889   Council on Social Work Education.   The advanced curriculum
       in social work education; workshop report of the 1956
       Annual Program Meeting.   New York: The Council, 1956.
       21p.

1890 _____. Social work education in the post-Master's pro-
gram--no. 1. Guiding principles. New York, The Council, 1953. 70p.

1891 _____. Social work education in the post-Master's pro-
gram--no. 2. Approaches to curriculum content. New
York: The Council, 1954. 81p.

1892 _____. Social Work education in the post-Master's pro-
gram--no. 3. Field work and related issues. New York:
The Council, 1953. 80p.

1893 Crow, Richard T. and Kenneth W. Kindelsperger. "The PhD
or the DSW?" Journal of Education for Social Work, v.
11, no. 3, fall 1975. 38-43.

1894 Deasy, Leila Calhoun. "Student and professor in the doctoral
program." Journal of Social Work Process, v. 15, 1966.
153-173.

1895 Germain, Carel. "Teaching an ecological perspective for social work practice." Teaching for competence in the delivery of direct services. Compiled by the Council on
Social Work Education. New York: The Council, 1976.
31-39.

1896 Gil, David G. "Implications for doctoral programs of an
examination of the concept of motivation." Education for
social work with "unmotivated" clients; proceedings of an
institute, Brandeis University, 1965. Waltham, Mass.:
Florence Heller Graduate School for Advanced Studies in
Social Welfare, Brandeis University, 1965. 198-211.

1897 Green, Rose and Maurice B. Hamovitch. "Education of social workers for mental health consultation." American
Journal of Orthopsychiatry, v. 32, no. 2, March 1962.
225-226.

1898 Green, Solomon H. "Jewish Identity Seminar: culture, commitment, service." Jewish Social Work Forum, v. 11,
spring 1975. 53-64.

1899 Levitt, Louis. "Toward an understanding of the theoretical
foundations of social work." Jewish Social Work Forum,
v. 11, spring 1975. 44-52.

1900 Levy, Charles S. "Learning and teaching ideology." Jewish
Social Work Forum, v. 11, spring 1975. 15-25.

1901 Loewenberg, Frank M. Doctoral students in schools of social
work. New York: Council on Social Work Education,
1972. 94p.

1902 Lyndon, Benjamin H. "The future of master's and doctoral programs in social work education." Undergraduate social work education for practice: a report on curriculum content and issues. Edited by Lester J. Glick. Washington, D. C.: Government Printing Office, 1972. 117-123.

1903 Marks, Rachel Bryant. "An examination of applications for admissions to programs of advanced education: analysis and interpretation." Social Work Education Reporter, v. 13, no. 1, March 1965. 6-7, 15.

1904 Parad, Howard J. and Lydia Rapoport. "Advanced social work educational programs in community mental health." Handbook of community mental health. Edited by Stuart E. Golann and Carl Eisdorfer. New York: Appleton-Century-Crofts, 1972. 873-887.

1905 _____ and _____. "Advanced social work educational programs in community mental health: a summary report." Social Work Education Reporter, v. 20, no. 2, April-May 1972. 57-61.

1906 "A proposed curriculum with a practice emphasis in doctoral programs." Social Work Education Reporter, v. 14, no. 3, Sept. 1966. 33-36, 41.

1907 Rapoport, Lydia and Robert Z. Apte. "Advanced education for practice in community mental health." Social Work Education Reporter, v. 16, no. 1, Dec. 1968. 24-28, 65.

1908 Regensburg, Jeanette, editor. Some educational patterns in doctoral programs in schools of social work. New York: Council on Social Work Education, 1966. 120p.

1909 Rosen, Aaron. "Doctoral education, professional culture and development of social work knowledge." Applied Social Studies, v. 1, no. 3, Oct. 1969. 151-159.

1910 Sacks, Joel G. "The strategy of research instruction in the doctoral program." Jewish Social Work Forum, v. 11, spring 1975. 26-37.

1911 Sales, Esther. "The doctoral student experience: a preliminary study." Journal of Education for Social Work, v. 11, no. 2, spring 1975. 102-108.

1912 Scher, Bernhard. "Future directions of the social work curriculum--Doctoral programs." Curriculum building for the continuum in social welfare education. Edited by Michael J. Austin, et al. Tallahassee, Fla.: State University System of Florida, 1972. 71-76.

1913 Setleis, Lloyd. "The doctoral program: rationale and de-
      velopment." Jewish Social Work Forum, v. 11, spring
      1975. 7-14.

1914 _____. "Patterns of practice seminar: development and
      discovery." Jewish Social Work Forum, v. 11, spring
      1975. 38-43.

1915 Shapiro, Iris. "An analytic assessment of recent graduates
      of social work doctoral programs: lessons for model build-
      ing." Doctoral dissertation, Catholic University of Amer-
      ica, 1973. 204p.

1916 Siporin, Max. "Doctoral education for direct-service practice
      in social work." Journal of Education for Social Work,
      v. 9, no. 3, fall 1973. 78-86.

1917 Turner, Frank J. "Some observations on the doctoral degree
      in social work." Social Worker-Travailleur Social, v. 37,
      no. 3, July 1969. 197-202.

1918 Weisman, Celia B. "From the 'Urban Crisis' to 'Urban Con-
      dition.'" Jewish Social Work Forum, v. 11, spring 1975.
      65-72.

1919 Wharf, Brian. "Some further observations on the doctoral
      degree in social work." Social Worker-Travailleur So-
      cial, v. 37, no. 4, Nov. 1969. 261-263.

IX. UNDERGRADUATE SOCIAL WELFARE EDUCATION

A. GENERAL [See also Section XII.]

1920 Adams, William T. and Frank Dell'Apa, editors. Selected papers from two institutes on undergraduate education for the helping services; papers presented at Pueblo, Colorado and Pocatello, Idaho, 1965. Boulder, Colo.: Western Interstate Commission for Higher Education, 1965. 98p.

1921 Barker, Robert L., Thomas L. Briggs and Dorothy Bird Daly. Educating the undergraduate for professional social work roles. Syracuse, N.Y.: Syracuse University Press, 1971. 11p.

1922 Bisno, Herbert. The place of the undergraduate curriculum in social work education. The social work curriculum study, v.2. New York: Council on Social Work Education, 1959. 273p.

1923 Brennen, E. Clifford, et al. "Social work education: expectations for baccalaureate social workers." Public Welfare, v.34, no.3, summer 1976. 19-23.

1924 Brooks, Theodore James. "An analysis of the methods of the Detroit Urban Adult Education Institute with implications for undergraduate social work education." Doctoral dissertation, Michigan State University, 1969. 109p.

1925 Conference on Education at the Undergraduate Level for the Helping Services. Proceedings of the Conference, Manchester, New Hampshire, 1967. Durham, N.H.: New England Board of Higher Education, 1967. 139p.

1926 Council on Social Work Education. Colleges and universities with accredited undergraduate social work programs. New York: The Council, annual.

1927 _____. Continuities in undergraduate social welfare education. New York: The Council, 1969. 90p.

1928 _____. Observations on undergraduate social welfare education. New York: The Council, 1966. 36p.

1929 _____. Recent thoughts on undergraduate social welfare

179

education; three papers presented at the 1964 Annual Program Meeting, Toronto, by Mereb E. Mossman, Sue W. Spencer and John Melling. New York: The Council, 1964. 39p.

1930 _____. Social welfare content in undergraduate education; a guide to suggested content, learning experiences and organization. New York: The Council, 1962. 16p.

1931 _____. Undergraduate programs in social welfare; a guide to objectives, content, field experience, and organization. New York: The Council, 1967. 23p.

1932 _____. Undergraduate programs in social work; guidelines to curriculum, content, field instruction, and organization. New York: The Council, 1971. 27p.

1933 Cox, Cordelia. "Characteristics of undergraduate programs in social work education." Undergraduate social work education for practice: a report on curriculum content and issues. Edited by Lester J. Glick. Washington, D. C.: Government Printing Office, 1972. 7-21.

1934 Dolgoff, Ralph. "Administrative auspices for undergraduate social welfare programs: advantages and disadvantages of various alternatives." Social Work Education Reporter, v. 17, no. 3, Sept. 1969. 22-24.

1935 Fausel, Donald F. "The general practitioner in the undergraduate social welfare program." The social work general practitioner: a book of readings for the undergraduate social work major. Edited by Donald F. Fausel with assistance of Ross A. Klein. New York: MSS Information Corporation, 1973. 131-134.

1936 Feldstein, Donald. Undergraduate social work education: today & tomorrow. New York: Council on Social Work Education, 1972. 72p.

1937 Friedsam, Hiram Johnson. "Undergraduate education for social work." Social Work Education, v. 12, no. 3, June-July 1964. 7-9, 18.

1938 Galambos, Eva C. Undergraduate programs in the field of social welfare. Atlanta: Southern Regional Education Board, 1970. 36p.

1939 Goldstein, Howard. "The B. S. W. as the first professional degree: some opinions and questions." Canadian Journal of Social Work Education, v. 2, no. 1, spring 1976. 49-55.

1940 Guilford, Richard G. "A bachelor's degree in social welfare?"

Selected Biennial Round Table Conference papers: American Public Welfare Association, 1963. Washington, D. C.: The Association, 1964. 81-84.

1941 Guillot, Ellen Elizabeth. "Undergraduate education for social work." School and Society, v. 97, no. 2314, Jan. 1969. 25-27.

1942 Hales, William M., Jr. and Charles M. Hyder. "Human services: innovative education for a changing environment." Approaches to innovation in social work education. Compiled by the Council on Social Work Education. New York: The Council, 1974. 38-45.

1943 Harper, Ernest B. "The study of social work education: its significance for the undergraduate educational institutions." Social Work Journal, v. 32, no. 4, Oct. 1951. 178-183, 197.

1944 Hasan, Saiyid Zafar. "Social work education at the undergraduate level." Indian Journal of Social Work, v. 28, no. 1, April 1967. 63-69.

1945 Hollis, Ernest V. and Alice L. Taylor. "The undergraduate college in social work education." Social work education in the United States. New York: Columbia University Press, 1951. 155-209.

1946 Iberg, Lowell. "Undergraduate social welfare education--some community considerations." Public Welfare, v. 24, no. 3, July 1966. 203-207, 252.

1947 Kindelsperger, Kenneth W. An approach to the study of the public social services and its relationship to undergraduate education for social welfare. New York: Council on Social Work Education, 1956. 17p.

1948 Laughton, Charles W. "Multiple objectives in undergraduate social welfare programs: problems and issues." Journal of Education for Social Work, v. 4, no. 2, fall 1968. 43-51.

1949 Loewenberg, Frank M., editor. Essentials for undergraduate social welfare teachers. New York: Council on Social Work Education, 1969. 51p.

1950 _____. "Undergraduate education: a multi-purpose program." Public Welfare, v. 26, no. 2, April 1968. 151-154.

1951 _____. "Undergraduate social welfare education in a university: objectives and implementations." Social need and education for social welfare. Edited by Benjamin Lyndon. Syracuse, N. Y.: State University of New York, 1968. 38-44. Comments by Lowell Iberg. 45-48.

1952 Long, Margaret and Edward L. Protz, editors. Issues in planning for undergraduate social welfare education. Atlanta: Southern Regional Education Board, 1969. 34p.

1953 Lyndon, Benjamin H. Graduate professional schools of social work and undergraduate social welfare education, part I: Findings. Buffalo: State University of New York, 1965. 83p.

1954 McNickle, Roma K., editor. Undergraduate social service education; papers presented at the Regional Institute on Undergraduate Social Service Education, Salt Lake City, Utah, 1965. Boulder, Colo.: Western Interstate Commission for Higher Education, 1965. 78p.

1955 McPheeters, Harold L. and Robert M. Ryan. A core of competence for baccalaureate social welfare and curriculum implications. Atlanta: Southern Regional Education Board, 1971. 145p.

1956 Madison, Bernice. Undergraduate education for social welfare. San Francisco: San Francisco State College, 1960. 145p.

1957 Malhotra, Prema and Yahia Bin Mohammed. "Social work education at undergraduate level." Social Work Forum, v. 5, no. 2, April 1967. 10-15.

1958 Merle, Sherman and Arnulf M. Pins. "Study of research needs in undergraduate programs in social welfare." Social Work Education Reporter, v. 13, no. 3, Sept. 1965. 18-20, 34.

1959 _____. Survey of undergraduate programs in social welfare: programs, faculty, students. New York: Council on Social Work Education, 1967. 74p.

1960 Minnesota Resource Center for Social Work Education. Directions for undergraduate social work education; papers by Richard Broeker, et al. Minneapolis, Minn.: The Center, 1972? Various pagings.

1961 Mohsini, S. R. "Problems of undergraduate education in social work." Social Work Forum, v. 7, no. 2, July 1969. 63-70.

1962 Mossman, Mereb E. "A critical look at the current status of undergraduate social welfare programs." Education for social work; proceedings of the 1964 Annual Program Meeting, Council on Social Work Education. New York: The Council, 1964. 139-148.

1963 Parad, Howard J. "Form and substance in social work education." Child Welfare, v. 39, no. 2, Feb. 1960. 1-5.

1964 Perretz, Edgar A. "A critical review of undergraduate education for social work." Social Worker-Travailleur Social, v. 30, no. 4, Oct. 1962. 5-14.

1965 Pettijohn, Carl G. "Undergraduate social work education." Public Welfare, v. 23, no. 3, July 1965. 155-160.

1966 Pins, Arnulf M. An overview of undergraduate education in social welfare; past issues, current developments and future potentials. New York: Council on Social Work Education, 1968. 23p.

1967 _____. "Undergraduate education in social welfare." Social welfare forum, 1967; proceedings of the National Conference on Social Welfare. New York: Columbia University Press, 1967. 147-158.

1968 Reichert, Kurt and Elizabeth Reichert. "The relationship of undergraduate programs in social welfare to inner-city concerns, racial problems, and anti-poverty activities." Social Work Education Reporter, v. 16, no. 4, Dec. 1968. 16-17, 64-65.

1969 Romanyshyn, John M. "Undergraduate education in social welfare and the problem of the 'unmotivated' clients." Education for social work with "unmotivated" clients; proceedings of an institute, Brandeis University, 1965. Waltham, Mass.: Florence Heller Graduate School for Advanced Studies in Social Welfare, Brandeis University, 1965. 184-190.

1970 _____. "The undergraduate social welfare sequence." Public Welfare, v. 22, no. 3, July 1964. 202-206, 222.

1971 Ryan, Robert M. and Amy L. Reynolds, editors. Issues in implementing undergraduate social welfare education programs; a report of a regional conference for colleges and universities of the 15 Southern states. Atlanta: Southern Regional Education Board, 1970. 45p.

1972 Scheurell, Robert P. "Expectations of the baccalaureate social worker." Iowa Journal of Social Work, v. 5, no. 2, spring 1972. 3-7.

1973 Schwartz, Paul L. "On the self-directing professional in undergraduate social work education." Approaches to innovation in social work education. Compiled by the Council on Social Work Education. New York: The Council, 1974. 75-81.

1974 Sielski, Lester M. "The changing role of undergraduate social work education in relation to the graduate program." Curriculum building for the continuum in social welfare education. Edited by Michael J. Austin, et al. Tallahassee, Fla.: State University System of Florida, 1972. 62-65.

1975 Spencer, Sue W. "The director of a graduate school of social work looks at undergraduate education." Social Work Education, v. 12, no. 2, April-May 1964. 6-10.

1976 Stamm, Alfred M. An analysis of undergraduate social work programs approved by CSWE, 1971. New York: Council on Social Work Education, 1972. 26p.

1977 Stroup, Herbert H. "Social work and undergraduate colleges." Improving College and University Teaching, v. 11, no. 4, autumn 1963. 231-233.

1978 Stubbins, Henry. "The profession's expectations of undergraduate education." Social Worker-Travailleur Social, v. 35, no. 2, May 1967. 64-70.

1979 Teague, Dutton and Dorothy P. Buck, editors. Developing programs in the helping services: field experience, methods courses, employment implications. Boulder, Colo.: Western Interstate Commission for Higher Education, 1968. 42p.

1980 Thursz, Daniel. New areas of social work for the subprofessional. Arlington, Va.: ERIC Document Reproduction Service, 1967. 18p. ED 014755.

1981 An undergraduate social work education model for the multiversity (University of Minnesota); paper presented at the 1967 American Orthopsychiatric Association Convention, Washington, D. C. Arlington, Va.: ERIC Document Reproduction Service, 1967. 16p. ED 014756.

1982 Vidaver, Robert M. and James E. Carson. "A new framework for baccalaureate careers in the human services." American Journal of Psychiatry, v. 130, no. 4, April 1973. 474-478.

1983 Vigilante, Joseph L. "Legitimating undergraduate social work education: educational-administrative considerations." Undergraduate social work education for practice: a report on curriculum content and issues. Edited by Lester J. Glick. Washington, D. C. : Government Printing Office, 1972. 124-137.

1984 Walz, Thomas H. and John C. Kidneigh. Three year study of the undergraduate pre-social work program at the University of Minnesota; final report. Minneapolis: University of Minnesota, 1969. Various pagings.

1985 Warner, Dennis A. and Harvey Doerksen. "School of applied social science: an innovation." Improving College and University Teaching, v. 23, no. 3, summer 1975. 148-149.

1986 Western Interstate Commission for Higher Education. Undergraduate education and manpower utilization in the helping services. Boulder, Colo. : The Commission, 1967. 28p.

1987 Wetzel, Harold E. "New perspectives in school-agency teamwork: the undergraduate college." Public Welfare, v. 25, no. 2, April 1967. 150-154.

1988 Wiebler, James R. "Some perspectives on social work education at the undergraduate level in Hawaii, Minnesota and 'elsewhere.'" International Social Work, v. 18, no. 1, 1975. 27-35.

1989 Wisconsin. University. School of Social Welfare-Milwaukee. Progress report on an educational experiment: the undergraduate program. Milwaukee: The School, 1967. 22p.

1990 Witte, Ernest F. "The purposes of undergraduate education for social welfare." Journal of Education for Social Work, v. 1, no. 2, fall 1965. 53-60.

1991 _____. "Training social work associates." Education for social work; proceedings of the 1963 Annual Program Meeting, Council on Social Work Education. New York: The Council, 1963. 12-24. Discussions by Phyllis Osborn, Bertram M. Beck and John M. Romanyshyn. 24-32.

B. STUDENTS

1992 Davis, Anne J. "Self-concept, occupational role expectations, and occupational choice in nursing and social work." Nursing Research, v. 18, no. 1, Jan. -Feb. 1969. 55-59.

1993 _____. "Self concept, occupational role expectations, and occupational choice in nursing and social work." Doctoral dissertation, University of California, Berkeley, 1969. 177p.

1994 Fausel, Donald F. "Undergraduate social work recruitment and retention programs for ethnic minority and disadvantaged students." Doctoral dissertation, Columbia University, 1975. 247p.

1995 Gibbons, W. Eugene. "Undergraduate social work: the influence on values of undergraduate social work education." Doctoral dissertation, University of Utah, 1974. 183p.

1996 Goode, Norma Lee Montague. "Attitudes of professional and social work value orientations in undergraduate social welfare majors: a comparative study of professionalism attitudes and social work value orientations at two levels of professional social work education." Doctoral dissertation, University of Minnesota, 1974. 208p.

1997 Gross, Gerald M. "Student advising: a process to facilitate planning, integration, and use of educational experiences." Undergraduate social work education for practice: a report on curriculum content and issues. Edited by Lester J. Glick. Washington, D. C.: Government Printing Office, 1972. 62-70.

1998 Ho, Kam-fai. "Factors predictive of successful performance in social work education." Doctoral dissertation, Columbia University, 1974. 195p.

1999 Judah, Eleanor Hannon. "Acculturation to the social work profession in baccalaureate social work education." Journal of Education for Social Work, v. 12, no. 3, fall 1976. 65-71.

2000 Kohn, Ezra Asher. "Selected characteristics of social work students and education for social work at the University of Nebraska." Doctoral dissertation, University of Nebraska, 1972. 121p.

2001 Madison, Bernice. "The recruitment potential of undergraduate education for social welfare." Social Work Education Reporter, v. 8, no. 1, February 1960. 7-11.

2002 _____. "Undergraduate social welfare majors at San Francisco State College: their social characteristics and the influence of selected variables on their continuance in the program." Social Work Education Reporter, v. 17, no. 4, Dec. 1969. 52-55.

2003 Maslany, G. W. and C. F. Wiegand. "Reliability of a procedure for selecting students into a Bachelor of Social Work program." Canadian Journal of Social Work Education, v. 1, no. 1, fall 1974. 33-45.

2004 Moore, Jean E. and Gordon Welty. "A study of alternate admissions mechanism for undergraduate social welfare." Social Work Education Reporter, v. 21, no. 2, April-May 1973. 59-64.

2005 Mullen, Edward J. Evaluating student learning: baccalaureate programs and the community college transfer student. New York: Council on Social Work Education, 1976. 40p.

2006 Nowak, Mary Jane. "Admissions standards for undergraduate social work programs." Doctoral dissertation, Catholic University of America, 1973. 198p.

2007 Okin, Tessie Bregman. "Career choice and the undergraduate social welfare major: a study." Social Work Education Reporter, v. 19, no. 3, Sept.-Oct. 1971. 51-57.

2008 _____. "The development of career decisions by undergraduate social welfare majors." Doctoral dissertation, University of Pennsylvania, 1969. 215p.

2009 Polakoff, Dorothy P. "Social work--A career for the deaf person." Journal of Rehabilitation of the Deaf, v. 6, no. 2, Oct. 1972. 61-67.

2010 Rutchick, Irene Enid and Thomas H. Walz. A pilot study of the motivation and value profiles of students in the pre-social work sequence at the University of Minnesota. Minneapolis: University of Minnesota, 1968. 62p.

2011 Silvers, Sherry L. and Thomas H. Walz. A comparative study of female pre-social work and education students at the University of Minnesota, on N-ACH, N-AFF, N-POW, N-NUR, and N-SUC as projected into the Thematic Apperception Test. Minneapolis: University of Minnesota, 1969. 47p.

2012 Sturges, Jack and Roy D. Yarbrough. Ability of social work students to determine the appropriateness of solutions to problems encountered in social work practice. Arlington, Va.: ERIC Document Reproduction Service, 1975. 25p. ED 104273.

2013 _____ and _____. "Ability of social work students to identify and formulate helpful response statements." Journal of Social Welfare, v. 2, no. 3, winter 1975. 27-39.

2014 Walz, Thomas H. and Robert Edgren. The undergraduate social work student in the multiversity: a study of demographic and background characteristics of the pre-social work student at the University of Minnesota. Minneapolis: University of Minnesota, 1969. 27p.

2015 _____ and Barbara Tingley. "The undergraduate student in a pre-social work sequence." Social Work Education Reporter, v. 15, no. 1, March 1967. 20-21, 30-31.

2016 Wirtz (Willem) Associates. A limited scale study to determine some of the motivations which guide individuals into the field of social work. Philadelphia: Careers in Social Work, 1960.

2017 Zoet, Thomas and Thomas H. Walz. A comparative study of the pre-social work student with students in the College of Education and the College of Liberal Arts. Minneapolis: University of Minnesota, 1969. 45p.

C. CURRICULUM [See also Section IX. D.]

2018 Acker, Joan. "Content for methods courses in undergraduate curricula for the helping services." Developing programs in the helping services; field experience, methods courses, employment implications. Edited by Dutton Teague and Dorothy P. Buck. Boulder, Colo.: Western Interstate Commission for Higher Education, 1968. 25-35.

2019 Andrew, Gwen. "Associate and baccalaureate degree education for social work: a tentative proposal." Journal of Education for Social Work, v. 9, no. 1, winter 1973. 3-10.

2020 Bisno, Herbert. "Projections of curricular trends." Undergraduate education and manpower utilization in the helping services. Compiled by the Western Interstate Commission for Higher Education. Boulder, Colo.: The Commission, 1967. 13-23.

2021 Brennen, E. Clifford and Morton L. Arkava. "Students view the undergraduate curriculum." Journal of Education for Social Work, v. 10, no. 3, fall 1974. 9-16.

2022 Dea, Kay L. "Issues, problems, and approaches to curriculum development." Essentials for undergraduate social welfare teachers. Edited by Frank M. Loewenberg. New York: Council on Social Work Education, 1969. 7-13.

2023 Galaway, Burt, compiler. An annotated bibliography of text books suitable for undergraduate social welfare courses. Minneapolis: Minnesota Resource Center for Social Work Education, 1972. Unpaged.

2024 Geis, Gerbert. "Liberal education and social welfare: educational choices and their consequences." Journal of Education for Social Work, v. 1, no. 1, spring 1965. 26-32.

2025 Glick, Lester J. , editor. Undergraduate social work education for practice: a report on curriculum content and
issues. Washington, D. C. : Government Printing Office,
1972. 308p.

2026 Grosser, Shirley. "Educating the 'holistic' social worker:
a perspective and approach for practice." Canadian Journal of Social Work Education, v. 1, no. 2, spring 1975.
28-37.

2027 Jaffe, Lester D. "Building an undergraduate social work research sequence: an experiment and its implications."
Journal of Jewish Communal Service, v. 42, no. 1, fall
1965. 99-108.

2028 _____. "Developing an educational sequence in social work
research." International Social Work, v. 6, no. 1, 1963.
21-26.

2029 Johnson, H. Wayne. "Electives and undergraduate social work
education in a state university." Journal of Sociology and
Social Welfare, v. 1, no. 4, summer 1974. 225-232.

2030 Katz, Arnold. "Problem oriented education: an alternative
social work curriculum." Canadian Journal of Social Work
Education, v. 1, no. 2, spring 1975. 48-56.

2031 Koprowski, Eugene J. "A dynamic role-centered approach
for developing a generic baccalaureate curriculum in the
helping services." Undergraduate education and manpower
utilization in the helping services. Compiled by the Western Interstate Commission for Higher Education. Boulder,
Colo. : The Commission, 1967. 1-11.

2032 Lafferty, Sr. Nancy Ann. "A multidimensional curriculum
innovation model developed in an undergraduate social work
program." Doctoral dissertation, Washington University,
1974. 310p.

2033 Lawrence, Richard G. , Lawrence K. Northwood and Robert
Peterson. "Study of undergraduate courses in social work
and social welfare in 55 schools." Social Work Education,
v. 10, no. 4, Aug. -Sept. 1962. 9-11.

2034 Levin, Lester I. , editor. Student participation in social welfare education; report of a conference. Atlanta: Southern
Regional Education Board, 1972. 64p.

2035 _____, editor. Teaching social welfare, v. 1: Course
content and teaching methodology. Atlanta: Southern Reg-

ional Education Board, 1971. 126p.

2036 _____, editor. Teaching social welfare, v. 3: Issues
and trends in curriculum development. Atlanta: Southern
Regional Education Board, 1971. 118p.

2037 Loewenberg, Frank M. "Designing an undergraduate social
welfare program for the nineteen seventies." Continuities
in undergraduate social welfare education. Compiled by
the Council on Social Work Education. New York: The
Council, 1969. 51-59.

2038 _____. "Questions about curriculum content and organization." Essentials for undergraduate social welfare teachers. Edited by Frank M. Loewenberg. New York: Council on Social Work Education, 1969. 1-6.

2039 _____ and Ralph Dolgoff. Teaching of practice skills in
undergraduate programs in social welfare and other helping services. New York: Council on Social Work Education, 1971. 88p.

2040 Macarov, David. "Developing an educational sequence in social group work." International Social Work, v. 6, no. 1,
Jan. 1963. 13-20.

2041 McLean, Ann L. and Joan F. Robertson. "Systematic integration of consumer input into curriculum revision."
Journal of Education for Social Work, v. 11, no. 2, spring
1975. 84-90.

2042 McPheeters, Harold L. and Robert M. Ryan. A core of
competence for baccalaureate social welfare and curriculum implications. Atlanta: Southern Regional Education
Board, 1971. 145p.

2043 Madison, Bernice. The public assistance job and the undergraduate social work curriculum. San Francisco: San
Francisco State College, 1954. 103p.

2044 Marks, Rachel Bryant. "The place of the undergraduate
curriculum in social work education, by Herbert Bisno:
review." Social Service Review, v. 33, no. 4, Dec. 1959.
387-392.

2045 Mendes, Richard H. P. "An approach to the basic
undergraduate course." Education for social work:
proceedings of the 1963 Annual Program Meeting,
Council on Social Work Education. New York:
The Council, 1963. 183-196. Discussions by Eveline M. Burns, Katherine Handley and Herman Piven.
196-202.

2046 _____, et al. Social welfare as a social institution; illustrative syllabi for the basic course in undergraduate social welfare. New York: Council on Social Work Education, 1963. 111p.

2047 Mossman, Mereb E. "Social welfare content in undergraduate education." Education for social work; proceedings of the 1963 Annual Program Meeting, Council on Social Work Education. New York: The Council, 1963. 37-47.

2048 Pilcher, Donald M. and Irving B. Tebor. "Interim report of NIMH-funded research on undergraduate social welfare education: San Diego State College." Social Work Education Reporter, v. 17, no. 1, March 1969. 56-58.

2049 Romanyshyn, John M. "The basic social welfare course on the undergraduate level: some principles and some problems." Education for social work; proceedings of the 1961 Annual Program Meeting, Council on Social Work Education. New York: The Council, 1961. 109-122.

2050 Ryan, Robert M. and Amy Reynolds, editors. Creative curricula in undergraduate social welfare education. Atlanta: Southern Regional Education Board, 1970. 62p.

2051 Scheurell, Robert P. and Robert A. Holzhauer. "A model of an undergraduate program in social work." Iowa Journal of Social Work, v. 5, no. 2, spring 1973. 8-16.

2052 Schindler, Ruben. "A comparative study of social work curricula in selected community and four-year colleges in New York State." Doctoral dissertation, Yeshiva University, 1973. 247p.

2053 Schwartz, Paul L. "Curriculum for undergraduate social welfare." Curriculum building for the continuum in social welfare education. Edited by Michael J. Austin, et al. Tallahassee, Fla.: State University System of Florida, 1972. 38-50.

2054 Sielski, Lester M. "Undergraduate social welfare curriculum." Improving College and University Teaching, v. 18, no. 2, spring 1970. 110-111.

2055 Southern Regional Education Board. Curriculum in social work education; report of a region-wide conference, 1961. Atlanta: The Board, 1961. 52p.

2056 _____. Social Welfare Manpower Project. Administration and management for undergraduate social work: report of a conference, April 23-25, 1975. Atlanta: The Board, 1975. 79p.

2057 _____. Undergraduate Social Welfare Faculty Development
Project. Administration and management for undergraduate
social work: final report on a project. Atlanta: The
Board, 1976. 67p.

2058 Spiro, Shimon. "Development of the 'Community Work' Sequence in an undergraduate curriculum: the problem of
learning experiences in the field." International Social
Work, v. 5, no. 3, July 1962. 29-36.

2059 Tebor, Irving B. and Patricia B. Pickford. Social work: a
helping profession in social welfare; a syllabus. New
York: Council on Social Work Education, 1966. 86p.

2060 Thomas, Edwin J., J. W. McCulloch and Malcolm J. Brown.
"A design for research instruction in applied social studies." Applied Social Studies, v. 1, no. 1, Jan. 1969. 43-51.

2061 _____, _____, and _____. "An experiment to evaluate
research instruction for undergraduate social workers."
Applied Social Studies, v. 1, no. 2, June 1969. 93-105.

2062 Vasey, Wayne. "The Curriculum Study: implications for
graduate and undergraduate curricula." Social Casework,
v. 41, no. 1, Jan. 1960. 7-13.

2063 Walz, Thomas H., et al. Experimental curriculum in an
undergraduate social welfare program: a review of "A
Study of the Nature and Basis of Civil Disorders" and
other courses. Minneapolis: University of Minnesota,
1969. 52p.

2064 _____. "Interim report of NIMH-funded research on undergraduate social welfare education: University of Minnesota." Social Work Education Reporter, v. 17, no. 1, March
1969. 54-55, 60.

2065 Warner, Victoria. "The social welfare practitioner program
at Florida A&M University." Curriculum building for the
continuum in social welfare education. Edited by Michael
J. Austin, et al. Tallahassee, Fla.: State University
System of Florida, 1972. 59-61.

2066 Westby, Frithjof O. M. and Robert D. Mabbs. "Interim
report of NIMH-funded research on undergraduate social
welfare education: Augustana College." Social Work Education Reporter, v. 17, no. 1, March 1969. 51-53.

D. TEACHING AND LEARNING [See also Section IX. C.]

2067 Belzile, Louise, et al. "Teaching and learning--Conference

groups in a Bachelor's program." Social Worker-Travailleur Social, v. 40, no. 1, Feb. 1972. 43-49.

2068 Bisno, Herbert. "A theoretical framework for teaching social work methods and skills, with particular reference
to undergraduate social welfare education." Journal
of Education for Social Work, v. 5, no. 2, fall 1969.
5-17.

2069 Chapin, Rosemary and Nancy Waldman. The helping process.
Minneapolis: Minnesota Resource Center for Social Work
Education, 1972. 129p.

2070 Constable, Robert T. "Preparing for practice: field experience and course work in the undergraduate social work
program." Teaching for competence in the delivery of
direct services. Compiled by the Council on Social Work
Education. New York: The Council, 1976. 9-17.

2071 Crider, Charles C. , editor. Report of the Institute for College Faculty on Teaching a Social Welfare Course, Michigan State University, 1964. New York: Council on Social Work Education, 1966. 117p.

2072 Dea, Kay L. The instructional module: its uses for beginning teachers in undergraduate programs in social welfare.
New York: Council on Social Work Education, 1971. 50p.

2073 Ehlers, Walter H. and John C. Prothero. "Performances
and attitudes of social work students using programmed
instruction texts." Programmed Learning and Educational
Technology, v. 8, no. 4, Oct. 1971. 225-234.

2074 Enos, Richard Edward. "Selected characteristics of undergraduate social work education programs and faculty members and reports of job satisfaction." Doctoral dissertation, University of Utah, 1976. 232p.

2075 Gelman, Sheldon R. , compiler. Toward building the undergraduate social work library; an annotated bibliography.
New York: Council on Social Work Education, 1971. 39p.

2076 Kolevzon, Michael S. "The impact of undergraduate social
work education: a comparative study." Doctoral dissertation, University of California, 1973. 1 v. (various pagings)

2077 Levin, Lester I. , editor. Preparing faculty for the multi
roles of the social work educator. Atlanta: Southern
Regional Education Board, 1974. 139p.

2078 _____, editor. Student participation in social welfare education; report of a conference. Atlanta: Southern Regional Education Board, 1972. 64p.

2079 _____, editor. Teaching social welfare, v.1: Course content and teaching methodology. Atlanta: Southern Regional Education Board, 1971. 126p.

2080 Mossman, Mereb E. "Qualifications for teaching in undergraduate education for social work." Undergraduate education; a series of papers delivered at the 1958 Annual Program Meeting, Council on Social Work Education. New York: the Council, 1958. 11-18.

2081 Pearman, Jean R. and Irwin R. Jahns. "The diffusion of an innovative methods' model into course content." Social Work Education Reporter, v.21, no.2, April-May 1973. 65-68.

2082 _____, _____ and Ernest G. Gendron. "Some comparative profiles of undergraduate social welfare educators." Arete, v.2, no.2, fall 1972. 77-94.

2083 Pohek, Marguerite V. "Teaching media and teaching materials." Essentials for undergraduate social welfare teachers. Edited by Frank M. Loewenberg. New York: Council on Social Work Education, 1969. 14-20.

2084 Ruhl, Erving C. "The use of video tape systems in teaching social work practice." Doctoral dissertation, University of Southern California, 1975. 236p.

2085 Seidl, Frederick W. "An application of didactic and decision methods to teaching the initial course in undergraduate social work education." Doctoral dissertation, University of Wisconsin, 1970. 185p.

2086 Shell, Clarice. "A structured approach to interpersonal skill training." Canadian Journal of Social Work Education, v. 1, no.2, spring 1975. 38-47.

2087 Star, Barbara Gail. "An experimental study of the impact of videotape self-image confrontation of the self perceptions of social work students." Doctoral dissertation, Ohio State University, 1973. 196p.

E. FIELD EXPERIENCES AND INSTRUCTION

2088 Abel, Charles M. and H. Wayne Johnson. "A summer design for student experiential learning." Iowa Journal of Social Work, v.7, nos.2 and 3, August 1976. 78-82.

2089 Ames, Lois. "Use of a daily journal in supervision of undergraduate students' field work." Social Casework, v. 55,
no. 7, July 1974. 442-444.

2090 Austin, Michael J., Edward Kelleher and Philip L. Smith,
editors. The field consortium: manpower development
and training in social welfare and corrections. Tallahassee,
Fla.: State University System of Florida, 1972. 121p.

2091 Broom, Jean M. and Thomas H. Walz. An evaluation of the
apprentice-field experience project in undergraduate social
welfare at the University of Minnesota. Minneapolis: University of Minnesota, 1969. 66p.

2092 Corbett, Kathryn L. "Demonstration project workshop for
agency instructors of undergraduate field experience courses." Social Work Education Reporter, v. 16, no. 4, Dec.
1968. 61-62.

2093 Cox, Cordelia. "Some considerations in relation to undergraduate field experience in social welfare." Selected
papers from two institutes on undergraduate education for
the helping services. Edited by William T. Adams and
Frank Dell'Apa. Boulder, Colo.: Western Interstate
Commission for Higher Education, 1965. 64-73.

2094 Davis, Marie. "Field experience in social work with deaf
students." Journal of Rehabilitation of the Deaf, v. 6, no.
2, Oct. 1972. 76-77.

2095 Dawson, Betty Guthrie. "Supervising the undergraduate in a
psychiatric setting." The dynamics of field instruction:
learning through doing. Compiled by the Council on Social
Work Education. New York: The Council, 1975. 10-19.

2096 DeJong, Cornell R. "Field instruction for undergraduate social work education in rural areas." The dynamics of
field instruction: learning through doing. Compiled by
the Council on Social Work Education. New York: The
Council, 1975. 20-30.

2097 Dolgoff, Ralph and Donald Feldstein. "Developing undergraduate field instruction." Social Work Education Reporter,
v. 20, no. 1, Dec.-Jan. 1972. 19-22.

2098 Gadol, Morris. "Some observations on points of relevance
between undergraduate field experience and field instruction in the graduate school of social work." Social Work
Education Reporter, v. 14, no. 2, June 1966. 36, 51-52.

2099 Hester, Curtis. "Training the deaf in social work: an undergraduate program in a mental health setting." Journal of

Rehabilitation of the Deaf. v. 6, no. 2, Oct. 1972. 68-72.

2100 Levin, Lester I. , editor. Teaching social welfare, v. 2:
Field instruction. Atlanta: Southern Regional Education
Board, 1971. 85p.

2101 Lloyd, A. Katherine. "Field work as part of undergraduate
preparation for professional education." Social Service
Review, v. 30, no. 1, March 1956. 55-64.

2102 Maner, Virginia. "The establishment of field experience in
public welfare for the baccalaureate degree social worker."
Creative curricula in undergraduate social welfare education. Edited by Robert M. Ryan and Amy Reynolds. Atlanta: Southern Regional Education Board, 1970. 50-62.

2103 Matson, Margaret B. "Field experience for the undergraduate
social welfare student." Undergraduate social work education for practice: a report on curriculum content and
issues. Edited by Lester J. Glick. Washington, D. C. :
Government Printing Office, 1972. 80-92.

2104 _____ . Field experience in undergraduate programs in social welfare. New York: Council on Social Work Education, 1967. 64p.

2105 _____ . "Learning through field experience." Developing
programs in the helping services; field experience, methods courses, employment implications. Edited by Dutton
Teague and Dorothy P. Buck. Boulder, Colo. : Western
Interstate Commission for Higher Education, 1968. 15-
24.

2106 _____ . "Learning through field experience." Issues in
implementing undergraduate social welfare education programs; a report of a regional conference for colleges and
universities of the 15 Southern states. Edited by Robert
M. Ryan and Amy L. Reynolds. Atlanta: Southern Regional Education Board, 1970. 18-29.

2107 Mossman, Mereb E. "The values of an agency experience
in public welfare for undergraduate students interested
in social work." Social Work Education, v. 10, no. 5,
Oct. -Nov. 1962. 11-14.

2108 Owens, Evelyn. An approach to teaching the undergraduate
field experience course. Madison: University of Wisconsin, 1967. 14p.

2109 Paonessa, John J. "A new learning experience in undergraduate field observation." Social Work Education Reporter,
v. 18, no. 1, March 1970. 59-60, 64-65.

2110　Poe, William D. "Undergraduate field instruction in Veterans
　　　　Administration Hospitals: agency and school collaboration."
　　　　Doctoral dissertation, University of Utah, 1974. 168p.

2111　Reid, Nellie N. "Field experience in rural areas." Issues
　　　　in implementing undergraduate social welfare education
　　　　programs; a report of a regional conference for colleges
　　　　and universities of the 15 Southern States. Edited by Ro-
　　　　bert M. Ryan and Amy L. Reynolds. Atlanta, Southern
　　　　Regional Education Board, 1970. 38-42.

2112　St. John, David. "Goal-directed supervision of social work
　　　　students in field placement." Journal of Education for
　　　　Social Work, v. 11, no. 3, fall 1975. 89-94.

2113　Samoff, Zelda. "Developing field experiences in a metropol-
　　　　itan area." Issues in implementing undergraduate social
　　　　welfare education programs; a report of a regional con-
　　　　ference for colleges and universities of the 15 Southern
　　　　States. Edited by Robert M. Ryan and Amy L. Reynolds.
　　　　Atlanta: Southern Regional Education Board, 1970. 31-37.

2114　Scheurell, Robert P. and Robert A. Holzhauer. "The field
　　　　unit in undergraduate field experience: research as a
　　　　case example." Iowa Journal of Social Work, v. 3, no. 3,
　　　　summer 1970. 87-92.

2115　Smith, A. LaMont. "Field experience--the potential for learn-
　　　　ing." Selected papers from two institutes on undergraduate
　　　　education for the helping services. Edited by William T.
　　　　Adams and Frank Dell'Apa. Boulder, Colo.: Wes-
　　　　tern Interstate Commission for Higher Education, 1965.
　　　　18-23.

2116　Tingley, Barbara Wallis and Thomas H. Walz. Field exper-
　　　　ience in an undergraduate pre-social work program: a
　　　　study of its effectiveness. Minneapolis: University of
　　　　Minnesota, 1969. 99p.

2117　Turnbull, Anne. "Teaching family centered practice in a BSW
　　　　programme: a field experience." Social Worker-Travail-
　　　　leur Social, v. 43, no. 3, fall 1975. 153-155.

2118　Walz, Thomas H. "The community experience in undergra-
　　　　duate social work education." Undergraduate social work
　　　　education for practice: a report on curriculum content
　　　　and issues. Edited by Lester J. Glick. Washington, D.
　　　　C.: Government Printing Office, 1972. 71-79.

2119　_____. "Use of field experience in teaching Social Welfare
　　　　as a Social Institution." Social Work Education Reporter,
　　　　v. 13, no. 4, Dec. 1965. 23-25, 44-45.

2120 Wenzel, Kristen, editor. Curriculum guides for undergraduate
      field instruction programs. New York: Council on Social
      Work Education, 1972. 261p.

2121 _____, editor. Undergraduate field instruction programs:
      current issues and predictions. New York: Council on
      Social Work Education, 1972. 133p.

2122 Wilkens, Anne. Guides for field instruction for graduate
      schools of social work, field experience of undergraduate
      students, and summer employment of undergraduate
      students. Washington, D. C.: U. S. Bureau of
      Family Services and U. S. Children's Bureau, 1963.
      33p.

2123 Willigan, Barbara. "My training experience in social work
      at Gallaudet College and present employment." Journal
      of Rehabilitation of the Deaf, v. 6, no. 2, Oct. 1972. 78-
      79.

2124 Yamanaka, K. Morgan. "The undergraduate social welfare
      college-agency relationship." Social Work Education Re-
      porter, v. 18, no. 2, June 1970. 30-32, 49.

F. EVALUATION OF GRADUATES AND PROGRAMS

2125 Anderson, Eugene D. Accountability study of undergraduate
      social work education at East Tennessee State University.
      Johnson City, Tenn.: Department of Social Services, East
      Tennessee State University, 1974. 35p.

2126 Arkava, Morton L. and E. Clifford Brennen, editors. Com-
      petency-based education for social work: evaluation and
      curriculum issues. New York: Council on Social Work
      Education, 1976. 204p.

2127 _____, et al. Montana social work competence scales:
      a summative examination for baccalaureate social work-
      ers. Missoula, Mont.: Department of Social Work, Uni-
      versity of Montana, 1976. 36p.

2128 _____ and E. Clifford Brennen. "Toward a competency
      examination for the baccalaureate social worker." Jour-
      nal of Education for Social Work, v. 11, no. 3, fall 1975.
      22-29.

2129 Bucklew, Reba M. "An evaluation of seventeen years of under-
      graduate social work education at Texas Woman's Univer-
      sity." Social Work Education Reporter, v. 11, no. 1, Feb.
      1963. 19-20.

2130 Buran, Gretchen and Thomas H. Walz. A study of the differences in background and performance of pre-social work and non-pre-social work undergraduate majors in a graduate school of social work. Minneapolis: University of Minnesota, 1969. 41p.

2131 _____. A study of the performance of undergraduate social welfare majors on an examination for beginning positions in Minnesota county welfare agencies. Minneapolis: University of Minnesota, 1969. 74p.

2132 Dolgoff, Ralph. "Organizational structure and socialization: educational interaction and career choices in undergraduate social work education." Doctoral dissertation. Columbia University, 1974. 333p.

2133 Ellis, Helen. "The contribution of an undergraduate program to the field of social work." Catholic Charities Review, v. 45, no. 7, Sept. 1961. 8-12.

2134 Galambos, Eva C. and Xenia R. Wiggins. After graduation: experiences of college graduates in locating and working in social welfare positions. Atlanta: Southern Regional Education Board, 1970. 64p.

2135 Johnson, Walter B. "Indiana University Division of Social Service reports on study of 1950-1960 undergraduate grads." Social Work Education Reporter, v. 10, no. 1, Feb. 1962. 20-21.

2136 Kruse, Thomas Lee. "Adequacy of preparation for social work practice: self-assessment by students about to graduate with the baccalaureate degree in social work." Doctoral dissertation, Ohio State University, 1973. 184p.

2137 Miller, Joseph Pearce, Jr. "A study of career choice among undergraduate social science majors: social work, psychology and sociology, with emphasis upon social work." Doctoral dissertation, University of Pittsburgh, 1974. 132p.

2138 Nowak, Mary Jane and William E. Stilwell. Developmental models for accountability in undergraduate social work education. Arlington, Va.: ERIC Document Reproduction Service, 1974. 22p. ED 115149.

2139 Padberg, William Hugo. "The social welfare labor market attachment of the undergraduate social work major." Doctoral dissertation, Columbia University, 1974. 267p.

2140 Pearman, Jean R. and Ann L. McLean. "Some perceptual comparisons: BSW graduates, agency representatives, and instructors." Arete, v. 3, no. 1, spring 1974. 41-51.

2141 Rosenblatt, Aaron, Marianne Welter and Sophie Wojciechowski. The Adelphi experiment: accelerating social work education. New York: Council on Social Work Education, 1976. 189p.

2142 Turner, Robert O. and Alexis H. Skelding. "Results of a survey of June 1970 social welfare baccalaureate graduates." Curriculum building for the continuum in social welfare education. Edited by Michael J. Austin, et al. Tallahassee, Fla.: State University System of Florida, 1972. 124-126.

2143 Walton, Ellen G. and Thomas H. Walz. "A follow-up study of graduates of a pre-social work program: implications for education and practice." Social Work Education Reporter, v. 19, no. 1, Dec.-Jan. 1971. 54-57.

2144 _____ and _____. A follow-up study of pre-social work graudates from the University of Minnesota. Minneapolis: University of Minnesota, 1969. 136p.

2145 Waters, R. O. and R. M. Bartlett. "Bachelor's degree school social workers." Social Worker-Travailleur Social, v. 38, no. 3, July 1970. 11-15.

[See also Section XII.]

2146 Andrew, Gwen. "Associate and baccalaureate degree educa-
      tion for social work: a tentative proposal. " Journal of
      Education for Social Work, v. 9, no. 1, winter 1973. 3-10.

2147 Austin, Michael J. and Philip L. Smith. "New demands from
      the field for curriculum change. " Curriculum building
      for the continuum in social welfare education. Edited by
      Michael J. Austin, et al. Tallahassee, Fla. : State Uni-
      versity System of Florida, 1972. 150-156.

2148 Brawley, Edward Allan. "The associate-degree worker in
      the human services: an examination, synthesis, and ex-
      tension of current models of education and practice. "
      Doctoral dissertation, University of Pennsylvania, 1973.
      397p.

2149 _____ and Ruben Schindler. Community and social service
      education in the community college: issues and character-
      istics. New York: Council on Social Work Education,
      1972. 72p.

2150 _____. New human service worker; community college
      education and the social services. New York: Praeger,
      1974. 178p.

2151 _____. "A systems approach to the evaluation of a com-
      munity college program in mental health work. "   Ap-
      proaches to innovation in social work education. Compiled
      by the Council on Social Work Education. New York:
      The Council, 1974. 15-25.

2152 California Community Colleges. Office of the Chancellor.
      Social services--A suggested associate degree curriculum.
      Revised. Washington, D. C. : Government Printing Of-
      fice, 1973. 195p.

2153 Cameron, Donald A. "An examination of social service pro-
      grams in Ontario community colleges with special refer-
      ence to field instruction. " Doctoral dissertation, Univer-

sity of Toronto, 1975. 302p.

2154   Council on Social Work Education. The community services
        technician; guide for associate degree programs in the
        community and social services. New York: The Council,
        1970. 35p.

2155   Duplantie, Jean-Pierre L. "Differences between social ser-
        vice graduates and Bachelor of Arts graduates in their
        role as social welfare workers." Doctoral dissertation,
        University of Chicago, 1974. 237p.

2156   Eslinger, Troy R. Recruitment and training of social wel-
        fare assistants. Arlington, Va. : ERIC Document Repro-
        duction Service, 1968. 7p. ED 032869.

2157   Feldstein, Donald. Community college and other associate
        degree programs for social welfare areas. New York:
        Council on Social Work Education, 1968. 23p.

2158   _____ . "The paraprofessional and the community college."
        Social Work, v. 14, no. 1, Jan. 1969. 117.

2159   Florida. State University System, and Division of Community
        Colleges. Social Work Education Project; final report.
        Arlington, Va. : ERIC Document Reproduction Service,
        1972. 137p. ED 067978.

2160   Hall, Jeanette. Pilot "C" curriculum evaluation and inter-
        pretive analysis; phase II final report of the Social Ser-
        vice Aide Project for the Training and Education of Para-
        professionals. Arlington, Va. : ERIC Document Repro-
        duction Service, 1970. 44p. ED 047138.

2161   Lynch, Stanley and Marta Konik. "Curriculum for indigenous
        human service workers." Curriculum building for the
        continuum in social welfare education. Edited by Michael
        J. Austin, et al. Tallahassee, Fla. : State University
        System of Florida, 1972. 52-58.

2162   McLellan, Gordon. "Education for the social services in
        community colleges." Social Worker-Travailleur Social,
        v. 36, no. 3, July 1968. 191-194.

2163   McPheeters, Harold L. and James B. King. Plans for teach-
        ing mental health workers: community college curriculum
        objectives. Atlanta: Southern Regional Education Board,
        1971. 79p.

2164   Moed, Martin G. , Thomas Carroll and Marie Stewart. "Ex-
        perimenting with a Social Service Technology Program."
        Junior College Journal, v. 40, no. 6, March 1970. 45-49.

2165 Mullen, Edward J. Evaluating student learning: baccalaureate programs and the community college transfer student. New York: Council on Social Work Education, 1976. 40p.

2166 Olson, Irene. "Junior college education for social service assistant." Child Welfare, v. 45, no. 10, Dec. 1966. 599-600, 606.

2167 Queens College. New Human Services Institute. College programs for paraprofessionals; a directory of degree-granting programs in the human services. New York: Behavioral Publications, 1975. 135p.

2168 Reed, Selina E. "Developing a model social service curriculum in a community college." Social Work Education Reporter, v. 20, no. 3, Sept. -Oct. 1972. 70-73.

2169 Romney, Leonard S. "Challenges, concerns, and concepts in a community college education in social work." Approaches to innovation in social work education. Compiled by the Council on Social Work Education. New York: The Council, 1974. 62-74.

2170 _____. "Toward development of a generic model for human service field experience." Social Work Education Reporter, v. 19, no. 3, Sept. -Oct. 1971. 61-65.

2171 Schindler, Ruben. "A comparative study of social work curricula in selected community and four-year colleges in New York State." Doctoral dissertation, Yeshiva University, 1973. 247p.

2172 Segal, Brian. "Community college teaching and staff development: new linkages in the curriculum continuum." Curriculum building for the continuum in social welfare education. Edited by Michael J. Austin, et al. Tallahassee, Fla.: State University System of Florida, 1972. 137-149.

2173 _____ and Michael J. Austin. "Innovations in field instruction: community college teaching and staff development." Journal of Education for Social Work, v. 10, no. 1, winter 1974. 77-80.

2174 Soong, Robert K. Career ladders and core curriculum in human services; phase II final report of the Social Service Aide Project for the Training and Education of Paraprofessionals. Arlington, Va.: ERIC Document Reproduction Service, 1970. 23p. ED 047141.

2175 _____, et al. Human services course delivery systems. Arlington, Va.: ERIC Document Reproduction Service, 1971. 39p. ED 057001.

2176 _____, et al. Social Service Aide Project for the Education and Training of Paraprofessionals; phase I final report. Arlington, Va.: ERIC Document Reproduction Service, 1969. 149p. ED 035062.

2177 Swift, Joan. "Curriculum for human services career programs in community colleges." Curriculum building for the continuum in social welfare education. Edited by Michael J. Austin, et al. Tallahassee, Fla.: State University System of Florida, 1972. 27-37.

2178 _____. Human services career programs and the community college. Washington, D. C.: American Association of Junior Colleges, 1971. 81p.

2179 Turner, Robert O. "The community college and social welfare education." Curriculum building for the continuum in social welfare education. Edited by Michael J. Austin, et al. Tallahassee, Fla.: State University System of Florida, 1972. 131-136.

2180 _____ and Alexis H. Skelding. "Results of a survey of June 1970 community college graduates." Curriculum building for the continuum in social welfare education. Edited by Michael J. Austin, et al. Tallahassee, Fla.: State University System of Florida, 1972. 121-123.

2181 Warren, Barry. Pilot "B" curriculum evaluation and interpretive analysis; phase II final report of the Social Service Aide Project for the Training and Education of Paraprofessionals. Arlington, Va.: ERIC Document Reproduction Service, 1970. 91p. ED 047142.

2182 Wetzel, Jean. Pilot "A" curriculum evaluation and interpretive analysis; phase II final report of the Social Service Aide Project for the Training and Education of Paraprofessionals. Arlington, Va.: ERIC Document Reproduction Service, 1970. 43p. ED 047139.

XI. CONTINUING EDUCATION FOR SOCIAL WORK, CREDIT EXTENSION AND PART-TIME PROGRAMS

2183 Appelberg, Esther. "Mothers as social work students." Social Work Education Reporter, v. 13, no. 4, Dec. 1965. 26-30.

2184 Balint, Enid. "Training post-graduate students in social casework." British Journal of Medical Psychology. v. 32, part 3, Sept. 1959. 193-199.

2185 Baskett, H. K. "Rethinking the role of continuing education in the social welfare field." Dialogue, v. 1, no. 3, June 1974. 1-27.

2186 Brenner, Melvin N. and William H. Koch. "Continuing education among social workers: pattern and profiles." Approaches to innovation in social work education. Compiled by the Council on Social Work Education. New York: The Council, 1974. 26-37.

2187 Brown, Edwin G. "Continuing education." Assuring practitioner competence: whose responsibility? Edited by Dean H. Hepworth. Salt Lake City: Graduate School of Social Work, University of Utah, 1974. 61-64. Group discussion. 64-65.

2188 Catalyst. Survey of opportunities for part-time study in Master's degree programs in social work. New York: Catalyst, 1973. 18p.

2189 Council on Social Work Education. Guide to continuing education in schools of social work. New York: The Council, 1974. 40p.

2190 _____. On-going education; subject area workshop report of the 1954 Annual Program Meeting, Council on Social Work Education. New York: The Council, 1954. 23p.

2191 Dinerman, Miriam. "Social work training for unconventional students in Great Britain." Journal of Education for Social Work, v. 11, no. 2, spring 1975. 32-36.

2192 Faherty, Vincent E. "Continuing social work education: a

Delphi survey." Doctoral dissertation, University of Utah, 1976. 216p.

2193 Faruqee, Selima and Armand A. Lauffer, editors. Social work continuing education year book. Ann Arbor: School of Social Work, University of Michigan, 1973. 183p.

2194 Frey, Louise A. "The evaluation of teacher competence in continuing education." Social Work Education Reporter, v. 20, no. 3, Sept.-Oct. 1972. 43-47.

2195 Hoffer, Joe R. "Continuing education through social welfare conferences." Social welfare forum, 1969; official proceedings of the National Conference on Social Welfare. New York: Columbia University Press, 1969. 60-74.

2196 Howery, Victor I. "Continuing education: program development, administration, and financing." Journal of Education for Social Work, v. 10, no. 1, winter 1974. 34-41.

2197 Illinois. University, Dixon. Regional Office for Continuing Education and Public Service. A survey of student interest in a first year Master of Social Work program for the Greater Rockford, Illinois area: final report. Arlington, Va.: ERIC Document Reproduction Service, 1975. 12p. ED 115757.

2198 Johnson, Betty S. and Victoria Brown. "New approaches to training the alienated social worker." Public Welfare, v. 30, no. 3, summer 1972. 54-58.

2199 Koch, William H. and Melvin N. Brenner. "Continuing education for social service: implications from a study of learners." Journal of Education for Social Work, v. 12, no. 1, winter 1976. 71-77.

2200 Kurren, Oscar, Wilbur Finch and Sonja Matison. "One model for an interrelated program of in-service training and continuing education in social work." Social Work Education Reporter, v. 17, no. 1, March 1969. 31-34, 61-62.

2201 Lauffer, Armand A. "Continuing education as problem-focused extension." Journal of Education for Social Work, v. 8, no. 3, fall 1972. 40-49.

2202 Lewis, Verl S. "From housewife to social worker: the University of Maryland's Extended Study Program." Social Work Education Reporter, v. 17, no. 2, June 1969. 45-47, 57.

2203 _____. "Part-time students in professional schools." Social Work Education Reporter, v. 17, no. 4, Dec. 1969. 24, 61.

2204 Marantz, Ethel C. and Ethel B. Weinstein. "The story of an experiment: a school of social work trains volunteers." Social Work Education Reporter, v.13, no.3, Sept. 1965. 24-25, 28.

2205 Miller, Deborah. Continuing education programs of schools of social work; report of a survey. New York: Council on Social Work Education, 1969. 18p.

2206 Moore, Jean E. "Concepts of continuing education in higher education: implications for social work education." NUEA Spectator, v.39, no.20, June 1975. 24-29.

2207 National Association of Social Workers. Commission on Social Work Education. The development of programs of continuing education for social welfare personnel. New York: The Association, 1969. 64p.

2208 Robins, Arthur J. "Institutional linkages of continuing education." Approaches to innovation in social work education. Compiled by The Council on Social Work Education. New York: The Council, 1974. 51-61.

2209 Rothman, Beulah. "Perspectives on learning and teaching in continuing education." Journal of Education for Social Work, v.9, no.2, spring 1973. 39-52.

2210 Schaub, Elisabeth and Sandra Cohen. "Report on a national survey of 63 graduate schools of social work offering continuing education programs in social welfare administration and management." National project on education for management, v.1. Prepared by the School of Social Work, University of Pennsylvania. Philadelphia: The School, 1975. 8p. in buff covers.

2211 Southwick, Phyllis C. "Social work continuing education: a survey of administrative structures and programming in graduate schools of social work, 1975." Doctoral dissertation, University of Utah, 1976. 140p.

2212 Stein, Leonard S. Survey of St. Louis area social workers on their continuing education interests. Arlington, Va.: ERIC Document Reproduction Service, 1969. 18p. ED 040368.

2213 Swack, Lois G. "Continuing education and changing needs." Social Work, v.20, no.6, Nov. 1975. 474-480.

2214 _____. "The unique aspects of short-term teaching: how to teach the 'How to's' to the doers." Journal of Education for Social Work, v.10, no.1, winter 1974. 90-95.

2215   Taber, Merlin and Doris G. Baker.   "Testing innovations in practice: an experiment in continuing education." Social Work Education Reporter, v. 18, no. 1, March 1970. 42-44.

2216   United States.   National Institute of Mental Health. Mental health continuing education programs for long-term care providers. Washington, D. C. : Government Printing Office, 1975. 98p.

2217   Waldstein, Martha.   "Refresher course for married women reentering the casework field." Social Casework, v. 41, no. 8, Oct. 1960. 418-424.

2218   Walz, Thomas H.   "A continuing education curriculum for the graduate social worker." Journal of Education for Social Work, v. 9, no. 1, winter 1973. 68-78.

2219   Webster, Thomas G.   "Concepts basic to continuing education." Social Work Education Reporter, v. 19, no. 3, Sept. - Oct. 1971. 66-70.

2220   Wright, Marjorie Brown.   Educational model for social service administration and management: summary progress report. Arlington, Va. : ERIC Document Reproduction Service, 1975. 82p. ED 113283.

XII. CONTINUUM IN SOCIAL WORK EDUCATION

2221   Adelphi University. School of Social Work. Experimental
       project; accelerated continuum, undergraduate-graduate
       social work education. Garden City, N. Y. : The School,
       1968. 43p.

2222   Ammons, Paul. "Advanced placement in MSW programs."
       Journal of Education for Social Work, v. 11, no. 3, fall
       1975. 12-15.

2223   Andrew, Gwen. "Doing concepts: thoughts toward resolution
       of the continuum dilemma." Journal of Education for So-
       cial Work, v. 12, no. 1, winter 1976. 3-10.

2224   Austin, Michael J., et al., editors. Curriculum building for
       the continuum in social welfare education. Tallahassee,
       Fla. : State University System of Florida, 1972. 159p.

2225   Bisno, Herbert. "The relationship between the undergraduate
       and graduate phases of social work education." The place
       of the undergraduate curriculum in social work education.
       New York: Council on Social Work Education, 1959. 79-
       89.

2226   _____. Structure and quality in social work education; re-
       port of the Task Force on Structure and Quality in Social
       Work Education. New York: Council on Social Work Ed-
       ucation, 1974. 23p.

2227   Boehm, Werner W. "Continuum in education for social work."
       Evaluation of social intervention. Edited by Edward F.
       Mullen and James R. Dumpson. San Francisco: Jossey-
       Bass, 1972. 210-239.

2228   Coleman, Morton. "Continuing education as part of the social
       work continuum." Social work continuing education year-
       book, 1973. Edited by Selima Faruqee and Armand Lauf-
       fer. Ann Arbor, Mich. : University of Michigan School
       of Social Work, 1973. 20-26.

2229   Council on Social Work Education. Policy statements on so-
       cial work practice and education and structure and quality
       in social work education adopted by the House of Delegates,
       March 1976. New York: The Council, 1976. 1v. (var-
       ious pagings).

209

2230 _____ . Undergraduate and graduate courses in the social
services; an exploration of their interdependence; workshop
report of the 1962 Annual Program Meeting. New York:
The Council, 1962. 28p.

2231 _____ . The undergraduate department and the graduate
school--How can the integration of undergraduate and graduate education be more effectively accomplished? Workshop report no. 2 of the 1953 Annual Program Meeting.
New York: The Council, 1953. 16p.

2232 Deasy, Leila Calhoun. "Some comments on education for social work." Doctoral students look at social work education. Edited by Leila Calhoun Deasy. New York: Council on Social Work Education, 1971. 129-140.

2233 Dolgoff, Ralph. An analysis of the responses to the Reports
of the Task Force on Structure and Quality in Social Work
Education and the Task Force on Practice and Education.
New York: Council on Social Work Education, 1975. 49p.

2234 Dresser, Harriet. "Linkages between undergraduate and graduate social work education." Teaching social welfare,
v. 3: Issues and trends in curriculum development. Edited by Lester I. Levin. Atlanta: Southern Regional Education Board, 1971. 47-51.

2235 Dumpson, James R. "Social welfare education in a university: its objectives and implementation." Social need
and education for social welfare. Edited by Benjamin
Lyndon. Syracuse, N. Y.: State University of New York,
1968. 24-36.

2236 Eades, Joe C. "Starting where the student is: an experiment in accelerated graduate social work education."
Journal of Education for Social Work, v. 12, no. 3, fall
1976. 22-28.

2237 Feldstein, Donald. "The associate degree in the social services." Undergraduate social work education for practice: a report on curriculum content and issues. Edited
by Lester J. Glick. Washington, D. C.: Government
Printing Office, 1972. 96-105.

2238 _____ . "Heliocentric perspective on social work education." Evaluation of social intervention. Edited by Edward F. Mullen and James R. Dumpson. San Francisco:
Jossey-Bass, 1972. 240-250.

2239 Fike, David F. "Swing courses and their consequences."
Journal of Education for Social Work, v. 11, no. 3, fall
1975. 50-54.

2240 Gadol, Morris. "Some observations on points of relevance between undergraduate field experience and field instruction in the graduate school of social work." Social Work Education Reporter, v. 14, no. 2, June 1966. 36, 51-52.

2241 Gore, Marylyn. "Two goes into four: linkages between two and four year college programs in social welfare." Social Work Education Reporter, v. 17, no. 4, Dec. 1969. 11-13.

2242 Guilford, Richard G. "What is the best undergraduate preparation for entrance into graduate school? the viewpoint of the graduate school of social work." Social Work Education Reporter, v. 14, no. 2, June 1966. 33, 46-48.

2243 Hope, Martin. "The continuum of undergraduate-graduate social work education." Teaching social welfare, v. 3: Issues and trends in curriculum development. Edited by Lester I. Levin. Atlanta: Southern Regional Education Board, 1971. 61-73.

2244 Jones, Dorothy. "Recommendations for undergraduate preparation for graduate school--from the viewpoint of the undergraduate college." Social Work Education Reporter, v. 14, no. 2, June 1966. 32, 49, 51.

2245 Jones, Marshall E. "The undergraduate university and the graduate school of social work." Social Service Review, v. 18, no. 2, June 1944. 165-169.

2246 Lower, Katherine D. "Undergraduate preparation prerequisite to admission to graduate schools of social work--from the graduate point of view." Undergraduate education; a series of papers delivered at the 1958 Annual Program Meeting, Council on Social Work Education. New York: The Council, 1958. 6-10.

2247 Lustman, Claire R. "Implications of the continuum for agencies." Undergraduate social work education for practice: a report on curriculum content and issues. Edited by Lester J. Glick. Washington, D. C.: Government Printing Office, 1972. 138-154.

2248 Lyndon, Benjamin H. "Change and social work education's reaction: evolution or the 'big bang' approach?" Public Welfare, v. 27, no. 2, April 1969. 125-134.

2249 _____. "The creation of relevance: social welfare education in continuity." Continuities in undergraduate social welfare education. Compiled by the Council on Social Work Education. New York: The Council, 1969. 7-21.

2250 _____. Graduate professional schools of social work and undergraduate social welfare education, part I: Findings. Buffalo: State University of New York, 1965. 83p.

2251 Matson, Margaret B. "Undergraduate preparation prerequisite to admission to graduate schools of social work--from the undergraduate point of view." Undergraduate education; a series of papers delivered at the 1958 Annual Program Meeting, Council on Social Work Education. New York: The Council, 1958. 1-5.

2252 Meyerson, Erma. "Educational linkages between undergraduate education in social welfare and professional social work education." Journal of Education for Social Work, v. 5, no. 2, fall 1969. 31-37.

2253 Mossman, Mereb E. "The bachelor's degree program in the social work continuum." Undergraduate social work education for practice: a report on curriculum content and issues. Edited by Lester J. Glick. Washington, D. C.: Government Printing Office, 1972. 106-116.

2254 Mullen, Edward J. Evaluating student learning: baccalaureate programs and the community college transfer student. New York: Council on Social Work Education, 1976. 40p.

2255 Ripple, Lilian. Report of the Task Force on Structure and Quality in Social Work Education. New York: Council on Social Work Education, 1974. 68p.

2256 Roberts, Robert W. "An interim report on the development of an undergraduate-graduate continuum of social work education in a private university." Journal of Education for Social Work, v. 9, no. 3, fall 1973. 58-64.

2257 Rosenblatt, Aaron, Marianne Welter and Sophie Wojciechowski. The Adelphi experiment: accelerating social work education. New York: Council on Social Work Education, 1976. 189p.

2258 Samoff, Zelda. "The continuum revisited--The undergraduate underpinnings." Continuities in undergraduate social welfare education. Compiled by the Council on Social Work Education. New York: The Council, 1969. 23-39.

2259 _____. "Undergraduate-graduate: we-they or one school." Social Work Education Reporter, v. 20, no. 3, Sept. -Oct. 1972. 74-79.

2260 Witte, Ernest F. "Articulation between graduate and undergraduate education for the social services." Observations on undergraduate social welfare education. Compiled by the Council on Social Work Education. New York: The Council, 1966. 27-34.

2261 Wojciechowski, Sophie. "Continuum in social work education: Adelphi University School of Social Work experiment." Approaches to innovation in social work education. Compiled by the Council on Social Work Education. New York: The Council, 1974. 92-104.

XIII. EDUCATION FOR FIELD OF PRACTICE AND SOCIAL PROBLEM AREAS

A. AGING AND THE AGED

2262 Aldridge, Gordon J. "Training for work with older people." Gerontologist, v. 4, no. 2, June 1964. 78-79, 103.

2263 Beckman, C. Wesley. "Aging: attitudes of social work students as predicted by selected socio-demographic variables, life, and educational experiences." Doctoral dissertation, University of Utah, 1974. 170p.

2264 Brewer, Jack L. "Working with older people--A field placement program for second-year graduate social work students." San Diego, Calif.: Graduate School of Social Work, San Diego State College, 1970. 20p.

2265 Brody, Elaine M. "Serving the aged: educational needs as viewed by practice." Social Work, v. 15, no. 4, Oct. 1970. 42-51.

2266 Cohen, Ruth G. "Graduate social work training in a multi-purpose geriatric center." Gerontologist, v. 11, no. 4, winter 1971. Part I, 352-355.

2267 _____. "Student training in a geriatric center." Issues in human services. Edited by Florence Whiteman Kaslow. San Francisco: Jossey-Bass, 1972. 168-184.

2268 Council on Social Work Education. Social work education for better services to the aging; proceedings of the Seminar on the Aging, Aspen, Colorado, 1958. New York: The Council, 1959. 93p.

2269 _____. Teacher's source book on aging. New York: The Council, 1964. 1 folder.

2270 Donahue, Wilma. "Training in social gerontology." Geriatrics, v. 15, no. 11, Nov. 1960. 801-809.

2271 Guttmann, David, Frances L. Eyster and Garland Lewis. "Improving the care of the aged through interdisciplinary effort." Gerontologist, v. 15, part 1, Oct. 1975. 387-392.

2272 Hartford, Margaret E. "The MSW-MPA dual degree program in gerontology: a new model for the preparation of social work administrators." Journal of Education for Social Work, v. 12, no. 3, fall 1976. 51-58.

2273 Kosberg, Jordan I. "A social problems approach to gerontology in social work education." Journal of Education for Social Work, v. 12, no. 1, winter 1976. 78-84.

2274 Kushner, Rose E. and Marion E. Bunch, editors. Graduate education in aging within the social sciences. Ann Arbor: Division of Gerontology, University of Michigan, 1967. 118p.

2275 Linn, Margaret W., et al. "The C. A. R. E. Project: interdisciplinary and community-oriented approach to training social work students." Journal of Education for Social Work, v. 10, no. 2, spring 1974. 47-50.

2276 Lowy, Louis. Training manual for human service technicians working with older persons, part I: Trainers. Boston: Boston University Bookstores, 1968. 107p.

2277 Maxwell, Jean M. "Improving social work services to older people through education." Education for social work; proceedings of the 1963 Annual Program Meeting, Council on Social Work Education. New York: The Council, 1963. 145-157.

2278 Mayadas, Nazneen S. and Douglas L. Hink. "Group work with the aging: an issue for social work education." Gerontologist, v. 14, no. 5, Oct. 1974. 440-445.

2279 Monk, Abraham. "A conceptual base for 'second-generation' programs in gerontological social work." Journal of Education for Social Work, v. 11, no. 3, fall 1975. 84-88.

2280 Mutschler, Phyllis. "Factors affecting choice of and perseveration in social work with the aged." Gerontologist, v. 11, no. 3, autumn 1971. Part I, 231-241.

2281 Pearlman, Lou W., Jerome Hammerman and Sheldon S. Tobin. Social casework--Field work training in a geriatric institutional setting: review of a five-year experience. Chicago: American Public Welfare Association, 1968. 16p.

2282 Saul, Shura. "Learning about aging." Social Work Education Reporter, v. 20, no. 1, Dec. -Jan. 1972. 70-73. Addendum by Florence Schwartz. 73-74.

2283 Sherman, Edith M. and Margaret R. Brittan. A plan to span: work-study in social gerontology; a demonstration project at the University of Denver. Edited by Ina Friedelson. Washington, D. C. : Government Printing Office, 1970. 49p.

2284 Shulder, Lois B. "A comparison of attitudes of law students, social work students, and gerontology students toward the aged and toward income-security programs and social welfare services for the aged." Doctoral dissertation, University of Southern California, 1973. 226p.

2285 Smith, Harold K. "Aging specializations in schools of social work: a curriculum-model for gerontology education in social work." Doctoral dissertation, University of Utah, 1976. 122p.

2286 Tobin, Sheldon S. "The educator as advocate: the gerontologist in an academic setting." Journal of Education for Social Work, v. 9, no. 3, fall 1973. 94-98.

2287 United States. National Institute of Mental Health. Mental health continuing education programs for long-term care providers. Washington, D. C. : Government Printing Office, 1975. 98p.

2288 White House Conference on Aging, 1961. Background paper on role and training of professional personnel. Washington, D. C. : Government Printing Office, 1960. 147p.

2289 _____. The role and training of professional personnel in the field of aging. Washington, D. C. : U. S. Department of Health, Education, and Welfare, 1961. 58p.

2290 White House Conference on Aging, 1971. Training: background and issues. Washington, D. C. : Government Printing Office, 1971. 81p.

B. ALCOHOLISM AND DRUG DEPENDENCE

2291 Bailey, Margaret B. "Attitude toward alcoholism before and after a training program for social caseworkers." Quarterly Journal of Studies on Alcohol, v. 31, no. 3, Sept. 1970. 669-683.

2292 _____. "Teaching experience and attitude change." Alcoholism and family casework: theory and practice. New York: Community Council of Greater New York, 1968. 125-133.

2293 Einstein, Stanley and Edward Wolfson. "Alcoholism curricula: how professionals are trained." International Journal of the Addictions, v. 5, no. 2, June 1970. 295-312.

2294 Garvin, Charles. "Social work education in alcoholism."
Annals of the New York Academy of Sciences, v. 178,
March 29, 1971. 52-57.

2295 Levy, Charles S. "Introducing social work students to alcoholism." Quarterly Journal of Studies on Alcohol, v. 24,
no. 4, Dec. 1963. 697-704.

2296 Lincoln, Lois, Margaret Berryman and Margaret W. Linn.
"Drug abuse: a comparison of attitudes." Comprehensive Psychiatry, v. 14, no. 5, Sept./Oct. 1973. 465-471.

2297 Manohar, Velandy, Joyce DesRoches and Ernest W. Ferneau,
Jr. "Education program in alcoholism for social workers--
Its impact on attitudes and treatment-oriented behavior."
British Journal of Addiction, v. 71, no. 3, Sept. 1976. 225-
234.

2298 Stein, Shayna R. and Margaret W. Linn. "The effect of drug
use on social work students' treatment attitudes." Journal of Education for Social Work, v. 11, no. 2, spring 1975.
109-115.

2299 Trader, Harriet. "A professional school's role in training
ex-addict counselors." Journal of Education for Social
Work, v. 10, no. 3, fall 1974. 99-106.

2300 Wilbur, Mary. "Training of social work students in a nar-
cotics treatment center: an impressionistic study." Drug
Forum, v. 1, no. 4, July 1972. 417-425.

C. CHILD AND FAMILY SERVICES

2301 Adler, Jack. "Social work education for foster care practice." Social Work Education Reporter, v. 20, no. 2,
April-May 1972. 18-22.

2302 Aikin, Dorothy. "Teaching family diagnosis in the social
work curriculum." Social Service Review, v. 34, no. 1,
March 1960. 42-50. Comments by Gertrude Leyendecker.
42-47; Sidney J. Berkowitz. 47-50.

2303 Albert, Gerald. "Advanced psychological training for marriage counselors--luxury or necessity?" Journal of Marriage and Family Living, v. 25, no. 2, May 1963. 181-183.

2304 Bardill, Donald R. "The simulated family as an aid to learning family group treatment." Child Welfare, v. 55, no. 10,

Dec. 1976. 703-709.

2305 Baxter, Edith S. "The agency's expectations from the beginning professional worker." Child Welfare, v. 43, no. 2, Feb. 1964. 76-79, 90.

2306 Beardon, Alan. "Group work training for child care officers." Social Service Quarterly, v. 42, no. 4, spring 1969. 136-140.

2307 Behre, Charlotte. "Management of the caseloads of child welfare graduate students." Child Welfare, v. 53, no. 8, Oct. 1974. 499-507.

2308 Bodin, Arthur M. "Family therapy training literature: a brief guide." Family Process, v. 8, no. 2, Sept. 1969. 272-279.

2309 Boehm, Bernice and Werner W. Boehm. "Social work education and child welfare practice." Child Welfare, v. 47, no. 3, March 1968. 143-153, 169.

2310 Boehm, Werner W. "The shape of things to come in child welfare: a social work educator's viewpoint." Child Welfare, v. 45, no. 1, Jan. 1966. 11-16.

2311 _____. "The Social Work Curriculum Study and its implications for family casework." Social Casework, v. 40, no. 8, Oct. 1959. 428-436.

2312 Clare, Morris. "An experiment in social work education." Adult Education (London), v. 43, no. 4, Nov. 1970. 229-231.

2313 Cleghorn, John M. and Sol Levin. "Training family therapists by setting learning objectives." American Journal of Orthopsychiatry, v. 43, no. 3, April 1973. 439-446.

2314 Costin, Lela B. and Jennette R. Gruener. "A project for training personnel in child welfare." Child Welfare, v. 43, no. 4, April 1964. 175-181.

2315 _____. "Training nonprofessionals for child welfare service." Children, v. 13, no. 2, March-April 1966. 63-68.

2316 Daly, Dorothy Bird. "The family as the unit of service in social work." Helping the family in urban society. Edited by Fred Delliquadri. New York: Columbia University Press, 1963. 170-184.

2317 Dumpson, James R., Swithun Bowers and Norris E. Class. "Child welfare as a field of social work practice: a discussion." Child Welfare, v. 39, no. 10, Dec. 1960. 29-33.

2318 Erickson, Gerald. "Teaching family therapy." Journal of Education for Social Work, v. 9, no. 3, fall 1973. 9-15.

2319 Forthman, Robert C. "Child welfare: searching for relevant learning on the undergraduate level." Child Welfare, v. 51, no. 4, April 1972. 231-240.

2320 Fradkin, Helen, editor. Use of personnel in child welfare agencies; proceedings of the Arden House Conference, 1966, Harriman, N. Y. New York: School of Social Work, Columbia University, 1966. 47p.

2321 Fuller, Annette and Marc Pilisuk. "Training the professional to serve in the youth culture." Social Work Education Reporter, v. 21, no. 1, Dec. -Jan. 1973. 28-30, 47-50.

2322 Gelfand, Bernard, Igor Starak and Patricia Nevidon. "Training for empathy in child welfare." Child Welfare, v. 52, no. 9, Nov. 1973. 595-600.

2323 Glover, E. Elizabeth. "Education, training, and manpower." Child Welfare, v. 45, no. 3, March 1966. 124, 158.

2324 _____. "The foster care agency: a unique resource for social work education." Child Welfare, v. 46, no. 2, Feb. 1967. 64, 103.

2325 Goldberg, Ruth L. and Sidney M. Grossberg. "The role of the learning center on family functioning in social work education." Family Coordinator, v. 24, no. 3, July 1975. 273-280.

2326 _____. "The social worker and the family physician." Social Casework, v. 54, no. 8, Oct. 1973. 489-495.

2327 Goldberg, Thelma. "Social work students in day-care settings." Children, v. 14, no. 3, May-June 1967. 113-116.

2328 Griffin, Patricia C. "A demonstration of new methods in child welfare: a student project." Child Welfare, v. 52, no. 7, July 1973. 462-469.

2329 Hromadka, Van G. "European concept of child care and what we can learn from it." Child Welfare, v. 43, no. 8, Oct. 1964. 427-430.

2330 _____. "How child care workers are trained in Europe." Children, v. 11, no. 6, Nov. -Dec. 1964. 219-222.

2331 Ireland, Eleanor. "The social worker's contribution to training in child psychiatry." Journal of Child Psychology and Psychiatry and Allied Disciplines, v. 8, no. 2, Nov. 1967. 99-104.

2332 Kadushin, Alfred. "Public perception of child welfare services--results of a student survey." Journal of Education for Social Work, v. 10, no. 1, winter 1974. 42-47.

2333 Kristenson, Avis. "The child welfare worker: strengths and limitations in his professional training." Child Welfare, v. 43, no. 2, Feb. 1964. 64-71.

2334 Lawder, Elizabeth A. "Education and training for child welfare: a realistic view." Child Welfare, v. 45, no. 3, March 1966. 133-136.

2335 Levande, Diane I. "Family theory as a necessary component of family therapy." Social Casework, v. 57, no. 5, May 1976. 291-295.

2336 Leyendecker, Gertrude. "A family agency reviews its educational program." Social Casework, v. 44, no. 4, April 1963. 185-192.

2337 Linford, Alton A. "Education and in-service training for the public family and children's services." Education for social work; proceedings of the 1963 Annual Program Meeting, Council on Social Work Education. New York: The Council, 1963. 81-92.

2338 Littner, Ner. "Is social work education keeping pace with our deepening knowledge of children?" Education for social work; proceedings of the 1962 Annual Program Meeting, Council on Social Work Education. New York: The Council, 1962. 135-151. Discussion by Charlotte Towle. 152-161.

2339 McCoy, Jacqueline. "Are the schools adequately training students for child welfare?" Child Welfare, v. 43, no. 2, Feb. 1964. 72-75.

2340 Madison, Bernice and Michael Schapiro. New perspectives on child welfare: services, staffing, delivery system. San Francisco, 1973. 177p.

2341 Matson, Margaret B. "Education and training for child welfare: from the point of view of the undergraduate school." Child Welfare, v. 45, no. 3, March 1966. 137-139.

2342 Mayer, Morris F. and John Matsushima. "Training for child care work: a report on a national conference." Child Welfare, v. 48, no. 9, Nov. 1969. 525-532.

2343 Mumford, Napoleon B. "Training graduate social work students for child advocacy in community mental health."
Journal of Education for Social Work, v. 11, no. 1, winter 1975. 113-120.

2344 Neubauer, Peter B. and Joseph Steinert. "The significance for social workers of the multidiscipline approach to child development." Social Service Review, v. 29, no. 4, Dec. 1950. 459-465. Discussion by Charlotte Towle. 466-468.

2345 O'Neill, John F. and Steven I. Pflanczer. Profiles in child welfare service: a study of differentially trained social workers. Milwaukee: University of Wisconsin Extension Division, 1965. 85p.

2346 Parad, Howard J. "Social work training for child welfare: some key issues." Child Welfare, v. 40, no. 1, Jan. 1961. 1-7.

2347 Schulman, Gerda L. "Teaching family therapy to social work students." Social Casework, v. 57, no. 7, July 1976. 448-457.

2348 Shapiro, Deborah. "Professional training and the child welfare worker: an exploratory study." Approaches to innovation in social work education. Compiled by the Council on Social Work Education. New York: The Council, 1974. 82-91.

2349 Stewart, George J. "Day care: an under-used resource in child welfare." Child Welfare, v. 47, no. 4, April 1968. 207-211.

2350 Swain, Doris D. "Social work education and manpower for child welfare." Child Welfare, v. 45, no. 8, Oct. 1966. 468-470.

2351 Towle, Charlotte. "The training of the social worker for child guidance." Handbook of child guidance. Edited by Ernest Harms. New York: Child Care Publications, 1947. 372-390.

2352 Turnbull, Anne. "Teaching family centered practice in a BSW programme: a field experience." Social Worker-Travailleur Social, v. 43, no. 3, fall 1975. 153-155.

2353 United Nations. Department of Economic and Social Affairs. A handbook of training for family and child welfare. New York: United Nations, 1969. 110p. ST/SOA/85.

2354 _____. Economic Commission for Asia and the Far East. Report of the Asian Seminar on Training for Family and

Child Welfare. Bangkok: The Commission, 1963. 51p.

2355 Walrond-Skinner, Sue. "Training for family therapy: the supervision of students in a specialist agency." Social Work Today, v. 5, no. 5, 30 May 1974. 149-154.

2356 Wasserman, Sidney and Paul Gitlin. "A child care training experience revisited." Child Welfare, v. 44, no. 1, Jan. 1965. 35-40.

2357 _____ and _____. "Child care worker training experience: a coordinated effort between classroom and agency." Child Welfare, v. 42, no. 8, Oct. 1963. 392-398.

2358 Woods, Thomas L. "Social work consultation and student training in day care centers." Child Welfare, v. 52, no. 10, Dec. 1973. 663-668.

2359 Younghusband, Eileen L. "Developments in social work training." Youth service and interprofessional studies. Edited by Inga Bulman, Maurice Craft and Fred Milson. New York: Pergamon Press, 1970. 108-120.

D. COMMUNITY AND SOCIAL ACTION PROGRAMS

2360 Beck, Bertram M. "Knowledge and skills in administration of an antipoverty program." Social Work, v. 11, no. 3, July 1966. 102-106.

2361 Brooke, Rosalind. "Which way for welfare rights teaching?" Social Work Today, v. 4, no. 13, 20 Sept. 1973. 390-392.

2362 Cypher, John and Ron Walton. "Welfare rights and social work education." Social Work Today, v. 4, no. 13, 20 Sept. 1973. 394-398.

2363 Faivre, Beatrice M. "Social work education at the crossroads." Catholic Charities Review, v. 45, no. 3, March 1961. 15-18.

2364 Forman, Mark, et al. "Learning and teaching in a community field laboratory." Social Work Education Reporter, v. 19, no. 2, April-May 1971. 32-37.

2365 Hathway, Marion. "Social action and professional education." Proceedings of the National Conference of Social Work, Cleveland, 1944. New York: Columbia University Press, 1944. 363-373.

2366 Kansas City Regional Council for Higher Education. Cooper-

ative Social Welfare Action Program; a report of the first
year of an undergraduate program in social welfare education. Kansas City, Mo.: The Council, 1971. 55p.

2367 King, Clarence. Working with people in community action;
an international casebook for trained community workers
and volunteer community leaders. New York: Association
Press, 1966. 192p.

2368 Lowy, Louis. "Social work and social statesmanship." Social Work, v. 5, no. 2, April 1960. 97-104.

2369 Meld, Murray B. "The political salience of education for
community organization practice." Journal of Education
for Social Work, v. 12, no. 3, fall 1976. 80-87.

2370 Paull, Joseph E. "Social action: So what's to teach?" Social Work Education Reporter, v. 19, no. 1, April-May
1971. 49-52.

2371 Slavin, Simon. "The role of schools of social work in educating social workers for anti-poverty programs." Personnel in anti-poverty programs: implications for social work
education. By Sherman Barr, et al. New York: Council on Social Work Education, 1967. 9-27.

2372 Todres, Rubin. "The professional socialization of attitudes
toward social action tactics among social work students."
Doctoral dissertation, University of Pittsburgh, 1974.
266p.

E. CORRECTIONS AND JUVENILE DELINQUENCY [See also Section XVI. B. 4.]

2373 Austin, Michael J., Edward Kelleher and Philip L. Smith,
editors. The field consortium: manpower development
and training in social welfare and corrections. Tallahassee, Fla.: State University System of Florida, 1972.
121p.

2374 Brennan, William C. and Shanti K. Khinduka. "Role discre-
pancies and professional socialization: the case of the
juvenile probation officer." Social Work, v. 15, no. 2,
April 1970. 87-94.

2375 Burbank, Edmund G. "Some problems and issues confronting
social work education in corrections." Social Work Education Reporter, v. 10, no. 4, Aug. -Sept. 1962. 1-7.

2376 _____. "What the schools of social work can do to increase

the pool of trained correctional personnel. " Education
for social work; proceedings of the 1961 Annual Program
Meeting, Council on Social Work Education. New York:
The Council, 1961. 163-177.

2377 Central Council for Education and Training in Social Work.
The social worker in the juvenile court: some suggestions
for training. London: The Council, 1974. 15p.

2378 Conference on Undergraduate Education for the Social Service.
An examination of the role of undergraduate education in
the preparation of personnel for corrections and social
welfare. Inglewood, Calif.: California State College,
1965. 99p.

2379 Council on Social Work Education. The education needs of
personnel in the field of corrections. New York: The
Council, 1956. 20p.

2380 _____. Social work education for personnel in the field of
corrections. New York: The Council, 1956. 24p.

2381 _____. Committee on Corrections. Perspectives and
guides in the expansion of social work education for the
correctional field. New York: The Council, 1958. 25p.

2382 Crow, Richard. "The perceptions of training needs of adult
probation and parole officers in Colorado." Doctoral dissertation, University of Denver, 1974. 253p.

2383 Johnson, Kenneth D. "The professional schools face the
challenge of correctional work." Focus, v. 29, no. 5,
Sept. 1950. 129-132, 149-151.

2384 Judge Baker Guidance Center, Boston. A pilot training program for the training of personnel for the field of juvenile delinquency. Boston: The Center, 1960. 3 vols.

2385 Kaslow, Florence and Stewart Werner. "Educating social
workers for evolving roles in corrections." Journal of
Sociology and Social Welfare, v. 3, no. 6, July 1976. 656-671.

2386 Knouff, Scotia B. "Descriptions of the joint multi-method
project implications for in-service training in probation
and graduate social work education." Social Work Education Reporter, v. 14, no. 2, June 1966. 31, 42-44.

2387 Meeker, Ben S. "The Curriculum Study: implications for
the field of corrections." Social Casework, v. 41, no. 1,
Jan. 1960. 24-29.

2388 Ohlin, Lloyd E. , Herman Piven and Donnell M. Pappenfort.

"Major dilemmas of the social worker in probation and parole." NPPA Journal, v. 2, no. 3, July 1956. 211-225.

2389 Panakal, J. J. "Training for correctional work." Indian Journal of Social Work, v. 28, no. 1, April 1967. 89-94.

2390 Polk, Kenneth. The university and corrections: potential for collaborative relationships. Washington, D. C. : Joint Commission on Correctional Manpower and Training. 1969. 78p.

2391 Prigmore, Charles S. , editor. The expansion of correctional field placements and internships. New York: Council on Social Work Education, 1965. 60p.

2392 _____ . "Fitting corrections into the curriculum." Social Work, v. 7, no. 1, Jan. 1962. 103-105.

2393 _____ , editor. Manpower and training for corrections; proceedings of Arden House Conference on Manpower and Trainings for Corrections, 1964. New York: Council on Social Work Education, 1966. 260p.

2394 Rothman, Beulah. "Contributions of probation to social work education emerging from a joint project on multi-methods." Social Work Education Reporter, v. 14, no. 2, June 1966. 30, 41-42.

2395 Sedio, Edward, Gordon Nelson and Beulah Compton. "Social work student placement in a probation setting." NPPA Journal, v. 2, no. 3, July 1956. 233-238.

2396 Senna, Joseph J. "The role of the graduate school of social work in criminal justice higher education." Journal of Education for Social Work, v. 10, no. 2, spring 1974. 92-98.

2397 Shelly, Joseph A. "Bringing the classroom into the courtroom: a program of undergraduate student training." Crime and Delinquency, v. 7, no. 1, Jan. 1961. 25-36.

2398 Shireman, Charles H. "Education for social workers in the correctional field, by Elliott Studt: review." Social Service Review, v. 33, no. 4, Dec. 1959. 404-408.

2399 _____ . "Education for social workers: the correctional field." Child Welfare, v. 39, no. 5, May 1960. 6-7.

2400 Sternbach, Jack C. "Issues in corrections from both sides of the bars." Social Casework, v. 54, no. 6, June 1973. 342-349.

2401 Studt, Elliot. "Building a program of social work educational services for the correction field." Education for social work; proceedings of concurrent sessions of the 1955 Annual Program Meeting, Council on Social Work Education. New York: The Council, 1955. 38-48.

2402 _____. A conceptual approach to teaching materials: illustrations from the field of corrections. New York: Council on Social Work Education, 1965. 243p.

2403 _____. "Contribution of correctional practice to social work theory and education." Social Casework, v. 37, no. 6, June 1956. 263-269.

2404 _____. Education for social workers in the correctional field. The social work curriculum study, v. 5. New York: Council on Social Work Education, 1959. 50p.

2405 _____. "Learning casework in a juvenile probation setting." Social Casework, v. 32, no. 8, Oct. 1951. 343-350.

2406 _____. "A school of social work build a program of correctional personnel." NPPA Journal, v. 2, no. 3, July 1956. 226-232.

2407 Treger, Harvey, et al. The police-social work team: a new model for interprofessional cooperation. Springfield, Ill.: Charles C. Thomas, 1975. 269p.

2408 _____. "Social work in the police agency: implications for education and practice." Journal of Education for Social Work, v. 12, no. 2, spring 1976. 43-50.

2409 United States. Children's Bureau. Training personnel for work with juvenile delinquents. Washington, D. C.: Government Printing Office, 1954. 90p.

2410 Viegas, Kenneth D. "Education for social work in the administration of justice." Journal of Education for Social Work, v. 10, no. 1, winter 1974. 105-108.

2411 Vigilante, Joseph L. and Milton Rector. "Arden House Conference on Corrections: implications for social work education." Social Work Education Reporter, v. 13, no. 1, March 1965. 8-9, 22-23.

2412 Wilson, Marguerite. "Strategies of teaching in corrections." Social Casework, v. 51, no. 10, Dec. 1970. 618-624.

2413 Younghusband, Eileen L. "Report on a survey of social work in the field of corrections." Social Work Education, v. 8, no. 4, Aug. 1960. Supplement. 24p.

F. FAMILY PLANNING

2414 Armitmahal, G. R. "Training of family planning workers. "
Social Work Forum, v. 4, no. 4, Oct. 1966. 47-51.

2415 Atkins, Jacqueline Marx, compiler. Audio-visual resources
for population education and family planning: an international guide for social work educators. New York: International Association of Schools of Social Work, 1975.
148p.

2416 Chilman, Catherine S. and Paul H. Glasser. Social work
roles and functions in family and population planning:
some implications for social work education. Ann Arbor:
Social Work Education and Population Planning Project,
School of Social Work, University of Michigan, 1974. 54p.

2417 Glasser, Paul H. , Helen J. Hunter and Henry J. Meyer. Social work education for family and population planning:
topical outlines and annotated references selected for social work educators. Ann Arbor: University of Michigan,
1973. Various pagings.

2418 Haselkorn, Florence. "Family planning content in the graduate social work curriculum. " The social worker and
family planning; based on the proceedings of the 1969
Annual Institute for Public Health Social Workers. Edited
by Joanna F. Gorman. Washington, D. C. : U. S. Public Health Service, 1970. 102-111.

2419 _____. "Family planning: implications for social work
education. " Journal of Education for Social Work, v. 6,
no. 2, fall 1970. 13-19.

2420 International Association of Schools of Social Work. A developmental outlook for social work education; a report
of a Seminar on "Maximizing Social Work Potentials for
Family Planning and Population Activities," Singapore,
1973. New York: The Association, 1974. 175p.

2421 Kendall, Katherine A. , editor. Population dynamics and
family planning: a new responsibility for social work
education; proceedings of an International Conference on
Social Work Education, Population, and Family Planning,
Honolulu, Hawaii, 1970. New York: Council on Social
Work Education, 1971. 159p.

2422 Manisoff, Miriam T. , editor. Family planning training for

social service. New York: Planned Parenthood/World
Population, 1970. 85p.

2423 Meisels, Joseph F. "Implications of population changes for
social work education." Education for social work; proceedings of the 1957 Annual Program Meeting, Council on
Social Work Education. New York: The Council, 1957.
71-78.

2424 Nanavatty, Meher C. Social work education, training and research in the field of family planning and population control. New York: International Association of Schools of
Social Work, 1971. 9p.

2425 Oettinger, Katherine Brownell and Jeffrey D. Stansbury, editors. Population and family planning: analytical abstracts
for social work educators and related disciplines. New
York: International Association of Schools of Social Work,
1972. 161p.

2426 _____ . The school of social work's responsibilities in
family planning education. Washington, D. C.: U. S.
Department of Health, Education, and Welfare, 1968. 16p.

2427 _____ . Social work in action: an international perspective
on population and family planning--The Asian contribution.
New York: International Association of Schools of Social
Work, 1975. 345p.

2428 Palacios, Teresita S. "De-emphasizing family planning in
social work education?" Social Work Education and Development Newsletter, no. 12, March 1975. 19-20.

2429 Pangalangan, Evelina A. "Family planning themes and crea-
tive literature: a social work educator's experience."
Social Work Education and Development Newsletter, no. 12,
March 1975. 17-18.

2430 Rapoport, Lydia. "Education and training of social workers
for roles and functions in family planning." Journal of
Education for Social Work, v. 6, no. 2, fall 1970. 27-38.

2431 Schlesinger, Benjamin. "Social work education and family
planning." Social Worker-Travailleur Social, v. 41, no. 2,
summer 1973. 93-99.

2432 Seldin, Nathan Everett. "Professional interaction and occupational identification: a national study of family planners,
social work educators, and field instructors." Doctoral
dissertation, University of Denver, 1973. 427p.

2433 Werley, Harriet H., et al. "Medicine, nursing, social work:

professionals and birth control: student and faculty attitudes." Family Planning Perspectives, v. 5, no. 1, winter
1973. 42-49.

G. HEALTH AND MEDICAL CARE [See also Sections XVI. B. 5, 6, 7.]

2434 American Association of Medical Social Workers. Education
for medical social work, the curriculum content. Washington, D. C.: The Association, 1951. 50p.

2435 American Public Health Association. Committee on Professional Education. "Educational qualifications of social
workers in public health programs." American Journal
of Public Health, v. 52, no. 2, Feb. 1962. 317-324.

2436 Anthony, Helen. "Training for medical social work." Medical social work: a career in hospital and community.
Reading, Eng.: Educational Explorers, 1968. 100-107.

2437 Assessment Conference on Social Work Education in Neuro-
logical and Sensory Disease. Proceedings of the Conference, State University of New York at Buffalo, 1967.
Buffalo, N. Y.: School of Social Welfare, State University of New York at Buffalo, 1967. 70p.

2438 Bartlett, Harriett M. "Frontiers of medical social work."
Social Work, v. 7, no. 2, April 1962. 75-83.

2439 _____. Social work practice in the health field. New York:
National Association of Social Workers, 1961. 280p.

2440 Bracht, Neil F. "Health Maintenance Organizations: legislative and training implications." Journal of Education
for Social Work, v. 11, no. 1, winter 1975. 36-44.

2441 Butrym, Zofia T. "Some implications for education and practice I." Medical Social Work (London), v. 19, no. 3, June
1966. 16-27.

2442 Hartshorn, Alma E. "Social work and the hospital: changing
concepts of training, generic and specialized." Australian
Journal of Social Work, v. 16, no. 1, Feb. 1963. 2-9.

2443 Health and disability concepts in social work education; proceedings of a workshop conference sponsored by the School
of Social Work, University of Minnesota. Minneapolis:
School of Social Work, University of Minnesota, 1964.
46p.

2444 Hookey, Peter. "Education for social work in health care organizations." Social Work in Health Care, v. 1, no. 3 spring 1976. 337-345.

2445   Jones, Kathleen. "Society as the client." Medical Social Work (London), v. 19, no. 3, June 1966. 2-8.

2446   Kindelsperger, Walter L. , et al. Responsibility of schools of social work to help meet the changing needs of medical care. New York: United Hospital Fund of New York, 1968. 39p.

2447   Kurtz, Richard A. and David J. Giacopassi. "Medical and social work students' perceptions of deviant conditions and sick role incumbency." Social Science and Medicine, v. 9, no. 4-5, April-May 1975. 249-256.

2448   Lustman, Claire R. "Development of social work education in the Veterans Administration: current trends and future plans." Social Work Education Reporter, v. 17, no. 3, Sept. 1969. 54-56, 60.

2449   Marshall, David B. "A doctor's reaction to 'The first two years.'" Medical Social Work (London), v. 19, no. 3, June 1966. 34-38.

2450   Mitchell, Florence. "'The first two years': review article." Medical Social Work (London), v. 18, no. 7, Nov. 1965. 209-212.

2451   Moon, Marjorie and Kathleen Slack. The first two years: a study of work experience of some newly qualified medical social workers. London: Institute of Medical Social Workers, 1965. 83p.

2452   Myers, Ruth Fey and Richard W. Soldo. "Program upgrades students' skills." Hospitals, v. 48, no. 2, 16 Jan. 1974. 50-52.

2453   Newton, George. "The impact of the first two years: a comparison with social work in other settings." Medical Social Work (London), v. 19, no. 3, June 1966. 9-15.

2454   Parlow, J. and A. Rothman. "Attitudes towards social issues in medicine of five health science faculties (Dentistry, medicine, nursing, pharmacy, and social work)." Social Science and Medicine, v. 8, no. 6, June 1974. 351-358.

2455   Perretz, Edgar A. "Social work education for the field of health." Social Work in Health Care, v. 1, no. 3, spring 1976. 357-365.

2456   Richards, Kay. "Comparison between a student's and a worker's caseload. " Medical Social Work (London), v. 19, no. 8, Jan. 1967. 259-266.

2457 Seminar on Public Health for Schools of Social Work. Public health concepts in social work education; proceedings of the seminar, Princeton University, 1962. New York: Council on Social Work Education, 1962. 295p.

2458 Smith, Esther B. , et al. "Social work education. " Community services and education: The heart and circulation, v. 2; proceedings of the National conference on Cardiovascular Diseases, Washington, D. C. , 1964. Edited by E. Cowles Andrus. Bethesda, Md. : Federation of American Societies for Experimental Biology, 1965. 916-926.

2459 Snelling, Jean M. The contribution of the Institute of Medical Social Workers to education for social work. Bradford, Eng. : Association of Social Work Teachers, 1970. Unpaged.

2460 Spencer, Ethel. "Some implications for education and practice II. " Medical Social Work (London), v. 19, no. 3, June 1966. 28-33.

2461 Spencer, Sue W. Education for social work practice in changing health programs. Boston: School of Social Work, Simmons College, 1969. 20p.

2462 Stamm, Isabel. "Social work education for practice in the health field. " Education for social work; proceedings of the 1963 Annual Program Meeting, Council on Social Work Education. New York: The Council, 1963. 115-122.

2463 Stites, Mary A. History of the American Association of Medical Social Workers. Washington, D. C. : American Association of Medical Social Workers, 1955. 132p.

2464 Wittman, Milton. "Social work manpower in the health services. " American Journal of Public Health, v. 55, no. 3, March 1965. 393-399.

H. MENTAL HEALTH [See also Section XVI. B. 8.]

2465 American Association of Psychiatric Social Workers. Education for psychiatric social work; proceedings of the Dartmouth Conference, 1949. New York: The Association, 1950. 233p.

2466 Bandler, Bernard. "Community mental health and the educational dilemmas of the mental health professions. " Jour-

nal of Education for Social Work, v. 8, no. 3, fall 1972.
5-18.

2467 Barter, John. "Mental health and social work training." Social Work Today, v. 7, no. 13, 16 Sept. 1976. 367-370.

2468 Blanchard, Myron and Rosa Felsenburg. "Social work education for community mental health center functioning." Social Work Education Reporter, v. 20, no. 1, Dec. /Jan. 1972. 51-55.

2469 Carlsen, Thomas, editor. Social work manpower utilization in mental health programs; proceedings of a workshop. Syracuse, N. Y.: Syracuse University Press, 1969. 41p.

2470 Chester, Robert, et al. "The gap in social work education." Mental Hygiene, v. 53, no. 1, Jan. 1969. 84-89.

2471 Dawson, Betty Guthrie. "Supervising the undergraduate in a psychiatric setting." The dynamics of field instruction: learning through doing. Compiled by the Council on Social Work Education. New York: The Council, 1975. 10-19.

2472 Dean, Robert L. "Intake as core learning for psychiatric social work students." Social Work, v. 3, no. 1, Jan. 1958. 62-67.

2473 Evans, Phyllis P. and Neil F. Bracht. "Meeting social work's challenge in community mental health." Mental Hygiene, v. 55, no. 3, July 1971. 295-297.

2474 French, Lois Meredith. Psychiatric social work. New York: The Commonwealth Fund, 1940. 344p.

2475 Glueck, Bernard. "Special preparation of the psychiatric social worker." Proceedings of the National Conference of Social Work, 1919. Chicago: Rogers & Hall, 1919. 599-606.

2476 Green, Rose and Maurice B. Hamovitch. "Education of social workers for mental health consultation." American Journal of Orthopsychiatry, v. 32, no. 2, March 1962. 225-226.

2477 Hambrecht, Leona. "Education for psychiatric social work to meet an evolving program of basic professional education." Journal of Psychiatric Social Work, v. 22, no. 1, Oct. 1952. 37-44.

2478 Hamilton, Margaret. "Learning to be a social worker with the mentally disordered." British Journal of Psychiatric

Social Work, v. 10, no. 4, autumn 1970. 178-183.

2479 Henry, William E. , John H. Sims and S. Lee Spray. The fifth profession: becoming a psychotherapist. San Francisco: Jossey-Bass, 1971. 221p.

2480 Institute on Teaching Psychiatric Social Work. Teaching psychiatric social work; proceedings of the Institute, Atlantic City, 1955. New York: American Association of Psychiatric Social Workers, 1955. 43p.

2481 Institute on the Use of the Case Method in Teaching Psychiatric Social Work. The case method in teaching social work; proceedings of the Institute, Atlantic City, 1957. Charlotte Towle, leader. New York: National Association of Social Workers, 1959. 78p.

2482 Jacobson, Doris Seder. "Instruction in mental health and illness: a report on an innovation in social work education." Social Work Education Reporter, v. 21, no. 2, April-May 1973. 53-58.

2483 Koegler, Ronald R. , Enery Reyes Williamson and Corazon Grossman. "Individualized educational approach to fieldwork in a community mental health center." Journal of Education for Social Work, v. 12, no. 2, spring 1976. 28-35.

2484 Kurtz, Nancy, Richard Kurtz and Robert Hoffnung. "Attitudes toward the lower- and middle-class psychiatric patient as a function of authoritarianism among mental health students." Journal of Consulting and Clinical Psychology, v. 35, no. 3, Dec. 1970. 338-341.

2485 Lee, Porter R. and Marion E. Kenworthy. "Education for psychiatric social work." Mental hygiene and social work. New York: The Commonwealth Fund, 1931. 155-263.

2486 McPheeters, Harold L. and James B. King. Plans for teaching mental health workers: community college curriculum objectives. Atlanta: Southern Regional Education Board, 1971. 79p.

2487 Mangum, Paul D. and Kevin M. Mitchell. "Attitudes toward the mentally ill and community care among professionals and their students." Community Mental Health Journal, v. 9, no. 4, winter 1973. 350-353.

2488 Mishne, Judith. "Reservations about The fifth profession: a redesign of training for clinical social work; essay review." Clinical Social Work Journal, v. 4, no. 2, summer 1976. 127-133.

2489 Mumford, Napoleon B. "Training graduate social work students for child advocacy in community mental health." Journal of Education for Social Work, v. 11, no. 1, winter 1975. 113-120.

2490 Myers, E. "What are we training psychiatric social workers for?" British Journal of Psychiatric Social Work, v. 8, no. 4, autumn 1966. 50-53.

2491 Neumann, Frederika. "The training of psychiatric social workers for individual psychotherapy." American Journal of Orthopsychiatry, v. 19, no. 1, Jan. 1949. 25-31.

2492 Parad, Howard J. and Lydia Rapoport. "Advanced social work educational programs in community mental health." Handbook of community mental health. Edited by Stuart E. Golann and Carl Eisdorfer. New York: Appleton-Century-Crofts, 1972. 873-887.

2493 _____ and _____. "Advanced social work educational programs in community mental health: a summary report." Social Work Education Reporter, v. 20, no. 2, April-May 1972. 57-61.

2494 Perlman, Helen Harris. "Classroom teaching of psychiatric social work." American Journal of Orthopsychiatry, v. 19, no. 2, April 1949. 306-315.

2495 Rapoport, Lydia and Robert Z. Apte. "Advanced education for practice in community mental health." Social Work Education Reporter, v. 16, no. 1, Dec. 1968. 24-28, 65.

2496 Sison, Mehelinda G. "Community development in a psychiatric setting: the Spring Grove experience." Doctoral dissertation, University of Pennsylvania, 1975. 150p.

2497 Southern Regional Education Board. Community mental health in social work education. Atlanta: The Board, 1975. 91p.

2498 Spaulding, Edith R. "The training school of psychiatric social work at Smith College." Proceedings of the National Conference of Social Work, 1919. Chicago: Rogers & Hall, 1919. 606-611.

2499 Swift, Sarah Howard. Training in psychiatric social work at the Institute for Child Guidance, 1927-1933. New York: The Commonwealth Fund, 1934. 177p.

2500 Towle, Charlotte. "The training of the social worker for child guidance." Handbook of child guidance. Edited by Ernest Harms. New York: Child Care Publications, 1947. 372-390.

2501 Vidaver, Robert M. and James E. Carson. "A new framework for baccalaureate careers in the human services."
American Journal of Psychiatry, v. 130, no. 4, April 1973.
474-478.

2502 Watkins, Ted R. "The comprehensive community health center as a field placement for graduate social work students."
Community Mental Health Journal, v. 11, no. 1, spring
1975. 27-32.

2503 Werner, Harold D. "Training social work students for an
expanding mental health clinic program." Mental Hygiene,
v. 47, no. 1, Jan. 1963. 103-107.

2504 Wittman, Milton. "Education for community mental health
practice: problems and prospects." Social Work, v. 3,
no. 4, Oct. 1958. 64-70.

2505 _____. "Significance of new scientific developments in
the mental health field for social work education." Social
Service Review, v. 31, no. 2, June 1957. 135-143.

I. MENTAL RETARDATION

2506 Barnhard, Stephanie. "Student learning patterns and problems
in a mental retardation setting." Social work and mental
retardation. Edited by Meyer Schreiber. New York: John
Day, 1970. 667-676.

2507 Begab, Michael J. "The effect of differences in curricula
and experiences on social work attitudes and knowledge
about mental retardation." Social work and mental retardation. Edited by Meyer Schreiber. New York: John
Day, 1970. 677-680.

2508 _____. The effect of differences in curricula and experiences on social work student attitudes and knowledge about
mental retardation. Washington, D. C.: National Institute of Child Health and Human Development, 1968. 135p.

2509 _____. "Impact of education on social work students'
knowledge and attitudes about mental retardation." American Journal of Mental Deficiency, v. 74, no. 6, May 1970.
801-808.

2510 _____. "Mental retardation content in the social work curriculum." Brown Studies, 1964. 1-16.

2511 _____. "New developments in mental retardation and their
implications for social work education." Education for social work; proceedings of the 1959 Annual Program Meeting,

Council on Social Work Education. New York: The Council, 1959. 62-70.

2512 Bertrand, Patricia T. Issues in social work education affecting the teaching of mental retardation content. Madison: School of Social Work, University of Wisconsin, 1967. 14p.

2513 Dana, Bess S. "Enriching social work education with mental retardation content." Journal of Education for Social Work, v. 1, no. 2, fall 1965. 5-10.

2514 Hindman, Darrell A. Cooperative programs of training and research in mental retardation. Yellow Springs, Ohio: Antioch Press, 1959. 160p.

2515 Hume, Marguerite, editor. Mental retardation: a new dimension in social work education. Louisville, Ky.: Kent School of Social Work, University of Louisville, 1967. 84p.

2516 Katz, Alfred H., editor. Mental retardation and social work education; proceedings of Conference on the Education and Training of Social Workers in Mental Retardation, Milford, Michigan, 1959. Detroit: Wayne State University Press, 1961. 56p.

2517 Krishef, Curtis and David L. Levine. "Preparing the social worker for effective services to the retarded." Mental Retardation, v. 6, no. 3, June 1968. 3-7.

2518 Landon, Lucy. A plan for orientation of incoming field instructors to an institution for the mentally retarded. New Brunswick, N. J.: School of Social Work, Rutgers University, 1965. 63p.

2519 Lewis, Verl S., editor. Field instruction in mental retardation settings serving children. Baltimore: School of Social Work, University of Maryland, 1967. 129p.

2520 McNary, Willette. The Jefferson County field course: report of a four-year project in mental retardation. Madison: School of Social Work, University of Wisconsin, 1967. 23p.

2521 Pisapia, Matthew L. "Mental retardation in the social work curriculum." Mental Retardation, v. 2, no. 5, Oct. 1964. 294-298.

2522 Prothero, John C. and Walter H. Ehlers. "Social-work students' attitude and knowledge changes following study of programmed materials." American Journal of Mental Deficiency, v. 79, no. 1, July 1974. 83-86.

2523 Schreiber, Meyer. "A selected list of teaching materials regarding mental retardation for faculty of schools of social
work. " Mental Retardation Abstracts, v. 4, no. 2, April-
June 1967. 181-187.

2524 Smith, Winifred E. "Issues in social work education affecting
the teaching of mental retardation content. " Social work
and mental retardation. Edited by Meyer Schreiber. New
York: John Day, 1970. 655-666.

2525 _____. "Service to the retarded as social work education. "
Children, v. 11, no. 5, Sept. -Oct. 1964. 189-192.

2526 Sterns, Caroline R. and Herbert H. Jarrett. "Mental retardation content in the curricula of graduate schools of social work. " Mental Retardation, v. 14, no. 3, June 1976.
17-19.

2527 Utah. University. Graduate School of Social Work. Mental
retardation content in the social work curriculum; proceedings of an institute for field instructors and campus faculty. Edited by Eleanor S. Stein. Salt Lake City: University of Utah Press, 1959. 43p.

2528 White, Grace. "What social work has to offer in the field
of mental retardation. " American Journal of Mental Deficiency, v. 65, no. 6, May 1961. 772-781.

J. PUBLIC WELFARE

2529 American Association of Schools of Social Work. Education
for the public social services. Chapel Hill: University
of North Carolina Press, 1942. 324p.

2530 Austin, David M. and Michael L. Lauderdale. "Social work
education: preparing public welfare administrators. " Public Welfare, v. 34, no. 3, summer 1976. 13-18.

2531 Brennen, E. Clifford, et al. "Social work education: expectations for baccalaureate social workers. " Public Welfare,
v. 34, no. 3, summer 1976. 19-23.

2532 Breul, Frank R. "Education for social workers in the public social services, by Irving Weissman and Mary R. Baker: review. " Social Service Review, v. 33, no. 4, Dec.
1959. 411-414.

2533 Chaturvedi, H. R. "Teaching of public welfare administration." Indian Journal of Social Work, v. 25, no. 3, Oct. 1964. 277-280.

2534 Cohen, Wilbur J. "Implications for the social work curriculum of poverty as we face it today." Education for social work; proceedings of the 1962 Annual Program Meeting, Council on Social Work Education. New York: The Council, 1962. 122-134.

2535 Fauri, David P. "Social work education for leadership roles in state government." Journal of Education for Social Work, v. 12, no. 1, winter 1976. 44-49.

2536 "Field instruction placements in public welfare agencies." Social Work Education, v. 9, no. 3, June 1961. 4-5.

2537 Johnson, Betty S. and Victoria Brown. "New approaches to training the alienated social worker." Public Welfare, v. 30, no. 3, summer 1972. 54-58.

2538 Kermish, Irving, Barbara Kohlman and Frank Kushin. The professionally educated social worker in public assistance programs; a California perspective. Berkeley: School of Social Welfare, University of California, 1970. 106p.

2539 Kindelsperger, Kenneth W. An approach to the study of the public social services and its relationship to undergraduate education for social welfare. New York: Council on Social Work Education, 1956. 17p.

2540 Madison, Bernice. The public assistance job and the undergraduate social work curriculum. San Francisco: San Francisco State College, 1954. 103p.

2541 Meyer, Rose and Virginia L. Tannar. "The use of the public assistance setting for field practice." Social Work, v. 4, no. 3, July 1959. 35-40.

2542 Pins, Arnulf M. "The public welfare worker 1965-1975: implications for social work education." Public Welfare, v. 25, no. 1, Jan. 1967. 21-27.

2543 Podell, Lawrence. "The impact of professional social work education upon public social service personnel." Public Welfare, v. 31, no. 2, spring 1973. 64-68.

2544 _____. "Professional experiences in public welfare." Social Work Education Reporter, v. 18, no. 3, Sept.-Oct. 1970. 51-54.

2545 _____. "Professional social workers in public social services." Public Welfare, v. 27, no. 2, April 1969. 140-147.

2546 Rosen, Aaron and Ronda S. Connaway. "Public welfare, so-
       cial work, and social work education." Social Work, v.
       14, no. 2, April 1969. 87-94.

2547 Schottland, Charles I. "Education for social workers: the
       public social services." Child Welfare, v. 39, no. 5, May
       1960. 7-9.

2548 Shannon, Ruth. "Developing a framework for field work in-
       struction in a public assistance agency." Social Casework,
       v. 43, no. 7, July 1962. 355-360.

2549 Thompson, Jane K. and Donald P. Riley. "Use of profession-
       als in public welfare: a dilemma and a proposal." So-
       cial Work, v. 11, no. 1, Jan. 1966. 22-27.

2550 Vasey, Wayne. "Implication for social work education."
       Multi-problem dilemma: a social research demonstra-
       tion with multi-problem families. Edited by Gordon
       E. Brown. Metuchen, N. J.: Scarecrow Press,
       1968. 32-46.

2551 Weissman, Irving and Mary R. Baker. Education for social
       workers in the public social services. The social work
       curriculum study, v. 7. New York: Council on Social
       Work Education, 1959. 170p.

2552 Wilkens, Anne. Guides for field instruction for graduate
       schools of social work, field experience of undergraduate stu-
       dents and summer employment of undergraduate students.
       Washington, D. C.: U. S. Bureau of Family Services and
       U. S. Children's Bureau, 1963. 33p.

2553 Winston, Ellen. "Future social work practices and services--
       implications for education." Public Welfare, v. 25, no. 1,
       Jan. 1967. 15-20.

2554 _____. "New dimensions in public welfare: implications
       for social work education." Social work education and
       social welfare manpower: present realities and future
       imperatives. By Ellen Winston, et al. New York: Coun-
       cil on Social Work Education, 1965. 1-25.

2555 Wolfe, Corinne H. "Changes in professional education for
       improving public social services." Higher education and
       the social professions. Edited by Henry M. Barlow.
       Lexington, Ky.: College of Social Professions, University
       of Kentucky, 1973. 53-76.

2556 _____. "The Curriculum Study: implication for the public
       social services." Social Casework, v. 41, no. 1, Jan. 1960.
       19-24.

2556a Yankey, John. "Social work education: Marketing strategy
as an aid to curriculum design." Public Welfare, v. 34,
no. 4, autumn 1976. 14-19.

K. REHABILITATION

2557 Central Council for Education and Training in Social Work.
People with handicaps need better trained workers; report
of a Working Party on Training for Social Work with Handicapped People. London: The Council, 1974. 68p.

2558 Cochintu, Anne W. "Education for social workers: rehabilitation of the handicapped." Child Welfare, v. 39, no. 5,
May 1960. 9.

2559 Cooper, Ruth. "Social work in vocational rehabilitation."
Social Work, v. 8, no. 1, Jan. 1963. 92-98.

2560 Dabelstein, Donald H. "Basic content in the field of rehabilitation." Education for social work; proceedings of the
1955 Annual Program Meeting, Council on Social Work Education. New York: The Council, 1955. 28-37.

2561 Dana, Bess S. "The Curriculum Study: implications for the
field of rehabilitation of the handicapped." Social Casework,
v. 41, no. 1, Jan. 1960. 29-33.

2562 Davis, Marie. "Field experience in social work with deaf
students." Journal of Rehabilitation of the Deaf, v. 6, no.
2, Oct. 1972. 76-77.

2563 Durfee, Richard. "Personality characteristics and attitudes
toward the disabled of students in the health professions."
Rehabilitation Counseling Bulletin, v. 15, no. 1, Sept. 1971.
35-44.

2564 Elwell, Mary Ellen. "Training undergraduate social workers
for work with the deaf." Journal of Education for Social
Work, v. 11, no. 1, winter 1975. 51-58.

2565 Godfrey, Beryl, editor. Orientation of social workers to the
problems of deaf persons. Washington, D. C. : Vocational
Rehabilitation Administration, U. S. Department of Health,
Education, and Welfare, 1964. 135p.

2566 Hester, Curtis. "Training the deaf in social work: an undergraduate program in a mental health setting." Journal of
Rehabilitation of the Deaf. v. 6, no. 2, Oct. 1972. 68-72.

2567 Horwitz, John J. Education for social workers in the rehabilitation of the handicapped. The social work curriculum study, v. 8. New York: Council on Social Work Education, 1959. 76p.

2568 _____. "How professional education can contribute to the preparation of social workers serving the handicapped." Social Worker-Travailleur Social, v. 27, no. 1, Jan. 1959. 29-38.

2569 James, Alice. "Education for social workers in the rehabilitation of the handicapped, by John J. Horwitz: review." Social Service Review, v. 33, no. 4, Dec. 1959. 415-419.

2570 Mayers, Friedericka. "Modifying attitudes and adjustment through social work training in an agency serving the visually handicapped." New Outlook for the Blind, v. 70, no. 2, Feb. 1976. 72-77.

2571 Pumphrey, Muriel W., editor. Rehabilitation in social work education; proceedings of a workshop, St. Louis, Missouri, 1960. St. Louis, Mo.: George Warren Brown School of Social Work, Washington University, 1960. 19p.

2572 Simmons College. School of Social Work. Proceedings of Workshop on Rehabilitation Content in Social Work Education, 1957. Boston: The School, 1957. 124p.

2573 Sprick, Heidemarie. "Helping social work students experience blindness." Social Work Education and Development Newsletter, no. 15, March 1976. 14-15.

2574 Turner, William H. and James E. Granberry. "Social work students in vocational rehab: an experience in learning and cooperation." Rehabilitation Record, v. 7, no. 2, Mar.-April 1966. 6-9.

2575 Whiteman, Martin and Irving F. Lukoff. "Attitudes toward blindness and other physical handicaps." Journal of Social Psychology, v. 66, no. 1, June 1965. 135-145.

2576 _____ and _____. "Attitudes toward blindness in two college groups." Journal of Social Psychology, v. 63, no. 1, June 1963. 179-191.

2577 Willigan, Barbara. "My training experience in social work at Gallaudet College and present employment." Journal of Rehabilitation of the Deaf, v. 6, no. 2, Oct. 1972. 78-79.

2578 Wojciechowski, Sophie. "Basic educational implications for rehabilitative social work training." New Outlook for the Blind, v. 59, no. 4, April 1965. 145-148.

L. SCHOOL SOCIAL WORK [See also XVI. B. 3.]

2579 Anderson, Richard J. "Introducing change in school-community-pupil relationships: maintaining credibility and accountability." Journal of Education for Social Work, v. 10, no. 1, winter 1974. 3-8.

2580 Austin, Michael J. , Jeffrey Lickson and Philip L. Smith, editors. Continuing education in social welfare: school social work and the effective use of manpower. Tallahassee, Fla. : State University System of Florida, 1972. 133p.

2581 Beck, Bertram M. "School social work: an instrument of education." Social Work, v. 4, no. 4, Oct. 1959. 87-91.

2582 Browning, Grace. "Discussion of the articles on school social work by Mildred Sikkema and Florence Poole." Helping the troubled school child. Edited by Grace Lee. New York: National Association of Social Workers, 1959. 415-419.

2583 Hawkins, Mable T. "Interdisciplinary team training: Social work students in public school field placement settings." The dynamics of field instruction: learning through doing. Compiled by the Council on Social Work Education. New York: The Council, 1975. 40-49.

2584 Jacobsen, Virginia. "Evaluating my social work training for visiting teacher work." Helping the troubled school child. Edited by Grace Lee. New York: National Association of Social Workers, 1959. 430-433.

2585 Janvier, Carmelite. "Essentials of a training program for school social workers." Helping the troubled school child. Edited by Grace Lee. New York: National Association of Social Workers, 1959. 407-414.

2586 Johnson, Arlien. School social work: its contribution to professional education. New York: National Association of Social Workers, 1962. 255p.

2587 Moore, Barbara M. "Challenge to colleges of education and schools of social work." Social work in schools: patterns and perspectives. Edited by John J. Alderson. Northbrook, Ill. : Whitehall, 1969. 118-126.

2588 Nesbit, Elsie. "Goals, recruitment, training, and staffing." School social work: a service of schools. Edited by Horace W. Lundberg. Washington, D. C. : U. S. Office of Education, 1964. 43-54.

2589 Ralphs, F. Lincoln, chairman. "Report of the Working Party on the Role and Training of EWOs (Ralphs report)." Social Work Today, v. 4, no. 11, 23 Aug. 1973. 338-340.

2590 Sarri, Rosemary C. and Frank F. Maple, editors. The school in the community. Washington, D. C.: National Association of Social Workers, 1972. 304p.

2591 Schulhofer, Edith, chairman. "Establishing basic social service in a parochial school within the context of an educational program of a school of social work: summary of a sectional meeting." Proceedings of the 52nd Annual Meeting of the National Conference of Catholic Charities, New Orleans, 1966. Washington, D. C.: Graphic Arts Press, 1968. 57-59.

2592 Smalley, Ruth E. "Some elements of supervision in school social work." Helping the troubled school child. Edited by Grace Lee. New York: National Association of Social Workers, 1959. 420-429.

2593 Vargus, Ione. "Developing, launching, and maintaining the school-community-pupil program." Social services and the public schools. Edited by DeWayne J. Kurpius and Irene Thomas. Urbana, Ill.: Jane Addams School of Social Work, University of Illinois, 1976. 61-73.

2594 Waters, R. O. and R. M. Bartlett. "Bachelor's degree school social workers." Social Worker-Travailleur Social, v. 38, no. 3, July 1970. 11-15.

2595 Wille, Jane. "Goals and values in education: their implications for social work education." Social Work, v. 5, no. 3, July 1960. 97-103.

M. URBAN AND RURAL SETTINGS

2596 Bristow, Thomas C., Jr. "Field placement in Williamsburg County." Arete, v. 2, no. 1, spring 1972. 31-41.

2597 Brooks, Michael P. and Michael A. Stegman. "Urban social policy, race, and the education of planners." Journal of the American Institute of Planners, v. 34, no. 5, Sept. 1968. 275-286.

2598 Butler, Mary P. "Developing field placements in rural community." Teaching social welfare, v. 2: Field instruction. Edited by Lester I. Levin. Atlanta: Southern Regional Education Board, 1971. 1-9.

2599 Chestang, Leon W. "Extending services to inner-city communities: The Afro-American Family and Community Services, Inc." Social Work Education Reporter, v. 20, no. 3, Sept.-Oct. 1972. 39-42.

2600 DeJong, Cornell R. "Field instruction for undergraduate social work education in rural areas." The dynamics of field instruction: learning through doing. Compiled by the Council on Social Work Education. New York: The Council, 1975. 20-30.

2601 Farman-Farmaian, Sattareh. "Community-focussed services: multi-purpose welfare centres as instruments of social change." Education for social change: human development and national progress; proceedings of the International Congress of Schools of Social Work, 1974. New York: The Association, 1975. 34-45.

2602 Ginsberg, Leon H. "Education for social work in rural settings." Social Work Education Reporter, v. 17, no. 3, Sept. 1969. 28-32, 60-61.

2603 _____, editor. Social work in rural communities: a book of readings. New York: Council on Social Work Education, 1976. 130p.

2604 Gore, Madhav S. "Contribution of social work education to the preparation of village level workers." International Social Work, v. 2, no. 2, April 1959. 22-26.

2605 Hendry, Charles E. "Implications from social work education abroad for work in small communities." Education for social work; proceedings of the 1960 Annual Program Meeting, Council on Social Work Education. New York: The Council, 1960. 119-130.

2606 Iliovici, Jean. "Urban development: implications for training social work personnel: In Europe and Africa." Urban development: its implications for social welfare; proceedings of the 13th International Conference of Social Work, Washington, D. C., 1966. New York: Columbia University Press, 1967. 296-299.

2607 Kaikobad, N. F. "Training of professional workers for urban community development." Social Welfare, v. 9, no. 7, Oct. 1962. 8-10.

2608 Myers, Clara Louise Hanser and Arthur J. Robins. "How social work education may more effectively serve nonurban America." Education for social work; proceedings of the 1960 Annual Program Meeting, Council on Social Work Education. New York: The Council, 1960. 100-118.

2609 Perlman, Robert. "Preparing social work students for a
      responsible role in urban development." Education for
      social work; proceedings of the 1962 Annual Program
      Meeting, Council on Social Work Education. New York:
      The Council, 1962. 162-166.

2610 Reichert, Kurt and Elizabeth Reichert. "The relationship of
      undergraduate programs in social welfare to inner-city
      concerns, racial problems and anti-poverty activities."
      Social Work Education Reporter, v. 16, no. 4, Dec. 1968.
      16-17, 64-65.

2611 Reid, Nellie N. "Field experience in rural areas." Issues
      in implementing undergraduate social welfare education
      programs; a report of a regional conference for colleges
      and universities of the 15 Southern States. Edited by Ro-
      bert M. Ryan and Amy L. Reynolds. Atlanta: Southern
      Regional Education Board, 1970. 38-42.

2612 Samoff, Zelda. "Developing field experiences in a metropo-
      litan area." Issues in implementing undergraduate social
      welfare education programs; a report of a regional con-
      ference for colleges and universities of the 15 Southern
      states. Edited by Robert M. Ryan and Amy L. Reynolds.
      Atlanta: Southern Regional Education Board, 1970. 31-37.

2613 Stokes, Carl B. "Social work education in the urban scene."
      Journal of Education for Social Work, v. 5, no. 1, spring
      1969. 91-95.

2614 Weber, Gwen K. "Preparing social workers for practice in
      rural social systems." Journal of Education for Social
      Work, v. 12, no. 3, fall 1976. 108-115.

2615 Weisman, Celia B. "From the 'Urban Crisis' to 'Urban
      Condition.'" Jewish Social Work Forum, v. 11, spring
      1975. 65-72.

2616 Winston, Ellen. "Urban development: implications for train-
      ing social work personnel." Urban development: its im-
      plications for social welfare; proceedings of the 13th In-
      ternational Conference of Social Work, Washington, D. C.,
      1966. New York: Columbia University Press, 1967.
      283-296.

XIV. ETHNIC MINORITIES AND WOMEN IN SOCIAL WORK EDUCATION

A. GENERAL

2617   Anderson, Ernest Frederick. "The manifest need for cooperation between ethnic groups in social work education." Social Work Education Reporter, v. 19, no. 3, Sept./Oct. 1971. 35-38.

2618   Armendariz, Juan. Social work education for economically disadvantaged groups in Texas. Austin: School of Social Work, University of Texas at Austin, 1973. 38p.

2619   Arnold, Howard D. "American racism: implications for social work." Journal of Education for Social Work, v. 6, no. 2, fall 1970. 7-12.

2620   Brown, Eddie F. "The inclusion of ethnic minority content in the curricula of graduate schools of social work." Doctoral dissertation, University of Utah, 1975. 148p.

2621   Brown, Patricia A. "Racial social work." Journal of Education for Social Work, v. 12, no. 1, winter 1976. 28-35.

2622   Crompton, Don W. "Minority content in social work education--promise or pitfall?" Journal of Education for Social Work, v. 10, no. 1, winter 1974. 9-18.

2623   Council on Social Work Education. Educationally disadvantaged students in social work education; opening and expanding opportunities in graduate schools of social work. New York: The Council, 1968. 168p.

2624   _____. "Systemic barriers to recruitment, retention, and promotion of ethnic minority faculty in schools of social work." Social Work Education Reporter, v. 20, no. 3, Sept.-Oct. 1972. 25-27.

2625   Fausel, Donald F. "Undergraduate social work recruitment and retention programs for ethnic minority and disadvantaged students." Doctoral dissertation, Columbia University, 1975. 247p.

2626   Goodman, James A., editor. Dynamics of racism in social

work practice. Washington, D. C.: National Association
of Social Workers, 1973. 375p.

2627 Greenberg, Harold I. and Carl A. Scott. "Ethnic minority-
group recruitment and programs for the educationally disadvantaged in schools of social work." Social Work Education Reporter, v. 17, no. 3, Sept. 1969. 32A-32D.

2628 Hamovitch, Maurice B. "Impact of federal agencies on in-
fluencing higher education for minority groups." Social
Work Education Reporter, v. 20, no. 2, April-May 1972.
43-46.

2629 _____. "One school's attack on institutional racism."
Social Work Papers, v. 12, Jan. 1974. 1-8.

2630 Hurst, Charles H., Jr. "The time of crisis--A challenge
for social work education everywhere." Journal of Education for Social Work, v. 7, no. 2, spring 1971. 19-24.

2631 Jackson, William S. "The Civil Rights Act of 1964: implications for social work education in the South." Social
Work Education Reporter, v. 14, no. 3, Sept. 1966. 27-
29, 44-45.

2632 Kagwa, G. Winifred. "Utilization of racial content in developing self-awareness." Journal of Education for Social Work,
v. 12, no. 2, spring 1976. 21-27.

2633 Levitt, Louis. "Recruiting minority group students to social
work." Manpower: a community responsibility; proceedings of the Arden House Workshop, 1967. New York:
National Commission for Social Work Careers, National
Association of Social Workers, 1968. 39-40.

2634 Loewenstein, Sophie F. "Integrating content on feminism and
racism into the social work curriculum." Journal of Education for Social Work, v. 12, no. 1, winter 1976. 91-96.

2635 Longres, John. "The impact of racism on social work education." Journal of Education for Social Work, v. 8, no. 1,
winter 1972. 31-41.

2636 McCann, Charles W., editor. Perspectives on ethnic minority content in social work education: report of a program
in continuing education for deans and faculties of graduate
schools of social work. Boulder, Colo.: Western Interstate Commission for Higher Education, 1972. 85p.

2637 Mirelowitz, Seymour and Leona Grossman. "Ethnicity: an
intervening variable in social work education." Journal
of Education for Social Work, v. 11, no. 3, fall 1975. 76-
83.

2638 Murase, Kenji. Project on Development of Ethnic/Cultural Content in the Social Work Curriculum; final report. Boulder, Colo.: Western Interstate Commission for Higher Education, 1974. Various pagings.

2639 Richan, Willard C. "The social work educator's dilemma: the academic vs. the social revolution." Journal of Education for Social Work, v. 9, no. 3, fall 1973. 51-57.

2640 Robertson, Mary Ella. "Attracting minority group members to social work--professional education's responsibility." Manpower: a community responsibility; proceedings of the Arden House Workshop, 1967. New York: National Commission for Social Work, National Association of Social Workers, 1968. 36-38.

2641 _____. "Inclusion of content on ethnic and racial minorities in the social work curriculum." Social Work Education Reporter, v. 18, no. 1, March 1970. 45-47, 66.

2642 Roth, Norman R. Ethnic content in the research component of the social work curriculum: a report of a survey of graduate schools of social work. Boulder, Colo.: Western Interstate Commission for Higher Education, 1973. 34p.

2643 Sanders, Daniel S. "Dynamics of ethnic and cultural pluralism: implications for social work education and curriculum innovation." Journal of Education for Social Work, v. 11, no. 3, fall 1975. 95-100.

2644 Scott, Carl A., editor. Ethnic minorities in social work education; a collection of papers highlighting developments and issues concerning faculty, students, and curriculum in social work education. New York: Council on Social Work Education, 1970. 89p.

2645 _____. "Ethnic minorities in social work education: issues, trends, and developments." The current scene in social work education. By Arnulf M. Pins, et al. New York: Council on Social Work Education, 1971. 15-27.

2646 Stempler, Benj L. "Effects of aversive racism on white social work students." Social Casework, v. 56, no. 8, Oct. 1975. 460-467.

2647 Turner, John B. "Education for practice with minorities." Social Work, v. 17, no. 3, May 1972. 112-118.

2648 Wells, Mabel G. "Report on a successful social work recruitment program." Journal of Education for Social Work, v. 10, no. 1, winter 1974. 109-117.

2649 Young, Whitney M. , Jr. "Minorities and social work career."
Careers in social work; 1967 annual review, National Commission for Social Work Careers. New York: The Commission, 1967. 9-10, 19.

B. AMERICAN INDIANS

2650 Brennan, Jere L. , compiler. The forgotten American--Amer-
ican Indians remembered; a selected bibliography for use
in social work education. New York: Council on Social
Work Education, 1972. 83p.

2651 Council on Social Work Education. American Indian Task
Force. American Indian Task Force report. Edited by
John E. Mackey. New York: The Council, 1973. 10p.

2652 Edwards, Eugene D. "A description and evaluation of American Indian social work training programs." Doctoral dissertation, University of Utah, 1976. 182p.

2653 Farris, Charles E. "The American Indian: social work education's neglected minority." Journal of Education for
Social Work, v. 11, no. 2, spring 1975. 37-43.

2654 Minnesota Resource Center for Social Work Education. Annotated bibliography of recommended American Indian resource
materials for human service educators. Minneapolis,
Minn.: The Center, 1974? 10p.

C. ASIAN AMERICAN

2655 Council on Social Work Education. Asian American Task
Force. Asian American Task Force report: problems
and issues in social work education. Edited by Kenji
Murase. New York: The Council, 1973. 48p.

2656 Ho, Man Keung. "Social work with Asian Americans." Social Casework, v. 57, no. 3, March 1976. 195-201.

2657 Kitano, Harry H. L. , compiler. Asians in America: a selected bibliography for use in social work education. New
York: Council on Social Work Education, 1971. 79p.

2658 Kuramoto, Ford H. "What do Asians want? an examination
of issues in social work education." Journal of Education for Social Work, v. 7, no. 3, fall 1971. 7-17.

2659 Kushida, Arlene Hori, et al. "A training program for Asian and Pacific Islander Americans." Social Casework, v. 57, no. 3, March 1976. 185-194.

D. BLACK

2660 Baker, Dorothy L. , Alexander Richberg and Isaac White. Black content in schools: a model of Black content in a school of social work's curriculum. Boulder, Colo.: Western Interstate Commission for Higher Education, 1973. 56p.

2661 Beckerman, Aaron Harry. "Ethnicity and graduate social work education: an exploratory study of first year full-time students enrolled in six Greater New York City schools of social work, 1965-1966." Doctoral dissertation, Columbia University, 1971. 448p.

2662 Billingsley, Andrew. "Black students in a graduate school of social welfare." Social Work Education Reporter, v. 17, no. 2, June 1969. 38-44, 60.

2663 Burt, Winston Donald. "Admission criteria for Black students in graduate social work education: traditional and non-traditional approaches." Doctoral dissertation, University of Michigan, 1973. 254p.

2664 Chavis, James M. "Educating for Black social development-- The role of social work education." Nation building time; proceedings of the 1973 Annual Conference of the National Association of Black Social Workers. Detroit: Multi-Tech Services, 1974. 142-145.

2665 Council on Social Work Education. Black perspectives on social work education: issues related to curriculum, faculty, and students. New York: The Council, 1974. 79p.

2666 _____. Black Task Force. Black Task Force report; suggested guides for the integration of Black content into the social work curriculum. Edited by E. Aracelis Francis. New York: The Council, 1973. 19p.

2667 De Anda, Raup and Vernon Lockett. "Introducing Black and Chicano content into a social work curriculum: a recommendation." Social Work Education Reporter, v. 20, no. 3, Sept. -Oct. 1972. 28-31.

2668 Dunmore, Charlotte, compiler. Poverty, participating, protest, power, and Black Americans; a selected bibliography for use in social work education. New York: Council on Social Work Education, 1970. 67p.

2669 Feldstein, Donald and Marylyn Gore. "The undergraduate social welfare program: Black studies and the new action
thrust." Social Work Education Reporter, v. 17, no. 4,
Dec. 1969. 18-19.

2670 Fluckiger, Fritz A. Minority group candidates for social work
education. New York, School of Social Work, Hunter College, 1971. 75p.

2671 Gary, Lawrence E. The Afro-American experience and the
social work curriculum: some specific suggestions. Washington, D. C.: Institute for Urban Affairs and Research,
Howard University, 1974. 67p.

2672 _____. "Educating Blacks for the 1970's: the role of
Black colleges." Diversity: cohesion or chaos--Mobili-
zation for survival; proceedings of the 1972 Annual Conference of National Association of Black Social Workers.
Nashville, Tenn.: Fisk University, 1973. 28-59.

2673 _____. "Social work education and the Black community:
a proposal for curriculum revisions." Social Work Education Reporter, v. 16, no. 4, Dec. 1968. 47-50, 68-69.

2674 Gilbert, Gwendolyn C. "The role of social work in Black
liberation." Black Scholar, v. 6, no. 4. Dec. 1974. 16-23.

2675 Glasgow, Douglas. "The Black thrust for vitality: the impact
on social work education." Journal of Education for Social Work, v. 7, no. 2, spring 1971. 9-18.

2676 Haynes, George E. "Cooperation with colleges in securing
and training Negro social workers for urban centers."
Proceedings of the National Conference of Charities and
Correction, 1911. Edited by Alexander Johnson. Fort
Wayne, Ind.: Fort Wayne Printing Co., 1911. 384-387.

2677 Kindelsperger, Kenneth W. "'To be (or not to be) equal.'"
Social Work Education, v. 12, no. 4, Aug.-Sept. 1964. 2,
7.

2678 Lucas-White, Lydia. "Blacks and education in Nova Scotia:
implications for social work education and practice." Social Work in Atlantic Canada, v. 1, 1975. 35-51.

2679 McClure, Jesse F. "Survival and beyond in the education of
Black social workers." Survival and beyond; proceedings
of the 1974 Annual Conference of the National Association
of Black Social Workers. Detroit: Multi-Tech Services,
1974. 90-95.

2680 Mathis, Thaddeus P. "Educating for Black social development:

the politics of social organization." Journal of Education for Social Work, v. 11, no. 1, winter 1975. 105-112.

2681 Sanders, Charles L. , editor. Black agenda for social work in the seventies; proceedings of the Class-Field Institute, School of Social Work, Atlanta University, Nov. 1970. Atlanta: The School, 1971. 55p.

2682 _____, editor. Crossing over; proceedings of 50th Anniversary at Atlanta University School of Social Work. New York: Afram Associates, 1971. 62p.

2683 Southern Regional Education Board. Enhancing human service programs in Black colleges. Atlanta: Southern Regional Education Board, 1970. 40p.

2684 "South's foremost school of social work: Atlanta U School is Dixie oldest and largest." Ebony, v. 14, no. 12, Oct. 1959. 84-88.

2685 Stukes, Sandra P. "Black students and schools of social work--issues and concerns." Nation building time; proceedings of the 1973 Annual Conference of the National Association of Black Social Workers. Detroit: Multi-Tech Services, 1974. 146-161.

2686 Tidwell, Billy J. "The Black community's challenge to social work." Journal of Education for Social Work, v. 7, no. 3, fall 1971. 59-65.

2687 Wallace, Joan S. "Black studies and social work education: new life styles for social workers." Journal of Black Studies, v. 6, no. 2, Dec. 1975. 208-216.

2688 Weisman, Irving. "More minority group candidates for social work education: an experimental program." Social Work Education Reporter, v. 16, no. 1, March 1968. 43, 55-57.

2689 Young, Whitney M. , Jr. "Social work education--For what end?" After fifty years; papers from the 50th anniversary year 1967-1968. Compiled by the School of Social Work, University of Minnesota. Minneapolis: The School, 1969. 14-34.

2690 _____. "To be equal." Social Work Education Reporter, v. 13, no. 2, June 1965. 16-17.

2691 Zober, Edith and Bill C. F. Snider. "A comparison of Iowa social work students with the general public in their perceptions of Black people and their struggle for equality." Iowa Journal of Social Work, v. 4, no. 1, winter 1971. 26-33.

E. CHICANOS

2692 Camarillo, Mateo R. and Antonio Del Buono. "Utilizing barrio expertise in social work education." La causa Chicana: the movement for justice. Edited by Margaret M. Mangold. New York: Family Service Association of America, 1972. 115-125.

2693 Chicano Training Center. Three perspectives on Chicano content in the social work curriculum. Houston: The Center, 1975. 37p.

2694 Council on Social Work Education. Chicano Task Force. Chicano Task Force report. Edited by Juliette Ruiz. New York: The Council, 1973. 24p.

2695 Curren, D. J., editor. The Chicano Faculty Development Program: a report. New York: Council on Social Work Education, 1973. 134p.

2696 De Anda, Raup and Vernon Lockett. "Introducing Black and Chicano content into a social work curriculum: a recommendation." Social Work Education Reporter, v. 20, no. 3, Sept.-Oct. 1972. 28-31.

2697 Dieppa, Ismael and Marta Sotomayor. Chicano ethnic content in the social work curriculum: a modular approach. Boulder, Colo.: Western Interstate Commission for Higher Education, 1974. 39p.

2698 _____. "Chicanos: issues in social work education regarding students, faculty, and curriculum enrichment." Social Work Education Reporter, v. 20, no. 1, Dec.-Jan. 1972. 56-59.

2699 Garcia, Alejandro. "The Chicano and social work." Social Casework, v. 52, no. 5, May 1971. 274-278.

2699a Gomez, Ernesto, Daniel E. Jennings and Yolanda Santos. Selective guide to materials related to the Chicano for human service training and education. San Antonio, Tex.: Worden School of Social Service, Our Lady of the Lake University of San Antonio, 1976. 251p.

2700 Navarro, Eliseo, compiler. The Chicano community; a selected bibliography for use in social work education. New York: Council on Social Work Education, 1971. 57p.

2701 San Diego State College. School of Social Work. Chicanos: a student report on social work education. San Diego: School of Social Work, San Diego State College, 1971. 81p.

2702 Sanchez, Rodolfo B. A Chicano perspective on social work curriculum development. Arlington, Va. : ERIC Document Reproduction Service, 1972. 21p. ED 072892.

2703 Sotomayor, Marta and Philip D. Ortego y Gasca, editors. Chicano content and social work education. New York: Council on Social Work Education, 1975. 94p.

2704 Souflee, Federico and Graciela Schmitt. "Educating for practice in the Chicano community." Journal of Education for Social Work, v. 10, no. 3, fall 1974. 75-84.

F. PUERTO RICANS

2705 Balian, Pereta, et al. "Induction of Puerto Rican faculty in New York City schools of social work." Social Work Education Reporter, v. 19, no. 1, Dec. -Jan. 1971. 41-42.

2706 Brooklyn College. Institute of Puerto Rican Studies. The Puerto Rican people; a selected bibliography for use in social work education. New York: Council on Social Work Education, 1973. 54p.

2707 Campos, Angel P. , editor. Puerto Rican Curriculum Development Workshop; a report. New York: Council on Social Work Education, 1974. 69p.

2708 Council on Social Work Education. Puerto Rican Task Force. Puerto Rican Task Force report. Edited by Magdalena Miranda. New York: The Council, 1973. 16p.

2709 Delgado, Melvin. "Social work and the Puerto Rican community." Social Casework, v. 55, no. 2, Feb. 1974. 117-123.

2710 Gonzales, Augustin and Sally Romero. "Inclusion of Puerto Rican curriculum content in social work training." Social Work Education Reporter, v. 19, no. 1, Dec. -Jan. 1971. 42-43.

2711 Longres, John. Perspectives from the Puerto Rican Faculty Training Project. New York: Council on Social Work Education, 1973. 64p.

2712 Marin, Rosa C. "Puerto Ricans are not being attracted to United States schools of social work." Social Work Education Reporter, v. 19, no. 1, Dec. -Jan. 1971. 45.

2713 Mizio, Emelicia. "Puerto Rican social workers and racism." Social Casework, v. 53, no. 5, May 1972. 267-272.

2714 Rivera, Julian. "Recruitment of Puerto Rican students into schools of social work." Social Work Education Reporter, v. 19, no. 1, Dec. -Jan. 1971. 43-44.

G. WOMEN [See also Sections I. C; III. D, E. 3.]

2715 Appelberg, Esther. "Mothers as social work students." Social Work Education Reporter, v. 13, no. 4, Dec. 1965. 26-30.

2716 Brager, George and John A. Michael. "The sex distribution in social work: causes and consequences." Social Casework, v. 50, no. 10, Dec. 1969. 595-601.

2717 Canada. Women's Bureau. A new career after 30; report of an enquiry into the experience of women who had taken professional social work training at thirty years of age or over. Ottawa: Department of Labour of Canada, 1960. 34p.

2718 Diangson, Pat and Diane F. Kravetz and Judy Lipton. "Sex-role stereotyping and social work education." Journal of Education for Social Work, v. 11, no. 3, fall 1975. 44-49.

2719 Gould, Ketayun H. and Bok-Lim C. Kim. "Salary inequities between men and women in schools of social work: myth or reality?" Journal of Education for Social Work, v. 12, no. 1, winter 1976. 50-55.

2720 Harris, Linda Hall and Margaret Exner Lucas. "Sex-role stereotyping." Social Work, v. 21, no. 5, Sept. 1976. 390-394.

2721 Herberg, Dorothy Chave. "Career patterns and work participation of graduate female social workers." Doctoral dissertation, University of Michigan, 1970. 266p.

2722 _____. "A study of work participation by graduate female social workers: some implications for professional social work training." Journal of Education for Social Work, v. 9, no. 3, fall 1973. 16-23.

2723 Lacerte, Judith. "If only Jane Addams had been a feminist." Social Casework, v. 57, no. 10, Dec. 1976. 656-660.

2724 Lewin, Thomas Fred. "The employment experience of married women social caseworkers: a study of one hundred graduates of the New York School of Social Work, Columbia University." Doctoral dissertation, University of Chicago, 1962. 124p.

2725   Lewis, Verl S.   "From housewife to social worker: the University of Maryland's Extended Study Program."   Social Work Education Reporter, v. 17, no. 2, June 1969.   45-47, 57.

2726   Meisel, Susan Schilling and Alice Perkins Friedman.   "The need for women's studies in social work education."   Journal of Education for Social Work, v. 10, no. 3, fall 1974. 67-74.

2727   Pascoe, A. W.   "Married women graduates in part-time practice."   Social Worker-Travailleur Social, v. 38, no. 3, July 1970.   8-10.

2728   Redfern, Margaret, Shirley B. Klass and Kaye M. Coleman. "A housewives' group in a university setting."   Social Work, v. 21, no. 6, Nov. 1976.   527-528.

2729   Schwartz, Mary C.   "Sexism in the social work curriculum." Journal of Education for Social Work, v. 9, no. 3, fall 1973.   65-70.

2729a   Silvers, Sherry L. and Thomas H. Walz.   A comparative study of female pre-social work and education students at the University of Minnesota, on N-ACH, N-AFF, N-POW, N-NUR, and N-SUC as projected into the Thematic Apperception Test.   Minneapolis: University of Minnesota, 1969. 47p.

2730   Waldstein, Martha.   "Refresher course for married women reentering the casework field."   Social Casework, v. 41, no. 8, Oct. 1960.   418-424.

2731   Walton, Ronald G.   "Women and social work education." Two decades of training 1951-71."   Women in social work.   London: Routledge & Kegan Paul, 1975. 57-65, 209-220.

H.   WORKING CLASS ETHNIC GROUPS

2732   Efthim, Alex.   "Serving the U. S. work force: a new constituency for schools of social work."   Journal of Education for Social Work, v. 12, no. 3, fall 1976. 29-36.

2733   Giordano, Joseph.   "Servicing and organizing the white ethnic working-class community."   Journal of Education for Social Work, v. 11, no. 1, winter 1975.   59-65.

2734   Palley, Howard A. and Marian L. Palley.   "Ethnicity, political coalition and the development of a megapolicy perspective in social work education." Journal of Sociology and Social Welfare, v. 2, no. 3, spring 1975.   365-371.

XV. SECTARIAN SOCIAL WORK EDUCATION

A. CATHOLIC

2735 Bateman, Richard. "Catholic charities: renewal and reform."
Catholic Charities Review, v. 47, no. 10, Dec. 1963. 5-14.

2736 Biestek, Felix P. "Objectives of a Catholic school of social
work." Catholic Charities Review, v. 36, no. 9, Nov. 1952.
208-211.

2737 Boylan, Marguerite T. "Personnel and training." Social welfare in the Catholic church: organization and planning
through Diocesan Bureaus. New York: Columbia University Press, 1941. 201-228.

2738 Geary, Leo A. "What the Catholic agency expects of the
Catholic school of social work." Proceedings of the 25th
Meeting of the National Conference of Catholic Charities,
Denver, 1939. Washington, D. C. : Ransdell, 1939.
405-413.

2739 Hannigan, Betty and Henry R. Evans. "What is Catholic social casework?" Catholic Charities Review, v. 47, no. 2,
Feb. 1963. 4-7.

2740 Harrington, Rev. John M. Problems of education in a Catholic school of social work; address delivered to Boston
College School of Social Work students and alumni, April
1950. Boston: School of Social Work, Boston College,
1950. 14p.

2741 Hynes, Eleanor Marie. "Some issues in Catholic social work
education, 1910-1955." Doctoral dissertation, Tulane
University, 1971. 174p.

2742 Lauerman, Lucian L. Catholic education for social work.
Washington, D. C. : Catholic University of America Press,
1943. 124p.

2743 Lawler, Loretto R. Full circle: the story of the National
Catholic School of Social Service, 1918-1947. Wạshington,
D. C. : Catholic University of America Press, 1951.
243p.

2744 McGuinn, Walter. "The task confronting the Catholic school of social work in meeting the demands of the Catholic agency." Proceedings of the 25th Meeting of the National Conference of Catholic Charities, Denver, 1939. Washington, D. C.: Ransdell, 1939. 413-420.

2745 Schulhofer, Edith, chairman. "Establishing basic social service in a parochial school within the context of an educational program of a school of social work: summary of a sectional meeting." Proceedings of the 52nd Annual Meeting of the National Conference of Catholic Charities, New Orleans, 1966. Washington, D. C.: Graphic Arts Press, 1968. 57-59.

2746 William J. Kerby: democracy through Christ. n. p., William J. Kerby Foundation, 1943. 32p.

B. JEWISH

2747 Balsam, Philip, chairman. "Graduates of the Wurzweiler School of Social Work look at the field of Jewish communal service: panel discussion." Jewish Social Work Forum, v. 6, no. 2, fall 1969. 46-59.

2748 Beckerman, Aaron and Helene Fishbein. "The parties to social work education: the school, the agency, the students: a case study." Conference papers: Annual Conference of the Association of Jewish Center Workers, 1971. New York: The Association, 1971. 37-56.

2749 Blum, Deborah Cardozo, Shmuel Lefkowitz and Neal Levy. "Jewish consciousness and social work values at Wurzweiler: a research study." Jewish Social Work Forum, v. 12, spring 1976. 67-78.

2750 Bubis, Gerald B. "Contributions of Jewish center practice to social work education." Conference papers: Annual Conference of the Association of Jewish Center Workers, 1971. New York: The Association, 1971. 57-60.

2751 _____. "Professional education for the Jewish component in casework practice." Journal of Jewish Communal Service, v. 52, no. 3, spring 1976. 270-277.

2752 Canter, Irving. "What research tells us about training for the Jewish component in the practice of group work in Jewish settings." Journal of Jewish Communal Service, v. 39, no. 3, spring 1963. 266-285.

2753 Cutter, William. "Thoughts on Jewish professional training."

Journal of Jewish Communal Service, v. 52, no. 4, summer 1976. 331-337.

2754 Dolgoff, Ralph. "The Jewish B.A. social worker: a new professional for Jewish communal services." Journal of Jewish Communal Service, v. 52, no. 1, fall 1975. 73-81.

2755 Feldstein, Donald. "The baccalaureate worker in the Jewish community center." Journal of Jewish Communal Service, v. 52, no. 4, summer 1976. 404-411.

2756 Gold, Bertram H. and Arnulf M. Pins. "Effective preparation for Jewish community center work." Journal of Jewish Communal Service, v. 39, no. 2, winter 1962. 121-141.

2757 Golden, Irwin. "The utilization of social work manpower in Jewish community centers: alternative models." Journal of Jewish Communal Service, v. 46, no. 1, fall 1969. 59-69.

2758 Green, Solomon H. "Jewish Identity Seminar: culture, commitment, service." Jewish Social Work Forum, v. 11, spring 1975. 53-64.

2759 _____. "Seeking Jewish dimensions in field instruction." Jewish Social Work Forum, v. 5, no. 1, spring 1968. 5-19.

2760 Greene, Allan, Barry Kasdan and Brian Segal. "Jewish social group work students view the Jewish community center field as a placement and career." Journal of Jewish Communal Service, v. 44, no. 2, winter 1972. 168-176.

2761 Hofstein, Saul. "Preparation of workers for casework practice in the Jewish agency." Journal of Jewish Communal Service, v. 45, no. 2, winter 1968. 156-164.

2762 Lauffer, Armand. "The future of social work in the Jewish community center; the case of the disinclined student." Journal of Jewish Communal Service, v. 46, no. 1, fall 1969. 45-58.

2763 Levy, Charles S. "Education for social work practice in Jewish communal service." Journal of Jewish Communal Service, v. 52, no. 1, fall 1975. 34-42.

2764 _____, editor. The role of the Jewish school of social work in preparing social work practitioners for Jewish communal service; papers presented at the National Conference of Jewish Communal Service, Atlantic City, 1962. New York: Wurzweiler School of Social Work, Yeshiva University, 1962. 23p.

2765 _____. "The special purpose of the Jewish School of Social Work." Jewish Social Work Forum, v. 1, no. 1, fall
1963. 7-16.

2766 Pins, Arnulf M. "The Jewish social work student: some
research data about him and their implications for the
shortage of Jewish community center workers." Journal
of Jewish Communal Service, v. 41, no. 1, fall 1964. 88-
100.

2767 _____ and Leon H. Ginsberg. "New developments in social
work education and their impact on Jewish communal service and community center work." Journal of Jewish
Communal Service, v. 48, no. 1, fall 1971. 60-71.

2768 _____ and _____. "New developments in social work
education and their impact on Jewish communal service
and Jewish community center work." Conference papers:
Annual Conference of the Association of Jewish Center
Workers, 1971. New York: The Association, 1971. 11-
24. Comments by Martin Levine, Bernard Reisman and
Arnold L. Feiner. 25-36.

2769 Reisman, Bernard. "An alternative perspective on training
Jewish communal workers." Journal of Jewish Communal
Service, v. 52, no. 4, summer 1976. 338-343.

2770 _____. "Social work education and Jewish communal service and Jewish community centers: time for a change."
Journal of Jewish Communal Service, v. 48, no. 4, summer
1972. 384-395.

2771 Rosen, Alex. "Critical issues in professional preparation
for the field of Jewish communal service." Journal of
Jewish Communal Service, v. 40, no. 3, spring 1964. 269-
279.

2772 Teicher, Morton I. "The Wurzweiler School of Social Work:
an historical overview." Jewish Social Work Forum, v.
11, spring 1975. 1-6.

C. PROTESTANT

2773 Chakerian, Charles G. "The particular needs of social services under religious auspices." Religious content in social work education; workshop report of the 1960 Annual
Program Meeting, Council on Social Work Education.
New York: The Council, 1961. 29-37.

2774 _____. "Professional education to meet the churches' re-

sponsibilities and services in social welfare." The churches and social welfare. Hartford, Conn.: The Hartford
Seminary Foundation, 1955. 13-18.

2775 Eckardt, Ralph W., Jr. "Evangelical Christianity and social
work: a study of the beliefs and practice of graduates of
the social work majors at Philadelphia College of Bible
and Temple University." Doctoral dissertation, University of Pennsylvania, 1974. 322p.

2776 Hall, M. Pennelope and Ismene V. Howes. "The recruitment
and training of workers." The church in social work:
a study of moral welfare work undertaken by the Church
of England. London: Routledge & Kegan Paul, 1965.
102-123.

XVI. INTERPROFESSIONAL EDUCATION AND INTERDISCIPLINARY STUDIES

A. GENERAL

2776a Bassoff, Betty Zippin. "Interdisciplinary education for health professionals: issues and directions." Social Work in Health Care, v. 2, no. 2, winter 1976-77. 219-228.

2777 Dana, Bess S. and Cecil G. Sheps. "Trends and issues in interprofessional education: pride, prejudice, and progress." Journal of Education for Social Work, v. 4, no. 2, fall 1968. 35-41.

2777a Kane, Rosalie Ann Smolkin. "Interprofessional education and social work: a survey." Social Work in Health Care, v. 2, no. 2, winter 1976-77. 229-238.

2778 _____. "The interprofessional team (with special reference to the role and education of the social worker)." Doctoral dissertation, University of Utah, 1975. 272p.

2779 Lees, Ray. "Education for social service." British Hospital Journal and Social Service Review, v. 81, 21 Aug. 1971. 1711.

2779a Linn, Margaret W. , et al. "The C. A. R. E. Project: inter-disciplinary and community-oriented approach to training social work students." Journal of Education for Social Work, v. 10, no. 2, spring 1974. 47-50.

2780 Maslach, George J. "The reorganization of educational resour-ces." Daedalus, v. 96, no. 4, fall 1967. 1200-1209.

2781 Neubauer, Peter B. and Joseph Steinert. "The significance for social workers of the multidiscipline approach to child development." Social Service Review, v. 29, no. 4, Dec. 1950. 459-465. Discussion by Charlotte Towle. 466-468.

2782 Ruhe, C. H. William and Paul L. McLain. "An interprofes-sional seminar at the University of Pittsburgh." Journal of Legal Education, v. 13, no. 4, 1961. 505-511.

2783 White, Grace. "Preparation of social workers for interprofes-

sional and inter-agency collaboration." Education for social work; proceedings of the 1960 Annual Program Meeting, Council on Social Work Education. New York: The
Council, 1960. 131-138.

B. INTERPROFESSIONAL EDUCATION

1. Architecture

2784 Wittman, Friedner D. and Milton Wittman. "Architecture
and social work: some impressions about educational
issues facing both professions." Journal of Education for
Social Work, v. 12, no. 2, spring 1976. 51-58.

2. Business Administration

2785 Pennsylvania. University. School of Social Work. National
project on education for management, v. 1. Philadelphia:
The School, 1975. 1 v. (various pagings)

2786 _____. _____. School of Social Work and the Wharton
Entrepreneurial Center, Wharton School. Management in
social welfare: casebook studies. Philadelphia: The
School and The Center, 1976. 234p.

2787 _____. _____. Wharton School. Wharton Entrepreneurial Center. National project on education for management, v. 2. Philadelphia: The Center, 1975. 183p.

3. Education

2788 Conference on Interprofessional Communication: Challenge to
Social Work and Education. Society and the school; communication challenge to education and social work; report.
Edited by Robert H. Beck. New York: National Association of Social Workers, 1965. 175p.

2789 Craft, Maurice. "Education and social work." Education and
social work: a symposium. Edited by F. H. Pedley.
New York: Pergamon Press, 1967. 1-27.

2790 _____ and Alma Craft. "The interprofessional perspectives
of teachers and social workers: a pilot inquiry." Social
and Economic Administration, v. 5, no. 1, Jan. 1971. 19-
28.

2791 _____. "Teaching social work and interprofessional training." Youth service and interprofessional studies. Edited
by Inga Bulman, Maurice Craft and Fred Milson. New
York: Pergamon Press, 1970. 121-140.

2792 Evans, Norman. "Together or apart? Teachers and social workers." Social Service Quarterly, v. 43, no. 3, winter 1970. 108-110.

2793 Everett, Edith M. "Teaching teachers." Family, v. 7, no. 3, May 1926. 71-75.

2794 Fox, Raymond. "Social agency and school: training educators to deliver helping services." Child Welfare, v. 53, no. 6, June 1974. 386-393.

2795 Hawkins, Mable T. "Interdisciplinary team training: social work students in public school field placement settings." The dynamics of field instruction: learning through doing. Compiled by the Council on Social Work Education. New York: The Council, 1975. 40-49.

2796 Kerry, Trevor and Carolle Kerry. "Social concern in teacher training." Spectrum, v. 4, Jan. 1972. 56-57.

2797 Kitson, G. M. "The more we are together." Education and Training, v. 14, Oct. 1972. 315-316.

2798 Lees, Sue and Ray Lees. "Social work and teacher training." Social Work Today, v. 3, no. 14, 19 Oct. 1972. 9-11.

2799 McGrath, Earl J. "Cooperation of education and social work." Social Welfare forum, 1949; official proceedings of the National Conference of Social Work. New York: Columbia University Press, 1950. 90-101.

2800 Moore, Barbara M. "Challenge to colleges of education and schools of social work." Social work in schools: patterns and perspectives. Edited by John J. Alderson. Northbrook, Ill.: Whitehall, 1969. 118-126.

2801 Olshansky, Bernard. "The community organization component in Jewish education." Journal of Jewish Communal Service, v. 44, no. 3, spring 1968. 271-279. Discussion by Louis Schwartzman. 280-283.

2802 Reid, Ivan. "Social science and teaching performance." Educational Research, v. 15, no. 1, Nov. 1972. 52-54.

2803 Tibble, J. W. "Interprofessional education." Youth service and interprofessional studies. Edited by Inga Bulman, Maurice Craft and Fred Milson. New York: Pergamon, 1970. 141-149.

2804 Wormald, Eileen. "Teachers and the social services." Social Service Quarterly, v. 44, no. 3, winter 1971. 112-114.

4. Law

2805 Bates, St. John and Maybel Bates. "The legal education of social workers." Social Work Today, v. 5, no. 23, 20 Feb. 1975. 710-712.

2806 Bradway, John S. "The social education of law students." Family, v. 13, no. 6, Oct. 1932. 198-202.

2807 Brenner, Ruth F. "Utilization of the court subculture in professional training." Social Casework, v. 40, no. 3, March 1959. 119-123.

2808 Cady, Francis C. "A successful experiment in interdisciplinary teaching and learning." Journal of Legal Education, v. 27, no. 4, 1976. 609-613.

2809 Central Council for Education and Training in Social Work. Legal studies in social work education; report of the Legal Studies Group. London: The Council, 1974. 63p.

2810 Ellingston, John R. "A sociologist's participation in criminal law instruction." Journal of Legal Education, v. 8, no. 2, 1955. 207-210.

2811 Foster, Henry H., Jr. "Social work, the law, and social action." Social Casework, v. 45, no. 7, July 1964. 383-392.

2812 Handler, Joel F. "The role of legal research and legal education in social welfare." Stanford Law Review, v. 20, no. 4, April 1968. 669-683.

2813 Harvey, Audrey. "Legal studies for social workers?" New Law Journal, v. 124, no. 5666, 19 Sept. 1974. 869.

2814 Hazard, Geoffred C., Jr. "Interdisciplinary courses and programs in law and social work--a survey." Family Law Quarterly, v. 6, no. 4, winter 1972. 423-440.

2815 Hyman, J. D. "Preface to the articles on the inter-relationship of social welfare and law disciplines." Buffalo Law Review, v. 17, no. 3, spring 1968. 717-718.

2816 Katkin, Daniel. "Law and social work: a proposal for interdisciplinary education." Journal of Legal Education, v. 26, no. 3, 1974. 294-317.

2817 Katz, Sanford N. "The lawyer and the caseworker: some observations." Social Casework, v. 42, no. 1, Jan. 1961. 10-15.

2818 Levitt, Louis. "Social work and the law--some curriculum approaches: a commentary on Dean Charles Schottland's article." Buffalo Law Review, v. 17, no. 3, spring 1968. 741-746.

2819 McClean, Harry Justus. "Legal training for social workers." Studies in Sociology, Sociological monographs no. 1, Sept. 1916. 15p.

2820 National Conference of Lawyers and Social Workers. Interprofessional relationships at the graduate school level: law and social work. Publication no. 8. New York: The Conference, 1969. 5p.

2821 Paulsen, Monrad G. "The law schools and the War on Poverty." Conference proceedings of the National Conference on Law and Poverty, Washington, D. C., 1965. Edited by Martin R. Wolf. Washington, D. C.: Government Printing Office, 1966. 77-88.

2822 Roberts, Gwyneth. "Teaching law to social workers." Social Work Today, v. 5, no. 12, 19 Sept. 1974. 353.

2823 Schottland, Charles I. "Social work and the law--some curriculum approaches." Buffalo Law Review, v. 17, no. 3, spring 1968. 719-731.

2824 Sloane, Homer W. "Relationship of law and social work." Social Work, v. 12, no. 1, Jan. 1967. 86-93.

2825 Smith, Audrey D. "The social worker in the legal aid setting: a study of interprofessional relationships." Social Service Review, v. 44, no. 2, June 1970. 155-168.

2826 Smith, N. J., J. W. McCulloch and Margaret Wardle. "Teaching law on professional social work courses: an exploratory study based on social workers' comments." Social Work Today, v. 6, no. 7, 26 June 1975. 201-205.

2827 Sparer, Edward V. "The place of law in social work education: a commentary on Dean Schottland's article." Buffalo Law Review, v. 17, no. 3, spring 1968. 733-740.

5. Medicine

2828 American Association of Medical Social Workers. Committee on Participation in Teaching of Medical Students. Medical social workers participate in medical education. Washington, D. C.: American Association of Medical Social Workers, 1954. 50p.

2829 Bartlett, Harriett M. The participation of medical social workers in the teaching of medical students. Chicago: American Association of Medical Social Workers, 1939. 68p.

2830 _____. Social work practice in the health field. New York: National Association of Social Workers, 1961. 280p.

2831 Beall, Patricia and Morris Green. "Role of the social worker in a children's diagnostic service." Social Work, v. 5, no. 1, Jan. 1960. 77-83.

2832 Bertino, Laura and Robert C. Jackson., editors. Social workers as trainers in health programs. Berkeley: Program in Public Health Social Work, University of California, 1972. 84p.

2833 Bloom, Samuel W. "Growth of the behavioral sciences in medical education: some implications for social workers." Journal of Medical Education, v. 39, no. 9, Sept. 1964. 820-827.

2834 Bracht, Neil F. and Inge Anderson. "Community field work collaboration between medical and social work students." Social Work in Health Care, v. 1, no. 1, fall 1975. 7-17.

2835 _____. "The contribution of public health social work in academic departments of community medicine." Milbank Memorial Fund Quarterly, v. 47, no. 1, Jan. 1969. Part I, 73-89.

2836 Dalgleish, Katherine B., Rosalie Ann Kane and James J. McNamara. "Rotating social work students within a medical center." Health and Social Work, v. 1, no. 2, May 1976. 166-171.

2837 Edelson, S. Eric. "The changing role of the social workers in medical education." Social Work, v. 10, no. 1, Jan. 1965. 81-86.

2838 Elliott, Valerie. "Social work and medical education." Social Worker-Travailleur Social, v. 40, no. 3, Sept. 1972. 163-168.

2839 Ellis, June. "The social worker as a clinical instructor of medical students." Journal of Medical Education, v. 43, no. 4, April 1968. 508-510.

2840 Gang, Stephen and Mary Brueton. "Social worker and general practitioner: an experiment in combined learning." Practitioner, v. 206, no. 1233, March 1971. 395-398.

2841 Grinnell, Richard M. , Jr. , Nancy S. Kyte and S. Hunter.
      "Social workers teaching in medical school. " Health and
      Social Work, v. 1, no. 2, May 1976. 151-165.

2842 _____, et al. "The status of graduate-level social workers
      teaching in medical schools. " Social Work in Health Care,
      v. 1, no. 3, spring 1976. 317-324.

2843 Haselkorn, Florence. "Some dynamic aspects of interprofes-
      sional practice in rehabilitation. " Social Casework, v. 39,
      no. 7, July 1958. 396-401.

2844 Hutter, M. J. , G. E. Zakus and C. I. Dungy. "Social work
      training of new health professionals. " Health and Social
      Work, v. 1, no. 2, May 1976. 125-136.

2845 Joint Committee of the Association of American Medical Col-
      leges and the American Association of Medical Social Work-
      ers. Widening horizons in medical education: a study of
      the teaching of social and environmental factors in medi-
      cine, 1945-1946. New York: Commonwealth Fund, 1948.
      228p.

2846 Kemple, David P. "Social worker graduates of schools of
      public health. " Doctoral dissertation, University of Pitts-
      burgh, 1971. 275p.

2847 Knight, Janet. "The medical social worker's participation in
      medical student teaching; conference report. " Medical
      Social Work (London), v. 20, no. 6, Oct. 1967. 212-214.

2848 Knox, Elspeth and John Rendle-Short. "The training of med-
      ical students in social paediatrics. " Australian Journal
      of Social Work, v. 19, no. 1, Feb. 1966. 7-10.

2849 Lambert, H. P. "The medical social worker's participation
      in medical student teaching: a doctor's view. " Medical
      Social Work (London), v. 20, no. 6, Oct. 1967. 214-216.

2850 Leon, Robert L. and Jane P. Friedman. "Method of orient-
      ing medical students in community social services. " Pub-
      lic Health Reports, v. 77, no. 9, Sept. 1962. 752-754.

2851 Liverman, Lonis and Nathalie Kennedy. "Social work parti-
      cipation in medical training. " Children, v. 7, no. 6, Nov. -
      Dec. 1960. 229-234.

2852 Loeb, Eleanor. "Some concepts for interdisciplinary prac-
      tice. " Social Work, v. 5, no. 4, Oct. 1960. 83-90.

2853 McGann, Leona M. and Margie Lutzker. "A new dimension
      in medical training. " Journal of Rehabilitation, v. 41, no.

2, March-April 1975. 35-36.

2854 _____, _____, and Count D. Gibson, Jr. "Primary responsibility for the psychosocial aspects of care: the role of the medical student." Journal of Medical Education, v. 48, no. 6, June 1973. 594-595.

2855 Moses, Mabel Benzion. "Role of medical social workers in medical education." Indian Journal of Social Work, v. 33, no. 4, Jan. 1973. 307-315.

2856 Muras, H. "The medical social worker's participation in medical student teaching: a social worker's view." Medical Social Work (London), v. 20, no. 6, Oct. 1967. 216-220.

2857 National Association of Social Workers. The psychiatric social worker teaches medical students; papers presented by the Committee on Participation in Medical Education. New York: The Association, 1957. 64p.

2858 _____. Joint Committee on Participation in Medical Education. Participation of social workers in medical education. New York: The Association, 1961. 60p.

2859 Prins, Herschel A. and Marion B. H. Whyte. Social work and medical practice. Oxford: Pergamon Press, 1972. 81p.

2860 Rehr, Helen, editor. Medicine and social work: an exploration in interprofessionalism. New York: Published for the Doris Siegel Memorial Fund of the Mount Sinai Medical Center by Prodist, 1974. 112p.

2861 Smith, David M. "The social work externship." Journal of the Royal College of General Practitioners, v. 23, no. 135, Oct. 1973. 692-696.

2862 Tanner, Libby A. and Lynn P. Carmichael. "The role of the social worker in family medicine training." Journal of Medical Education, v. 45, no. 11, Nov. 1970. Part I, 859-865.

2863 Thomson, Ruth. "Can the social worker teach the physician?" Journal of Medical Education, v. 48, no. 6, June 1973. 585-587.

2864 Ullmann, Alice. "A reappraisal of social work participation in medical education." Medical Social Work (London), v. 18, no. 6, Oct. 1965. 175-179.

2865 _____. "The role of the social worker in teaching fourth-year medical students." Journal of Medical Education,

v. 34, no. 3, March 1959. 239-246.

2866 _____. "Teaching medical students to understand stress in illness. " Social Casework, v. 57, no. 9, Nov. 1976. 568-574.

6. Nursing

2867 Benedikt, Lucie. "The social worker in practical nurse education. " Nursing Outlook, v. 13, no. 1, Jan. 1965. 60-62.

2868 Bergman, Rebecca, Tamar Krulik and Itzhak Ditzian. "Opinion on nursing. part III: social work students. " International Nursing Review, v. 23, no. 1, Jan. -Feb. 1976. 15-24.

2869 Dammann, Gloria L. A. "Interprofessional aspects of nursing and social work curricula. " Nursing Research, v. 21, no. 2, Mar. -April 1972. 160-163.

2870 Gordon, Eckka. Medical social work looks at nursing education. New York: American Association of Medical Social Workers, 1954. 44p.

2871 Guttmann, David, Frances L. Eyster and Garland Lewis. "Improving the care of the aged through interdisciplinary effort. " Gerontologist, v. 15, part 1, Oct. 1975. 387-392.

2872 Helper, Kathryn E. "The formal contribution of social work to a nursing education program. " Journal of Nursing Education, v. 3, no. 4, Nov. 1964. 23-27.

2873 Leiniger, Madeleine. "This I believe--About interdisciplinary health education for the future. " Nursing Outlook, v. 19, no. 12, Dec. 1971. 789-791.

2874 Mahar, Irene R. "Where there's a will. " Nursing Outlook, v. 17, no. 10, Oct. 1969. 55-57.

2875 Prock, Valencia. "A joint approach to education for the health professions. " Nursing Outlook, v. 9, no. 8, Aug. 1961. 472-474.

2876 Quartaro, Emma Giordano and Ruth Reagan Hutchison. "Interdisciplinary education for community health: the case for nursing and social work collaboration. " Social Work in Health Care, v. 1, no. 3, spring 1976. 347-356.

2877 Tanner, Libby A. and Ethel J. Soulary. "Interprofessional student health teams. " Nursing Outlook, v. 20, no. 2,

Feb. 1972. 111-115.

7. Pharmacy

2878 Kilwein, John, William T. Hall and Gerald C. St. Denis. "Social science, social work and pharmacy." Social Work in Health Care, v. 2, no. 1, fall 1976. 95-100.

8. Psychiatry

2879 Bandler, Bernard. "Interprofessional collaboration in training in mental health." American Journal of Orthopsychiatry, v. 43, no. 1, Jan. 1973. 97-107.

2880 Committee on Psychiatry and Social Work. "Psychiatrists as teachers in schools of social work." Group for the Advancement of Psychiatry, report no. 53, May 1962. 765-817.

2881 Firestein, Stephen K. "Teaching dynamic psychiatry to social work students." Social Casework, v. 57, no. 4, April 1976. 265-271.

2882 Graham, Norman and Sheldon I. Miller. "The social worker in undergraduate medical education." International Journal of Social Psychiatry, v. 20, no. 3-4, autumn-winter 1974. 265-268.

2883 Ireland, Eleanor. "The social worker's contribution to training in child psychiatry." Journal of Child Psychology and Psychiatry and Allied Disciplines, v. 8, no. 2, Nov. 1967. 99-104.

2884 "On psychotherapy and casework." Group for the Advancement of Psychiatry, v. 7, no. 71, March 1969. 27-42.

2885 Prince, G. Stewart. "The teaching of mental health in schools of social work." International Social Service Review, no. 8, March 1961. 31-35.

2886 Reece, Shirley A. "Social work participation in psychiatric training related to intake work." American Journal of Psychiatry. v. 121, no. 12, June 1965. 1183-1189.

2887 Sacks, Helen L. , Marian Henderson and Elizabeth C. Bellis. "Social work participation in training residents in psychiatry." American Journal of Orthopsychiatry, v. 38, no. 1, Jan. 1968. 25-30.

2888 Smith, Neilson F. "Interdisciplinary training for community mental health service." Journal of Education for Social Work, v. 10, no. 2, spring 1974. 106-113.

2889 Thomson, Hope and Dorthea Lane. "Teaching of psychotherapy: the social worker." International Psychiatry Clinics,
v. 1, no. 2, April 1964. 319-329.

9. Public Administration

2890 Hartford, Margaret E. "The MSW-MPA dual degree program
in gerontology: a new model for the preparation of social
work administrators." Journal of Education for Social
Work, v. 12, no. 3, fall 1976. 51-58.

2891 Kurren, Oscar and Paul Lister. "Social work internship in
public housing: an interdisciplinary experience." Journal
of Education for Social Work, v. 12, no. 3, fall 1976. 72-
79.

2892 Winthrop, Henry. "Policy and planning programs as goals of
scientific work: interdisciplinary training for social planning as a case study in applied social science." American Journal of Economics and Sociology, v. 34, no. 3, July
1975. 225-245.

C. INTERDISCIPLINARY STUDIES

1. Behavioral and Social Sciences

2893 Ancona, Leonardo. "Problems arising in the teaching of
psychology in schools of social work." International Social Service Review, no. 8, March 1961. 27-30.

2894 Ashton, Elwyn Thomas. Social work and the social sciences.
Bala, North Wales, Eng.: A. J. Chapple, 1966. 96p.

2895 Bisno, Herbert. "The use of social science content in social
work education: some problems and possibilities." International Social Service Review, no. 8, March 1961. 43-49.

2896 Boehm, Werner W. "Contribution of psychoanalysis to social
work education." Social Casework, v. 39, no. 9, Nov. 1958.
487-494.

2897 _____. "Social work and the social sciences." Journal
of Psychiatric Social Work, v. 21, no. 1, Sept. 1951. 4-8.

2898 Brennan, Tom. "Teaching of sociology to social workers."
Australian Journal of Social Work, v. 23, no. 4, Dec. 1970.
7-13.

2899 Council for Training in Social Work. The teaching of sociology in social work courses; report of the Sociology Study

Group. London: Central Council for Education and Training in Social Work, 1972. 32p.

2900 Coyle, Grace L. "New insights available to the social worker from the social sciences." Social Service Review, v. 26, no. 3, Sept. 1952. 289-304.

2901 _____. Social science in the professional education of social workers. New York: Council on Social Work Education, 1958. 69p.

2902 _____. "Some considerations in relating social science and social work education." Education for social work; proceedings of the 1958 Annual Program Meeting, Council on Social Work Education. New York: The Council, 1958. 88-94.

2903 Dixon, George I. J. "About cooperative programs in social work education." Wisconsin Sociologist, v. 2, no. 2, fall 1963. 11-16.

2904 Fellin, Phillip A., Edwin J. Thomas and Clarice Freud. "Institutes on behavioral science knowledge for field instructors." Journal of Education for Social Work, v. 4, no. 1, spring 1968. 5-13.

2905 Frankel, Charles. "Social philosophy and the professional education of social workers." Social Service Review, v. 33, no. 4, Dec. 1959. 345-359.

2906 Greenwood, Ernest. "Social sciences and social work: a theory of their relationship." Social Service Review, v. 29, no. 1, March 1955. 20-33.

2907 Halmos, Paul. "Problems arising in the teaching of sociology to social workers." International Social Service Review, no. 8, March 1961. 19-26.

2908 _____, editor. The teaching of sociology to students of education and social work. Keele, Eng.: University College of North Staffordshire, 1961. 133p.

2909 Hartford, Margaret E. and Grace L. Coyle. Social process in the community and the group: significant areas of content in a social work curriculum. New York: Council on Social Work Education, 1958. 89p.

2910 Leonard, Peter. "Application of sociological analysis to social work training." British Journal of Sociology, v. 19, no. 4, Dec. 1968. 375-384.

2911 Lund, Bernt H. "The teaching of social sciences in schools of social work." International Social Work, v. 3, no. 1, Jan. 1960. 1-8.

2912 Maas, Henry S. "Collaboration between social work and the social sciences." Social Work Journal, v. 31, no. 3, July 1950. 104-109.

2913 _____. "Use of behavioral sciences in social work education." Social Work, v. 3, no. 3, July 1958. 62-69.

2914 Maria Mercedes, Sr. "Contributions of sociology to undergraduate preparation for social work." Sociological Analysts, v. 21, no. 3, fall 1960. 201-207.

2915 Marshall, T. H. "The social sciences in the training of social workers." International Social Service Review, no. 8, March 1961. 11-17.

2916 National Science Board. Special Commission on the Social Sciences. "The social sciences and the professions: social work." Knowledge into action: improving the Nation's use of the social sciences. Washington, D. C.: Government Printing Office, 1969. 44-50.

2917 Pearman, Jean R. Social science and social work: applications of social science in the helping professions. Metuchen, N. J.: Scarecrow Press, 1973. 214p.

2918 Sherman, Sanford N. "The influence of social science on casework practice." Journal of Jewish Communal Service, v. 41, no. 1, fall 1964. 55-59.

2919 Stein, Herman D. "Issues in the relationship of social science to social work education." International Social Work, v. 4, no. 1, Jan. 1961. 10-18.

2920 _____. "Social science in social work practice and education." Social Casework, v. 36, no. 4. April 1955. 147-155.

2921 _____. "Social work and the behavioral and social sciences: reflections on developments." Journal of Jewish Communal Service, v. 41, no. 1, fall 1964. 16-28.

2922 Stroup, Herbert H. "Contribution of anthropology to social work education." Social Casework, v. 31, no. 5, May 1950. 189-194.

2923 Sylvain, Jeanne. "Problems arising in the teaching of cultural anthropology to social workers." International Social Service Review, no. 8, March 1961. 37-41.

2924 Towle, Charlotte. "Notes on the teaching of psychology to social work students." Some reflections on social work education. London: Family Welfare Association, 1956. 43-55.

2925 Tucker, Murray A. "Interfacing economics with social work education." Journal of Education for Social Work, v. 10, no. 1, winter 1974. 96-104.

2926 United Nations Educational, Scientific and Cultural Organization. The contribution of social sciences in social work training. Paris: UNESCO, 1961. 90p.

2927 Younghusband, Eileen L. "The social sciences and social work education; a report on the United Nations - U. N. E. - S. C. O. seminar." International Social Work, v. 4, no. 2, April 1961. 41-42.

2. History

2928 Chambers, Clarke A. "The discipline of history in a social welfare curriculum." Journal of Education for Social Work, v. 9, no. 1, winter 1973. 11-22.

2929 De Schweinitz, Karl. "Social values and social action--the intellectual base as illustrated in the study of history." Social Service Review, v. 30, no. 2, June 1956. 119-131.

2930 Seed, Philip. "The place of history in social work." Case Conference, v. 15, no. 10, Feb. 1969. 407-408.

2931 Stroup, Herbert H. "Use of biography in pre-professional social work education." Social Casework, v. 33, no. 5, May 1952. 179-186.

3. Humanities

2932 Aldridge, Gordon J. and Earl J. McGrath. Liberal education and social work. New York: Teachers College Press, 1965. 102p.

2933 "Asian creative literature for social work education." Social Work Training and Teaching Materials Newsletter, no. 4, July 1972. 1-18.

2934 Blake, M. L. "Language and social work: an experiment in Thailand." International Social Work, v. 14, no. 2, 1971. 43-52.

2935 Edman, Irwin. "Contribution of the humanities and the professional schools." Social work as human relations; anniversary papers of the New York School of Social Work and the Community Service Society. New York: Columbia

University Press, 1949. 93-100.

2936 Finnegan, Edward J. "Great literature and social work education." Social Work Education Reporter, v. 14, no. 3, Sept. 1966. 32, 45-47, 49.

2937 Greene, Maxine. "The humanities and social work education." Journal of Education for Social Work, v. 2, no. 1, spring 1966. 21-31.

2938 Mandell, Betty. "Social work as a liberal art." Social Work, v. 12, no. 3, July 1967. 102-106.

2939 Moore, Stewart. "Concepts and exercises in the classroom use of Canadian literature." Canadian Journal of Social Work Education, v. 2, no. 1, spring 1976. 3-11.

2940 _____. "Use of Canadian literature in social work education." Canadian Journal of Social Work Education, v. 1, no. 1, fall 1974. 14-25.

2941 Pangalangan, Evelina A. "Creative literature: a new dimension in social work education." International Social Work, v. 17, no. 1, 1974. 62-68.

2942 _____. "Creative literature: its use in social work education." Social Work (Manila), v. 12, no. 2, April-Dec. 1972. 21-27, 38.

2943 United Nations. Economic and Social Commission for Asia and the Pacific. Asian creative literature in social work education: a review of eight country workshops. New York: United Nations, 1975. 111p. E/CN. 11/1216.

2944 Valk, Margaret A. "Learning to feel the client's predicament: creativity in social work student training through the teaching of imaginative literature." Social Work Today, v. 4, no. 5, 31 May 1973. 150-153.

2945 _____. "Teaching creatively through literature and the arts." Social Work Training and Teaching Materials Newsletter, no. 6, March 1973. 13-20.

2946 Yasas, Frances Maria. "Asian creative literature for social work education." Curriculum development and teaching; proceedings of the South East Asian Seminar for Social Work Educators. Edited by Armaity Sapur Desai and Angelina C. Almanzor. Bombay: Athenaeum Press, 1972. 88-106.

4. Religion
[See also Section XV.]

2947   Council on Social Work Education. Religious content in social
       work education; workshop report of the 1960 Annual Program
       Meeting. New York: The Council, 1961. 85p.

2948   Liyanage, Mathu H. "Buddhism and social work education."
       Social Work Education and Development Newsletter, no. 11,
       Nov. 1974. 8-12.

2949   Spencer, Sue W. "Religion and social work." Social Work,
       v. 1, no. 3, July 1956. 19-26.

2950   . "What place has religion in social work education?"
       Social Service Review, v. 35, no. 2, June 1961. 161-170.

2951   Weil, Frank L. "Cooperation of church and social work."
       Social welfare forum, 1949: official proceedings of the
       National Conference of Social Work. New York: Columbia
       University Press, 1950. 125-134.

XVII. INTERNATIONAL SOCIAL WORK EDUCATION AND SOCIAL WORK EDUCATION IN FOREIGN COUNTRIES

A. INTERNATIONAL SOCIAL WORK EDUCATION [See also Section III. E. 7.]

2952 Allen, Theodora and Genevieve C. Weeks. "Undergraduate summer study in social welfare in England. " Social Work Education Reporter, v. 14, no. 4, Dec. 1966. 23-25, 62.

2953 Altmeyer, Arthur J. "Training for international responsibilities. " America's role in international social welfare. By Alva Myrdal, Arthur J. Altmeyer and Dean Rusk. Gloucester, Mass.: Peter Smith, 1967. 57-91.

2954 Anders, J. R. "Internationalism in social work education. " Journal of Education for Social Work, v. 11, no. 1, winter 1975. 16-21.

2955 Ankrah, E. Maxine. "Report on the International Congress of Schools of Social Work. " Development and participation: operational implications for social welfare; proceedings of the 17th International Conference on Social Welfare, Nairobi, Kenya, 1974. New York: Columbia University Press, 1975. 368-382.

2956 Aptekar, Herbert H. "The preparation of Americans for social work abroad. " Social Work Education Reporter, v. 13, no. 2, June 1965. 18-19.

2957 Bishop, Julia Ann. "On being a Fulbright lecturer in Scotland. " Journal of Social Work Process, v. 13, 1962. 9-31.

2958 Blackey, Eileen. "Summary report of group discussions on curriculum planning for social work in newly developing communities. " International Social Work, v. 4, no. 3, July 1961. 4-7.

2959 Bowers, Swithun. "Similarities and differences in social work education. " International Social Work, v. 2, no. 2, April 1959. 27-29.

2960 _____. "Social work's 'multi-coloured garment. '" Social Work Education Reporter, v. 16, no. 1, March 1968. 47-48.

2961 Branscombe, Martha. "Curriculum planning for social work

in newly developing communities." International Social
Work, v. 4, no. 3, July 1961. 1-3.

2962 Breen, Mary Lurie. "How adequate is American training for
practice overseas?" Social Work, v. 8, no. 4, Oct. 1963.
18-25.

2963 Bye, Lilian and Gerda De Bock. "Highlights of the 14th International Congress of Schools of Social Work." Social welfare and human rights; proceedings of the 14th International
Conference on Social Welfare, Helsinki, Finland, 1968.
New York: Columbia University Press, 1969. 276-297.

2964 Clarkson, Elizabeth. "The contribution of British social work
to developing countries." International Social Work, v. 19,
no. 1, 1976. 3-8.

2965 Conference on International Social Welfare Manpower. Proceedings of the Conference, 1964, Washington, D. C.
Washington D. C. : Government Printing Office, 1965.
112p.

2966 Council on Social Work Education. The essential task: training social welfare manpower. New York: Published by
Council on Social Work Education for International Association of Schools of Social Work and International Council
on Social Welfare, 1969. 56p.

2967 Cowan, Barbara and Frank J. Turner. "Overseas field placement: an educational experiment." Journal of Education
for Social Work, v. 11, no. 2, spring 1975. 18-24.

2968 Eaton, Joseph W. "The international dimension in social work
education." International Social Work, v. 16, no. 2/3,
1973. 56-60.

2969 Friedlander, Walter A. "Education for social work." International social welfare. Englewood Cliffs, N. J. : Pren-
tice-Hall, 1975. 199-214.

2970 Ginsberg, Leon H. , et al. "An experiment in overseas field
instruction." Journal of Education for Social Work, v. 8,
no. 2, spring 1972. 16-24.

2971 Howard, Donald S. "Schools of social work and social policy;
a summary of National Association Reports." International
Social Work, v. 7, no. 3, July 1964. 14-31.

2972 Intercultural exploration: universals and differences in social
work values, functions, and practice; report of the Intercultural Seminar, the East-West Center, Hawaii, 1966.
New York: Council on Social Work Education, 1967. 184p.

2973   International Association of Schools of Social Work.   Educa-
       tion for social change: human development and national
       progress; proceedings of the 17th International Congress
       of Schools of Social Work, Nairobi, 1974. New York:
       The Association, 1975. 167p.

2974   _____. New themes in social work education; proceedings
       of the 16th International Congress of Schools of Social
       Work, The Hague, The Netherlands, 1972. New York:
       The Association, 1973. 197p.

2975   _____. Social work education in the seventies; papers
       presented at the 15th International Congress of Schools of
       Social Work, 1970, Manila, Philippines. New York: The
       Association, 1970. 90p.

2976   Interprofessional Conference on Training of Personnel for Over-
       seas Service. Interprofessional training goals for techni-
       cal assistance personnel abroad; report of the conference,
       Ithaca, New York, 1959. Prepared by Irwin T. Sanders.
       New York: Council on Social Work Education, 1959. 198p.

2977   Katz, Arthur. "Social work's contribution to the Peace Corps."
       Education for social work; proceedings of the 1962 Annual
       Program Meeting, Council on Social Work Education. New
       York: The Council, 1962. 75-85.

2978   Kendall, Katherine A. "Highlights of the new CSWE program
       of international cooperation in social work education."
       Social Work Education Reporter, v. 15, no. 2, June 1967.
       20-23, 37, 42.

2979   _____. No quiet place; the Elizabeth Wisner lecture. New
       Orleans, School of Social Work, Tulane University, 1971.
       16p.

2980   _____. "Social work training around the world." Social
       Service Review, v. 34, no. 2, June 1960. 203-213.

2981   _____, editor. Teaching of comparative social welfare; a
       workshop report. New York: Council on Social Work Ed-
       ucation, 1969. Various pagings.

2982   Khinduka, Shanti K. Manpower for United Nations technical
       assistance. Waltham, Mass.: Florence Heller Graduate
       School for Advanced Studies in Social Welfare, Brandeis
       University, 1968. 51p.

2983   _____ and Richard J. Parvis. "On teaching international
       social welfare." Social Work Education Reporter, v. 17,
       no. 1, March 1969. 35-38, 65-66.

2984 _____ . "Reflections of an Indian student on American social work and his culture. " Social Work Papers, v. 9,
1962. 45-48.

2985 _____ . "Social work and the third world. " Social Service
Review, v. 45, no. 1, March 1971. 62-73.

2986 Lally, Dorothy. National social service systems; a comparative study and analysis of selected countries. Washington,
D. C. : U. S. Social and Rehabilitation Service, 1970.
78p.

2987 Leaper, R. A. B. "Highlights of the International Congress
of Schools of Social Work. " Urban development: its implications for social welfare; proceedings of the 13th International Conference of Social Work, Washington, D. C. ,
1966. New York: Columbia University Press, 1967.
311-318.

2988 Lee, Hei-Man. "Culture learning fieldwork: an educational
experiment for the development of intercultural understanding. " Social Work Education and Development Newsletter,
no. 15, March 1976. 10-15.

2989 Lightman, J. B. "The community organization approach in
training for international social work. " Social Work Review, v. 10, July 1963. 1-6.

2990 _____ . "A unified field work theory of training for international social work. " Social Worker-Travailleur Social,
v. 26, no. 3, April 1958. 37-45.

2991 Lochhead, Andrew. "Social welfare courses at Swansea: a
ten-year review. " Social Service Quarterly, v. 36, no. 4,
spring 1963. 154-158.

2992 _____ . "Training for social work. " Report of the Seminar
on Social Welfare in a Developing Economy, Delhi, 1963.
New Delhi: Planning Commission, Government of India,
1964. 40-52.

2993 Lodge, Richard. "Process in international consultation for
professional education. " Journal of Social Work Process,
v. 14, 1964. 147-161.

2994 Madison, Bernice. "Comparative studies in social welfare:
review of a course. " Social Work Education Reporter,
v. 18, no. 2, June 1970. 36-38, 48.

2995 _____ . "Social welfare in international perspective: review of an undergraduate course. " Journal of Education
for Social Work, v. 12, no. 1, winter 1976. 97-104.

2996   Manis, Francis. "Education for social work: field work in developing nations." International Social Work, v. 14, no. 2, 1971. 17-20.

2997   _____. Field practice in social work education; perspectives from an international base. Fullerton, Calif.: Sultana Press, 1972. 160p.

2998   Marks, Rachel Bryant. "Some thoughts on the social worker's preparation for work abroad." Some aspects on social work training. Compiled by the Swedish Association of Graduates from Schools of Social Work and Public Administration. Kumla, Sweden: The Association, 1969. 66-73.

2999   Masi, Fidelia A. "International field placements." Journal of Education for Social Work, v. 10, no. 1, winter 1974. 55-59.

3000   Miller, Paul. "Social work education and the International Education Act." Social Work Education Reporter, v. 16, no. 2, June 1968. 34-37.

3001   Morris, Robert. "Overcoming cultural and professional myopia in education for human service." Journal of Education for Social Work, v. 6, no. 1, spring 1970. 41-51.

3002   Moses, Dorothy. "Social work education in North America: its applicability to other countries." Proceedings of the Canadian Conference on Social Work, 1958. Toronto: The Conference, 1958. 19-25.

3003   Neipris, Joseph. "The International Congress of Schools of Social Work: highlights." New strategies for social development; role of social welfare; proceedings of the 15th International Conference on Social Welfare, Manila, 1970. New York: Columbia University Press, 1971. 198-209.

3004   Paglia, Emma Fasolo. "Teaching Americans in America." Journal of Education for Social Work, v. 9, no. 2, spring 1973. 31-38.

3005   Pettiss, Susan T. "Whither international education exchange? A social worker's perspectives and recommendations." International Educational and Cultural Exchange, v. 6, no. 1, summer 1970. 57-70.

3006   Rees, Stuart. "International co-operation in community work training." International Social Work, v. 15, no. 1, 1972. 29-33.

3007   Robertson, Jean M. "Observations on some aspects of social work education in developing countries." International Social Work, v. 6, no. 2, April 1963.   19-21.

3008   Salomon, Alice.   Education for social work; a sociological
       interpretation based on an international survey.   Zurich,
       Switz.: Verlag für Recht und Gesellschaft, 1937.   265p.

3009   Schneiderman, Leonard.   "The goals of social work education
       in the developing nations."   International Social Work, v.
       11, no. 4, Oct. 1968.   30-34.

3010   Sikkema, Mildred.   "Issues in social work education at the
       Ninth International Congress of Schools of Social Work."
       Social Service Review, v. 34, no. 2, June 1960.   214-222.

3011   Stein, Herman D.   "Highlights of the International Congress
       of Schools of Social Work."   Social progress through so-
       cial planning--The role of social work; proceedings of the
       12th International Conference of Social Work, Athens,
       Greece, 1964.   New York: International Conference of
       Social Work, 1965.   183-189.

3012   Stickney, Patricia J. and Rosa Perla Resnick, editors.   World
       guide to social work education.   New York: International
       Association of Schools of Social Work, 1974.   297p.

3013   Training programs in social welfare for international social
       workers.   Washington, D. C.: U. S. Social Security
       Administration, 1959.   24p.

3014   United Nations.   Report of the Interregional Workshop on
       Training for Administration of Social Services, Geneva,
       1964.   New York: United Nations, 1966.   60p. ST/TAO/-
       SER. C/92.

3015   _____. Bureau of Social Affairs.   Training for social work;
       second international survey.   New York: United Nations,
       1955.   160p. ST/SOA/25.

3016   _____. Department of Economic and Social Affairs.   Train-
       ing for social work; third international survey.   New York:
       United Nations, 1958.   349p. ST/SOA/37.

3017   _____.   _____.   Training for social welfare; fifth inter-
       national survey; new approaches in meeting manpower needs.
       New York: United Nations, 1971.   88p. ST/SOA/105.

3018   _____.   _____.   Training for social work; fourth inter-
       national survey.   New York: United Nations, 1964.   120p.
       ST/SOA/57.

3019   _____. Department of Social Affairs.   International direc-
       tory of schools of social work.   New York: United Nations,

1954. 127p. ST/SOA/20.

3020 _____ . _____ . Training for social work; an international survey. New York: United Nations, 1950. 248p.
E/CN.5/196/Rev.1.

3021 U. S. Social Security Administration. Observation as a way
of learning for international social workers. Washington,
D. C.: The Administration, 1955. 19p.

3022 Vakharia, Parin. "Problems in adapting social work education obtained in the United States to practice at home."
Professional education of students from other lands. Edited by Irwin T. Sanders. New York: Council on Social
Work Education, 1963. 244-251.

3023 Van Stegeren, Willemina F. "Returning to social work from
foreign study: a reintegration process." Journal of Social Work Process, v.15, 1966. 133-146.

3024 Watson, Elizabeth V. "Training and utilization of social work
manpower." International social welfare research and
demonstration. Los Angeles: Regional Research Institute
in Social Welfare, School of Social Work, University of
Southern California, 1974. 121-137.

3025 Younghusband, Eileen L. "The Curriculum Study: international implications for social work education." Social
Casework, v.41, no.1, Jan. 1960. 33-38.

3026 _____ . Social work and social change. New York: Council on Social Work Education, 1964. 166p.

3027 _____ . "Some international aspects of education for social
work." Education for social work; proceedings of the 1963
Annual Program Meeting, Council on Social Work Education. New York: The Council, 1963. 66-77.

3028 _____ . "Tasks and trends in education for social work:
an international appraisal." Social Work (London), v.20,
no.3, July 1963. 4-11.

B. AFRICA

1. General

3029 Brown, Malcolm J. "Social work values in a developing country." Social Work, v.15, no.1, Jan. 1970. 107-112.

3030 Clifford, W. Social work training in Africa; a paper presented at the Seminar of Social Work Training in Africa, Lusaka, 1963. Addis Ababa, Ethiopia: United Nations Economic Commission for Africa, 1963. 21p. E/CN. 14/-SWTA/4.

3031 Diallo, Hawa. Essential conditions in the development of a school of social work; statement presented at Seminar on Social Work Training in Africa, Lusaka, 1963. Addis Ababa, Ethiopia: United Nations Economic Commission for Africa, 1963. 11p. E/CN. 14/SWTA/3.

3032 Hardiman, Margaret G. W. Social work training needs in East Africa; report on regional seminar in Uganda, Dec. 1967. London: Commonwealth Foundation, 1968. 11p.

3033 Hodge, Peter. "Problems of social work education in Africa." Case Conference, v. 13, no. 4, August 1966. 118-122.

3034 Iliovici, Jean. "Urban development: implications for training social work personnel: In Europe and Africa." Urban development: its implications for social welfare; proceedings of the 13th International Conference of Social Work, Washington, D. C. , 1966. New York: Columbia University Press, 1967. 296-299.

3035 Nabwire, Constance R. The transferability of North American social work to Black Africa. Kampala, Uganda: Milton Obote Foundation, Adult Education Centre, 1968. 62p.

3036 Neely, Ann Elizabeth. "Social work education in a changing Africa." International Social Work, v. 9, no. 2, April 1966. 25-29.

3037 Omari, T. Peter. "Training and research in social welfare in West Africa." Social work in West Africa; report of the Seminar on Social Work in West Africa, Legon, 1962. Edited by St. Clair Drake and T. Peter Omari. Accra, Ghana: Department of Social Welfare and Community Development, 1963. 111-116.

3038 Riby-Williams, J. "Education for social change." Education for social change: human development and national progress; proceedings of the International Congress of Schools of Social Work, 1974. New York: The Association, 1975. 82-95.

3039 Shawky, Abdel H. "Social work education in Africa." International Social Work, v. 15, no. 3, 1972. 3-16.

3040 _____. "Training needs and problems in social welfare services in Eastern and Central Africa." International Social Work, v. 11, no. 4, Oct. 1968. 35-42.

3041 Sylvain, J. G. Training for social work in French-speaking African countries; paper presented at the Seminar on Social Work Training in Africa, Lusaka, 1963. Addis Ababa, Ethiopia: United Nations Economic Commission for Africa, 1963. 24p. E/CN. 14/SWTA/7.

3042 "Training for social work in Africa." International Social Service Review, no. 9, April 1963. 29-35.

3043 United Nations. Economic Commission for Africa. The development and use of teaching materials in social work training with special reference to the African Region. Addis Ababa, Ethiopia: The Commission, 1971. 17p. E/CN. 14/SW/34.

3044 _____. _____. Report of Consultant Team for the Study of Schools of Social Work in Africa, 19 October-20 December 1964. Addis Ababa, Ethiopia: The Commission, 1966. 88p. E/CN. 14/SWSA/3/Add. 1.

3045 _____. _____. Report of Expert Group Meeting on Social Welfare Training and Administration (Teaching Materials), Addis Ababa, 1971. Addis Ababa, Ethiopia: The Commission, 1971. 22p. E/CN. 14/514 (E/CN. 14/SW/35).

3046 _____. _____. Report of the Expert Working Group of Social Work Educators, Addis Ababa, 1969. Addis Ababa, Ethiopia: The Commission, 1969. 28p. E/CN. 14/454.

3047 _____. _____. Report of the Seminar for Social Work Educators in Africa. Addis Ababa, Ethiopia: The Commission, 1966. 91p. E/CN. 14/SWTA/42/Rev. 1.

3048 _____. _____. Report of the Seminar on Social Work Training in Africa, Lusaka, Northern Rhodesia, 1963. Addis Ababa, Ethiopia: The Commission, 1964. 51p. E/CN. 14/SWTA/35.

3049 _____. _____. Social work training in a changing Africa. Addis Ababa, Ethiopia: The Commission, 1965. 84p. E/CN. 14/SWTA/41.

3050 _____. _____. Training for social work in Africa. New York: United Nations, 1964. 50p. E/CN. 14/SWSA/3.

3051 _____. Office of Social Affairs, Geneva. European cooperation in training for social welfare in Africa; report of the expert group, Cesenatico, Italy, 1965. Geneva: United Nations, 1965. 82p. SOA/ESWP/EG/Rep. 6.

2. Egypt

3052 United Arab Republic. Ministry of Social Affairs. Training for social welfare. Cairo: The Ministry, 1967. 63p.

3. Ethiopia

3053 Gerima, Yohannes Wolde. "Personnel and training for social
welfare; with special reference to the School of Social Work
of University College, Addis Ababa." International Social
Service Review, no. 9, April 1963. 36-40.

3054 Sedler, Rozanne F. "Social welfare in a developing country:
the Ethiopian experience, part III: The role of social
work education." International Social Work, v. 11, no. 2,
April 1968. 36-44.

4. Kenya

3055 Ilan, Issacher and Miriam Hoffert. "Training social workers
for East Africa: a personal account." il Kidma, v. 1,
no. 2, 1973. 24-28.

3056 Weisner, Stanley. Professional social work in Kenya: training and performance. Lower Kabete: Kenya Institute of
Administration, 1972. 71p.

3057 _____ and Constance Meyer Weisner. "Professional social
work in Kenya--Training and performance--A critical evaluation." Social Work Forum, v. 10, no. 4, Jan. 1973.
3-12.

5. Zambia

3058 Brown, Peter T. "Social work education in Zambia: an integrated approach." International Social Work, v. 14, no. 1,
1971. 42-47.

3059 Dunning, Arthur W. "'... Limits to the amount of noise...:'
relationships between agency and school in a developing
country." International Social Work, v. 15, no. 2, 1972.
4-7.

C. ASIA AND PACIFIC AREA

1. General

3060 Almanzor, Angelina C. "Gearing social work education to
development, with special reference to poverty and the
problems of the family in Asian society." Social Work
Education and Development Newsletter, no. 12, March 1975.
11-17.

3061 Desai, Armaity Sapur and S. H. Pathak. "A report on the Seminar on Developmental Aspects of Social Work Training Curricula: ECAFE-UNICEF (EAPRO), Bangkok, Nov. 14-15, 1972." Social Work Forum, v. 10, no. 3, Oct. 1972. 18-28.

3062 Desai, M. M. "Role of field work supervisor in training of professional social workers in Asiatic countries." Ceylon Journal of Social Work, v. 4, no. 3, 1963. 25-29.

3063 International Association of Schools of Social Work. Asian social problems: new strategies for social work education; proceedings of the Third Asian Regional Seminar, "Development of Teaching Resources and Interdisciplinary Communication," 1975, Hong Kong. New York: The Association, 1976. 168p.

3064 Moses, Dorothy. "Trends in social work education in Asia." Indian Journal of Social Work, v. 28, no. 1, April 1967. 1-10.

3065 "Objectives of professional social work and social work education in the context of national development and problems." Indian Journal of Social Work, v. 30, no. 1, April 1969. 73-85.

3066 "The relationship of social work education to developmental needs and problems in the ECAFE region; excerpts from the final report of a United Nations seminar." International Social Work, v. 12, no. 2, 1969. 27-37.

3067 "Relationship of social work education to developmental needs in the ECAFE Region." Indian Journal of Social Work, v. 29, no. 4, Jan. 1969. 327-339.

3068 United Nations. Economic and Social Commission for Asia and the Pacific. Asian creative literature in social work education: a review of eight country workshops. New York: United Nations, 1975. 111p. E/CN. 11/1216.

3069 _____. _____. Some guidelines for institutions of higher learning in social work: report of the Expert Group Meeting on the Determination of Social Development Content in Social Work Education Curricula, 1974, Bangkok. Bangkok: The Commission, 1974. 60p. SD/SW/-ExIn-7.

3070 _____. Economic Commission for Asia and the Far East. Problems and prospects in schools of social work contributing to development in the ECAFE region; report of the ECAFE/UNICEF Seminar on Developmental Aspects of Social Work Training Curricula, part I. Bangkok: The

Commission, 1972. 48p. E/CN. 11/SD/Sem. SWT/L. 3.

3071 _____ . _____ . Report of the Asian Seminar on Training for Family and Child Welfare. Bangkok: The Commission, 1963. 51p. E/CN. 11/L. 116.

3072 _____ . _____ . Report of the Regional Training Centre
for Social Work Educators and Field Work Supervisors,
Bangkok, 1966, part I. Bangkok: The Commission, 1967.
156p.

3073 _____ . _____ . Report of the Seminar on the Relation-
ship of Social Work Education to Developmental Needs and
Problems in the ECAFE Region, Bangkok, 1968. Bangkok:
The Commission, 1968. 55p. E/CN. 11/SD/DNP/L. 2.

3074 _____ . _____ . Report of the Working Group on the
Development of Indigenous Teaching Material for Social
Work. Bangkok: The Commission, 1964. 183p. E/CN. -
11/672.

3075 _____ . _____ . Support materials for the ECAFE/UNI-
CEF Seminar on Developmental Aspects of Social Work
Training Curricula; a collection of in-country reports on
selected topics; project proposals from participants; and
a report on communication for the seminar, part II. Bangkok: The Commission, 1972. 135p. SD/Sem/SWT/R. 1.

3076 _____ . Technical Assistance Programme. Report of the
United Nations Asia and the Far East Seminar on Training
for Community Development and Social Work, Lahore, West
Pakistan, 1957. New York: United Nations, 1958. 86p.
TAO/AFE/4.

2. Australia

3077 Australian Council of Social Service. Social welfare education
in Australia; report of the Joint Committee on Social Welfare Education in Australia. Sidney: The Council, 1973.
199p.

3078 Cutcher, R. , et al. "Social service training in Commonwealth
tertiary institutions. " Social Service, v. 19, no. 3, Nov. -
Dec. 1967. 10-15.

3079 Einspinner, P. G. "Welfare work education at the vocational
level. " Social Service, v. 25, no. 4, Jan. -Feb. 1974. 2-7.

3080 "The graduate diploma in social and administrative studies--
Oxford University. " Australian Journal of Social Work,
v. 21, no. 3, Sept. 1968. 21-22.

3081 Green, Solomon H. "Social work in Australia." Australian Journal of Social Work, v. 23, no. 3, Sept. 1970. 1-11.

3082 Hyde, Alice. "Group Project: an Australian experiment in social work training." Case Conference, v. 9, no. 1, May 1962. 4-8.

3083 Lawrence, R. John. "The future role and development of social work in Australia." Australian Journal of Social Work, v. 15, no. 2, Dec. 1962. 1-7.

3084 _____. Professional social work in Australia. Canberra: Australian National University, 1965. 241p.

3085 Parker, Norma. "Developments in professional education." Australian Journal of Social Work, v. 19, no. 2, May 1966. 1-4.

3086 Pavlin, Frank. "Generation gap: student social worker and the A. A. S. W." Australian Journal of Social Work, v. 22, no. 4, Dec. 1969. 35-36.

3087 Stockbridge, M. E. "Graduate diplomas in social work: seventeen months." Australian Journal of Social Work, v. 21, no. 3, Sept. 1968. 15-21.

3088 Tauss, Walter. "Are there limits to the demand for social workers?" Australian Journal of Social Work, v. 23, no. 3, Sept. 1970. 15-16.

3. Ceylon

3089 Hooker, Elbert L. "Professional education for social work." Ceylon Journal of Social Work, v. 6, no. 1, 1962. 13-17.

3090 Pillai, G. R. "The training programme for professional social workers in Ceylon." Ceylon Journal of Social Work, v. 4, no. 4, 1963. 9-11.

4. Hong Kong

3091 Chaisson, Josephine D. , Alan F. Klein and Martha Moscrop. A training programme for social work in Hong Kong; report on a training programme for social work with proposals for the future development of social work training in Hong Kong. Hong Kong: Hong Kong Government Printer, 1963. 2 vol.

3092 Ho, Kam-fai. "Factors predictive of successful performance in social work education." Doctoral dissertation, Columbia University, 1974. 195p.

3093   Riches, Graham. "Community work placements in social
        work training: the experience of Hong Kong." Social
        Work Today, v. 2, no. 9, 29 July 1971. 9-11.

3094   Younghusband, Eileen L. A report on employment and train-
        ing for social work in Hong Kong. Hong Kong: Social
        Welfare Department, 1971. 50p.

3095   _____. Training for social work in Hong Kong; a report
        prepared for the Government of Hong Kong. Hong Kong:
        The Government of Hong Kong, 1960. 42p.

5. India

3096   Ansari, Nazir Ahmad. An appraisal of the training program-
        mes for social education workers in India. Delhi: Central
        Institute of Education, 1970. 54p.

3097   Aptekar, Herbert H. "Generic and specific in social work
        training." Social Work Review, v. 8, July 1961. 11-21.

3098   Baker, Dorothy M. "Training to solve people problems: the
        Bombay School of Social Work." Worldmission, v. 23, no.
        1, spring 1972. 22-25.

3099   Banerjee, G. R. "Training for medical and psychiatric so-
        cial work." Indian Journal of Social Work, v. 28, no. 1,
        April 1967. 79-87.

3100   Berkowitz, Monroe and Philip Thomas. "The training of
        labour welfare officers." Indian Journal of Social Work,
        v. 21, no. 2, Sept. 1960. 181-190.

3101   Chatterjee, Prabodh Kumar. "The growth and development
        of community organization education in schools of social
        work in India, 1936-1969: an historical analysis." Doc-
        toral dissertation, Bryn Mawr College, 1972. 456p.

3102   Dadlani, G. G. "Survey of social work education in India
        as preparation for work in the field." Baroda, India:
        Faculty of Social Work, Maharaja Sayajirao University of
        Baroda, 1961. 63p.

3103   Delhi School of Social Work. Field records in group work
        and community organization. Delhi: The School, 1958.

3104   _____. Field work practices in schools of social work in
        India. Delhi: The School, 1958.

3105   _____. Field work supervision in an Indian school of so-
        cial work. Delhi: The School, 1957.

3106 Desai, Armaity Sapur. "Role of the Association of Schools of Social Work in the development of the profession of social work in India." Social Work Forum, v. 11, no. 2, July 1973. 8-12.

3107 Desai, M. M. "Training for family and child welfare." Indian Journal of Social Work, v. 28, no. 1, April 1967. 115-119.

3108 Gokhale, S. D. , editor. Social welfare, legend and legacy: silver jubilee commemoration volume of the Indian Council of Social Welfare. Bombay: Popular Prakashan, 1975. 432p.

3109 Gore, Madhav S. "The cultural perspective in social work in India." International Social Work, v. 9, no. 3, July 1966. 6-16.

3110 _____. "Current trends in social work education." Social Work Review, v. 10, July 1963. 22-26.

3111 _____. "Education for social work." Encyclopedia of social work in India, v. 1. New Delhi: Planning Commission, Government of India, 1968. 254-263.

3112 _____. "A note on recruitment to schools of social work." Social Work Forum, v. 1, no. 1, Jan. 1963. 25-26.

3113 _____. Social work and social work education. New York: Asia Publishing House, 1966. 155p.

3114 Grangrade, K. D. "The India Project seen through the eyes of a Delhi participant." Social Work Education Reporter, v. 10, no. 2, April 1962. 7-10.

3115 Hartman, Nelie M. "A team member reviews the CSWE India Project." Social Work Education Reporter, v. 10, no. 2, April 1962. 1-5.

3116 Hasan, Saiyid Zafar. "Social work education at the undergraduate level." Indian Journal of Social Work, v. 28, no. 1, April 1967. 63-69.

3117 India. Planning Commission. "Training programmes." Plans and prospects of social welfare in India. Faridabad, India: Government of India Press, 1963. 216-225.

3118 _____. University Grants Commission. Social work education in Indian universities. New Delhi: The Commission, 1965. 98p.

3119 Jacob, K. K. Methods and fields of social work in India.

New York: Asia Publishing House, 1965. 264p.

3120 Jagannadham, V. and S. P. Nandwani. Training for social welfare work: courses and institutions. New Delhi: Indian Institute of Public Administration, 1960. 97p.

3121 Kaikobad, N. F. "Training for community development." Indian Journal of Social Work, v. 28, no. 1, April 1967. 95-107.

3122 _____. "Urban development: implications for training social work personnel: In India." Urban development: its implications for social welfare; proceedings of the 13th International Conference of Social Work, Washington, D. C., 1966. New York: Columbia University Press, 1967. 306-310.

3123 Khinduka, Shanti K. "Recruitment of students--some reflections." Social Work Forum, v. 1, no. 1, Jan. 1963. 19-24.

3124 Kudchedkar, L. S. "Problems in selecting students to schools of social work in India." Social Work Forum, v. 1, no. 1, Jan. 1963. 29-32.

3125 _____. "Training for labour welfare." Indian Journal of Social Work, v. 28, no. 1, April 1967. 71-78.

3126 Kumaran, V. C. "Reflections on undergraduate social work education." Social Welfare, v. 18, no. 2, Feb. 1972. 11-12.

3127 Malhotra, Prema and Yahia Bin Mohammed. "Social work education at undergraduate level." Social Work Forum, v. 5, no. 2, April 1967. 10-15.

3128 Mehta, Vera D. "Issues of social group work in India." Social Work Training and Teaching Materials Newsletter, no. 7, July 1973. 3-12.

3129 Mhetras, V. G. "Teaching of labour welfare administration." Indian Journal of Social Work, v. 25, no. 3, Oct. 1964. 281-284.

3130 Mohsini, S. R. "Problems of undergraduate education in social work." Social Work Forum, v. 7, no. 2, July 1969. 63-70.

3131 Moses, Dorothy. "University education for social work." Indian Journal of Social Work, v. 12, no. 1, June 1951. 91-96.

3132 Muzumdar, Ammu M. "Selection of students to the schools of social work--A challenge to social work educators." Social Work Forum, v. 1, no. 1, Jan. 1963. 27-28.

3133 Nagpaul, Hans. "Appraisal of social work specialities." Indian Journal of Social Work, v. 31, no. 2, July 1970. 135-154.

3134 _____. "The diffusion of American social work education to India: problems and issues." International Social Work, v. 15, no. 1, 1972. 3-17.

3135 _____. "Dilemmas of social work education in India." Indian Journal of Social Work, v. 28, no. 3, Oct. 1967. 269-284.

3136 _____. "Social work as a profession in India: a sociological analysis." Indian Journal of Social Work, v. 32, no. 4, Jan. 1972. 387-411.

3137 _____. "Social work education in India." Social work in India. Edited by S. K. Khinduka. Allahabad, India: Kitab Mahal, 1965. 241-268.

3138 _____. The study of Indian society; a sociological analysis of social welfare and social work education. New Delhi: S. Chand, 1972. 510p.

3139 Nanavatty, Meher C. "Growth and problems of the profession of social work in India." Indian Journal of Social Work, v. 28, no. 1, April 1967. 55-62.

3140 _____. "Social work education in India: a critique." Social Work Forum, v. 4, no. 2, April 1966. 67-74.

3141 Panakal, J. J. "Training for correctional work." Indian Journal of Social Work, v. 28, no. 1, April 1967. 89-94.

3142 Pathak, S. H. "Training for social work: a new pattern." Social Work Forum, v. 3, no. 4, Oct. 1965. 46-52.

3143 _____. "Training for social work in the Fourth Five Year Plan." Social Welfare, v. 13, no. 5, Aug. 1966. 23-24, 30.

3144 Ramachandran, P. and A. Padmanabha. Professional social workers in India: their employment position and functions. Bombay: United Asia Publications, 1969. 182p.

3145 _____. "Social work education--some data many doubts." Indian Journal of Social Work, v. 29, no. 3, Oct. 1968. 241-253.

3146 _____ . "Training for social research." Indian Journal
of Social Work, v. 28, no. 1, April 1967. 109-114.

3147 Ranade, S. N. "Recruitment to social work." Social Work
Forum, v. 1, no. 1, Jan. 1963. 13-18.

3148 Roy, Asoke Mohan. "Training of social servants." Indian
Journal of Social Work, v. 24, no. 4, Jan. 1964. 235-246.

3149 Schlesinger, Benjamin. "American training for Indian social
worker: cure or curse?" Indian Journal of Social Work,
v. 21, no. 3, Dec. 1960. 261-265.

3150 Sethi, D. P. "Social work curricula in India." Social Welfare, v. 15, no. 1, April, 1968. 6-8, 15.

3151 Singh, Surendra. "Social welfare administration: need for
trained personnel." Social Welfare, v. 18, no. 3, June
1971. 7-9.

3152 "Social work education in India." Social Work Forum, v. 4,
no. 2, April 1966. 63-66.

3153 Srivastava, S. P. "Issues before India's social work educators." Social Work Forum, v. 11, no. 1-2, July 1973.
1-7.

3154 _____ . "Some issues relating to field work and research
in education for correctional work in India." Social Work
Forum, v. 12, no. 1, April 1974. 15-27.

3155 Tellis-Nayak, Jessie. "Training personnel for social welfare
and development projects in India." Social Work Training
and Teaching Materials Newsletter, no. 6, March 1973.
4-8.

3156 Thomas, P. T. "Problems of social work education in India."
Indian Journal of Social Work, v. 28, no. 1, April 1967.
41-53.

3157 _____ . "Professional training in social work." Towards
a philosophy of social work in India. Edited by Sugata
Dasgupta. New Delhi: Popular Book Services, 1967.
52-73.

3158 _____ . "Social work education and training." Report of
the Seminar on Social Welfare in a Developing Economy,
Delhi, 1963. New Delhi: Planning Commission, Government of India, 1964. 62-75.

3159 _____ . "Social work education and training in India."
Social Action (Indian), v. 14, no. 1, Jan. 1964. 19-27.

3160 Vakharia, Parin. "University education for social work." Indian Journal of Social Work, v. 12, no. 1, June 1951. 97-103.

3161 Vasudeva Moorthy, M. Social work: philosophy, methods and fields. Dharwar, India: Karnatak University, 1974. 116p.

3162 Viswanathan, N. "Schools of social work and social policy in India." Indian Journal of Social Work, v. 25, no. 3, Oct. 1964. 233-242.

3163 Wadia, A. R., editor. History and philosophy of social work in India. 2nd edition. New Delhi: Allied Publishers Private Ltd., 1968. 464p.

3164 Wright, Helen R. "Similarities and differences in social work education as seen in India and North America." International Social Work, v. 2, no. 1, Jan. 1959. 1-10.

3165 Yesas, Frances Maria. "Gandhian values in professional social work education in India." Indian Journal of Social Work, v. 25, no. 1, April 1964. 1-28.

3166 Yelaja, Shankar A. "Schools of social work in India: an overview of their present status." Indian Journal of Social Work, v. 30, no. 1, April 1969. 2-21.

3167 _____. "Schools of social work in India--historical development, 1936-1966." Indian Journal of Social Work, v. 29, no. 4, Jan. 1969. 361-378.

3168 _____. "Social Welfare Policy and Services curriculum in Indian schools of social work." Doctoral dissertation, University of Pennsylvania, 1967. 329p.

6. Iran

3169 Farman-Farmaian, Sattareh. "Social work education and training." Report of the Seminar on Social Welfare in a Developing Economy, Delhi, 1963. New Delhi: Planning Commission, Government of India, 1964. 53-61.

3170 Prigmore, Charles S. Social work in Iran since the White Revolution. University, Ala.: University of Alabama Press, 1976. 194p.

7. Israel

3171 Blackey, Eileen. "The development of the social work curriculum in Israel." International Social Work, v. 5, no. 2, April 1962. 1-7.

3172 Ickowicz, Miriam. The Institute for Training Social Workers: rationale and program. Jerusalem: n. p. , 1965. 29p.

3173 _____. Training social workers for rural and development areas. Jerusalem: Israel Ministry of Social Welfare, 1963. 23p.

3174 Jaffe, Eliezer David. "The social work establishment and social change in Israel." Social Work, v. 15, no. 2, April 1970. 103-109.

3175 Jaffe, Lester D. "Developing an educational sequence in social work research." International Social Work, v. 6, no. 1, Jan. 1963. 21-26.

3176 Lappin, Ben W. "Social work education in Israel." Community workers and the social work tradition; their quest for a role examined in Israel and in Canada. Toronto: University of Toronto Press, 1971. 190p.

3177 Macarov, David. "Developing an educational sequence in social group work." International Social Work, v. 6, no. 1, Jan. 1963. 13-20.

3178 Moscrop, Martha. "The social worker as an agent of change." Canadian Welfare, v. 44, no. 1, Jan. -Feb. 1968. 35-39.

3179 Rosenfeld, Jona M. "Training for social welfare and development in Israel: policies and programmes for the Seventies." International Social Work, v. 14, no. 1, 1971. 48-55.

3180 Spiro, Shimon. "Development of the 'Community Work' Sequence in an undergraduate curriculum: the problem of learning experiences in the field." International Social Work, v. 5, no. 3, July 1962. 29-36.

8. Japan

3181 Dessau, Dorothy, editor. Glimpses of social work in Japan. Revised edition. Kyoto, Japan: Social Workers' International Club of Japan, 1968. 260p.

3182 Japan. Working Committee on Social Work Education. New social work education: an interim report. Tokyo: The Committee, 1975. 16p.

3183 Maeda, Kei Kudo. "An experience in teaching social group work in Japan." Social Work Training and Teaching Materials Newsletter, no. 7, July 1973. 13-14.

3184 Shinomiya, Kyoji. "Similarities and differences in social work education as seen from Japan." International Social Work, v. 2, no. 1, Jan. 1959. 21-24.

3185 Wakabayashi, Tatsuo. "Study of the social work curriculum in Japan." International Social Work, v. 5, no. 1, Jan. 1962. 20-24.

9. Korea

3186 Korea (Republic). Ministry of Health and Social Affairs. Introduction on the National Social Workers Training Institute. Seoul: The Ministry, 1960. 16p.

10. New Guinea

3187 O'Collins, Maev. "Introducing social work education at the University of Papua New Guinea." International Social Work, v. 14, no. 1, 1973. 20-25.

11. New Zealand

3188 Robb, J. H. "Similarities and differences in social work education as seen from New Zealand." International Social Work, v. 2, no. 1, Jan. 1959. 11-14.

12. Pakistan

3189 Chaudhry, Mohammad Afzal. "Issues of group work in Pakistan." Social Work Training and Teaching Materials Newsletter, no. 7, July 1973. 14-17.

3190 Dumpson, James R. Training for social work in Pakistan; prepared for the Government of Pakistan, appointed by the UN Technical Assistance Administration. New York: United Nations, 1955. 50p. TAA/PAK/3 Rev. 1.

3191 Khan, Jahangir and S. M. Anwer. An experiment in social work; a report on the orientation programme of college students in social work. Peshawar: West Pakistan Academy for Village Development, 1962. 132p.

3192 Livingstone, Arthur S. Social work education in Pakistan; prepared for the Government of Pakistan, appointed under UN Programme for Technical Assistance. New York: United Nations, 1960. 40p. TAA/PAK/18/Rev. 1.

3193 Sahibzada, Mohammad Idris. Social work education and training in the former N. W. F. P. Peshawar, Pakistan: Board of Economic Enquiry, Peshawar University, 1965. 28p.

13. Philippines

3194 Almanzor, Angelina C. "The applicability and non-applicability of western social concepts to social work education and practice in the Philippines." Social Work (Manila), v. 10, nos. 1 & 2, Jan. / Feb. 1965. 126-127, 132-134.

3195 _____. "Philippine experiences in the development of indigenous teaching materials for social work." Social Work (Manila), v. 9, nos. 11 & 12, Nov. / Dec. 1964. 98-99, 108-109.

3196 Lasan, Dolores B. "Integrated methods--retrospect and prospect." Social Work Training and Teaching Materials Newsletter, no. 10, June 1974. 2-5.

3197 _____. "Issues of social group work in the Philippines." Social Work Training and Teaching Materials Newsletter, no. 7, July 1973. 17-19.

D. CANADA

3198 Armitage, W. A. J. "Education, competence and utilization." Social Worker-Travailleur Social, v. 39, no. 4, Nov. 1971. 179-183.

3199 Barnes, John. "An overview of the one-year M. S. W. programme in Canada." Social Worker-Travailleur Social, v. 44, nos. 2-3, summer-fall 1976. 34-42.

3200 Bolte, Gordon L. "Current trends in doctoral programs in schools of social work in the United States and Canada." Doctoral students look at social work education. Edited by Leila Calhoun Deasy. New York: Council on Social Work Education, 1971. 109-126.

3201 Cameron, Donald A. "An examination of social service programs in Ontario community colleges with special reference to field instruction." Doctoral dissertation, University of Toronto, 1975. 302p.

3202 Canada. Statistics Canada. Student Information Section. Statistical information on schools of social work in Canada. Ottawa: Information Canada, annual.

3203 _____. Women's Bureau. A new career after 30; report of an enquiry into the experience of women who had taken professional social work training at thirty years of age or over. Ottawa: Department of Labour of Canada, 1960. 34p.

3204 Canadian Association for Education in the Social Services.

The first university degree in social work--A statement on objectives, content and organization. Ottawa: The Association, 1971. 48p.

3205 Canadian Association of Schools of Social Work. Educational policy for university programmes of social work. Ottawa: The Association, 1974. 13p.

3206 _____. Employment of social service graduates in Canada; task force report on policy issues and implications. Ottawa: The Association, 1975. 25p.

3207 _____. Manual of standards and procedures for the accreditation of programmes of social work education. Ottawa: The Association, 1975. 50p.

3208 Conference on Manpower Needs and Education in the Field of Social Welfare. Manpower needs in the field of social welfare; papers. Ottawa: Association of Universities and Colleges of Canada, 1967. 131p.

3209 Conference on Social Services Manpower. Proceedings of the Conference, Quebec, 1971. Ottawa: Association of Universities and Colleges of Canada, 1972. 88p.

3210 Crane, John A. Employment of social service graduates in Canada. Ottawa: Canadian Association of Schools of Social Work, 1974. 138p.

3211 Eubank, Earl E. "The schools of social work of the United States and Canada: some recent findings." Social Service Review, v. 2, no. 2, June 1928. 263-273.

3212 Govan, Elizabeth S. L. "The Canadian study of social work education--A mutual project of schools and agencies." Education for social work; proceedings of the 1955 Annual Program Meeting, Council on Social Work Education. New York: The Council, 1955. 57-63.

3213 Hendry, Charles E. Fiftieth Anniversary, 1914-1964: School of Social Work, University of Toronto. Toronto: School of Social Work, University of Toronto, 1964. 63p.

3214 Hutton, Miriam. "Education for the social services." Canadian Journal of Higher Education, v. 5, no. 2, 1975. 23-37.

3215 Kerry, Esther W. "Early professional development in Montreal." Social Worker-Travailleur Social, v. 29, no. 3, June 1961. 35-42.

3216 Kinanen, Karl. "Social work competence and use of manpower." Social Worker-Travailleur Social, v. 39, no. 4,

Nov. 1971. 184-189.

3217 King, Dorothy. "Canadian schools of social work in wartime."
Family, v. 23, no. 5, July 1942. 180-185.

3218 Lappin, Ben W. Community workers and the social work
tradition; their quest for a role examined in Israel and in
Canada. Toronto: University of Toronto Press, 1971.
190p.

3219 Lucas-White, Lydia. "Blacks and education in Nova Scotia:
implications for social work education and practice." Social Work in Atlantic Canada, v. 1, 1975. 35-51.

3220 Maslany, George W. Social service manpower project. Regina, Sask.: School of Social Work, University of Saskat-
chewan-Regina Campus, 1973. 3 vol.

3221 Melichercik, John. "Social work education and social work
practice." Social Worker-Travailleur Social, v. 41, no.
3, spring 1973. 22-27.

3222 Moore, Stewart. "Concepts and exercises in the classroom
use of Canadian literature." Canadian Journal of Social
Work Education, v. 2, no. 1, spring 1976. 3-11.

3223 _____. "Use of Canadian literature in social work education." Canadian Journal of Social Work Education, v. 1,
no. 1, fall 1974. 14-25.

3224 Mumm, Louise N. , editor. Student financial aid for master's
program in graduate schools of social work in the U. S.
A. and Canada. New York: Council on Social Work Education, 1968. 184p.

3225 National Commission for Social Work Careers. Social work
fellowships and scholarships in Canada and the United
States for the academic years 1965-66 and 1966-67. New
York: The Commission, 1964. 91p.

3226 Perretz, Edgar A. "A critical review of undergraduate education for social work." Social Worker-Travailleur Social, v. 30, no. 4, Oct. 1962. 5-14.

3227 Rose, Albert. "Teaching Social Welfare Policy and Services
in the social work curriculum of Canadian schools." Canadian Journal of Social Work Education, v. 1, no. 3, summer 1975. 4-12.

3228 Schlesinger, Benjamin. "Social work education and family
planning." Social Worker-Travailleur Social, v. 41, no. 2,
summer 1973. 93-99.

3229 Segal, Brian. "Dilemmas in the social work education--social
      work manpower equation." Canadian Journal of Social
      Work Education, v. 1, no. 2, spring 1975. 4-12.

3230 Seminar on Training Programmes in the Social Services at
      the Post-Secondary, Non-University Level. Proceedings
      of the Seminar, Ottawa, 1968. Ottawa: Association of
      Universities and Colleges of Canada, 1969. 198p.

3231 Stubbins, Henry. "The profession's expectations of undergra-
      duate education." Social Worker-Travailleur Social, v. 35,
      no. 2, May 1967. 64-70.

3232 _____. "The undergraduate social worker and the manpower
      crisis." Social Worker-Travailleur Social, v. 34, no. 4,
      Nov. 1966. 256-259.

3233 Wharf, Brian. "Future role of the graduate social worker."
      Canadian Welfare, v. 42, no. 3-4, July-Aug. 1966. 132-
      139.

3234 Woodsworth, D. E. "Politics and social work education."
      Canadian Journal of Social Work Education, v. 2, no. 3,
      1976. 15-22.

E. EUROPE

1. General

3235 Council of Europe. Social Committee. Social workers: role,
      training and status. Strasbourg, France: The Council,
      1967. 79p.

3236 De Jongh, J. F. "A European experiment in casework teach-
      ing." Social Casework, v. 34, no. 1, Jan. 1953. 9-17.

3237 Iliovici, Jean. "Urban development: implications for training
      social work personnel: In Europe and Africa." Urban
      development: its implications for social welfare; proceed-
      ings of the 13th International Conference of Social Work,
      Washington, D. C., 1966. New York: Columbia Univer-
      sity Press, 1967. 296-299.

3238 Lyndon, Benjamin H. Graduate professional schools of social
      work and undergraduate social welfare education, part I:
      Findings. Buffalo: State University of New York, 1965.
      83p.

3239 Sailer, Erna. "Similarities and differences in social work
      education as seen from Europe." International Social Work,

v. 2, no. 1, Jan. 1959. 15-20.

3240 United Nations. European Social Development Programme.
      Report of Expert Group on Manpower Needs in the Social
      Welfare Field and Implications for Training Programmes,
      Hellebaek, Denmark, 1969. New York: United Nations,
      1969. 71p. SOA/ESDP/1969/2.

3241 Younghusband, Eileen L. "Some international aspects of ed-
      ucation for social work in Europe." Some aspects on so-
      cial work training. Compiled by the Swedish Association
      of Graduates from Schools of Social Work and Public Ad-
      ministration. Kumla, Sweden: The Association, 1969.
      144-150.

2. Denmark

3242 Katz, Arnold. "Problem oriented education: an alternative
      social work curriculum." Canadian Journal of Social Work
      Education, v. 1, no. 2, spring 1975. 48-56.

3243 Valbak, Age. "Social training in Denmark in the melting pot."
      Some aspects on social work training. Compiled by the
      Swedish Association of Graduates from Schools of Social
      Work and Public Administration. Kumla, Sweden: The
      Association, 1969. 115-130.

3. Finland

3244 Niemi, Veikko. "Training for social work in Finland." In-
      ternational Social Work, v. 5, no. 3, July 1962. 25-28.

4. Great Britain

3245 Ainsworth, Frank and Nan Bridgford. "Student supervision
      in residential social work." British Journal of Social
      Work, v. 1, no. 4, winter 1971. 455-462.

3246 Association of Community Workers. Knowledge and skills
      for community work. London: The Association, 1975.
      39p.

3247 Association of Social Work Teachers. Social work education
      in the 1970's. Bradford, Eng.: The Association, 1971.
      112p.

3248 Aves, Geraldine. "United Kingdom experience in the expan-
      sion." International Social Work, v. 11, no. 1, Jan. 1968.
      1-8.

3249 Bamford, Terry. "Training--a realistic objective." Social
      Work Today, v. 8, no. 10, 7 Dec. 1976. 1.

3250 Barter, John. "Mental health and social work training." So-
      cial Work Today, v. 7, no. 13, 16 Sept. 1976. 367-370.

3251 Baxter, A. D. "'Younghusband' workers: a relative experi-
      ment in supervision." Almoner, v. 14, no. 6, Sept. 1961.
      247-260.

3252 Bessell, Robert. "New development in social work education."
      Case Conference, v. 15, no. 10, Feb. 1969. 404-406.

3253 Bilston, W. G. "Groupwork training for social workers."
      Social Work (London), v. 25, no. 3, July 1968. 2-5.

3254 British Association of Social Workers. "Policy statement on
      basic professional education for social work." Social Work
      Today, v. 2, no. 23, 9 March 1972. 15-18.

3255 Brown, Sibyl Clement and E. R. Gloyne. The field training
      of social workers: a survey. London: Allen & Unwin,
      1966. 148p.

3256 Browne, Megan. "Education for change." British Journal of
      Psychiatric Social Work, v. 8, no. 2, autumn 1965. 15-19.

3257 Butler, Barbara. "The two months' placement for social stu-
      dies students." Case Conference, v. 8, no. 2, June 1961.
      35-38.

3258 Cavenagh, Winifred E. Four decades of students in social
      work. Birmingham, Eng. : University of Birmingham,
      n. d. 97p.

3259 Central Council for Education and Training in Social Work.
      Legal studies in social work education; report of the Legal
      Studies Group. London: The Council, 1974. 63p.

3260 _____. People with handicaps need better trained workers;
      report of a Working Party on Training for Social Work
      with Handicapped People. London: The Council, 1974.
      68p.

3261 _____. Setting the course for social work education 1971-
      1973. London: The Council, 1973. 36p.

3262 _____. Social work education 1973-74. London: The
      Council, 1975. 48p.

3263 _____. Social work, residential work is a part of social
      work; report of the Working Party on Education for Resi-
      dential Social Work. London: The Council, 1974. 48p.

3264 _____. The social worker in the juvenile court: some

suggestions for training. London: The Council, 1974. 15p.

3265 _____. The teaching of community work; a study group discussion paper. London: The Council, 1975. 84p.

3266 _____. Training for residential social work: a new pattern suggested by the Working Party on Residential Social Work, with implications for training and education in entire social services field. London: The Council, 1973. 61p.

3267 Central Training Council in Child Care. Community placements: some experiments in social work education. London: The Council, 1970. 36p.

3268 _____. Playgroups: the development of dual purpose groups in social work education. London: The Council, 1970.

3269 _____. The residential placement in the training of social workers. London: The Council, 1970.

3270 _____. The structure of courses: some implications for the pattern of fieldwork training. London: The Council, 1970. 24p.

3271 _____. The supervision of fieldwork practice: some aspects of its adaptation to new developments in social work education. London: The Council, 1971. 39p.

3272 _____. Working with groups: the development of experience of groupwork as a basic part of social work education. London: The Council, 1970. 32p.

3273 Cheetham, Juliet. "Social work education and the departments of social work." Social Work Today, v. 1, no. 12, March 1971. 5-10.

3274 Christopherson, Derman. "CCETSW: the work of the new Central Council for Education and Training in Social Work." The year book of social policy in Britain, 1971. Edited by Kathleen Jones. London: Routledge & Kegan Paul, 1972. 3-15.

3275 Collis, Arthur. "Social work--A current assessment of training and related topics." Social Work (London) v. 18, no. 3, July 1961. 5-9.

3276 Community Work Group. Current issues in community work. London: Routledge & Kegan Paul, 1973. 180p.

3277 Council for Training in Social Work. Human growth and behavior as a subject for study by social workers; report of the Working Party on Human Growth and Behavior. London: The Council, 1967.

3278 _____. The teaching of fieldwork; report of the Working Party on Fieldwork. London: The Council, 1971. 44p.

3279 _____. The teaching of sociology in social work courses; report of the Sociology Study Group. London: Central Council for Education and Training in Social Work, 1972. 32p.

3280 Davies, D. C. G. "An experiment in social work training." Coombe Lodge Reports, v. 7, no. 9, 1974. 622-632.

3281 Deed, D. M. "Dangers of stereotypes in student supervision." Case Conference, v. 9, no. 1, May 1962. 10-15.

3282 Dinerman, Miriam. "Social work training for unconventional students in Great Britain." Journal of Education for Social Work, v. 11, no. 2, spring 1975. 32-36.

3283 Donnison, D. V. "Teaching of social administration." British Journal of Sociology, v. 12, no. 3, Sept. 1961. 203-223.

3284 Edwards, M. Elizabeth and Moy Thomas. "Education for social casework: a comparative study of a university and a technical college casework course." Social Work (London), v. 21, no. 3, July 1964. 18-25.

3285 _____. "Selection of students." Coombe Lodge Reports, v. 7, no. 9, 1974. 582-598.

3286 _____. "A study of the social work tutor's expectations of fieldwork agencies and his responsibilities towards them." Social Work (London), v. 23, no. 1, Jan. 1966. 17-25, 32.

3287 Gore, Thomas. "Training of social workers in Britain." Social Casework, v. 43, no. 6, June 1962. 297-303.

3288 Great Britain. Department of Health and Social Security. Manpower and training for the social services; report of the Working Party, R. A. Birch, chairman. London: HMSO, 1976. 182p.

3289 _____. _____. Advisory Council on Child Care. Fieldwork training for social work. London: HMSO, 1971. 215p.

3290 Gulbenkian (Calouste) Foundation, Lisbon. Community work and social change; a report on training. London: Long-man Group Ltd., 1968. 171p.

3291 Hack, Kenneth A. "A study of predictors of success on a social work course." British Journal of Social Work, v. 3., no. 2, summer 1973. 189-207.

3292 Halmos, Paul. "Preprofessional practical training in social science." Case Conference, v. 8, no. 2, June 1961. 39-44.

3293 Jones, Howard, editor. Towards a new social work. London: Routledge and Kegan Paul, 1975. 176p.

3294 Jones, Kathleen. The teaching of social studies in British universities. Hitchin, Hertforshire, Eng.: Codicote Press, 1964. 87p.

3295 Jones, Neville. "Selection of students for social work train-ing." Social Work (London), v. 27, no. 3, July 1970. 16-20.

3296 Jones, Robin Huws. "The National Institute for Social Work Training." Medical Social Work (London), v. 19, no. 2, May 1966. 44-48.

3297 _____. "The National Institute for Social Work Training." Social Work (London), v. 20, no. 3, July 1963. 12-15.

3298 _____. "The National Institute for Social Work Training in Britain." International Social Work, v. 7, no. 2, April 1964. 5-7.

3299 Jordan, Malcolm. "Education and social work." Social Work Today, v. 3, no. 14, 19 Oct. 1972. 5-6.

3300 Leaper, R. A. B. "An experiment in community work train-ing." Social Service Quarterly, v. 41, no. 2, autumn 1967. 63-66.

3301 _____. "Immediate issues in training for community work." Social Work Today, v. 2, no. 1, April 1971. 21-23.

3302 Leonard, Peter. "Experiments in post-professional education." Social Work Today, v. 1, no. 4, July 1970. 5-9.

3303 Livingstone, Arthur S. The overseas student in Britain, with special reference to training courses in social welfare. Manchester, Eng.: University Press, 1960. 169p.

3304 McCulloch, J. W., R. J. W. Foren and P. J. Hitch. "Mo-tivation and academic performance as factors in the selection of social work students." Educational Research, v. 11, no. 3, June 1969. 207-211.

3305 McDougall, Kay. "Thinking aloud--On basic social work teaching." Case Conference, v. 8, no. 10, April 1962. 266-269.

3306 _____. "Thinking aloud--On generic training." Case Conference, v. 8, no. 8, Feb. 1962. 201-204.

3307 _____. "Thinking aloud--On the social science courses." Case Conference, v. 8, no. 9, March 1962. 233-237.

3308 Masi, Fidelia A. "Observations on British social work education." Iowa Journal of Social Work, v. 6, no. 2 and 3, Dec. 1975. 137-152.

3309 Moon, Marjorie and Kathleen Slack. The first two years: a study of work experience of some newly qualified medical social workers. London: Institute of Medical Social Workers, 1965. 83p.

3310 Munday, Brian. "Emergency training for mature students." Social Work Today, v. 2, no. 2, 22 April 1971. 21-23.

3311 National Institute for Social Work Training. An introductory account, 1961-1974. London: The Institute, 1974. 32p.

3312 Nursten, Jean P. "Applied social studies: a curriculum for a degree course." Social Service Quarterly, v. 40, no. 2, autumn 1966. 58-60, 72-74.

3313 _____ and John Pottinger. "Social work training--The consumer's view." Social Service Quarterly, v. 43, no. 4, spring 1970. 152-154.

3314 Parsloe, Phyllida, Elizabeth Warren and Judy Gauldie. "Social work as taught." New Society, v. 35, no. 4, March 1976. 488-491.

3315 Pierce, Rachel, Renee Roseman and Bob Parsons. "Change of career students in social work." Social Work Today, v. 4, no. 23, 21 Feb. 1974. 741-743.

3316 Ralphs, F. Lincoln, chairman. "Report of the Working Party on the Role and Training of EWOs (Ralphs report)." Social Work Today, v. 4, no. 11, 23 Aug. 1973. 338-340.

3317 Rodgers, Barbara N. The careers of social studies students. Hitchin, Hertfordshire, Eng.: Codicote press, 1964. 75p.

3318 _____. A follow-up study of social administration students at Manchester University, 1940-60. Manchester: Manchester University Press, 1963.   44p.

3319 _____ and June Stevenson.   A new portrait of social work:
a study of the social services in a northern town from
Younghusband to Seebohm.   London: Heinemann Education
Books, 1973.   363p.

3320 Sainsbury, Eric.   "Education for social work in Britain."
Indian Journal of Social Work, v. 28, no. 1, April 1967.
25-40.

3321 _____, editor.   Field work in social administration courses: a guide to the use of field work placements in the
teaching of social administration in basic social studies
courses.   London: Published for the National Institute
for Social Work Training by the National Council of Social
Service, 1966.   78p.

3322 Seebohm, Frederick, Chairman.   Report of the Committee on
Local Authority and Allied Personal Social Services.   London: HMSO, 1969.   370p.

3323 Smith, Marjorie J.   Professional education for social work
in Britain; an historical account.   London: Allen & Unwin,
1965.   114p.

3324 Snelling, Jean M.   "Changes in training."   Medical Social
Work (London), v. 18, no. 3, June 1965.   71-75.

3325 _____.   The contribution of the Institute of Medical Social
Workers to education for social work.   Bradford, Eng. :
Association of Social Work Teachers, 1970.   Unpaged.

3326 _____.   "Implications for training and further education of
comprehensive social services."   Medical Social Work
(London), v. 22, no. 2, May 1969.   42-51.

3327 _____.   "The management of curriculum development."
Coombe Lodge Reports, v. 7, no. 9, 1974.   599-607.

3328 _____.   "Robbins and social work."   Almoner, v. 16, no.
9, Dec. 1963.   262-269.

3329 _____.   "Training of social workers."   Proceedings of the
Royal Society of Medicine, v. 67, no. 9, Sept. 1974.   943-
945.

3330 Spencer, John.   "Social work education and the social services outside Canada: the British experience."   Canadian
Journal of Social Work Education, v. 2, no. 3, 1976.   23-31.

3331 Stevenson, Olive.   "Social work and training: the next phase."

Case Conference, v. 12, no. 7, Jan. 1966. 235, 239.

3332 _____ . "Some dilemmas in social work education." Oxford Review of Education, v. 2, no. 2, 1976. 149-155.

3333 Thorpe, Ellis and Stuart J. Rees. "Community work training." Social Work Today, v. 2, no. 5, 3 June 1971. . 25-27.

3334 Walton, Ronald G. "Women and social work education." "Two decades of training 1951-71." Women in social work. London: Routledge & Kegan Paul, 1975. 57-65, 209-220.

3335 Ward, Marjorie L. "The first three years: some personal reflections on the Certificate Courses in Social Work." Case Conference, v. 11, no. 6, Nov. 1964. 181-186.

3336 Wright, Reginald C. "The British Council for Training in Social Work." International Social Work, v. 8, no. 3, July 1965. 19-20.

3337 _____ . "The Certificate in Social Work courses and their implication for the medical social worker." Almoner, v. 17, no. 10, March 1965. 321-325.

3338 Young, Priscilla H. "Current developments in social work education." Coombe Lodge Reports, v. 7, no. 9, 1974. 577-581.

3339 Younghusband, Eileen L., chairman. Community work and social change; the report of a study group on training. London: Longman, 1968. 171p.

3340 _____ . Report on the employment and training of social workers. Dunfermline, Eng.: Carnegie United Kingdom Trust, 1947. 180p.

3341 _____ , chairman. Report of the Working Party on Social Workers in the Local Authority Health and Welfare Services. London: HMSO, 1959. 375p.

3342 _____ . Social work in Britain; a supplementary report on the employment and training of social workers. Dunfermline, Eng.: Carneige United Kingdom Trust, 1951. 256p.

3343 _____ . "Social work training and staffing implications of community care." Social Work (London), v. 22, nos. 2-3, April and July 1965. 22-28.

5. Greece

3344 Smith, Joan M. "Recent developments in social work education in Greece." International Social Work, v. 7, no. 2, April 1964. 1-4.

3345 _____, editor. "Social work curriculum planning in Greece." International Social Work, v. 5, no. 1, Jan. 1962. 15-19.

6. Italy

3345a Education for social welfare planning: an Italo-American project; proceedings of a Conference held under the joint auspices of the Florence Heller School for Advanced Studies in Social Welfare, Brandeis University and the Graduate School of Social Work, Rutgers University, 1970. New Brunswick, N. J. : Graduate School of Social Work, Rutgers University, 1971. 50p.

3346 Fasolo, Emma A. "Social work education in Italy." International Social Work, v. 3, no. 4, Oct. 1960. 1-4.

3347 Masi, Fidelia A. Exploring Italian social work: Columbus "in reverse." Rockville, Md. : National Institute of Mental Health, 1972. 96p.

3348 Morris, Robert. "Italo-American social work exchange: a one or a two-way street?" Social Work Education Reporter, v. 14, no. 4, Dec. 1966. 34-38, 55.

3349 O'Reilly, Charles T. "Italian social work education: observations after a decade." Catholic Charities Review, v. 46, no. 7, Sept. 1962. 4-10.

3350 Visalberghi, Aldo. "Structure of university education and education for social work in Italy." Journal of Education for Social Work, v. 6, no. 1, spring 1970. 61-68.

7. Netherlands

3351 Haan, Pieterdiena M. "A study of the activity of the supervisor of group work students in the first year of advanced social work education in the Netherlands." Doctoral dissertation, University of Pennsylvania, 1974. 229p.

8. Sweden

3352 Almquist, Marja. "The reorganization of the Swedish schools of social work and public administration." International Social Work, v. 6, no. 4, Oct. 1963. 31-37.

9. West Germany

3353 North, Maurice. "The training of social workers in West

Germany." Social Work Today, v. 5, no. 8, 11 July 1974. 233-236.

F. LATIN AMERICA

1. General

3354 Jones, Robert C. Schools of social work in Latin America. Washington, D. C. : Division of Labor and Social Information, Panamerican Union, 1942.

3355 Ospina-Restrepo, Gabriel and Eliana de Cataldo. Some aspects of the situation of the schools of social work in Latin America. Washington, D. C. : Pam American Union, 1963. 17p.

3356 Paraiso, Virginia A. "Education for social work in Latin America." International Social Work, v. 9, no. 2, April 1966. 17-24.

3357 _____. "Selecting students: requisites of current social work responsibilities." International Social Work, v. 10, no. 1, Jan. 1967. 18-28.

3358 _____. "Urban development: implications for training social work personnel: In Latin America." Urban development: its implications for social welfare; proceedings of the 13th International Conference of Social Work, Washington, D. C. , 1966. New York: Columbia University Press, 1967. 300-306.

3359 Resnick, Rosa Perla. "Conscientization: an indigenous approach to international social work." International Social Work, v. 19, no. 1, 1976. 21-29.

2. Argentina

3360 Vittorioso, Lidia C. Hernandez De. "Trends and patterns in social welfare and in social work education in Argentina." Doctoral dissertation, Catholic University of America, 1971. 376p.

3. Brazil

3361 Smith, Joan M. "The social work curriculum in Brazil." International Social Work, v. 5, no. 2, April 1962. 8-11.

4. Colombia

3362 Ginsberg, Leon H. "Social work in Colombia." Social Casework, v. 56, no. 10, Dec. 1975.   614-618.

5. Honduras

3363   Walz, Thomas H.   "Adaptation of the North American model
of social work education to Honduras: a study of attitude
change in Hondurian social workers resulting from their
professional education."   Doctoral dissertation, University of Minnesota, 1966.   285p.

6. West Indies

3364   Schlesinger, Benjamin, editor.   Social work education at the
University of the West Indies.   Nona, Jamaica: University of Appointment Service, 1967.   40p.

AUTHOR INDEX

Abbott, Edith 1, 57, 58, 129, 130, 399, 1528
Abel, Charles M. 2088
Abels, Paul 1817, 1869
Abrahamson, Arthur C. 1606
Abramowitz, Martin 1436
Abramowitz, Naomi R. 1177
Acker, Joan 2018
Ackerman, Nathan W. 1250
Ad Hoc Committee on Manpower Issues of the Council on Social Work Education and National Association of Social Workers 337
Adams, David M. 922
Adams, Frankie V. 190
Adams, William T. 1920
Addams, Jane 131
Adelphi University. School of Social Work 2221
Adler, Jack 338, 2301
Ahearn, Frederick L. , Jr. 1350
Aikin, Dorothy, 2302
Ainsworth, Frank 1502, 3245
Albert, Gerald 2303
Alderson, John 1118
Aldridge, Gordon J. 2262, 2932
Alexander, Chauncey A. 339
Alexander, Gayle 581
Allan, Eunice 1251
Allen, Jo Ann 1607
Allen, Theodora 2952
Almanzor, Angelina C. 973, 1039, 3060, 3194, 3195
Almquist, Marja 3352
Alpine, George C. 1252
Altmeyer, Arthur J. 2953
Amacher, Kloh-Ann 951, 1608, 1609
American Association of Group Workers 1323
American Association of Medical Social Workers 2434
American Association of Medical

Social Workers. Committee on Participation in Teaching of Medical Students 2828
American Association of Psychiatric Social Workers 2465
American Association of Schools of Social Work 261, 2529
American Association of Schools of Social Work. Committee on Faculty Work Loads and Salaries 589
American Public Health Association. Committee on Professional Education 2435
Ames, Lois 2089
Ammons, Paul 499, 2222
Ancona, Leonardo 2893
Anders, J. R. 2954
Anderson, Claire M. 1452
Anderson, Delwin 400
Anderson, Ernest Frederick 2617
Anderson, Eugene D. 2125
Anderson, G. Lester 544, 1019
Anderson, Inge 2834
Anderson, Mary E. 1780
Anderson, Richard J. 2579
Andrew, Gwen 952, 1020, 2019, 2146, 2223
Andrews, F. Emerson 74
Ankrah, E. Maxine 2955
Ansari, Nazir Ahmad 3096
Anthony, Helen 2436
Anwer, S. M. 3191
Appelberg, Esther 1253, 2183, 2715
Apte, Robert Z. 1907, 2495
Aptekar, Herbert H. 191, 302, 953, 1870, 1881, 2956, 3097
Archinard, Enolia B. 1178
Arden House Workshop on Man-

315

705, 3192, 3303
Liyanage, Mathu H. 2948
Llewellyn, Grace M. 1557
Lloyd, A. Katherine 2101
Lloyd, Gary A. 582, 1517
Lochhead, Andrew 2991, 2992
Lockett, Vernon 2667, 2696
Lockhart, George 1391
Lodge, Richard 2993
Loeb, C. Peter 30
Loeb, Eleanor 2852
Loeb, Martin B. 360
Loeser, Drake 1558
Loewenberg, Frank M. 277, 373,
517, 672, 680, 1901, 1949-
1951, 2037-2039
Loewenstein, Sophie F. 1202,
2634
Logan, Frances Walker 1720
Lombardo, Robert A. 495
Long, Margaret 1952
Longres, John 612, 1445, 2635,
2711
Lopez, Manuel D. 1168
Lovata, William M. 432
Lovejoy, Eunice 1169
Lowenstein, Jane 1829
Lower, Katherine D. 613, 824,
1482, 2246
Lowy, Louis 494, 887, 1058,
1059, 2276, 2368
Lubove, Roy 433
Lucas, Leon 434
Lucas, Margaret Exner 876,
2720
Lucas-White, Lydia 2678, 3219
Lukoff, Irving F. 916, 917,
2575, 2576
Lund, Bernt H. 2911
Lundberg, Emma Octavia 155,
156
Lundberg, Horace W. 668, 888
Lundy, Lawrence Allen 319
Lunt, Sally Herman 94
Lurie, Abraham 435
Lurie, Harry L. 1392, 1559
Lustman, Claire R. 2247, 2448
Lutzker, Margie 2853, 2854
Lynch, Stanley 2161
Lyndon, Benjamin H. 31, 518,
1902, 1953, 2248-2250, 3238
Lyndon B. Johnson School of Pub-
lic Affairs 32

- M -

Maas, Henry S. 228, 229, 994,
1203, 2912, 2913
Mabbs, Robert D. 2066
Macadam, Elizabeth 95, 96
Macarov, David 614, 1060-
1062, 1420, 1638, 2040, 3177
McBroom, Elizabeth 1204
McCall, Laura 1672
McCann, Charles W. 519, 2636
McClean, Ann L. 2140
McClean, Harry Justus 2819
McClure, Jesse F. 417, 2679
McConnell, T. R. 552
McCormick, Mary J. 157, 320,
321
McCoy, Jacqueline 2339
McCuan, Patrick 734, 1574
McCulloch, J. W. 2060, 2061,
2826, 3304
McCune, Shirley Dickinson 673
McDaniel, Clyde O., Jr. 615,
616, 990, 1483
MacDonald, Mary E. 322, 1484
McDonnell, David John 1597
McDougall, Kay 3305-3307
McGann, Leona M. 2853, 2854
McGee, Ruth 933
McGlothlin, William J. 33, 520
McGrath, Earl J. 2799, 2932
McGrath, Frances C. 991
MacGuffie, Robert A. 1826
McGuinn, Walter 2744
McGuire, Rita A. 1639, 1822
MacIntyre, J. McEwan 1063
Mackey, William J. 760, 761,
868, 869
McLain, Paul L. 2782
MacLauchin, Anna Margaret
230
MacLaughlin, Curtis P. 1438
McLean, Ann L. 2041, 2140
McLellan, Gordon 2162
McLeod, Donna L. 323
McMillen, Wayne 158
McNabola, F. Marie 694
McNamara, James J. 2836
McNary, Willette 1745, 2520

Woodcock, G. D. C. 1659, 1867
Woods, Thomas L. 2358
Woodsworth, D. E. 3234
Wooller, B. E. 1143
Wormald, Eileen 2804
Wright, Helen R. 187, 258, 3164
Wright, Lucy 188
Wright, Marjorie Brown 2220
Wright, Reginald C. 3336, 3337
Wu, Y. C. 55

- Y -

Yabura Lloyd 189
Yamanaka, K. Morgan 2124
Yankey, John 2556a
Yarbrough, Roy D. 259, 779,
  780, 2012, 2013
Yasas, Frances Maria 336, 2946,
  3165
Yeakel, Margaret 949, 950
Yelaja, Shankar A. 128, 260,
  640, 1242, 1408, 3166-3168
Young, Priscilla H. 1868, 3338
Young, Whitney M., Jr. 190,
  660, 2649, 2689, 2690
Youngdahl, Benjamin E. 542,
  543, 1018
Younghusband, Eileen L. 56, 498,
  630, 1104, 1407, 2359, 2413,
  2927, 3025-3028, 3094, 3095,
  3241, 3339-3343
Youth Service Information Center
  1146

- Z -

Zakus, G. E. 2844
Zimbalist, Sidney E. 1501
Zimmerman, Jerome 1677
Zober, Edith 921, 2691
Zoet, Thomas 2017
Zweig, Franklin M. 1409, 1605